CADOGAN GUIDES

Other titles in the Cadogan Guides series:

AUSTRALIA
BALI
BERLIN
THE CARIBBEAN
ECUADOR, THE GALÁPAGOS
  & COLOMBIA
GREEK ISLANDS
INDIA
IRELAND
ITALIAN ISLANDS
MEXICO
MOROCCO
NEW YORK
NORTHEAST ITALY
NORTHWEST ITALY
PORTUGAL
PRAGUE
ROME
SCOTLAND
SOUTH OF FRANCE:
  PROVENCE, CÔTE D'AZUR &
  LANGUEDOC-ROUSSILLON

SOUTH ITALY
SOUTHERN SPAIN:
  GIBRALTAR &
  ANDALUCÍA
SPAIN
THAILAND
TUNISIA
TURKEY
TUSCANY, UMBRIA &
  THE MARCHES
VENICE

Forthcoming:

CENTRAL AMERICA
GERMANY
ISRAEL
JAPAN
LONDON
MADRID & BARCELONA
MOSCOW & LENINGRAD
PARIS

For Schoffie

CADOGAN CITY GUIDES

AMSTERDAM

RODNEY BOLT

INDE·OVDE·SCHANS

CADOGAN BOOKS
London

THE GLOBE PEQUOT PRESS
Chester, Connecticut

Cadogan Books Ltd
Mercury House, 195 Knightsbridge, London SW7 1RE

The Globe Pequot Press
138 West Main Street, Chester, Connecticut 06412, USA

Cover design by Ralph King
Cover illustration by Tracey Bush

Maps © Cadogan Books, drawn by Ruth Hodkinson
Index by Dorothy Groves

Editor: Antony Mason
Managing Editor: Victoria Ingle
Series Editor: Rachel Fielding

First published in 1992

A catalogue record for this book is available from the British Library
ISBN 0–947754–43–1

Library of Congress Data available

ISBN 1–56440–001–8

Photoset in Ehrhardt on a Linotron 202
Typeset, printed and bound in Great Britain by
Redwood Press Ltd, Melksham, Wiltshire

CONTENTS

v

The Walks *Pages 86–196*
Pick of Amsterdam *87*

LIST OF MAPS

ABOUT THE AUTHOR

Rodney Bolt grew up in Africa and was educated at Cambridge University where he read English. He has travelled throughout Europe and has lived and worked in Greece and the Netherlands. He also writes and directs for the stage, and for some years ran a London pub theatre. In 1991 he packed his bags and headed for Amsterdam again.

ACKNOWLEDGEMENTS

Many thanks to my editor Antony Mason for his support, encouragement and healing touches, and to Paula Levey for plucking me from the vast unknown. Also to Hannah Oyen and Ido Vunderink without whose hospitality life would have been very difficult indeed; to Karen Lancel and Frank Oorthuys whose friendship and Amsterdam secrets are much treasured; to Annalies Basie and Iris Korfker for some wonderful trips into the countryside; to Arjen Lancel for an apartment and supportive *pilsjes*; to Patrick Beerepoot for all the running about; to Juanito Wadhwani for heroically braving the elements; to Sicco Heyligers for the strongest bicycle in Amsterdam; and to Chardmore Road, from whence cometh my strength.

I would also like to thank the Netherlands Tourist Board, the Amsterdam VVV and VVV offices in Gouda, Haarlem, Leiden and The Hague, and Caroline van Raamsdonk of Archivisie for their help and advice, and KLM Airlines for assistance with transport.

INTRODUCTION

The City coat of arms

You're walking late at night along the Amstel. A frill of gables ends abruptly against the hard lines of the vast new opera house which cut across the evening skyline. A lone junkie in ragged red jeans and a flat Spanish hat sways and dances to a frail tune that no-one else can hear. A young woman stands up to pedal her heavy black bicycle over a hump-backed bridge, her toddler asleep in a custom-built wicker carrier on the back. Just ahead an ancient man wearing a chauffeur's cap manoeuvres a wheelchair along the uneven pavement. Its incumbent, a *grande dame* swathed in black fur, nods as they pass with a gracious '*Goedenavond*'. In Amsterdam three strands of life continually interweave: reminders of the wealthy Golden Age trading city dominated by a few Calvinist families, the sleazy port, and the radical hippie mecca of the 1960s grown comfortably liberal.

As a visitor you'll find Amsterdam at once familar and curious. It has an edge and verve that will keep you on your toes. As Henry James wrote after a visit to the Netherlands in the 1870s, it will 'at least give one's regular habits of thought the stimulus of a little confusion'. You'll be daily launched into a farrago of sleek business people, droves of tourists, scruffs, bohemians and persons of decidedly ill repute. Yet everyone seems to get on remarkably well together; and the chance encounters with people here will be one of the lasting pleasures of your visit.

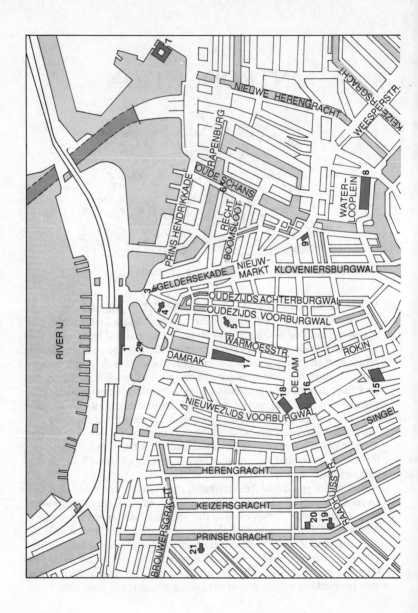

RIVER IJ

NIEUWE HERENGRACHT

KEIZERSGRACHT

WEESPERSTR.

RAPENBURG

OUDE SCHANS

WATER-
LOOPLEIN 8

RECHT
BOOMSLOOT

9

PRINS HENDRIKKADE

GELDERSEKADE 3

NIEUW-
MARKT KLOVENIERSBURGWAL

OUDEZIJDS ACHTERBURGWAL

4

OUDEZIJDS VOORBURGWAL

5

WARMOESSTR.

1

2

DAMRAK

17

ROKIN

DE DAM

18 16

15

NIEUWEZIJDS VOORBURGWAL

SINGEL

HERENGRACHT

KEIZERSGRACHT

RAADHUISSTR.

PRINSENGRACHT

20 19

BROUWERSGRACHT

21

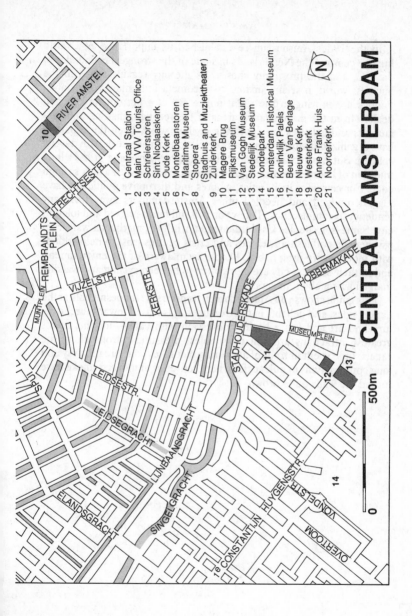

CENTRAL AMSTERDAM

1 Centraal Station
2 Main VVV Tourist Office
3 Schreierstoren
4 Sint Nicolaaskerk
5 Oude Kerk
6 Montelbaanstoren
7 Maritime Museum
8 'Stopera'
 (Stadhuis and Muziektheater)
9 Zuiderkerk
10 Magere Brug
11 Rijksmuseum
12 Van Gogh Museum
13 Stedelijk Museum
14 Vondelpark
15 Amsterdam Historical Museum
16 Koninklijk Paleis
17 Beurs Van Berlage
18 Nieuwe Kerk
19 Westerkerk
20 Anne Frank Huis
21 Noorderkerk

RIVER AMSTEL

REMBRANDTS
PLEIN
MUNTPLEIN
UTRECHTSESTR.
VIJZELSTR.
KERKSTR.
LEIDSESTR.
LEIDSEGRACHT
LIJNBAANSGRACHT
SINGELGRACHT
ELANDSGRACHT
STADHOUDERSKADE
HOBBEMAKADE
MUSEUMPLEIN
1e CONSTANTIJN HUYGENSSTR.
VONDELSTR.
OVERTOOM

0   500m

In the 1980s Amsterdam re-established its importance as a world finance centre. The Netherlands has one of the strongest economies in the EC, and the prosperity shows. As the city regains status in the business world, it seems anxious to become a little more respectable. Politics are moving to the right, police are clearing out junkies and dealers from the more squalid areas of the red-light district, and restaurants and galleries are appearing in their wake. Even the squatters have organized themselves into an association to make deals with the city council. But Amsterdam will never lose its alternative tang. It has a long tradition of liberal tolerance and is, after all, a port—with a port's rough edge. For centuries its heretics, whores and disruptive politicians have tugged, nudged and needled other Amsterdammers away from any tendency to complacency. Today you will still find a relaxed and tolerant city. Same-sex couples kiss in the street, whiffs of marijuana waft from psychedelic coffeeshops, clinics and crisis centres exist to help addicts with more severe drug habits. People seem aware of the environment, and in their spotless city are more often to be seen cycling and walking than whizzing about in cars.

This guide shows you Amsterdam in its diversity. It doesn't balk at the darker sides, and delights in the treasures. It is biased towards architecture and art and has a healthy obsession with cafés—for the town's greatest attractions are still its simplest pleasures: strolls along the canals, time spent in front of a painting that takes your breath away and long conversations in quiet cafés where centuries of tobacco smoke have turned the walls quite brown.

Travel

Het Lieverdje

Arriving in Amsterdam

By Air: In 1921 the world's first air travel booking office opened at Amsterdam's **Schiphol Airport**. The dashing Captain Jerry Shaw would fly intrepid passengers, two at a time in a fragile De Havilland, across the Channel to Croydon near London (Heathrow and Gatwick were still meadows). These days Schiphol enjoys a reputation as one of the world's sleekest and most user-friendly airports, and has an impressive mall of duty-free shops. It serves direct flights from London, Manchester, New York, Los Angeles, Toronto, Vancouver and Sydney as well as many other airports around the UK and Americas.

Flights from London take about 45 minutes, from New York about 8 hours. In 1984 the British and Dutch governments passed legislation that broke the monopoly held by KLM and BA over the Amsterdam–London route and the number of airlines offering flights rocketed. A browse through the travel ads in the British press (such as *Time Out* or the *Evening Standard*) will divulge any number of return flights priced below £100. Even scheduled airlines charge only a little more than that if you take advantage of a special offer (which usually involves staying over one Saturday night). American travellers thinking of stopping over in London might find it cheaper to buy a ticket to Amsterdam in the UK.

1

TWA offers only one direct route from the USA to Amsterdam—from JFK Airport in New York to Schiphol, but KLM, the Dutch national airline, flies to a number of American cities including New York, Baltimore, Los Angeles and Miami.

Schiphol Airport (General Information): tel 601 0966

Air UK UK:	tel (0345) 666777
Amsterdam:	tel 601 0633
American Airlines Amsterdam:	tel 664 8686
British Airways UK:	tel (081) 897 4000
Amsterdam:	tel 685 2211
British Midland UK:	tel (071) 589 5599
Amsterdam:	tel (06) 0222426
Canadian Airlines Amsterdam:	tel 685 1721
Dan Air UK:	tel (0293) 820222
Amsterdam:	tel 617 1754
KLM UK:	tel (081) 750 9000
Amsterdam:	tel 674 7747
Transavia UK:	tel (0293) 538181
Amsterdam:	tel 604 6518
TWA Amsterdam:	tel 626 2277

Transport from the Airport

Taxis will cost you at least *f*60, and hardly seem worth it given the ease, frequency and price of public transport. **Trains** leave for Centraal Station every 15 minutes (until 1 am, then hourly until 5 am). The journey takes about 20 minutes and tickets cost *f*4.75.

Alternatively, you can swan into town on the plush **KLM Hotel Bus**. The service is available to anyone, even if you sneaked over on a bucket flight and intend sleeping in the Vondelpark. Buses leave at 30-minute intervals from 6.25 am–11.25 pm and tickets cost *f*15. The *yellow line* stops at the Ibis, Amsterdam Hilton, Barbizon Centre, Parkhotel and the Amsterdam Apollo (i.e. Leidseplein and southern areas). The *orange line* covers the area around the Dam, stopping at the Pulitzer, Sonesta, Victoria, Krasnapolsky and Barbizon Palace hotels.

By Train: British Rail offers a choice of two routes from London to Amsterdam's **Centraal Station**: Victoria Station via Dover and Ostend,

2

and Liverpool Street Station via Harwich and the Hook of Holland (a longer channel crossing). The journey takes 10–12 hours, whichever option you decide on. Overnight trips are possible, and more comfortable if you book a cabin on the boat (from £10). There are discounts if you're under 26, or stay no more than 5 days. Return fares are currently:

From Liverpool Street: Standard £78, Youth £68, 5-day special £62.
From Victoria: Standard £83.50, Youth £60, 5-day special £57.

For British Rail European enquiries telephone (071) 834 2345. There's a talking timetable for Amsterdam on (071) 828 4264. Centraal Station's European enquiries number is 620 2266.

Travelling around Holland by rail is cheap. You don't have to book as services are frequent, and you can hop off a train to explore towns *en route* to your destination without paying extra. The information desk at Centraal Station can give you details of the various cheap tickets and passes offered by the network—a good idea if you're planning a lot of day trips.

By Bus: This is the cheapest way to go, but it can also be the nastiest. Overnight journeys, in particular, seem maliciously planned so that you're woken at a border crossing every few hours. National Express/Eurolines (tel (071) 730 0202) offer two options from London daily. On the morning departure you cross the channel by Hovercraft. The overnight trip involves the ferry and takes 2 hours longer. The current return price for either choice is £51.

By Car: To bring your car into the Netherlands you'll need a valid insurance document (such as the EC 'green card'), current registration and road safety test certificates, an international identification disc and an EC or international driving licence. Speed limits are 50 kph (31 mph) in built up areas, 80 kph (50 mph) on the open road, and 100 kph (75 mph) on motorways. Drive on the right, and give way to traffic approaching from the right, except where you have clear right of way. In Amsterdam be wary of sight-seeing pedestrians, give way to cyclists and remember that the yellow trams give way to no-one. The shortest ferry crossings are Harwich–Hook of Holland (Sealink; tel (0255) 243333) and Sheerness–Vlissingen (Olau Lines; tel (0795) 666666)—though, depending on where you're setting off from, you might find other lines more convenient: North Sea Ferries (Hull–Rotterdam; tel (0482) 77177); P&O (Dover–Zeebrugge/Ostend, Felixstowe–Zeebrugge; tel (081) 575 8555).

Entry requirements

Visas: EC nationals and citizens of Australia, Canada, New Zealand and the USA need only a valid passport to visit the Netherlands if their stay is for less than 3 months. British citizens can also use the temporary British Visitor's Passport (obtainable from Post Offices). If you intend to stay for longer than 3 months you should get your passport stamped on entry, and will need a **residence permit** (see Living and Working in Amsterdam).

Customs: If you buy goods at the **duty-free** shops, and are over 17, you can enter the Netherlands with 200 cigarettes (or 50 cigars or 250 g/8.82 oz of tobacco), 1 litre of spirits (or 2 litres of fortified wine) and 2 litres of non-sparkling wine, 50 g/1.76 oz of perfume and *f*125's worth of gifts. If you've bought goods tax-paid, allowances are higher, and if you live outside Europe they're doubled. You should leave any meat, fruit, plants, flowers, illegal radio transmitters and offensive weapons at home. If you bring in your dog or cat it must be accompanied by a certificate stating it's been inoculated against rabies.

The **exporting of flower bulbs** is permitted to the UK, but you need an inoculation certificate for the USA. It's best to have bulbs posted home to avoid border hassles. Most reputable dealers will do this, and all the necessary paperwork, for you.

Getting Around Amsterdam

Amsterdam is a sedate, compact and intimate city. Pedestrians and cyclists set the pace, and you'll find most places you want to visit within comfortable walking distance. If your legs are tired, or you're in a hurry, yellow trams will whisk you to almost anywhere you want to go. A car is a liability. Parking is expensive (when it's possible), and driving in the narrow streets, which throng with bicycles and jaywalking tourists, is a nightmare.

Public transport is efficient, safe and cheap. Maps, information and tickets are available from the **GVB (Amsterdam Municipal Transport Authority)** (Stationsplein 15, opposite Centraal Station; open Mon–Fri 7 am–10.30 pm, Sat 8 am–10.30 pm, Sun 8.30 am–4.30 pm; tel 627 2727). There's another branch at Amstel Station (open Mon–Fri 7 am–8.30 pm, Sat and Sun 10.15 am–5 pm) and in the summer there's often a mobile branch on Leidseplein. Once you've grasped the quirky logic behind it, the ticketing system seems quite sensible. Although you can buy **single tickets** on boarding, it's cheaper and easier to buy a **strip ticket** (*strippenkaart*, *f*9.35). This is valid on the metro and on all buses and trams throughout Holland. The *strippenkaart* is divided into 15 units. Each time you make a journey allow 1 unit for 'boarding', then one *more* for each zone you travel through: a journey in one zone needs 2 units, through two zones needs 3 units, and so on. Fold the card over at the appropriate unit and slip it into the slot of the stamping machine (on board buses and trams and at the entrance to metro stations). Your card is then stamped with the zone and time and is valid for an hour, even if you swap lines. Most tourist sights are within the central zone, but there are maps at all stations and stops, should you be in any doubt.

Strippenkaarten have no expiry date. You can buy them from stations, newsagents and the GVB. Bus and tram drivers can also sell you an **hourly ticket** (*uurnetkaart*, pronounced 'oornetkart') for *f*2.85 which allows you to travel anywhere in Amsterdam within an hour of its validation. If you intend to use a lot of public transport, the most economical ticket will be a **day ticket** (*dagkaart*). This allows unlimited travel in Amsterdam and costs *f*9.50 for 1 day, *f*12.60 for 2 days, *f*15.60 for 3 days, *f*18.50 for 4 days and an extra *f*2.90 for each additional day up to 9 days. You can buy *dagkaarten* from drivers or the GVB. Weekly, monthly or annual **season tickets** (*sterabonnement*) are also available from the GVB, starting from *f*12.50.

Uniformed and plain-clothes inspectors will spot-fine you *f*100 if they catch you travelling without a valid ticket. Playing the confused foreigner will get you nowhere.

By Tram: Trams run from 6 am Mon–Fri, 6.30 am Sat and 7.30 am Sun. Last trams are around midnight. They hurtle about, bells clanging, scattering cyclists and pedestrians and forcing passengers to hang on for dear life. You can get on or off through any one of the three doors (which open after you press the adjacent metal button). If it looks as if you're the only person due to get off, you'll need to tell the driver to stop by pushing one of the bell nipples inside (on older trams these are unmarked and can be quite obscure). Tram stops have yellow boards showing the numbers of the trams they serve and listing further destinations along the route.

By Bus: Buses work on the same system as trams, though you must board at the front door. You're much less likely to use them, unless you need a **night bus**. A black square with the bus number printed on it is

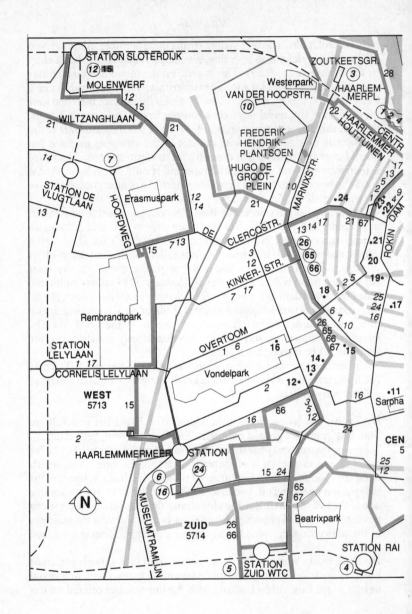

TRANSPORT IN AMSTERDAM

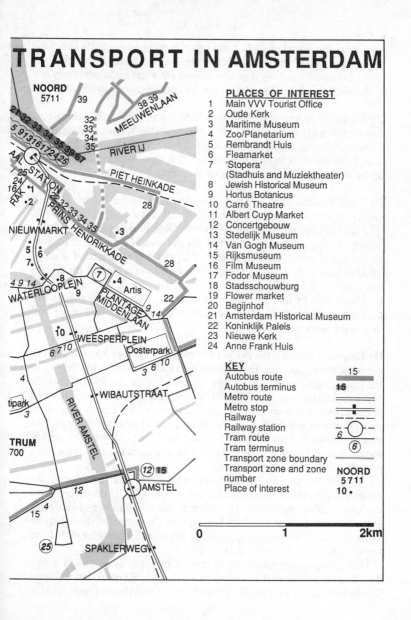

PLACES OF INTEREST

1. Main VVV Tourist Office
2. Oude Kerk
3. Maritime Museum
4. Zoo/Planetarium
5. Rembrandt Huis
6. Fleamarket
7. 'Stopera'
   (Stadhuis and Muziektheater)
8. Jewish Historical Museum
9. Hortus Botanicus
10. Carré Theatre
11. Albert Cuyp Market
12. Concertgebouw
13. Stedelijk Museum
14. Van Gogh Museum
15. Rijksmuseum
16. Film Museum
17. Fodor Museum
18. Stadsschouwburg
19. Flower market
20. Begijnhof
21. Amsterdam Historical Museum
22. Koninklijk Paleis
23. Nieuwe Kerk
24. Anne Frank Huis

KEY

Autobus route	15
Autobus terminus	**15**
Metro route	
Metro stop	
Railway	
Railway station	6
Tram route	
Tram terminus	6
Transport zone boundary	
Transport zone and zone number	NOORD 5711
Place of interest	10 •

0   1   2km

shown on the board of night bus stops. By some inscrutable logic, the night buses stop running at about the time the bars close (2 am) and don't start again until 4 am. So your alternatives are a late night out, a *very* late night out, or walking home. You can, of course, always catch a taxi.

By Metro: The metro is used mainly by commuters from the eastern and south-eastern suburbs. There are only two lines, both terminating at Centraal Station. Running times and ticketing are the same as for trams. The trains are refreshingly free of advertisements—except for signs put up by the National Council Against Swearing.

By Taxi: You can't hail an Amsterdam cab in the street, but have to pick one up at a rank, or telephone the 24-hour central control (677 7777). The main ranks are at Centraal Station, Rembrandtsplein and Leidseplein. Cafés, restaurants or nightclubs will usually phone a cab for you, and one will arrive within minutes. The city has its share of grumpy middle-aged male cabbies, familiar the world over, but, on the whole, taxi drivers are friendly and honest. When you set off, the meter should be blank, except for the minimum charge. Even short journeys are expensive, working out at about *f*2.30 a kilometre (*f*3.70 a mile) and increasing after midnight.

By Bicycle: Cycling is the perfect means of transport in Amsterdam. It's convenient and gets you about at just the right speed to enjoy the city to the full. It's also a very Dutch way to travel. There are 700,000 people living in Amsterdam, and 550,000 bicycles. Hundreds end up dumped in the canals, and from time to time a dredger with a massive iron claw floats round to fish them out. The curious crowd that invariably gathers to watch remains impassive as the crane hauls out old tyres and stringy lumps of mud, but bursts into a patter of applause at the appearance of a mangled, barnacle-encrusted bike.

The city has an excellent network of cycle-lanes, and motorists are either considerate or outnumbered and intimidated. (Amsterdam drivers have a saying that it would be better to run over a queue of old ladies at the bus stop than one cyclist.) Bicycles are cheap to hire, though it can be more economical to pick up a second-hand one. This you can do from markets or cycle shops for around *f*100.

Hire charges vary according to season, but start at around *f*8 a day. You'll need to take your passport, and a deposit. **Rent-A-Bike** (Pieter Jacobsdwarsstraat 11; tel 625 5029) takes major credit cards and asks for a *f*50 deposit. **The Bulldog** (Oudezijds Voorburgwal 126; tel 624 8248) and **Take-A-Bike** (Stationsplein 6, near Centraal Station; tel 624 8391) are a little cheaper, but require a *f*100 and *f*200 deposit respectively. Neither accepts credit cards.

Bicycle theft is endemic in Amsterdam. *Never* leave your bike unlocked. The best way to secure it is with a solid metal U-shaped lock (thieves go armed with clippers that cut through chains in seconds). Lock the front wheel *and* the frame to a railing or high post. It's a good idea, when you're hiring a bike, to check on your liabilities under the rental firm's terms of insurance.

By Water: If you have the time for the leisurely journeys, canal trips can give you an eye-opening perspective on the city. The moment you step on a boat, you seem to cross a mysterious boundary. People on shore carry on with their lives—nicking bicycles, arguing, making love—apparently oblivious of you sailing past only a few feet away.

The **Canal Bus** takes you on a gentle dawdle along some fine stretches of canal between the Rijksmuseum and Centraal Station, stopping at Leidseplein, Leidsestraat/Keizersgracht and the Anne Frank Huis. Buses leave at 45-minute intervals between 10 am and 6 pm. A day ticket costs *f*12.50, a 2-day ticket is *f*20.

The new **Water Taxis** can be great fun if you're in a party mood—the company will even lay on a guide, food and drink for appropriate extra charges. If you're lucky you can hail an empty water taxi as it putters past (they can stop anywhere along the canalside). You can also order them from the **Water Taxi Centrale** (Stationsplein 8; tel 622 2181; open daily 9 am–1 am; major credit cards accepted). Fares are metered—an eight-seater boat works out at around *f*60 for half an hour irrespective of the number of passengers.

If you're feeling energetic you can hire a **Canal Bike** (a pedalboat that seats two or four people; costs *f*18.50 per hour for a two-seater and *f*27.50 for a four-seater; deposit *f*50; no credit cards). Explore the canals for a while, then drop it off at any one of the hire company's five moorings—at Leidseplein (between the Marriott and American Hotels), between the Rijksmuseum and the Heineken Brewery, at the Westerkerk on Prinsengracht, on the Keizersgracht near Leidsestraat and near Centraal Station. Remember to keep to the right, and keep an ear open for warning hoots emitted by the long canal boats as they approach sharp corners or narrow tunnels.

By Car: If you find yourself lumbered with a car in Amsterdam, you can find **covered carparks** (indicated by a white P on blue background) at De Bijenkorf (on Beursplein), Byzantium (Stadhouderskade, opposite Leidseplein), Europarking (Marnixstraat 250), RAI (on the Europa Boulevard) and under the Muziektheater (Waterlooplein). Charges are around *f*3 an hour, and none of these carparks is open 24 hours. Parking meters also work out at *f*3 an hour. If you park illegally your car will be towed away before you've had a chance to buy an icecream. It will cost you at least *f*200 to get it back from the pound (Oostelijke Handelskade 2, near Centraal Station—this *is* open 24 hours), and they won't take credit cards. If you overstay your time at a meter, your car will be clamped. A yellow sticker on the windscreen tells you where to pay the fine (which works out at about *f*3 per hour). Meters are free after 7 pm, as are uncovered carparks (such as the one on Museumplein) after midnight.

The national **emergency car-repair service** is *ANWB Wegenwacht* (tel 626 8251 or 06 08 08; open 24 hours daily). The most convenient **24-hour petrol stations** are at Marnixstraat 250 and Sarphatistraat 225.

If you'd like to **hire a car**, you'll find the international companies well represented: Avis (Nassaukade 380, tel 683 6061); Budget (Overtoom 121, tel 612 6066) and Hertz (Overtoom 85, tel 612 2441). Local companies provide a good service, sometimes at less than half the price. Try Diks (Van Ostadestraat 278–280, tel 662 3366); Kaspers & Lotte (Van Ostadestraat 232, tel 679 9809) or Kuperus (Middenweg 175, tel 693 8790). Some companies prefer an international driving licence, though an EC one is valid. You'll also need your passport and a credit card (to pay a deposit).

Travellers with Disabilities

Amsterdam's cobbled streets and tiny houses with narrow doorways and steep stairs pose problems for those with limited mobility. **Trams** have high steps, and are not accessible at all. There is, however, a special **taxi service** for wheelchair users (tel 613 4134) and the **metro** (with the exception of Waterlooplein station, which has no lifts) is accessible. The **Netherlands Railways** publishes timetables in braille and a detailed booklet on *Rail Travel for the Disabled*, available at Centraal Station, or through their London office (tel (071) 630 1735).

The Dutch government takes an enlightened and constructive view of the problems faced by disabled people. They have, for example, introduced banknotes with dots in the corner that indicate their value to the visually impaired. You'll find nearly all museums, cinemas and churches have wheelchair access and many have facilities for the visually impaired and hard of hearing. The VVV (near Centraal Station; see Practical A–Z: Tourist Information) or the London Branch of the **Netherlands Board of Tourism** (25–28 Buckingham Gate SW1; tel (071) 630 0451) has lists of accommodation, restaurants, museums and tourist attractions with facilities for the disabled. For information on specialized holidays contact the British organization RADAR, 25 Mortimer St, London W1M 8AB, tel (071) 637 5400.

Maps

Wandering about Amsterdam's labyrinth of canals, you get the feeling that you could set off in *any* direction, and eventually end up where you need to be. (Very often this is true.) It will take some time before you can zig-zag through the backstreets with a local's accomplishment, but some moments studying a good map will help. Practically every free tourist leaflet has some sort of street-plan of Amsterdam. If you need more detail, *Falk* publish a variety of maps ranging from simple fold-outs to the origami-inspired 'patent-folded' version. These are available at souvenir shops and stationers.

Practical A–Z

Addresses

Houses on the main canals are numbered from west to east, even numbers on the outer circumference. The Dutch write the house number *after* the street name, and follow it by Roman numerals indicating the storey: Bloemstraat 56 II would be an apartment two floors above street level at no. 56 Bloemstraat. An apartment at street level is shown by the letters 'hs' (*huis*, house).

Amsterdammers seem to have run out of imagination when naming their streets. If they think they've hit on a good name they'll use it again and again—so you get not only Eerste/1e (first) Helmersstraat but also Tweede/2e (second) Helmersstraat and Derde/3e (third) Helmersstraat. Transverse streets get the epithet 'dwars', and also appear in multiples, so Tweede Egelantiersdwarsstraat will be the second street off Egelantiersstraat. A bit of a mouthful, but useful for finding your way around. The Oudezijd (old side of the city, east of Damrak) and the Nieuwezijd (new side, west of Damrak) are abbreviated in addresses to OZ and NZ—Oudezijds Voorburgwal, for example, is usually written OZ Voorburgwal. Postcodes are written *before* the word 'Amsterdam'. (Postcode directories are available in post offices.)

Climate and Packing

The songs, and all the clichés, about tulips and the spring are right. It's a heady time to be in Amsterdam. The city looks sharp and fresh in the clear light that glints off the canals, café owners tentatively put out a few tables and chairs to catch the new sun, there are flowers *everywhere* and everyone seems to be in a good mood. In summer the atmosphere becomes almost feverish. Tourists crowd the streets and bars, the air gets heavy and humid and mosquitoes breed abundantly on the canals. Gable-spotters enjoy autumn and early winter, as long lines of canalhouses reappear from behind the summer foliage. Brick, cobblestone and leaves mingle in a subtle spectrum of browns. January and February can be punishing. As you teeter along the slippery pavements, you're assassinated by the icy blasts of wind that howl down the narrow streets and lash around corners. But as the door bangs behind you in a warm café or *proeflokaal*, you'll discover the true meaning of the Dutch word *gezelligheid* ('cosiness' and 'friendliness' are about as close as English can get).

The one thing common to all seasons is rain—sudden showers more frequently than the monotonous drenching sort. It's a good idea to pack an umbrella at any time of the year. The temperature can drop rather suddenly, even in summer, so a few warm clothes are a wise precaution.

Amsterdammers are not ostentatious dressers. The **dress code** seems to be that if it feels good, it looks good—and no-one's going to bother you wherever you wear it. Nightclubbing youth is less self-conscious about fashion than in other cities, you'll find bank clerks wearing jeans to work, and T-shirts as well as black bow-ties at the opera.

English-language **books** are readily available, though expensive, so it's better to buy your holiday reading before you go.

Children

Amsterdam is a diminutive city, perfectly tailored to a small person's needs. Parents don't have to go to extraordinary expense or exercise great feats of imagination to give children a good time. Cycle lanes make bicycling about quite safe, a pedalo on the canal can while away a few hours blissfully, even a ride on a rattling, clanging tram can be an event. (If trams prove to be a hit, try one of the antique trolleys that go out to the

Amsterdamse Bos, a woody parkland where the children can ride horses, eat pancakes, swim and run about and shout to their hearts' content; see Day Trips.)

Walk VI is a good one for children—it takes in carnivorous plants, the Anne Frank House, a Money Box Museum and a quirky and eventful Theatre Museum. You can start off the walk in the **Zoo** (Plantage Kerklaan 40; tel 523 3400; open 9–5 daily; entrance adults f16, under-10s f9). It's green and quite attractive, as zoos go, with some interesting outcrops of 19th-century architecture. The complex includes a Planetarium, a museum and a children's farm, where you can stroke and be chewed by various animals (open daily 10–1 and 2–4.30; entrance to both included in the zoo ticket). There's another city farm in the Rembrandtpark, with free horse rides and a playground (*De Uylenburg*, Staalmeesterlaan 420; open Sept–Apr 10–4 daily, May–Aug 10–5 daily; entrance free; tel 618 5235).

Some **museums** have special facilities for children. The **NINT Museum of Science and Technology** is a paradise for young computer enthusiasts. All the high-tech displays have explanations in English and most of them invite fiddling fingers. At the other end of the scale is the **TM Junior** at the Tropenmuseum (Tropical Museum; Linnaeusstraat 2; tel 568 8300; open on Sun only noon–4 pm during term time, during holidays also Mon–Fri 11–4; special events some Saturdays; entrance adults f6, children f3—only one adult is admitted with each child). Staff, who have all had experience of a third world country, create a village-like environment where children can spend time learning first hand about aspects of another culture—such as drumming, rice making or dancing.

Of the **theme parks** out of town, by far the most exciting is **De Efteling** (Europaweg 1, Kaatsheuvel, Noord Brabant, 110 km from Amsterdam; tel (04167) 088111; open Easter–Oct 10–6 daily; entrance f21—Dutch Railways offer a special excursion ticket). This is a surreal fantasy-land with an enormous Enchanted Forest, flying carpets, mysterious boat journeys, a Sleeping Beauty whose breasts heave and all the usual (and some very unusual) rides. The VVV has information about other parks. If you visit The Hague then the **Madurodam Mini-town** is a welcome diversion (see Day Trips).

Over Christmas there's a popular **circus** at the Carré Theatre (see Entertainment). Other **children's theatre** is usually in Dutch, but you might be lucky enough to catch the odd mime or puppet show. Check the listings magazines under the following venues: Kindertheater Elleboog, De Krakeling, Poppentheater Diridas, Mirakel Poppentheater.

If you've had enough of the little darlings, you can get hold of vetted and reliable **babysitters** from Babyzitcentrale Babyhome (tel 616 1119; open for booking Mon and Thur 3–5 pm) or the more expensive Oppascentrale Kriterion (tel 624 5848; open 24 hours). Prices start at about ƒ5 an hour and you're expected to provide drinks, food for long sessions and the cost of transport home after midnight.

Consulates and Embassies

Australia, Koninginnegracht 23, The Hague, tel (070) 363 0983
Canada, Sophialaan 7, The Hague, tel (070) 361 4111
Great Britain, Koningslaan 44, tel 676 4343
New Zealand, Mauritskade 25, The Hague, (070) 346 9324
USA, Museumplein 19, tel 664 5661

For the telephone numbers of other consulates consult the VVV (see Tourist Information below) or one of the listings magazines.

Crime and Drugs

Amsterdam is one of the safest places in Europe. You need have little fear of serious street crime at any time of day or night (though women walking alone would be well advised to avoid red-light districts after midnight). At one time the area around Zeedijk in the city centre prickled with drug dealers and junkies and was quite creepy to walk through. A massive police clean-up has made the area safer, but despite council efforts to encourage shops and galleries to move there, it can still seem seedy and tense.

Contrary to received opinion **soft drugs** are *not* legal in Holland, though an official blind eye is turned to the possession of under 28 g (1 oz) of cannabis. The tolerance goes as far as allowing some coffeeshops to sell cannabis over the counter (see under Food and Drink); here people smoke marijuana on the premises. But this is *not* true of all coffeeshops and cafés, nor of areas outside Amsterdam. Anyone found in possession of **hard drugs**, such as heroin or cocaine can expect swift prosecution.

Bicycle theft, theft from cars and **pickpocketing** are something of a problem. You'll often see quite abusive signs on car windows informing all who might be tempted that there is nothing at all inside to steal.

Amsterdammers sometimes spend more on a lock than on their bicycle ('And I'd *just* bought a new lock!' is a common wail after a bike has been stolen). A favourite trick of pickpockets is to sidle up close and offer to sell you something illicit. In your annoyed efforts to get rid of them (or keenness to see what they've got) you don't notice that your wallet is being gently removed. Sensible vigilance is the only way to avoid these petty crimes: don't leave valuables in your car, always lock your bike securely (see p. 9) and don't carry a wallet in your back pocket or leave it on top of a shop counter when paying. Keep traveller's cheques and stubs separate and don't carry large amounts of money in one pocket.

Amsterdam's police generally keep a low profile and are a relaxed and sympathetic lot. If you do need them, the **emergency number is 06–11**. Main **police stations** are at Elandsgracht 117 and Warmoesstraat 44. Report any theft immediately, and get a written statement for your insurance claim. If you find yourself **in trouble** with the police, phone your consulate as soon as you can (but remember that Dutch police are under no legal obligation to allow you a phone call, and can detain you without charge for up to 24 hours). (For other useful numbers see under Emergencies.)

Discounts

The **Holland Leisure Card** entitles you to all sorts of discounts on transport, car rental, theatres and excursions. It costs *f*25 and is valid for a year—though it can pay for itself within a few days. It's available from the VVV (see Tourist Information below) or your local branch of the Netherlands Board of Tourism. Museums in The Netherlands are seldom free, but for *f*40 (*f*15 for under-18s and *f*25 for pensioners) you can buy an **Annual Museum Card** (*Museumjaarkaart*) which gets you into most museums in Holland for nothing, or at a substantial discount. If you're under 26 the **CJP** (*Cultureel Jongeren Passport*) entitles you to discount at museums, theatres and cultural events. It's available from the AUB Uitburo (Leidseplein 26, tel 621 1211, open Mon–Sat 10–6) for *f*15. You'll need a photograph for all these discount cards, and proof of age for the CJP.

Electricity

The **voltage** in The Netherlands is 220 AC, which is compatible with the UK, but you'll need a transformer for American electrical equipment. Wall sockets take rather flimsy two-pronged plugs.

Emergencies

Police, ambulance or fire brigade, telephone 06–11. The operators speak English.

If you are a victim of **rape or sexual abuse** contact *Tegen Haar Wil* (Against Her Will) on 625 3473 (24 hours). You'll find main **Police Stations** at Elandsgracht 117 and Warmoesstraat 44. It's a good idea, for insurance purposes, to report lost or stolen property to the police as soon as possible. There are **lost property offices** at Centraal Station, GVB Head Office (Prins Hendrikkade 108–114; open Mon–Fri 9–4; for items lost on public transport), and at Waterlooplein 11 (open Mon–Fri 11–3.30; for items lost in parks and on the streets). It's best to allow a day or two for your property to filter through the system before trying to reclaim it. For **medical emergencies**, see under Medical Matters below. **Lost or stolen credit cards** can be reported on the following numbers: American Express, 642 4488; Diners Club 627 9310; Mastercard/Access 01 04 57 0887; Visa 520 5534.

Festivals and Events

Perhaps because of Amsterdam's Puritan heritage, you'll find little civic or royal pomp. Instead, the city lets its hair down at a number of fairs, arts festivals and street parties—the best celebration of all being *Koninginnedag* on 30 April. Here are some dates to aim for:

February	**Carnival**: Though it's more a southern, Roman Catholic tradition, Amsterdammers (always in the market for a party) have also taken to the traditional dressing up and last-minute boozing before Lent.
25th	**Commemoration of the February Strike**—a solemn gathering at the *Dokwerker* statue on J.D. Meijerplein (see p. 131).
March	The **Stille Omgang** (Silent Procession) takes place at night on the Sunday closest to the 15 March. Roman Catholics from all over the world walk in silence along the Heiligeweg and up to Sint Nicolaaskerk to celebrate Amsterdam's 'Miracle' (see p. 31).
	Also in March, the Meervaart Theatre hosts a **Blues Festival** (see Entertainment) and there's a **boat show**

17

featuring the latest pleasure craft at the RAI Congress Centre (on Europaplein).

April **National Museum Weekend** is usually the third weekend in April. All the city's museums allow free entry and get *very* crowded. Unless you're exceptionally hard-up, this is a date to avoid.

30th **Koninginnedag** (Queen's Day—a national holiday to celebrate the Queen's birthday). Amsterdam declares a 'free market'. Anyone can sell anything anywhere and all bar and restaurant takings are tax free. The whole city turns into a cross between the Notting Hill Carnival and a fleamarket. Holland converges on the town to eat, drink, dance and be exceptionally merry, but with the usual charming Dutch relaxed tolerance. Up to three million people throng the streets (Amsterdam's population is only 700,000), yet you hardly see a policeman, there are no barricades, no rules and no problems—seldom upward of ten arrests over the whole day, and those are usually for pickpocketing. The best time to join in is after midnight on the 29th, when everyone is setting up stalls and people are as fresh and excited as children on Christmas Eve.

An internationally respected **World Press Photo Exhibition** displays the pick of newspaper and magazine photography from the preceding year. (In the Nieuwe Kerk from mid-April to mid-May.) Watch out also for **GRAP Day** at *De Melkweg* (see Entertainment), when Amsterdam's best new bands blast away well into the night.

May 4/5 **Herdenkingsdag** (Remembrance day) and **Bevrijdingsdag** (Liberation Day) are not the pompous, jingoistic affairs such occasions often become. Queen Beatrix lays a wreath at the National Monument at 8 pm on Remembrance Day and the whole city observes a moving 2-minute silence. The next day erupts in street parties, live music and another free market. Vondelpark and Leidseplein are the best places to be.

18

June   The **Holland Festival** and its fringe, the **Off-Holland Festival** run for the whole month of June. This is Amsterdam's (and The Hague's) answer to the Edinburgh Festival, with an impressive constellation of international performers booked into opera, dance and theatre venues around both cities.

On the second Sunday in June, 5000 people go for a jog around the canals in the **Echo Grachtenloop** (see Sport).

Around the beginning of the month (or at the end of May) the RAI Congress Centre plays host to **Kunst RAI**, an international contemporary art fair. Later in the month, the **World Roots Festival**—nine days of music, dance and theatre from non-Western cultures takes place at *De Melkweg*.

July   If the Holland Festival sounds too staid for your tastes, try the July **Summer Festival**—a bonanza of the avant-garde that goes on all over town (sometimes in the strangest places).

August   The **Uitmarkt** (Entertainment Market) takes place in the last week of August. Groups from all over the Netherlands offer tantalizing snippets of what the coming cultural season has to offer. It's free, and takes place in theatres, in the open air—in fact anywhere a company can find a suitable space.

More open-air music is played during the **Prinsengracht Concert**—this time from boats opposite the Pulitzer Hotel (Prinsengracht 315–31; also in the last week of August).

September   **Bloemen Corso** (Flower Parade) is a parade of floats from Aalsmeer ('the flower capital') to Amsterdam on the first Saturday of the month. Check with the VVV (see Tourist Information below) for details of the route and arrival times. Vijzelstraat and the Dam are the best places to watch from.

The **Jordaan Festival** is the liveliest of a series of neighbourhood street parties. All over the Jordaan, the

19

residents come out into the streets to booze, barbecue and try their luck in the often unabashedly dire local talent contests.

November   In mid-November St Nicholas (Sinterklaas/Santa Claus) arrives by steamboat at Centraal Station (supposedly from his home in Spain). He parades through the city on a white horse with his slave Black Pete (an oddly persistent tradition in modern, racially aware Amsterdam) and is given the keys of the city by the *burgemeester* on the Dam. Relax with a coffee on Rembrandtsplein and watch the early part of the procession in relative comfort.

December 5   **Pakjesavond** (Parcel Evening) is the traditional Dutch time to give presents—rather than Christmas Day. It's usual to make up a short rhyme which caricatures the recipient. It's very much a family occasion, and unless you have Dutch friends you'll find the city awfully quiet.

Oudejaarsavond (New Year's Eve), on the other hand, is the perfect excuse for more wild partying. People take to the streets with bottles of champagne, some bars stay open all night and there are fireworks *everywhere*.

Insurance

It is always advisable to take out **travel insurance** before any trip abroad—and to do so as soon as you buy your tickets. Specially tailored travel insurance packages cover medical expenses, lost luggage and theft, and also offer compensation for cancellation and delayed departure. The cost of travel insurance is steadily rising, but is still insignificant when compared to the potential costs of a serious emergency, or even the value of your tickets should you have to cancel your trip. Consult your insurance broker or travel agent. In the event of needing to make a claim, be sure to check the small print of your policy to see what documentation (police report, medical forms, invoices etc.) is required by the insurance company.

That said, EC nationals are entitled to receive free or reduced-charge medical treatment in the Netherlands: British visitors will need a form

E111 (fill in application form SA30, available from DSS branches or post offices). Theoretically you should organize this 2 weeks before you leave, though you can usually do it over the counter in one visit. The E111 does not insure personal belongings.

Medical Matters

Ambulance, tel 06–11.

The most useful place to ring if you are ill or need a dentist is the **Central Medical Service** on 664 2111/679 1821. This 24-hour service will refer you to a duty practitioner. The **Tourist Medical Service** on 673 7567 will do the same. The most central **hospital** with an outpatients department is *Onze Lieve Vrouwe Gasthuis* (Eerste Oosterparkstraat 179, tel 599 9111). **Chemists** (*drogisterij*) sell non-prescription drugs and toiletries. If you need a prescription made up you should go to an *apotheek*. The Central Medical Service can also advise you on this. If you've crushed your contact lenses or dropped your specs in a canal, try **York International Optical** (Leidsestraat 32; tel 618 2102; open Mon–Fri 9.30–6, Sat 9.30–5; appointment advisable, major credit cards accepted). If your dentures take a crunch try Accident (Amstelveenseweg 51; tel 664 4380; open Mon–Sat 9.30–5). There's a free and confidential **VD clinic** at Groeneburgwal 44 (tel 622 3777; open Mon–Fri 8.30–5, but arrive before 10.30 am for first consultation; appointment not necessary). The *Polikliniek Oosterpark* (Oosterpark 59; tel 693 2151; open Mon, Wed, Fri 9–5) offers **contraception, abortion and morning after pills**, but its services are not free.

For insurance to cover medical costs, see Insurance above.

Media

Don't be surprised if you find yourself chatting over a coffee with an Amsterdammer about the previous night's **BBC** TV soap-opera. Amsterdam gets BBC1 and 2, Radio 4 (198 kHz AM) and the World Service (6045 kHz AM). Even on Dutch television British and American shows tend to be sub-titled rather than dubbed. Most homes and hotels are connected to **cable**. You can get about 20 stations (including CNN) and can decide what to watch by flicking through to *Infokanaal*—two alternating screens with simultaneous broadcasts of what's on offer on all channels. Non-Dutch speakers might like to tune in to Netherlands

Radio 3 (96.8 mHz) for **pop** or Radio 4 (98.9 mHz) for **classical music**. There are also a number of smaller and pirate music stations—Amsterdam FM (106.8FM) plays the hippest dance music.

International newspapers are available all over Amsterdam, usually on the day of publication. If you want to pigeon-hole the Amsterdammer opposite you on the tram by the newspaper he's reading, here's a short list: *De Telegraaf* is right-wing, sensationalist press (though it has good accommodation ads on Wednesdays). It was the only paper allowed to publish during the Nazi occupation. The *NRC Handelsblad* is the favourite of intellectuals. *Het Parool* started life as a Resistance news-sheet during the war. *Trouw* also went underground, and *De Volkskrant* was banned. These three now form the nucleus of the left-wing press. *Het Financieel Dagblad* gives business news, and has an English summary.

Money

The unit of Dutch currency is the **guilder**, which is abbreviated as *f*, f, fl or Hfl (for the old Dutch term florin). A guilder is divided into 100 **cents** (shortened to 'c'). There are around *f*3 to the pound sterling, and just under *f*2 to the US dollar. The notes are said to be the prettiest in Europe, and come in *f*10, *f*25, *f*50, *f*100, *f*250, *f*500 and *f*1000 denominations. There are six types of coin: a **stuiver** (5c, copper); the **dubbeltje** (10c), **kwartje** (25c), *f*1 and **rikjsdalder** (*f*2.50)—all silver-coloured; and the *f*5 (gold-coloured). All prices are rounded up to multiples of five. Once you've got used to counting in 25s and 2.5s, it's pretty straightforward.

Credit Cards are not as widely accepted as you might expect. It's always a good policy to double check. (For lost credit cards, see under Emergencies). **Eurocheques** and **traveller's cheques** are a better idea. If you have appropriate identification, many establishments will accept them direct.

Banks are the best places to change your money. They're open from 9–4/5 Mon–Fri. (Some stay open until 7pm on Thursdays.) Head offices of the main Dutch banks are:

ABN AMRO, Vijzelgracht 32, tel 629 9111
NMB Postbank, Bijlmerplein 88, tel 563 9111
Rabobank, Wilhelminaplantsoen 124, tel 569 0569
Verenigde Spaarbank, Singel 548, tel 520 5911

Some foreign bank head offices are:

Barclays Bank, Weteringschans 109, tel 626 2209
Citibank NA, Herengracht 545, tel 551 5911
Lloyds Bank, Leidseplein 29, tel 626 3535

Bureaux de change often offer the same rates as banks, but take more commission. There are bureaux open until midnight on Leidsestraat, and the **GWK** exchanges at Centraal Station and Schiphol (both open 24 hours daily) are a better bet than the deals offered by hotel receptions.

If you exchange travellers' cheques at a company branch, you don't have to pay commission at all. You'll find offices of **American Express** at Amsteldijk 166, Damrak 66 (with 24-hour cash dispenser for cardholders and automatic travellers' cheque refund service) and at Koningsplein 10; and **Thomas Cook** at Dam 23–25, Damrak 1–5 (open until 10.30 pm weekdays and also on Sun 9.30–7), and at Leidseplein 31a and Muntplein 12a.

Post Offices

The Dutch postal service logo is a white *ptt post* on a red background. **Post offices** are generally open Mon–Fri 8.30–5. Larger branches may also open on Saturdays from 9–12 noon. Here you can buy stamps, and send letters, express letters and telegrams (make sure you're in the right queue—each counter is labelled). The **Main Post Office** is at Singel 250 (open Mon–Fri 8.30–6, Sat 9–12; late opening Thurs until 8.30; tel 556 3311) and, as well as the usual facilities, has phones, photocopiers, a gift shop and a philately counter. **Parcels** can be sent only through this office, or the sorting office (Oosterdokskade 3, near Centraal Station; open Mon–Fri 8.30–9, Sat 9–12 noon; tel 555 8911). **Stamps** (*post-zegels*) can also be bought from tobacconists. At the time of writing it costs 55c to send a postcard to the UK, 75c to send an airmail letter to the UK or a postcard to the USA and *f*1.30 to send an airmail letter to the USA (prices for letters under 20 grammes). The slot for overseas mail on **post boxes** is marked *Overige*. A **Poste Restante** service is available. Letters should be addressed to: Post Restante, Hoofdpostkantoor ptt, Singel 250, 1012 SJ Amsterdam. You'll need a passport to claim your mail.

Public Holidays

New Year's Day, Good Friday, Easter Sunday and Monday, Queen's Day (30 April), Ascension Day, Whit Sunday and Monday, Christmas Day and Boxing Day. On these days most things close, and Amsterdam can be very quiet indeed.

Religious Affairs

Roman Catholic services in English are held at an old clandestine church: St John and St Ursula (Begijnhof 30; tel 622 1918; Sun 12.15 pm). There's a **Latin High Mass** at Onze Lieve Vrouwekerk (Keizersgracht 220; Sun 11.15 am).

Protestant services in English are held in the serene English Reform/Scottish Presbyterian Church (Begijnhof 48; tel 624 9665; Sun 10.30 am) and at the Anglican Church (Groeneburgwal 42; tel 624 8877; Sun 10.30 am and 7.30 pm). Times of **Jewish** services vary. You can contact the Liberal Community at Jacob Soetendorpstraat 8 (tel 642 3562) and the Orthodox Community at PO Box 7967, Van der Boechorstraat 26, 1008 AD (tel 646 0046).

Telephones

Amsterdam's telephone boxes are green, with a white *ptt telecom* logo. **Payphones** take 25c, *f*1 and *f*2.50 coins. Queues are shorter at the **cardphones**, largely because phonecards are such a bother to buy. You can get them, after waiting in another long queue, only at post offices and railway stations. Instructions in phone boxes are clear, but don't be confused by the local ringing tone—a long continuous sound rather like the British 'engaged' signal. A busy line in Holland is indicated by rapid tones. Another confusing surprise is the dalek voice you get when phoning popular numbers such as airports or taxis. You're told: *Er zijn nog drie (three)/twee (two)/een (one) wachtenden voor u*—an indication of how many people are patiently waiting ahead of you in an electronic queue. The **Telehouse** (Raadhuisstraat 46–50; open 24 hours) offers fax, telex and telegram facilities. You can also phone abroad direct from phones that, as you speak, rather disconcertingly flash up the amount your call is costing. Private phone centres like the Teletalk Center (Leidsestraat 101; open 10–midnight) offer the same sevice as the Telehouse, but are pricier. Phoning direct from hotel rooms is usually outrageously expensive.

All numbers given in this book which are not preceded by a bracketed code are Amsterdam numbers.

Directory Enquiries: 008
International Operator (also for collect calls): 06 0410
International Directory Enquiries: 06 0418
Direct dialling code: USA 09–1- area code without 0
Direct dialling code: UK 09–44- area code without 0

When making international calls you must wait for a second dialling tone after dialling 09. International calls are cheaper between 8 pm and 8 am, but calls to other European countries don't count as international.

Time

Amsterdam is 2 hours ahead of Greenwich Mean Time in the spring and summer, and 1 hour ahead in winter and autumn.

Tipping and Etiquette

Restaurant and bar bills in Holland are inclusive of tax and service, so a tip isn't really necessary. It's customary, though, to round the amount up to the nearest guilder (or 5 guilders for a big bill). If the service has been exceptional, it's quite acceptable to add a little more. Don't leave money on the bar counter after buying your drink. Amsterdammers will either think it a little vulgar, or take it for a tip. **Taxi Drivers** expect 10 per cent—especially if they've helped with luggage.

Queuing at supermarket delicatessens, some banks and public institutions is controlled by an electronic ticketing system. You tear off a ticket as you enter and wait for your number to flash up on a screen. At cash machines and bank and post office counters, the rest of the queue keeps a polite metre or so's distance from the person transacting business. Sometimes there's a boundary line painted on the floor. Step over this mark (visible or otherwise) and the atmosphere turns icy.

English is spoken almost as a second mother-tongue in Amsterdam. Some Hollanders seem to resent this, but many (especially those working in restaurants, bars and shops) seem insulted if you ask 'Do you speak English?' One way round this is to open with a cheery *dag!* ('darhg'— good day) and then speak English. *'Dag'*—called out with a friendly upward lilt in the voice—is used at all times of day or night, entering *and* leaving shops, when speaking to barmen, policemen, cabbies and tram drivers.

When you meet a Dutch person for the first time, it's polite to shake hands and say your name clearly.

Toilets

Amsterdam is dotted with rather attractive, but foul-smelling, curved, green metal **urinoirs**. These are right on the pavement, and blot out only the mid-torso from public gaze. All passers-by see is a pair of feet and a face trying desperately to look nonchalant. In the 1970s, feminists—less out of pissoir-envy than anger at the lack of facilities for women—bound up a few of the offending privies in swathes of pink ribbon. The protest had no effect. Apart from those at railway stations, there are still no normal public toilets in Amsterdam. For women, or men who balk at the idea of peeing *al fresco*, the best option is to duck into a café. This is perfectly acceptable practice, though bars in some of the busier tourist areas discourage it. The better hotel foyers provide classier options, but this takes a certain amount of poise, as you have to stroll through the lobby as if you're a resident, all the time darting your eyes about for the relevant sign—not easy if you're caught in a last-minute dash. Station loos—and sometimes those in larger cafés—are guarded by fierce women, who require you to drop at least 25 cents into a saucer before passing.

Tourist Information

The *Vereniging Voor Vreemdelingenverkeer* (literally 'the Association for Alien Traffic') is known everywhere by it's initials **VVV** (pronounced fay fay fay). The English-speaking staff help with information about tourist sights, events and transport. They can change money and (for a *f*3.50 fee) arrange hotel and theatre bookings. They sell a range of maps and brochures and can suggest tours and walks. The main Amsterdam branch is opposite Centraal Station at Stationsplein 10 (open Easter–June, Sept Mon–Sat 9 am–11 pm, Sun 9 am–9 pm; July, Aug 9 am–11 pm daily; Oct–Easter Mon–Fri 9–6, Sat 9–5, Sun 10–1 and 2–5). A branch at Leidsestraat 106 has similar opening hours for most of the year (except Oct–Easter, Mon–Fri 10.30–5.30, Sat 10.30–9).

Information about public transport is given by the **GVB (Amsterdam Municipal Transport Authority)** (Stationsplein 15; open Mon–Fri 7–10.30, Sat 8–10.30, Sun 8.30–4.30).

The **AUB Uitburo** (Leidseplein 26; tel 621 1211; open Mon–Sat 10–6) gives information and sells advance tickets (booking fee ƒ2) for the city's **theatres and concert halls** and for many other cultural events. It also distributes leaflets and **listings magazines** (see Entertainment).

The information desk at Schiphol Airport can give you a free English copy of the **Visitors Yellow Pages**, a slim book of useful telephone numbers.

The **Netherlands Board of Tourism** offices can give you details of hotels and events and can sell you a Holland Leisure Card (see Discounts above):

UK 25–28 Buckingham Gate, London SW1E 6LD;
    tel (071) 630 0451
USA 355 Lexington Ave, 21st Floor, New York, NY 10017;
    tel (212) 370 7367
    225 N. Michigan Ave, Suite 326, Chicago, IL 60601;
    tel (312) 819 0300
    605 Market Street, Room 401, San Fransisco, CA 94105;
    tel (415) 543 6772
Canada 25 Adelaide Street East, Suite 710, Toronto, Ontario, M5C 1Y2;
    tel (416) 363 1577
Australia Suite 302, 5 Elizabeth Street, Sydney NSW 2000;
    tel (2) 276921

Tours

On the jetties around Centraal Station you'll find a cluster of boat companies offering **canal tours**, candlelight cruises and dinner cruises. Prices and standards are almost uniform, but Lovers Rondvaarten (Prins Hendrikkade 25–27; tel 622 2181) has the best reputation.

The VVV (see Tourist Information above) not only takes bookings for canal cruises, but constantly comes up with new ideas for touring the city—its staff can suggest all sorts of walking and cycling routes in and about Amsterdam, including a Walkman tour (ƒ30; you'll need your own personal stereo). **Yellowbike** (NZ Voorburgwal 66; tel 620 6940) also offers guided cycle tours around the city and surrounding waterlands.

More rewarding than the commercially organized tours are the informal walkabouts with old Amsterdam residents offered by **Mee in Mokum** (tel 625 1390; Mon–Fri 1–4 pm). The guides aren't professional, but give a homely, resident's touch that you're unlikely to find elsewhere. The tours are usually done in Dutch, but since the groups are small (about eight people), it's often possible to arrange an English alternative.

Archivisie is a small, overworked but dynamic new organization that offers specialist architectural tours for professionals or interested lay-people. It gets you into buildings that other tourists cannot reach (for information, tel 625 8908).

History

Watery Beginnings

A 17th-century English pamphleteer scoffed that the Dutch were 'bred and descended from a horse turd which was enclosed in a butter-box'. Our knowledge of the origins of the first Amsterdammers is only a shade more enlightened. For much of its early history Amsterdam was a swamp. The River Amstel petered out in the vast tidal flats of the IJ. There was a Roman settlement in the dunes near Leiden (Pliny was miserable there in AD 50), but they weren't too keen on the marshes to the north. The first inhabitants of the area we now call Amsterdam were probably intrepid adventurers who came floating down the Rhine in hollowed-out logs around AD 1000, looking for better land. Luck was certainly not on their side, but they made the best of a boggy lot, built huts on muddy mounds and drained the land around them, creating the first polders.

In the 12th century a local bigwig, **Gijsbrecht**, built himself a castle at the spot where the River Amstel was dammed (on the site of the present day Dam Square). He called himself the first Lord of Amstel and laid claim to the countryside emerging from the water around him. The Lords of Amstel were answerable to the **Bishops of Utrecht**, and rather resented it. In the late 13th century Gijsbrecht IV felt he was powerful enough to rebel, but he didn't reckon on his neighbour, Floris V, the

Count of Holland joining in the fray. Floris had wooed popular support in 1275 by granting special **toll privileges** to the people who lived beside 'the Aemstelle Dam'. Floris defeated Gijsbrecht, but later Gijsbrecht crept up on Floris and murdered him. The Bishop of Utrecht took advantage of the confusion and confiscated Gijsbrecht's land. In 1300 he granted the town of 'Aemstelledamme' its **first charter**. When he died in 1317 he ceded Amsterdam and the surrounding countryside to his nephew, William III, the new Count of Holland. The people of Amsterdam took full advantage of their toll privileges and of William's wide influence and settled down to serious trading and money-making.

Growing Prosperity

The growth of Amsterdam as a trading post owes itself to **herring and beer**. In 1323 the Count of Holland granted Amsterdam the sole right to import beer from Hamburg—at that time northern Europe's largest brewing town and a prominent member of the powerful alliance of Baltic trading ports, the **Hanseatic League**. As most people drank beer rather than the poisonous local water, Amsterdam merchants began to get rich. Then in 1384 one **Willem Beukels** hit upon a way of preserving herring more efficiently—by gutting them before salting. This meant that ships could stay out at sea even longer and travel further afield. At about the same time, as if obeying some cosmic plan, the herring moved their spawning ground from the Baltic to the North Sea. The industry prospered. It needed salt (from Portugal) and wood for the barrels (from Germany and Scandinavia). Amsterdam merchants had no qualms, as they moved further into the Baltic, about breaking in on the Hanseatic League's trade and developing new routes. Soon the city's ships were also carrying furs, iron ore, cloth, wine and enormous quantities of grain to feed Europe's growing population (bread was still the staple diet). Wily merchants began building warehouses all over the city to store goods until the best price could be fetched. Amsterdam became a thriving commercial centre and a nexus for European trade. It fought a bitter trade war with the Hanseatic towns, but, by the mid-15th century, was indomitable.

During medieval times the town remained small—a cosy cluster of wooden houses stretching along the banks of the Amstel. In 1300 Amsterdam had one church (the Oude Kerk) and two streets—the present day Warmoesstraat and Nieuwendijk. The town was razed by **great fires** in 1421 and 1452. Wooden buildings were forbidden after the second blaze, and only two remain today (see p. 105 and p. 153). By the 15th century the boundaries extended as far as Oudezijds Voorburgwal, Nieuwezijds Voorburgwal and Spui. There was a new church as well as a clump of monasteries, chapels and inns built to cope with pilgrims flocking to the scene of the **Amsterdam Miracle**. In 1345 a dying man had vomited up the host after his last communion. It was thrown on a fire but didn't burn. Later it developed healing powers, and would transport itself overnight between churches. A chapel of its own seemed to make it stay in one place and, though this burnt down, the host survived. It became an object of worship, and is still honoured today in the **Stille Omgang** (Silent Procession, see p. 17). One of those healed by the magic wafer was **Maximilian I**, Emperor of Austria (later Holy Roman Emperor). Amsterdam had further earned his gratitude by supporting his faction, the Kabeljauwen (Codfish), against the conservative Hoeken (Hooks) in the struggle for domination of the Low countries. In 1489 he upped Amsterdam's prestige by granting the city the right to use his royal insignia in its coat of arms. Trade flourished, and by 1500 Amsterdam bustled with 9000 inhabitants contained within its first city wall (following the line of the present day Gelderskade, Kloveniersburgwal and Singel canals).

Reformation and Revolt

At the beginning of the 16th century Europe was firmly in the grip of the Roman Catholic Church. But on 31 October 1517 a hitherto obscure Augustinian monk called **Martin Luther** calmly walked up to the chapel of Wittenberg Castle and nailed his '95 Theses' to the door. The 'Theses' condemned superstition in the Church and the practice of indulgences. Luther's act marked the beginning of the Reformation—theologians everywhere became braver and more audible in their criticism. In Rotterdam **Erasmus** propounded an idealized man as the pinnacle of creation, rather than the miserable sinner after the Fall. In Geneva **Calvin** appealed to the Age of Reason with his impeccably logical 'Institutes': the State should be separated from the Church, and in the hands of morally upright citizens. The Catholic Church responded swiftly and thousands were tried for heresy.

Trade ships carried new ideas quickly to Amsterdam. The revolutionary theology caught on, and there were many heresy trials, but the city fathers were traditionally tolerant and didn't always carry out sentences they were obliged to impose. In fact Calvin's austere doctrines, and the notion of civil power, rather appealed to a number of wealthy merchant families. The city became ruffled only when the lower-class sect of **Anabaptists** began to jostle the status quo. In 1534 Melchior Hoffman became convinced that mankind was on the brink of a new world order. Münster in Germany, was to be the New Jerusalem. He styled himself 'King of Münster' and sat back to await the Second Coming. Fervent crowds of believers joined him. Soon he was sending 'prophets' to Amsterdam, where people were easily convinced that they too lived in a chosen city. The city fathers were at first benign, but on 11 February 1535 a frenzied handful of Anabaptists stripped naked and cavorted about the Dam. Then, on 10 May, 40 members of the sect took advantage of the celebrations of the feast of the Guild of the Cross and occupied the town hall, while the councillors were 'far gone in drink'. It took the (probably inebriated) Civic Guard until the following morning to get them out. Heresy was bad enough, but civil unrest was intolerable. Normally mild Amsterdam came up with horrible death sentences for the usurpers: 'The chest is to be opened up while they are still alive, the heart removed and thrust into their faces, whereupon they are to be beheaded and quartered. Their heads are to be mounted on stakes on the town gates, and their parts are to be hung outside the gates.' Pictures were commissioned of the Anabaptists' acts of 'raving insanity', and were hung in the town hall as a warning to anyone else who might think of toppling the sacred city institutions. The lax city fathers were almost immediately replaced on orders from above.

At this time the Netherlands was ruled, as a consequence of marriages made in the stratosphere of the royal courts of Europe, by **Philip II** of Spain (later husband of Mary Tudor). Philip was head of the mighty Austro-Spanish Catholic house of Hapsburg which dominated much of Europe, owned most of South America and even laid claim to the English crown. Unlike his reassuringly named predecessors (Philip the Good, Charles the Bold and Philip the Fair), Philip II was a cruel and fanatical despot. He also took ages to reach decisions—so his subjects spent most of their lives in a terrified limbo. Action was dangerous, no orders came from above and awkward political situations had the habit of deteriorating around the protagonists. This was particularly aggravating in territories as far flung as the Netherlands. Even Dutch Catholics, outraged by the horrors of the Inquisition and this distant monarch's cruel repression, became antagonistic. Opposition to Philip began to grow along nationalist as well as religious lines. Philip took a quiet step back, leaving his sister, **Margaret of Parma**, to deal with any unpleasantness. Angry city regents persuaded her to sign the **'Moderation'**, which implied some measure of religious tolerance. Protestants from around Europe began to see the Netherlands as the only safe haven outside Germany and Switzerland. Calvinist preachers came to Amsterdam, where Protestant services were permitted outside the city walls. During the summer of 1566, hundreds of people left the city's churches to listen to these open air **'hedge-sermons'**.

A crop failure the previous winter had caused a **famine**. Amsterdam was already the largest town in Holland, with a population of over 30,000 and some appalling slums where people often froze to death or were stricken with diseases from the stinking canals. All this gave an even sharper edge to the religious rancour being stirred up in the polders outside the city. On 30 August some Amsterdam sailors brought back fragments of marble statues smashed by Puritans in Flemish churches. This sparked off a frenzy of destruction. The **iconoclasts** smashed the windows of the Oude Kerk and battered or burnt all popish treasures and artworks. A brave group of women encircled the chapel of the Heilige Stede (where the miraculous host was kept) and fended off furious attackers, but the violence spread. The rabble was diverted by the discovery of the wine cellars at the friary of the Friars Minor, but was only subdued when the city fathers offered up the Franciscan church for Protestant worship.

Even Protestant Amsterdammers, suddenly brought face to face with a wrathful populace, were shaken. Philip II was livid. He sent an army of 10,000 men under the **Duke of Alva**—the 'Iron Duke'—to punish the heretics. Most of the Protestant leaders, sensing what was coming, hastily left the country. When the Duke arrived in Amsterdam, 170 merchants' houses lay empty. He moved in style into a house on the prestigious, but desolate, Warmoesstraat and borrowed vast amounts of money to pay his army (including ƒ14,000 from his landlord). A reign of terror began. So many people were executed by his **Council of Blood** that the city was nicknamed 'Murderdam'. In 1568, the date taken as the beginning of the **Eighty Years' War** with Spain, the exiled **William of Orange** attempted a campaign against Alva. (William's previous discretion about his Protestant sympathies had earned him the name 'William the Silent'). Terrified local Protestants gave him little support and the invasion was a failure. William didn't have enough money to pay his soldiers and had to creep away from them in the night. He wandered around France gathering another army, and by 1572 was meeting with a little more success. He was assisted by the **Sea-beggars**, a rough and ready bunch of quasi-pirates, who proved an embarrassment to their sober general by pillaging churches, massacring clergy, dressing up in desecrated vestments and getting drunk (but they was later to form the basis of the Dutch navy). Soon William controlled all the towns around Amsterdam. Meanwhile, the populace was turning against Alva—less as a result of his vicious persecutions than because of the **10th penny tax** he had imposed (which diverted 10 per cent of all citizens' income into the Duke's coffers). Alva slipped away one night in 1573, just a few hours before he was due to face a meeting of angry creditors.

In the winter of 1575–6 William laid **siege** to the city. The town officials were so worried about infiltrators that they banned skating on the canals and even stood guard at important gates themselves. Cattle from the fields were brought within the city walls and stabled in the deserted merchants' houses. Priceless silver was melted down and minted into coins in an attempt to keep business ticking over. The ever-prudent Amsterdam city fathers had only been supporting Philip II because Spain seemed the stronger side. After a long siege, it became clear that William was going to win the war, so, in 1578, the city judiciously swapped allegiance and made peace with William. This signalled the virtual end of Spanish dominion over the Netherlands (though they were to retain sovereignty for another 70 years). Exiles streamed back into the city and on 26 May all the Catholic officials and most of the clergy (who had expected retaliatory executions) were bundled into a boat, escorted to the outskirts of the city and cast off to find their way to more hospitable climes. A Protestant city government was set up by members of leading Calvinist families. With characteristic Amsterdam grace, the events of 26 May were tactfully referred to as the 'Alteration'.

In 1579 the southern, Catholic and largely French-speaking, provinces signed the **Union of Arras** and declared their allegiance to Spain. This gave Spain a base for attacks on the north (most notably the punishing **Siege of Antwerp** in 1584–5). Seven northern provinces responded with the **Union of Utrecht**, a Protestant military federation with The Hague as the centre of power. The Union upheld the 'freedom of religious belief': this meant that you could *be* a Roman Catholic, but still weren't allowed to worship openly. Amsterdam, however, turned a blind eye to the clandestine churches that opened up in attics and behind domestic façades all over town.

Amsterdam was now by far the most economically powerful city in the federation. The siege of Antwerp had not only wiped out a major trade rival, but had despatched droves of refugees who made straight for the haven in the north. Amsterdam's tolerance paid off. The newcomers brought skills, like diamond cutting, that fired the city's crafts and industries into a new life.

Though the war had closed off normal trade routes, local merchants had kept rich by supplying both sides in the conflict. Through much of its history Amsterdam seemed to operate on the principle that 'if we didn't supply the enemy, we couldn't afford to fight them'. Arms dealers would support entire wars all over Europe, and brokers of marine insurance (introduced in the late 15th century) had no qualms about insuring both sides in a battle. Amsterdammers excelled at making money. At the end of the 16th century they were on the brink of the most resplendent era of their history.

The Golden Age (17th century)

A map worked into the floor of Amsterdam's 17th-century *Stadhuis* (town hall) places the city at the centre of the universe—and for much of the century that must have seemed true. Goods flowed into the port from around the world, paused for a while in one of the hundreds of brimming warehouses and, as soon as prices went up, were packed off to distant and lucrative markets. Guilds flourished as the abundance of raw materials attracted craftsmen from around Europe, and even the lowliest workers earned nearly twice as much as their English counterparts. The **Bours** (Exchange) thronged with merchants from countries as far away as India and Turkey. They conducted a resounding trade in property and shares, and merchandise of all sorts. **Isaac le Maire** had the bright idea of trading *in blanco*—dealing in paper with goods he didn't yet own—and the first futures market was begun. In 1609 the city council founded the **Amsterdam Wisselbank** (Bank of Exchange) in the cellar of the town hall. It drew up bank drafts to replace coins (which could be clipped, melted down or stolen), gave quick mortgages and lent at a good rate of interest. (An encouraging $3^1/2$–4 per cent; England dragged behind at 6 per cent). Amsterdam notes of exchange were accepted throughout the world. The bank was stable and efficient and foreign governments and monarchs used it to finance their campaigns and stash away nest-eggs in case they were toppled.

People flooded into the city and by 1650 the population had shot past the 200,000 mark. As early as 1613, far-sighted town planners had begun an extension of three new canals around the perimeter of the city. Initially the Herengracht (Gentleman's Canal), Keizersgracht (Emperor's Canal) and Prinsengracht (Prince's Canal) went only as far as the present day Leidsegracht, but further construction in 1662 gave Amsterdam its familiar half-moon shape. Malodorous industries and the poor were banished to the fields beyond, to the area now known as the Jordaan (see pp. 139–40). The wealthiest merchants built themselves grand mansions along the new canals and the city built a *Stadhuis* that was proclaimed the eighth wonder of the world (see pp. 102–3). The arts and intellectual life flourished. Not only were Rembrandt, Vermeer and Frans Hals kept busy, but lesser painters (craftsmen of the Guild of St Luke) churned out an estimated 20 million pieces of work during the first part of the century. Even the poorest houses had paintings. Books suppressed elsewhere rolled off Amsterdam's uncensored presses—and if you hung about the right cafés you could bump into Spinoza or Descartes.

The city's economy was solidly based on the Baltic grain trade (it filled four-fifths of the warehouses), but the spirit of the Golden Age shines clearest in the romance, daring and glamour of the trade with the East. Initially Amsterdam hadn't bothered to send ships further than Lisbon, relying on intrepid Portuguese sailors for booty from the spice islands. In 1580, however, Philip II conquered Portugal and closed its ports to his arch-enemy. It was clear that Amsterdam would have to send her own ships to the East. Jews fleeing the Inquisition brought valuable inside information about trade routes, and in 1595 Jan Huyghens published *Itinerario*, a book which told temptingly of the precariousness of Portuguese government in the colonies. Later that year **Cornelis de Houtman** set off with four ships and 200 men on a voyage of discovery. Only 99 men limped back in battered ships on 23 August 1597, and investors just managed to break even, but the port buzzed with excitement. When a second voyage realized a profit of 400 per cent, merchants exploded into action. In 1597 the romantically named 'Compagnie van Verre' (Far Away Company) began direct trade with the East Indies. Everybody wanted to get in on the act. So many new companies were formed that they looked likely to put each other out of business before they'd really started. On 20 March 1602 they all united to form the **Vereinigde Oostindische Compagnie** (United East India Company—VOC). All of Amsterdam seemed greedily caught up in the spirit of adventure. Domestic servants and seamstresses were among the thousands of early shareholders. The company had the monopoly of Dutch trade from the

Cape of Good Hope to Cape Horn, and at the peak of its influence it had over 150 merchant vessels protected by 40 fighting ships and its own army of 10,000 soldiers. It sailed all over the East Indies and also to India, Ceylon, China, the South Pacific Islands and South Africa. For nearly two centuries it was the most powerful trade organization in the world. The VOC could establish colonies, sign treaties and declare war and it became the cutting edge of Dutch colonialism. A contemporary English traveller remarked that it was 'a commonwealth within a commonwealth'.

In 1624 the West India Company was formed. It was a copy-cat venture, smaller and much less prosperous than the VOC, and had the trade monopoly over the seas between Africa and the Americas. It teetered along largely on the profits of the slave trade, but exhausted its coffers waging colonial wars against the Portuguese and Spanish. The company's main claim to fame was that it administered the American colony of New Amsterdam—later captured by the British and renamed New York.

The trading companies' economic clout gave Amsterdam tremendous sway over the rest of the Netherlands. Eight of the Chamber of Seventeen, the powerful governing body of the VOC, had to be Amsterdam citizens, and managers were appointed by the *burgemeester*. Power in the city itself was grasped by a handful of patrician families. The Catholic clique ousted during the Alteration was replaced by a Protestant oligarchy that became known as the **Magnificat**. Family names like Hooft, Pauw, Bicker, van Beuningen and Six can still raise an Amsterdammer's eyebrow. Wives and daughters sat on the boards of charities and almshouses (housed in confiscated monasteries) and sons would serve in the civil guard on their way up to becoming *burgemeesters* or magistrates. The city was ruled by the **Heren (Lords) XLVIII**, a council of four *burgemeesters*, a sheriff, seven jurists and 36 advisers. These 'regents' often came into conflict with national government. After the Union of Utrecht, the Netherlands was governed by the **States General**, a body of representatives that met at The Hague. Each province was headed by a *stadhouder* (an ancient title that was previously used for the king's deputy). In practice, *all* the provinces chose William of Orange as their *stadhouder*. Successive generations continued to elect heirs to the House of Orange, so the title became all but hereditary. William's son, Maurits, was called 'Prince', and soon the family was considered grand enough for a match with an English princess.

The *stadhouder* was commander-in-chief of the country's armed forces, and this brought him into conflict with the regents. Peace was better for business than war, and after the final defeat of the Spanish in 1648, the Amsterdam merchants wanted to cut back on military spending. William II wanted to keep his armies. The traditional unease between Amsterdam and the House of Orange bristled into tension. On 23 June 1650 the *stadhouder* visited Amsterdam and demanded an official reception. The regents refused, and condescendingly invited him for dinner instead. 'If we are to wine and dine together,' sniffed a piqued William, 'then we would have to be better friends than we are at present.' He left the next day, gathered troops and sent them to take Amsterdam by surprise. Civil war was narrowly averted. The invading army got lost in a fog and were spotted by a postman on his way over from Hamburg. The city was warned, and William was forced to negotiate. When he died of the pox some months later, the States General passed a law forbidding anyone from the House of Orange ever to become *stadhouder* again—a resolution that was only to last a few decades.

The Decline

In the first half of the 17th century Germany was battling through the Thirty Years' War, the Roundheads and Cavaliers were roughing each other up in England, and France had been left rather limp by the war with Spain. Around 1650 the dust began to settle, and the pugnacious neighbours turned their attention to the prosperous little country in their midst. The conflicts of the late 17th and 18th centuries drained the United Provinces' (and especially Amsterdam's) coffers and gave the warfaring House of Orange a useful step-up back to power.

Squabbles over herring and punitive anti-Dutch import laws led to wars with England in 1652 and 1664. Rather unwillingly, the Provinces found themselves fighting France in the **War of the Spanish Succession** (1701–14). There was another war in 1780 when England discovered the Dutch had secretly been trading with rebel American colonies. London and Hamburg began to take over as mercantile centres, while Amsterdam's old trade routes were threatened. England's increasing sea power began to erode the East Indies trade, and in 1791, after years of false accounting, the VOC went into liquidation. The River Schelde was re-opened as a trade route, putting Antwerp back on the map as an important port. Trade became a less important part of the economy, and while Amsterdam focussed its attention on banking, the early industrial revolution passed it by.

As the money business boomed, the Amsterdam oligarchy became increasingly corrupt and complacent. Children of influential families would be given public posts as christening presents. (They would draw the salary while a menial did the work.) The city fathers happily pocketed a large portion of the taxes they collected. The rich got ostentatious, and the poor got angry and subversive. On 24 June 1748 an Amsterdam merchant noticed a 'shameless slut' in the buttermarket who turned her back on a guard and 'several times raised her skirt, smacking her bare buttocks saying "that's for you"'. The guard shot her ('in her bare fundament') and she later died. This was all that was needed to spark off some well-organized street violence. Armed with lists of tax collectors' addresses, a mob stormed the grand canals, sacking houses and destroying anything of value. The **Tax Farmers' Riot** was swiftly suppressed, but the civil guard had to beat drums below the scaffold to drown out the slogans shouted by the ringleaders as they went to the gallows.

Vociferous, fantastically dressed bands of volunteers, heady with Rousseau's ideas, began to roam the countryside spreading the gospel of democracy. They had the support of some sympathetic patricians, such as Hendrik Hooft (affectionately known as 'Father Hooft'). Soon these **Patriots** had taken over the governments of many smaller towns, and on 27 April 1787 they staged a coup in Amsterdam. The Prince of Orange had had enough. With the armies of his brother-in-law, the King of Prussia, he sent the Patriots packing. Many fled to France, where they were just in time for the revolution. In 1795 a French Republican army, with the support of exiled Patriots, crossed the frozen Rhine and advanced on Amsterdam. There was, by this time, strong pro-French feeling in the Netherlands, especially in Amsterdam. The invading armies were seen as liberators, and the Regents were bloodlessly deposed in what became known as **The Velvet Revolution**. A 'Freedom Tree' was erected on the Dam and Amsterdammers danced around it celebrating the newly declared **Batavian Republic** (the Batavians were the ancient tribe of the Netherlands). Amsterdam got its first elected city government, but the *liberté, égalité* and *fraternité* were not to last for long. In 1806 Napoleon created his younger brother, **Louis Bonaparte**, King of the Netherlands. Louis converted Amsterdam's prized *Stadhuis* into a palace and demolished the ancient public weighhouse on the Dam because it spoiled his view. The city wasn't consoled by the fact that it was now the new capital.

Though he had started off on the wrong foot, Louis soon endeared himself to the people by visiting the stricken during smallpox epidemics, actively supporting the arts and sciences and rather foolishly standing up to his older brother. (He allowed Dutch smugglers to break Napoleon's blockade of British ports). Napoleon hadn't expected his young sibling to be such an upstart, so in 1810 he deposed him and incorporated the Netherlands into the French Empire. But Waterloo was just around the corner. Even before that battle, in 1813 (after Napoleon's retreat from Moscow) the French garrison withdrew from Amsterdam and the Netherlands was proclaimed a constitutional monarchy under the House of Orange. The 1814 **Congress of Vienna** united all the Netherlands provinces (north and south) for the first time—though this lasted only until 1831, when Belgium became an independent kingdom.

From Gloom to Light

Historian Jan Romein describes 19th-century Amsterdam as 'drabness piled on drabness'. After months of bickering with The Hague, Amsterdam had become the capital of the new Dutch Republic and home to the Netherlands Bank, but it was a stuffy and threadbare town. The city's coffers were empty. Napoleon's blockade of English ports and the British occupation of Dutch colonies during the Napoleonic wars had strangled trade, the money market had slipped across the channel to London, and Amsterdam's entrepreneurs had disdained the inventions of the Industrial Revolution. The trading companies' dainty sailboats were soon to be eclipsed by heavy steamships, too bulky to negotiate the Zuider Zee. In 1824 the North Holland Canal (between Amsterdam and Den Helde) was given a festive opening, but the bravado was misplaced. The numerous bends and locks compelled such creeping progress that it was hardly worth the merchants' while.

The sagging city almost collapsed under the burden of a population that doubled in the last half of the century. Living conditions were horrific. Whole families were crammed into dank cellars. Areas like the Jordaan and De Pijp became squalid, overcrowded slums, ravaged by cholera. (There were 2273 victims of the 1848/9 epidemic alone.) Amsterdam had fallen far from the glory-days of the Golden Age. In 1838, with deft symbolism, the piles under the Stock Exchange gave way and the building collapsed.

As the disconsolate city limped through the early decades of the 19th century, a few valiant paladins of the new industries tried to revitalize her. The king set up the Nederlandse Handelsmaatschappij (Netherlands Trading Company) to perk up the drooping trade in tropical products. In 1825 **Paul van Vlissingen** started running regular steamship services to London and Hamburg and built an engineering works on Oostenburg island in east Amsterdam. Almost single-handedly he nudged the city into the industrial age. But the man most personally responsible for rousing Amsterdam from her torpor was the peppy doctor and philanthropist, **Samuel Sarphati**. With his motto *Amsterdam Vooruit!* (Amsterdam Advance!), he was bent on pushing the town headlong into another Golden Age. He founded a commercial college, several banks, a construction company, the city's first hygienic bread factory, the Amstel Hotel (still one of the best in town) and an efficient and profitable refuse disposal service (the city's stinking waste was shipped out in sealed barges, composted and sold to farmers). He founded the *Vereniging voor Volksvlijt* (Industrial Society) to knock new life into the city's flagging manufacturers and to inject new technology into the factories. His sparkling glass Palace of Industry rose up dramatically on Frederiksplein and was home to countless displays, exhibitions and concerts until it burnt down in 1929.

Towards the end of the century Amsterdam began to thrive once more. New industries—even a motor car factory—flourished. The opening of the Suez Canal in 1869 meant easier access to the Orient, and in 1876 the North Sea Canal was cut through the dunes to give proper access to bigger ships. Amsterdam became the main supplier to a newly unified Germany, and manufacturing and shipbuilding industries revived. The discovery of diamonds in South Africa led to a boom in the diamond cutting trade, with workers becoming deliriously rich overnight. In 1839 the first railway in the Netherlands ran from Amsterdam to Haarlem; fifty years later there were nearly 200 trains running to destinations all over Europe and the city had a grand new railway station that obliterated the view of the harbour. During the 1880s the first trams and bicycles made their appearance. (Lady cyclists had to attend special riding schools, as it was thought undignified, if not lewd, for them to be seen wobbling along beside the canals). The Vondelpark was laid out on the edge of the city and the élite scurried to live around it. The arts blossomed. The Rijksmuseum, Concertgebouw, Carré Theatre, Amsterdamse Schouwburg and Stedelijk Museum all sprang up in the last two decades of the century. By 1883 Amsterdam had regained enough of her former grace to host the World Exhibition.

The 19th century saw an increase in parliamentary democracy in the Netherlands. The 1848 revolts in the rest of Europe made King William

II nervous. Amsterdam was tense. The slum area of the Jordaan, in particular, regularly erupted into violence—a tradition that continued for generations (it was the first part of town to get tarred streets, after Jordaaners had pelted the young Queen Wilhelmina with cobbles as she drove through). In 1848 the king set up a reform committee under the liberal Rudolph Thorbecke and changes were hurried through after a mob stormed around the Dam in 1849, with the alarming proclamation that 'All men are brothers'. As the franchise was extended, support grew for the socialist movement. In 1902 Henri Polak took up the first seat for the **Social Democratic Labour Party** (SDAP) on the city council. By 1915 the SDAP was the largest party in Amsterdam, housing associations had been formed, a 1901 Housing Act had stipulated minimum living conditions, and council houses established all over the city helped to relieve the pressure on areas like De Pijp and the Jordaan.

Amsterdam entered the 20th century on the crest of a boom. The Netherlands remained neutral in the First World War. Amsterdam happily traded in arms with both sides, and emerged comparatively unscathed—though the rest of her trade had taken a blow and food shortages in 1917 had provoked the Jordaaners into riots. The city's population was again growing fast. Canals were filled in to cope with burgeoning road traffic and in 1920 two converted De Havillands, carrying two passengers a piece, began to fly regularly to London. The world's first air travel booking office opened at **Schiphol** in the following year. In 1928 Amsterdam hosted the Olympic Games, but the 1929 Wall Street crash slid the city into an economic depression. Gangs of unemployed were set to work creating the Amsterdamse Bos (Amsterdam Forest) outside the city, and when, in 1934, the council tried to lop 25c off the dole pay, the Jordaaners again rioted. The 1930s also saw the growth of a small, but vociferous, **Dutch Nazi Party** (NSB).

The Second World War

The Netherlands hoped to remain neutral in the Second World War, as they had in the first. But on 10 May 1940 the Germans attacked Dutch airports and military barracks. Queen Wilhelmina and the Dutch government lost little time in skipping across the channel to the relative safety of England. They left Supreme Commander Winkelman to deal with the advancing Germans. He held out for five days during which Rotterdam was mercilessly bombed from the air. On 15 May the German army occupied the Netherlands and Hitler declared the cool

Austrian Nazi, **Arthur Seyss-Inquart**, *Rijkscomissaris* (State Commissioner). Members of the NSB who had collaborated with the invaders were catapulted to positions of high office.

At first life in Amsterdam carried on much the same as before, with Amsterdammers exercising their indefatigable capacity to turn a blind eye to anything that threatens to ruffle the smooth flow of daily business. However, when Seyss-Inquart's early softly-softly attempt to *nazificeren* ('nazify') Holland met with stolid Dutch inertia, he became more brutal. Young Dutchmen were sent off to work in Germany, soldiers who had been captured during the invasion and then released were re-arrested as prisoners-of-war. Jews, especially, were the butt of systematic oppressive decrees. The wearing of yellow stars was compulsory and Jews were banned from driving or from using trams. They had to hand in their bicycles, be indoors by 8 o'clock (not even out in their own gardens), were allowed to shop only in Jewish shops between 3 and 5 o'clock in the afternoon, and couldn't visit theatres, cinemas or sports grounds. Soon they were forbidden to visit Christians, had to go to separate schools and were fenced off in ghettos. On 22 February 1941 German trucks rumbled into the Jodenhoek (Jewish Quarter) and the first round-up of Jews began. In the years that followed nearly all of Amsterdam's Jews (10 per cent of the city's population) were transported, along with gypsies and homosexuals, to concentration camps in Germany. Hardly any survived.

The February *razzia* (raid on Jews) sparked off a spontaneous Amsterdam-wide strike that was viciously put down. Right through the occupation heroic Resistance fighters sabotaged German munitions and supplies stores, attempted to assassinate Nazi leaders, spawned batches of false documents and reeled off secret newspapers to keep the public properly informed. Nazi retaliation was diabolic. If they couldn't dig out the ringleaders, whole groups of innocent people would be shot in reprisal for any Resistance activity. Opposition also went on in quieter, but no less courageous ways. Many non-Jews wore yellow stars in sympathy and thousands gave shelter to *onderduikers* ('divers')—members of the Resistance, or Jews (like the Frank family), who went into hiding around the city. On Prince Bernhard's birthday, thousands imitated his habit of wearing a white carnation, much to the confusion of the Nazis who didn't know quite what to legislate against. Queen Wilhelmina re-established herself in the the good opinion of many Amsterdammers by broadcasting cheering messages to her people from the security of a BBC studio.

By the winter of 1944—'Hunger Winter'—the fabric of the city had collapsed. Everybody was starving (especially those sharing ration books with *onderduikers*), as the Germans had restricted the flow of food in retaliation for a Dutch railwaymen's strike. The famous Port of Cleve Restaurant on Spuistraat became a soup kitchen. Walking was the only means of transport and rubbish bins and sewers overflowed. Fuel was impossible to come by, so Amsterdammers stole any wood they could lay their hands on. Sleepers were torn from the tram tracks, parks thinned out mysteriously overnight and any empty houses were stripped of furniture, beams and floorboards. The Jodenhoek began to crumble.

On 5 May 1945 the Netherlands was liberated. On 7 May jubilant crowds crammed the streets of Amsterdam to greet the Canadian liberation force. In a final lash of malice, German soldiers opened fire on the crowd, killing 22 people.

Post-war Amsterdam

The Netherlands was devastated by the war. Its transport system was paralysed, industrial production had slumped by 30 per cent and the Germans had broken dikes, flooding much of the countryside. Despite chronic shortages of almost everything, Amsterdammers bounced back with a lively resilience, enthusiastic for a quick recovery. They even managed city-wide street parties in 1948 to celebrate Queen Juliana's coronation and Dutch victories in the Olympic Games. The granting of independence to former colonies knocked the edge off the tropical trade, but Amsterdam soon got down to the more mundane business of keeping the hungry new Ruhr industries fed. After the widening of the North Sea Canal and construction of the new **Amsterdam–Rhine Canal** in 1952, regeneration was meteoric. Garden-city suburbs sprang up around Amsterdam to house the swelling population. The 1960s vision of air, light and towering concrete gave birth to the Bijlmermeer (vast open stretches of concrete dotted with towerblocks that nobody wanted to live in).

Old patterns began to emerge. The solid Calvinist burgers were still very much in control, but the traditional tolerance of minorities and deviants soon made space, not for the naked dancing Anabaptists of yore, but for a new phenomenon of dreamy **hippies** and tatty youth. In the 1960s Amsterdam became a mecca of the blossoming youth culture. Troupes of long-haired, denim-clad, gently stoned young people hung out and slept around Centraal Station, the National Monument on the

Dam and in Vondelpark. In 1969 John Lennon and Yoko Ono staged their week-long 'Bed-in' for world peace in the Hilton Hotel. An old church near Leidseplein was converted into the Paradiso—a place where you could puff away on marijuana without fear of arrest, and have your ears blasted by the latest music. Homosexuals began to join the party, and soon Amsterdam was known as the gay capital of Europe.

At the centre of the Amsterdam counter-culture was a group of flamboyant jesters, the **Provos** (from *provocatie*—provocation: see Topics pp. 78–80). Philosophy student Roel van Duyn, and magician and one-time window cleaner Robert Jasper Grootveld, with a motley gang of accomplices staged 'happenings' on the Dam and around the statue of the *Lieverdje* (Little Darling) on the Spui. The Provos were against capitalism, traffic and tobacco, and for free bicycles and free sex. The demonstrations were light-hearted, theatrical and endearing. Whenever the police were needled into retaliation, onlookers in the elegant cafés around the square branded them bullies. However, when **Crown Princess Beatrix** married a German, Claus von Amsberg, in the Westerkerk in March 1966, the mood soured. The royal family was, to the Provos, the distillation of the Establishment. Not only the Provos were angry. There was a traditional coolness between Amsterdam and the House of Orange, and ratepayers resented having to foot the bill for the celebrations. The older generation—still raw from the Occupation—were appalled that their princess could marry a German. Demonstrators lined the route of the wedding procession waving banners demanding 'Republic' and 'Give me my bike back' (the Nazis had confiscated bicycles during the war). Smoke bombs were thrown and, though the day passed without serious incident, discontent bubbled on right through the spring. One hot June day a minor industrial dispute over construction workers' holiday pay erupted into violence. During a scuffle with the police in the Jordaan (as always), one worker, Jan Weggelar, died of a heart attack. Rumour spread that the police had killed him, and a full scale riot spread right across the city sucking in Provos, Nozems (youth gangs) and anyone who enjoyed a good fight. Shops were looted, cars burned and parking meters ripped out of the ground. By nightfall the *burgemeester* was about to call in the army, but Chief Commissioner van der Molen of the Amsterdam Police took the matter in hand. He donned full dress uniform, called for his sword and strode out bravely into the midst of a bemused crowd. At midnight he met union leaders and, though he didn't entirely defuse the situation, the disruption fizzled out two days later after the mob had stormed the Port van Cleve Restaurant and the offices of the right-wing newspaper, *De Telegraaf*.

Later that year, violence broke out again over proposals to build a huge bank on Vijzelstraat. Amsterdammers felt that big money was destroying the heart of the city by denuding it of anything but banks and offices. Again it was not only the Provos and Nozems who were objecting. Concerned burghers held a 'Teach-In' at the Hotel Krasnapolsky to debate the issue. In putting the case for the bank, Dr W. F. Heinemeyer, a local academic, hit upon what, for many people, is Amsterdam's charm: '... most Amsterdammers want a closely mixed-up network of streets and squares ... where there's a great variety of possibilities for doing things one doesn't have to do, shopping, going to films and plays, sitting on terraces, in cafés, looking around, wandering about ... a place where one can be *out* and at the same time *at home*, where it's a pleasure simply to *be*.... One can call it the "forum" nature of the inner city, and this is something so precious that no administration must be indifferent about it.' The city regents seemed to feel they could be. Three days later they debated the proposal and voted in favour of the bank by 30 votes to 14.

Meanwhile, the crowds camping out, especially those around the new National Monument (a war memorial), had begun to test the patience of upright, patriotic citizens. In 1967 off duty Marines had descended on unsuspecting hippies outside the Centraal Station and cut off their hair. The mess left by the impromptu campsites was an affront to the obsessively neat Amsterdammers and a bye-law passed in the summer of 1969 banned sleeping around national monuments. Initially it wasn't enforced—though the police would occasionally hose everyone down. In 1970, after violent clashes with the police had failed to oust the Dam drop-outs, the Marines once again decided on unofficial unilateral action. Bands of strapping lads singing barrack-room songs belted arm-in-arm down the Damrak, and frightened the hippies away forever. Good burghers looked on from the surrounding balconies and cheered, though the next morning the establishment press felt compelled to condemn, ever so lightly, the Marines' behaviour. Amsterdam's youth culture survived the attack, but was more formally accommodated in hostels and Sleep-Ins around town.

The Provos had broken up in 1967 'in order to avoid bloodshed', but Roel van Duyn went on to establish the **Kabouters** ('helpful gnomes')—a whimsical party of idealists with occasional flashes of common sense. In May 1970 they gathered, wearing pixie hats, on the Dam, planted an orange tree and issued a proclamation. They declared an Orange Free State (with van Duyn as its ambassador) that would soon link up in a fairy circle with other socialist elf cities around the world. Theirs was no longer to be 'the socialism of the clenched fist, but of the intertwined fingers, the erect penis, the escaping butterfly'. They wanted more trees, fewer banks and polluting industries, a ban on traffic in central Amsterdam, free white bikes for all—and improved psychiatric services. In the summer election they polled 11 per cent of the vote and won five seats on the city council. As the decade wore on, they lost their appeal and were finally disbanded in 1981.

Though the Provos were no more, and the Kabouters were on the wane, the late 1970s and early 1980s saw some spectacular street battles. The council's plan to build a **Metro**—largely to serve the outer suburbs—met with outrage. It was expensive, and meant pulling down more houses in the inner city. Many people refused to move and on 25 March 1975—'Blue Monday'—there were violent demonstrations when officials tried to clear the first houses for demolition. Police fired tear gas through the windows and drove armoured cars into the doors. The ferocity of the opposition increased until 1978, when the council agreed to build new homes and renovate areas of the inner city. Skirmishes went on right up until the opening of the Metro in 1980.

In 1980 13 per cent of the city's population was on the housing list. **Squatting** had become a popular solution to the chronic shortages. Properties that had been vacated for the Metro, factories left empty when companies moved outside the city and houses bought by speculative investors (and then left to rot and fall down so that the land could be developed more profitably) were occupied by the paint-pot and hammer-wielding homeless. A lot of work went into the renovation of squatter homes, and the building of accompanying studios and cafés. The network became highly organized, and, with 10,000 members by 1982, was a force to be reckoned with. Police attempts to evict squatters were heavy handed (they used tanks on a squat in the Vondelstraat) and not always successful. Battles would rage for days, and at one point the *burgemeester* had to declare a state of emergency. By 1984 the last of the big squats had fallen. On others a compromise had been reached—the council bought up the property, renovated it and let it back cheaply to the inhabitants. Squatting, and evictions, still go on, but in a calmer atmosphere.

Amsterdam still has a severe housing shortage. The present (socialist) *burgemeester*, Ed van Thijn, was tough on squatters when he first came to office, but has initiated a strong programme of *stadsvernieuwing* (urban renewal). As 1990s budgets begin to squeeze, however, the focus seems to be changing from housing to transforming Amsterdam into a tourist metropolis. (It is already Europe's fourth tourist city after London, Paris and Rome). Vast new development is going on around Centraal Station, but only one recent development—the building of the 'Stopera', a combined city hall and opera house on Waterlooplein—has aroused anything near the fervour of opposition of the 1960s and 1970s (see pp. 72–6). The notorious drugs problem seems more under control. Heroin dealers have been cleared out of the tourist areas around Zeedijk and Nieuwmarkt and now hole out in the south of the city. The *stads-wacht* (modern day equivalents of the Civil Guards in the Old Masters' portraits) wander about, unarmed, in smart uniforms with red trimmings, keeping an eye on public behaviour and making sure that buskers don't sing too loudly. Amsterdam seems headed for a quiet, rather comfortable, moment in its history, but its age-old tolerance of mischief remains the finest antidote to complacency. A flourishing gay community, the bustling red-light district, the newest wave of immigrants (from Turkey and Surinam), the Kabouters' heritage of environmental awareness and the Amsterdammers' nose for disruptive politics keep the cafés alive and the old port rough beneath its smooth veneer.

Art and Architecture

Windows and brick work of the 'Amsterdam School'

Dutch Painting

Sacheverell Sitwell wrote that painting and architecture are as endemic among the Dutch as poetry is among the English. During the 17th-century Golden Age (a high-watermark for painting, as well as an economic boom) an estimated 20 million paintings were executed. Even the humblest homes had the odd oil tacked up on the wall. A 17th-century English traveller observed that 'many times blacksmiths, cobblers etc. will have some picture or other by their forge or in their stall. Such is the general notion, inclination and delight that these country natives have to painting.'

These days Amsterdam is still the centre of a flourishing art trade, with nearly 150 commercial galleries that sell anything from Picasso to post-art school hopefuls. There's an enormous annual art fair at the RAI Congress Centre (usually in June) and open-air art markets spring up around town in the summer. Here you often find inspired work nestling among more predictable ceramics and watercolours—but never the sort of kitsch and tat that's draped on the railings of London's Hyde Park on a Sunday afternoon. Artists' *ateliers* are everywhere: in the red-light district, on boats, stretched out in glass-walled grandeur in the posher parts of town. Clusters of studios in the same area have open days from time to time, when (clutching a rough, photocopied map) you can wander in and out, look at work in progress and chat with the artists. Sunday afternoons are the favoured time for 'openings'. Relaxed, chatty crowds of friends, critics and hangers-on tipple free wine and spill out of galleries onto the deserted streets. These affairs seem less over-dressed, tense and po-seur-ridden than is usual in other parts of the world.

And, of course, there are all the Old Masters in the Rijksmuseum, a whole building full of Van Goghs and the go-getting Stedelijk Museum. Even in the Stedelijk, however, you're quite likely to find something by the latest American whizz-kid or the Dutch boy-next-door tucked in among the Chagalls and Mondriaans. In Amsterdam there's a feeling that art matters, is part of everyday life and that even the zaniest of new painters belongs to a long continuum of artists working in Holland.

Before the Golden Age

It is important to draw a distinction between Dutch and Flemish art. In 1579 the Netherlands polarized into a Flemish, predominantly Roman Catholic south, and an alliance of seven Dutch, Protestant northern provinces. Eugène Fromentin, the 19th-century art critic, observed that 'Holland had never possessed many national painters.... While she was blended with Flanders, it was Flanders that took upon herself to think, invent and paint for her.' Early Flemish art resounds with familiar names like Breughel, Bosch and van Eyck, while Holland musters Cornelis Ketel, a portrait painter who grew bored with his craft and, as a ruse to liven up his technique, started painting with his toes, with no noticeable loss in quality. However, in the 17th century migrations of prominent painters to the Protestant north, a blossoming national confidence and snowballing economic prosperity stimulated a new Dutch School. This exclusively Dutch painting was influenced by Flemish artists, but also by Italians and a small heritage of local painters less disgruntled with their lot than Cornelis Ketel.

In his *Book of Famous Men*, the 15th-century humanist Barolemmo Fayio lists only two Flemish artists: Jan van Eyck and Rogier van der Weyden— painters we still consider pivots of the period. Both had a strong influence on later Dutch painting. **Jan van Eyck** (1385–1441) and his shadowy brother, Hubert (some say they collaborated, some say that Hubert never existed) are credited with the discovery of oil paint. In reality, they merely perfected a technique that northern European pain-ters had been using for some time. Oil paints, which can be applied in layers, give a rich, deep tone which was much favoured by artists who were fascinated by *appearances*—the glowing colours of objects as they were touched by light. Italian artists, on the other hand, tended to be more concerned with *structure*, bodies and movement: they worked in tempera (egg-shell based paint) which rendered sharper, brighter colours—but soon latched onto the practical and artistic merits of oils.

Early Netherlandish art was mainly devotional. Static groups of bodies crowded pictures crammed with detail and heavily symbolic bric-a-brac. **Rogier van der Weyden** (1399–1464) swept the canvas clean. He focussed tightly on a few figures and injected a passionate, authentic emotional intensity into his work. This was extremely rare in religious art of the time, and had a powerful impact on later Dutch painters.

Albert Ouwater (active 1450–80) was the man who took these ideas north. He settled in Haarlem around the time that a book by the Florentine Leon Battista Alberti was being passed around painters' studios. Alberti argued that *historia* (narrative) was crucial to good art. Dutch painting became less static; small dramas and conflicts began to emerge from the canvas. **Geertgen tot Sint Jans** (about 1460–95) was much influenced by Ouwater. He painted bright, beautiful pictures, still laden with symbolic references but with a much freer arrangement of figures. The figures themselves, however, were still rigid, with little real eloquence of human movement. **Lucas van Leyden** (1489–1553), a child prodigy who was already engraving in his native Leiden at the age of nine, burst onto the scene with sparkling, dynamic, densely peopled paintings that revolutionized Dutch art. As these various strands combine we can see, in the work of painters like Lucas van Leyden and **Jan Mostaert** (1475–1555), the first signs of a separate Dutch school of painting.

In 1604 Karel van Mander, a painter and theorist working in Haarlem, published *Het Schilderboek*—a collection of biographies and a theoretical handbook for artists. It was the first full-scale work of art theory to delineate Dutch and Flemish traditions. Van Mander exalted Haarlem as the cradle of Dutch art. The school of painters working there was developing its own style of Italian Mannerism. The Mannerists believed their work shouldn't slavishly imitate Nature, but improve upon it with imagination and Art. Paintings (even those with innocent titles like *John the Baptist Preaching*) swarm with lumpy nude musclemen and elongated female figures. They sport about in exotic settings in which piled-up fragments of Roman art, stylized plants and fabulous beasts abound.

The first Dutch painter to travel to Renaissance Italy (it later became *de rigueur* for any artist who wanted to be taken seriously) was Jan van Scorel (1495–1562). He passed through Germany and Venice on a pilgrimage to Jerusalem. On his way back he visited Rome, and was given the job of curator of the massive papal art collection by Hadrian VI, the only Dutch pope in history. This experience changed his painting style completely, and he returned to Haarlem (as van Mander puts it) as 'the lantern-bearer and road-paver of the Arts in the Netherlands'. Others would claim that honour for Lucas van Leyden, but van Mander thought that Van Leyden was a show-off—and, besides, he didn't come from Haarlem. Van Scorel's pupil **Martin van Heemskerck** (1498–1574) also travelled to Italy and was one of the main propagators of Mannerist ideas in Holland.

Mannerism made Dutch painting far more lively and flexible, but painters began to tire of its ornament. A move to greater realism and narrative clarity—more Nature, less Art—can be seen in the works of **Hendrik Goltzius** (1558–1616), another member of Van Mander's Haarlem mafia.

By the 1620s another school of painters had sprouted in Utrecht. Artists such as **Hendrick Terbrugghen** (c.1588–1629) and **Gerrit van Honthorst** (c.1590–1624) were ardent followers of the Italian painter, Caravaggio. Caravaggio's *chiaroscuro* technique (strong contrasts of light and shadow) influenced successive waves of Dutch painters all the way through to Rembrandt and Vermeer. Terbrugghen was the first Dutch Caravagist to return to Holland (after a ten-year stay in Italy), but he was self-effacing and a bit of a misfit—he wasn't even elected to office in the Utrecht guild. The flattering and flamboyant Van Honthurst, on the other hand, ran up impressive lists of patrons wherever he went and became the best known of the Dutch Caravagists. His beautiful nocturnal scenes—candlelight and shadow playing over huddles of faces—earned him the nickname 'Gherardo delle Notti'.

The Golden Age

> France has shown a great deal of inventive genius, but little
> real faculty for painting. Holland has not imagined anything,
> but it has painted miraculously well.
> —*Eugène Fromentin, art critic, writing in 1875*

In 1565 mobs stormed through the Netherlands breaking church windows and destroying religious paintings and statues. In their enthusiasm to eliminate idolatry, these iconoclasts wiped out much of the country's artistic heritage. There seemed little call to replace it. The austere Calvinists who took control of the northern provinces after 1579 whitewashed the insides of churches and had no time for papish decoration. Italy and its art went out of fashion. The rising merchant classes seemed suspicious of unprofitable aristocratic foibles like patronage of the arts. Artists were in a dilemma: what *were* they to paint, and who would pay them for it. Eugène Fromentin comes right to the point:

> The problem was this: given a *bourgeois* people, practical, not
> inclined to dreams, very busy withal, by no means mystic, of
> anti-Latin tendency, with broken traditions, a worship
> without images, parsimonious habits—to find an art to
> please [them] ... there remained nothing for such a people
> to propose to themselves but a very simple and daring thing
> ... to paint its own *portrait*.

And so the Dutch set about painting 'the portrait of Holland, its external image, faithful, exact, complete, life-like, without any adornment'. In the Golden Age that followed, you find few flamboyant devotional paintings or pompous, heroic battle scenes. Instead, you are given portraits of merchants, town squares, street scenes, glimpses of daily life, breakfast tables, brothels, taverns, the countryside, or moments in history. No other nation has managed a more intimate and beautifully executed chronicle of its life and times.

Genre Painting: Early English critics called the pictures of scenes from everyday life 'drolleries'—nowadays we refer to them as genre paintings. By the mid-17th century, genre was one of the most popular art forms in Holland, and the cheapest to buy. These were straightforward, unembellished paintings of taverns, brothels and family life, but they often contained a covert moral message. Sometimes the signal was crude—wildly copulating dogs in a doorway behind a flirting couple refer to the saying 'As with the woman, so with her dog'. Sometimes complex allegorical references and obscure symbols were knitted into the apparently simple pictures. Unravelling these was, for an educated 17th-century viewer, half the fun of genre paintings.

There are examples of genre work in the paintings of the Caravagists Hendrick Terbrugghen and Gerrit van Honthorst, and in the work of some Mannerists, but it was the writing and painting of **Willem Buytewech** (1591–1624) in Haarlem, and the short visit to the town of

Flemish painter **Adriaen Brouwer** (1605–38), that really established the style in Holland. Brouwer was a disorderly bohemian and a popular painter. Both Rubens and Rembrandt went to great lengths to add his work to their collections, though Haarlem society took some time to recover from his high spirits. He was strongly influenced by his compatriots Breughel and Bosch, and would sit about in pothouses knocking off cruelly realistic sketches of the clientele. The grotesque portrayal of peasants appealed to his Haarlem pupil **Adriaen van Ostade** (1610–85), and became a feature of one strain of Dutch genre painting. (As Van Ostade grew older and richer, however, his work became calm, cosy and far more respectable.)

Another style of genre grew up in Leiden around the painter **Gerard Dou** (1613–75). His meticulous, highly finished, almost slick work was widely imitated and gave rise to the school of Leiden *fijnschilders* ('fine painters'). The paintings, often of genteel middle-class interiors, have subtle chiaroscuro lighting effects and some very abstruse symbolic references. Leiden seemed to enjoy especially difficult allusions, maybe because it was a university town. Dou's pupils **Gabriel Metsu** (1629–67) and **Frans van Mieris** (1635–81) excelled in elegant genre work.

In far-away Deventer **Gerard ter Borch** (1619–81) was developing his own style—highly attentive to detail and with an especially fine touch in painting fabrics. In Delft **Jan Vermeer** (1632–75) was painting the hushed, softly lit interiors that have earned him the reputation (with Rembrandt and Frans Hals) of being one of the three great painters of the age. Vermeer produced eleven children, and only three times that many paintings in his life. In the midst of his tumultuous household, he would lock himself away and work painstakingly on tranquil portraits of Dutch homes without a single child in sight. The reticent, and poor, painter would even hide from influential art dealers when they came to call.

The best recorder of riotous domestic uproar was tavern-keeper **Jan Steen** (1625–79). He paints the lewd, sozzled and wanton inhabitants of his sitting-rooms, taverns and brothels with such verve and good humour, that it's difficult to judge just what his moral attitude really is. The paintings of **Pieter de Hooch** (1629–after 1688) and **Nicholaes Maes** (1629–93), on the other hand, are closer to the subdued interiors of Vermeer. De Hooch is especially known for his sensitive portrayals of mothers and children. His paintings of the dark interiors of burgher homes with, somewhere in the picture, a door opening onto the bright outdoors, set a pattern for many other genre painters.

Historical and Biblical Painting: The 16th-century Mannerists had used Biblical and historical subjects as a pretext for fanciful flights of imagination, an excuse to adorn paintings with naked bodies and elaborate ornamentation. As we have seen, there was no place for this in respectable 17th-century merchants' sitting rooms, and the austere Calvinists proscribed art in churches. Most artists were launched into an open market of more acceptable styles—portraits, landscapes and genre scenes—but a few soldiered on in the grand old style. Many of these painters were simply out of touch with the spirit of the new age, but others came up with an innovative, more realistic style of historical painting.

The Dutch Caravagists (see above) were prime movers in the new direction. Their bold realism appealed to painters in this Age of Reason. The new style of historical painting leant on experience, rather than invention, and had a much clearer narrative. Unlike the Mannerists, who had indulged themselves in flashy virtuoso performances without any deference to period, 17th-century painters painted scenes from the Bible or from history (especially banquet scenes or intimate group studies of Christ with the apostles), attempting to portray clothing, buildings and utensils with some sort of historical accuracy. (They were, however, usually quite spectacularly off the mark.)

The Amsterdam painter **Pieter Lastman** (1583–1633) was the spearhead of the new generation of history painters. It was to study as his pupil that **Rembrandt van Rijn** (1606–69, see pp. 112–14) went to Amsterdam in 1624. Rembrandt clearly wanted to be part of the modern movement of realism. Kenneth Clark calls him 'the great poet of that need for truth and that appeal to experience which had begun with the Reformation'. His quest was for naturalness and authenticity. He used his neighbours in the Jewish Quarter for Biblical paintings, and infused his pictures with a powerful psychological realism. By the 1640s he was undoubtedly the best history painter in Holland, but it was a lonely mission, as the style remained unpopular during his lifetime. Only one of his pupils, the last, **Aert de Gelder** (1645–1627) concentrated exclusively on history painting. He worked in a lighter, more sentimental style than Rembrandt would ever have allowed himself to fall into.

Portraiture: Portraiture is the most conservative of all the categories of visual art. Painters commissioned to record the wealthy, pompous and important for posterity usually opt for well-tried, acceptable forms. The Golden Age brought some exciting innovators—especially with double and group portraits—but the changes were subtle and the style soon hardened once more into an emptier, more formalized genre.

Anthonie Mor (1519–74), who Italianized his name to Antonio Moro, spent some time in the court of Emperor Charles V, and introduced the fashionable classical style of Italian portraiture to the Netherlands. It was taken up by **Michiel Miereveld** (1567–1641). He had a comfortable job in the court of Frederick Henry in The Hague, churned out competent, formal pictures and became the leading portraitist of the early Dutch Republic. It was **Frans Hals** (1585–1666) who brought verve to portrait painting. His acute psychological perception, comic wickedness and lightness of touch give his portraits an unprecedented vibrancy. For the first time the sitters seem unconstricted, even friendly. Though his work became very dark towards the end of his life, his early group portraits are exuberantly stage-managed and really capture the high spirits and optimism of Holland's new-found freedom.

Rembrandt's portraits are more introspective, with subtle nuances of light and mood, but portraiture was, for him, primarily a source of income. The earlier 'jugs on a shelf' approach to sitters had been corrected by Hals, but it was Rembrandt who gave canvasses real vitality, particularly in larger works. His dynamic arrangement of the guardsmen in the *Nightwatch* (1642; see p. 113) revolutionized group portraiture. Although he brings his full artistic weight to the task, he reserves any radical experimentation for pictures of himself and his family. In these you find a sensitivity and flair quite beyond the formal traditions of the art.

Govert Flinck (1615–60) and **Ferdinand Bol** (1616–80), both students of Rembrandt, are admired as portraitists. Bol followed Rembrandt so slavishly that even art historians can't always tell them apart. Flinck had the awkward honour of being commissioned to paint for Amsterdam's new town hall after his teacher's preliminary sketches had been turned down. He died before completing his sketches, and Rembrandt was one of the painters employed to finish the job.

Frans Hals and Rembrandt gave portraiture a fresh burst of life, but, by the middle of the century other artists were cementing their innovations into a new repertory of poses and gestures. Dutch society was becoming grander and more pompous, and the artists it commissioned to paint its picture—like **Bartholomeus van der Helst** (1613–70)—thought Hals's and Rembrandt's work too plain. Once again the portraits lost spontaneity and energy and, though often stylish, became formalized and rhetorical.

Landscape, Still Life and Specialist Paintings: In his *Natural History*, Pliny marvels at the exactness with which some ancient painters could imitate Nature: birds would crash into a wall on which Zeuxis or Apelles had painted a still life. Early Netherlandish painters were impressed by this idea and paid loving attention to background rocks, trees and landscapes—so much so that Sir Henry Wotton, a 17th-century English Ambassador to the Low Countries, could marvel at the 'Artificiall Miracles' they created. (Michelangelo, however, is reputed to have scoffed at the mundaneness and literalness of this Netherlandish style, saying it was fit only for young or very old women, monks, nuns and certain tone-deaf members of the aristocracy.) Although no painters actually took an easel out of doors until the 19th century, this interest in realism did mean that landscape established a sturdy niche for itself in Dutch art during the Golden Age.

The 16th-century Mannerists used natural scenery, laced with fantastical creatures, as an exotic backdrop to biblical and classical scenes. The well-travelled **Gillis van Coninxloo** (1544–1607) painted very much in the Mannerist style, but is generally regarded as the first Dutch landscapist. Mannerist pictures were usually painted from a high view-point. It was **Esaias van de Velde** (1591–1632) who, quite literally, brought things down to earth. He painted dry, rather matter-of-fact country scenes from a low, more naturalistic, view-point—a style adopted by practitioners of what became known as the **tonal phase** of Dutch landscape painting.

Paintings of the tonal phase, which lasted until the 1640s, are delicate, almost monochromatic and are animated by the atmosphere they create. The 17th-century poet and critic Constantijn Huygens praised the school for its ability to evoke 'the warmth of the sun and the movement caused by a cool breeze'. The first tonal painter was Esaias's pupil **Jan van Goyen** (1596–1656). Although he began painting in the bolder colours of his master, he was soon producing translucent worlds of hazy greens, browns and greys. **Salomon van Ruysdael** (1600–70) painted refined, spacious landscapes and is considered the second major tonal painter.

Hercules Seghers (b.1590) painted some inspired and original scenes of waterfalls, desolate valleys and stormy mountains. Although he worked at the same time as the tonal painters, his unique style evoked the power of a much grander Nature. He had a reputation for being drunk and depressed, and disappeared in 1633. Nowadays the whereabouts of only 15 of his works are known, though there are records of another 30.

Rembrandt was a great admirer of Seghers, and owned eight of his paintings. His small *oeuvre* of landscapes strongly reflects Seghers's influence.

From the 1650s a new generation of landscape painters started producing rugged, grandiose works with more solid forms and stronger contrasts of light and colour than the rather pale pictures of the tonal phase artists. Leaders of this new **classical phase** were **Jacob van Ruisdael** (1628–82; Salomon's nephew, though they spelled their names differently) and **Albert Cuyp** (1620–91). Ruisdael is acknowledged as the greatest Dutch landscapist and is especially admired for his stormy skies. Cuyp combined clarity and a firm classical structure with (especially in his late work) Italianate lighting that suffuses his pictures with a soft glow. Ruisdael's pupil **Meindert Hobbema** (1638–1709) produced paintings very much derivative of his master's work before marrying the *burgemeester's* kitchen maid and becoming a wine gauger in the Amsterdam customs house, abandoning painting almost entirely.

Cuyp, like many other Dutch landscapists, fell under the spell of Italy. Many Hollanders were drawn south by the warmth and shimmering light. Right from the beginning of the century **Italianate** landscapes existed alongside the more typically Dutch pictures. (The term, however, refers more to the subject matter than to the influence of Italian art). The escapist, rather nostalgic paintings by artists like **Jan Both** (*c.*1618–52) and **Nicolaes Berchem** (1620–83) were very popular with the Dutch public. The landscapes are imaginary (some of these painters didn't even visit Italy) and are populated by the beautiful shepherdesses and antique ruins also found in the pastoral literature of the time. By the 19th century the style was beginning to lose favour. The English painter John Constable, in a lecture in 1836 berated Both and Berchem as specious painters whose reputation was propped up by dealers demanding high prices. When, reeling from the vehemence of the attack, an avid collector remarked that he had better sell his Berchems, Constable replied: 'No, sir, that will only continue the mischief, *burn them*.'

The English term **'still life'** comes from the Dutch 'stilleven', the word that began to be used around the 1650s to describe a theme in Dutch painting that was very typical of the 17th-century taste for the domestic and realistic. The stylistic development of still life painting parallels that of landscapes. Early works are 'tonal'—suspended against a plain background, suffused by a transparent, dull light. The objects painted are simple everyday things. The *ontbijtje* (breakfast piece) with bread, cheese and pewter mug is a favourite subject. Later *Vanitas* still lifes, reminding us of the ephemerality of life and earthly pleasures, became popular. Fruit is seen at its *toppunt*, the point of ripeness just before it goes bad, and darker symbols like skulls and snuffed out candles make an appearance. As the Golden Age society prospered, the simple *ontbijtjes* were replaced by *pronkstilleven* (*pronk* means ostentation). The style of these luxurious pieces is similar to that of the classical phase of landscape painters. Colours are brighter and each object seems sharply picked out, as if by spotlight. Gold, silver, china, expensive seafood and exotic fruit replace the simpler fare of earlier work.

Paintings of flowers were a specialized branch of still life. Real blooms were often cripplingly expensive, and short-lived. The 17th-century Dutch preferred *pictures* of flowers in their houses. The paintings were often complete fantasies—exotic blooms from all over the world, that flowered at different times of the year, would all be arranged in one vase. **Ambrosius Bosschaert the Elder** (1573–1621) and his three sons were the most prolific flower painters of the period. By the time he died, Bosschaert could command 1000 guilders a painting.

Despite Holland's reliance on the sea, **marine painting** doesn't occupy an important position in its art. Early painters like **Jan Porcellis** (1584–1632) seem primarily concerned with atmosphere of the sea and sky, while later artists like **Willem van de Velde the Younger** (1633–1707) begin to reflect the nation's pride in the ships themselves. Of the **architectural paintings**, **Pieter Saenredam's** (1597–1695) exquisitely executed church interiors are the most pleasing—and so accurate that they are still used as blueprints for restoration work. The most interesting **animal painter** is **Paulus Potter** (1625–54) whose bulls and cows have an intense reality that is almost nightmarish.

The 18th and 19th Centuries
After decades of entrepreneurial adventure, Amsterdam settled back to enjoy its wealth, and seemed to lose the drive that had propelled it through the Golden Age. Society began to look to France as a model of graceful living, and associations for the promotion of French ideas and culture sprang up.

With the deaths of Frans Hals (1666), Rembrandt (1669) and Vermeer (1675), the Golden Age of Dutch painting also came to an end.

The achievements of the 17th century were so great that they seemed to haunt 18th-century painters, who didn't dare do anything new. Paintings became over-refined and uniform in their imitation of French styles and reworking of old ideas. Much 17th-century painting had reflected the stern ethics of Calvinism, but the 18th century began to shed the moral sobriety that had been the dominant humour of the previous age. The freshest painting of the period comes from the few artists who reflected this change in mood and worked playfully with the established Dutch styles. The most impressive of these lighter-hearted painters was **Cornelis Troost** (1697–1750), whose delicately composed satires have earned him the title of the 'Dutch Hogarth'.

Much work was to be had painting the ceilings of grand mansions and decorating the interiors of new public buildings. **Gerard de Lairesse** (1640–1711) was the market-leader in this field. His somewhat over-enthusiastic admirers dubbed him the 'Dutch Raphael'. His successor, **Jacob de Wit**, (1695–1754) excelled as a *trompe l'oeil* artist and a decorator of churches. Protestant churches were still bare, but Catholicism was tolerated provided that (a 1730 decree cautioned) care was taken 'that the meeting places of the Catholics do not have the appearance of churches or public buildings, nor should they strike the public eye'. There were no such restrictions, however, on interiors, and De Wit made his fortune on commissions from wealthy parishes.

During the 19th century, painting became more documentary—any allegorical meaning or high moral purpose disappeared entirely. Romantic painters such as **Jozef Israëls** (1824–1911) and **A. H. Bakker Korff** (1824–82) did imbue their work with emotion, but it was of the sober, cosy Dutch variety rather than anything explosive or passionate. Landscapists ploughed on in a neo-classical or grand Romantic manner, though in the work of **A. G. Bilders** (1838–65) you can see the beginnings of a simpler naturalism. In place of the distant, artificially constructed views found in previous paintings, the landscape is seen from close to. This radical change, which gave paintings the sort of perspectives seen in photographs, characterized much work later in the century. (This is particularily evident in the city scenes of the Amsterdam Impressionist **G. H. Breitner** (1857–1923).) The landscapes and seascapes of **Johann Barthold Jongkind** (1819–91), drawn from the 17th-century tonal tradition, influenced later French Impressionists and Dutch artists of the Hague School.

The Hague School was active between 1870 and 1890, an Art-for-Art's-Sake movement made up of an enthusiastic group of Impressionistic painters. They became famous for their grey skies, and paintings of the long flat beaches and rain-swept polders (reclaimed land) around The Hague. Subject matter was less important than personal feelings and style. **Anton Mauve's** (1838–88) gently coloured landscapes are the best known. **Hendrik Mesdag** (1831–1915) was a skilled seascapist, and painted the impressive Panorama in The Hague (see p. 273). The brothers **Maris—Jacob** (1837–99), **Matthijs** (1839–1917) and **Willem** (1844–1910)—contributed fine landscapes and nature studies to the movement.

Undoubtedly the greatest painter of the century was the man that a director of the Stedelijk Museum called 'the lowliest, most human', **Vincent Van Gogh** (1853–90). During his short, troubled painting career, Van Gogh produced work quite unlike any other Dutch artist; his work also takes its own quite individual course in the stream of Post-Impressionist painting in general. (For a fuller account of Van Gogh and his work, see Walk VI, pp. 181–7).

Jan Toorop (1858–1928) trailed along with the stylistic changes of the century—from Pointillism to Expressionism. His best work, like that of his contemporary **Johan Thorn Prikker** (1868–1932), was in a delicate, almost fairytale Symbolist style that begins to point towards Art Nouveau.

The 20th Century

The individualism of the late 19th century undermined the supportive strength of the great painting traditions of the past. Twentieth-century Dutch artists were left not only with the question that had dogged their 17th-century forebears (*what* to paint), but also by a new problem: *how* to paint. There was no longer a framework of assumptions within which they could make their decisions. Twentieth-century art fragments into splinter-groups trying to find their way through the dilemma.

The artists of *De Stijl* ('Style', or 'The Way') came up with a new set of assumptions, a theory they believed would take the place of the old traditions. This theory was propounded in a series of polemical articles in the periodical from which they got their name (published from June 1917 to January 1932). They claimed that they were getting rid of all the inaccuracies, obscurity and casual accidents of individualism, and had discovered the essence of art—a Platonic ideal that the world could understand. The best known visual expression of this great universal principle are the straight black lines and blocks of primary colours in the work of **Piet Mondriaan** (1872–1944). (He dropped the second 'a' in his name in order to appear more French—a pretension that most Dutch Museums ignore.) Mondriaan gives us a one-man lesson in the development of abstract art. Even in early, recognizable landscapes you can see the germs of his fascination with horizontal and vertical lines. Gradually the figurative images dissolve and you're left with the dashes and criss-cross lines of what is aptly known as his 'plus-minus' period. Then the lines get straighter and bolder, and the colours resolve into bright, flat reds, yellows and blues. Mondriaan claimed he was aiming for the 'lucid tidiness' that the new age demanded. In this he is, paradoxically, very much part of a Dutch tradition of stillness and quiet, careful composition. As Kenneth Clark suggests: Mondriaan is Vermeer without the light.

The prime motivator of *De Stijl*, and editor of the periodical, was **Theo van Doesberg** (1883–1931). His paintings were more dynamic than Mondriaan's, and caused the final rift between the two artists (see p. 166). The work of a third member of the group, **Bart van der Leck** (1876–1958), is instantly recognizable—coloured triangles scattered on a white canvas. Van Doesberg was the real energy behind the movement. When he died the magazine ceased publication and formal contacts between members dissolved. Though *De Stijl* lasted only fifteen years, its impact was felt all over the world, not only in painting, but also in architecture, interior design, typography and even literature and music. The images are still plagiarized by trendy designers for company logos, coffee mugs and T-shirts.

Most of the major art movements of the early 20th century seemed to pass Holland by. There were, however, two Dutch schools of Expressionists active before the Second World War. The **Bergen School** centred on the recalcitrant work of **Charley Toorop** (1891–1955; daughter of the 19th-century painter Jan Toorop). **De Ploeg** ('The Plough'), was led by **Jan Wiegers** (1893–1959) and influenced by Van Gogh and the German Expressionists. They painted angular and explosively coloured pictures, often of the countryside around Groningen.

The hard, nightmarish quality of the Dutch **Magic Realists** is reminiscent of Salvador Dali's Surrealism, but their scenes are not as hallucinatory as Dali's. **Pyke Koch** (b.1901) paints alluring, pithy works with awe-inspiring technical prowess. He is shamefully little known outside the Netherlands. **Carel Willink** (1900–83) and **Raoul Hynckes** (b.1893) are two other prominent Magic Realist painters, if not quite as inspired.

The most exciting movement to emerge after the war was **COBRA** (made up of artists from *Co*penhagen, *Br*ussels and *A*msterdam). These painters were inspired by primitive art and children's paintings to develop a *volwassen kinderstijl* (grown-up child style). Their keywords were vitality and spontaneity. **Karel Appel** (b.1921) remarked 'I just mess about' and 'I paint like a barbarian in a barbarous age.' The gaudy, vibrant and topsy-turvy paintings of COBRA appear to represent a purposeful effort to wipe out any vestige of classical tradition.

During the 1960s minimalistic monochrome canvasses and white reliefs made an appearance. Work by **Jan Schoonhoven** (b.1914) was influenced by the German **Zero/Nul** movement, which was trying to create a new beginning for art by reducing individual influence to nothing. **Ad Dekkers** (1938–74) and **Edgar Fernhout** (1912–74; Charley Toorop's son) produced similar work, but were more in the abstract geometrical tradition of Mondriaan.

The technological revolution has had its impact on Dutch art. **Peter Struycken** (b.1939) began very much in the vein of Dekkers, but since 1968 has been using a computer to generate the colour and patterns of his work. **Jan Dibbets** (b.1941) uses montages of photographs geometrically arranged on clean white canvasses, in a way that seems to link him to Mondriaan and Saenredam (the 17th-century painter of church interiors).

Among other contemporary artists, keep an eye open for witty sculptures by **Servaas**, innovative painting by **Aldert Mantje** and **Ger van Elk**, and **Gijs Bakker's** poised mixed-media pieces. **Seymour Likely** lurks on the horizon. Likely is the creation of three Amsterdam artists. He berates Gallery Directors and collectors in long letters, and produces works that tweak at the Art Establishment with a refreshingly cheeky iconoclasm.

Architecture

Amsterdam is just what we imagine when we do not dream
of a northern Venice whose *Amstel* would be the *Giudecca*,
whose *Dam* another *Saint Marc's Square*.... It is oldish-
looking, middle-class, stuffy, busy, swarming.... The
colours are strong and sad, the forms symmetric, the façades
kept new.... We feel that it belongs to a people eager to
take possession of the conquered mud—anxious about its

business, commerce, industries, labour, rather than its
well-being, and which never, even in its greatest days, ever
thought of building palaces there.
—*Eugène Fromentin, 19th-century art critic*

The delights of Amsterdam's architecture are small-scale, domestic ones. It's a city of little corners and quiet surprises. Wealthy merchants over the centuries have built some grand mansions, but they're not gargantuan. Though you're unlikely to be bowled over by the sheer magnificence of some glittering edifice, you're sure to be stopped in your tracks, suddenly captivated by an ornamented gable, a witty façade decoration or a neat, perfectly poised little house.

Amsterdam is built on treacherously soft soil. Buildings are prevented from gracelessly subsiding into the bog by a centuries-old method, perfected in the 1750s and little changed since. Rows of piles are sunk, in twos, along the line of a proposed wall, right down to one of two hard sand levels (at 14 m or 20 m below the surface). Planks are fastened to the piles, and the walls are built on top. As old piles rot or sink, so buildings lean, bulge, crack or collapse. You can see houses listing at precarious angles, propped up by wooden beams. Over the gap left by the demise of one structure, two others will incline towards each other until they're stoutly pushed apart (by more wooden beams). There are a few sad cases where owners have had to make do with propping up the first floor and amputating the rest.

The first houses in Amsterdam were made of wood, but after fires nearly destroyed the city (in 1421 and 1452), people began building in brick. At first only the lower walls were of brick. The gables (which formed the outer walls of attics and were often shaped to give more interesting definition to steep triangular roofs) were still wooden. The shapes of early brick gables are a direct reflection of their wooden ancestry. Favourite Renaissance façade decorations were scrolls, vases and masks. The ornamentation reached a high point in the playful work of **Hendrick de Keyser** (1565–1621; responsible, also, for most of Amsterdam's delicate towers). It took until the end of the 17th century for people to stop building in the Renaissance style, but the adventurous were already experimenting with a purer form of Classicism in the 1620s. Dutch architects pored over recently translated Italian pattern books, and imitated the designs they found. Fruit, flowers, animals and human figures join the gable adornments; garlands and festoons appear under windows and the larger houses begin to resemble temple fronts.

Notable architects of the period are **Jacob van Campen** (1595–1657), who built the town hall on the Dam (see p. 102), and **Philips Vingboons** (1607–78) and his brother **Justus** (1620–98), famed for their domestic architecture. Towards the end of the century austerity set in, and architects wisely began to emphasize simplicity and harmony. **Adriaan Dortsman** (1625–82) is the master of the school of what became known as Restrained Dutch Classicism.

The 18th century saw the advent of the standardized, pre-fabricated gable—a sort of architectural mix-and-match. Unfortunately, plot widths were inconveniently irregular, so little disguises to hide the shortfall in the gable width—like vases on corners—were introduced. The century is marked by a fascination with things French. Gables became draped with acanthus leaves (Louis XIV), encrusted with asymmetrical fripperies (Louis XV) or strung with modest garlands (Louis XVI). Windows were made larger and brick façades were plastered or replaced by sandstone.

Amsterdam was a poor and sorry city for most of the 1800s. Little building went on until money began to dribble back into the coffers in the last decades of the century. The city's first social housing estates went up in areas like De Pijp and the Jordaan, but the period is remembered more for public buildings than for domestic architecture.

The driving force behind 19th-century Dutch architectural innovation was **P.J.H. Cuypers** (1827–1921), the designer of the Centraal Station and Rijksmuseum (see p. 93 and p. 110). He based his work on indigenous brick and wood architecture, but was easily lured towards neo-Gothic extravagance. His belief that the entire building, from basic structure to the smallest detail of decoration, should be governed by a single coherent principle became the basis for modern Dutch architecture. Two other styles dominated 19th-century building: the upstarts of the **Architectura et Amicitia** society went in for idiosyncratic fantasies that outdid even Cuypers' ornamentation, while the more conservative members of the **Maatschappij ter Bevordering der Bouwkunst** (Society of Architects) favoured an eclectic approach, resulting in a mixture of diluted styles. Most of the interesting 19th-century buildings in Amsterdam today come from the boom period of the latter part of the century, and reflect this divergence of taste. On the one hand you'll see buildings like A. N. Godefroy's Adventskerk (Keizersgracht 676), which manages to lump together a classical rusticated base, Romanesque arches, Lombardian moulding on the façade and imitation 17th-century lanterns. On the other hand, there are wildly ornamented buildings like J. L. Springer's Stadsschouwburg (see p. 191). In the last decades of the century architects began to reject eclecticism and work in a neo-Renaissance style. This led to a revival of indigenous Dutch brick architecture.

H.P. Berlage (1856–1934), the designer of the Beurs (see p. 95), is known as the father of modern Dutch architecture. Like Cuypers, he used traditional Dutch materials. He relished displaying a building's structure with graceful brickwork, but was never tempted into frivolous ornamentation. The most exciting 20th-century school of architecture arose as a reaction to Berlage's homespun, rational buildings. Younger architects, many of them in the employ of the city's housing department, began experimenting with decorative folds and turrets of brickwork shaped around a more solid inner skeleton of concrete. These modern, quirky brick fantasies of the **Amsterdam School** (active from around 1912 to 1924, see pp. 156–7) have, until recently, been neglected, but a recent exhibition of photographs and architects' drawings at the Stedelijk Museum has shot them back into fashion.

Under the influence of *De Stijl* (see pp. 61–2), Bauhaus in Germany, Frank Lloyd Wright in the USA and Le Corbusier in France, a new style of building emerged—all sharp edges, concrete, steel and glass. Known in the Netherlands as **Nieuwe Zakelijkheid** (Functionalism), it dominated the middle decades of the century. Though it produced some neat and attractive buildings such as the Round Blue Teahouse (1937; see p. 189) and some fine domestic architecture by Gerrit Rietveld, it must also take the blame for the thinking behind high-rise 1960s horrors, such as the estates at Bijlmermeer. Amsterdam has suffered more than its fair share of architectural atrocities in recent years—tacky façades of insensitively used modern materials and buildings hugely out of scale. Notable exceptions are the colourful **Moederhuis** (built in 1981 by the imaginitive modernist, Aldo van Eyck, winner of the 1990 Royal Gold Medal for Architecture—the world's most prestigious architectural award), the monumental new **Muziektheater** (1985; see p. 74–6) and the **NMB Bank Headquarters** (1987). This extraordinary brick building in Bijlmermeer has hardly a right-angle in sight, mineral water fountains instead of air-conditioning, a system that warms the building by recycling the heat generated by computers, and installations of mirrors and stone that play light tricks at the solstices. (It's sometimes possible to be taken on a guided tour: see Archivisie in Practical A–Z: Tours).

A Gable-spotter's Guide

A check-list to carry with you on canal walks. Architectural terms are explained on pp. 68–70.

Gables with roll ornaments (*c.*1570–1600). A rare, early type of gable. The only two remaining examples are at Singel 423 and at St Annenstraat 12 (off Warmoesstraat).

Step-gables (*c.*1600–65) were the most common of the first brick gables. Often the street-front below would still be wooden. Decoration was usually limited to designs in the brickwork of the façade itself. At Prinsengracht 2–4, you can see an unusual corner house with two step-gables.

Spout-gables (*c.*1620–1720) are a direct imitation of their pointed wooden predecessors. They were rarely used in front façades, except in the case of warehouses, but are common at the backs of buildings. The tops are often ornamented with a fronton, and volutes bedeck the upper corners. The façades of the warehouses at Prinsengracht 211–217 are virtually in their original form.

Elevated neck-gables (*c.*1640–70). A cross between a step-gable and a neck-gable. It has two steps (as opposed to the neck-gable's one) which are filled in with decorative sandstone claw-pieces. Other common ornamentation includes *oeils-de-boeuf*, pilasters and frontons. You'll find good examples at Herengracht 281–283.

Neck-gables (*c.*1640–1770) were invented by Philips Vingboons, and were extremely popular. In the 17th century they were decorated with fruit and flower claw-pieces and festoons. Eighteenth-century neck-gables are taller, and the decorations more voluptuous. Vingboon's first neck-gable (built in 1638) is at Herengracht 168.

Bell-gables (*c.*1660–1790) have a similar bell-shaped silhouette to neck-gables, but are filled out entirely with brick (rather than sandstone claw-pieces). Bell-gables usually have a sandstone trim and in the 18th century (when they were most popular) were often topped with a crest. There's a beautiful example at Keizersgracht 546.

Façades with straight cornices (17th–19th centuries) were cheaper to build, and particularly popular in the 19th century. As prosperity waned, architecture became more sober. Many old gables were 'modernized' into straight cornices—Keizersgracht 610 is one that got the chop.

Façades with elevated (i.e. decorated) cornices (18th century). After 1790, no more step, neck or bell-gables were built. The majority of old houses still intact in Amsterdam today have straight cornices. In the 18th century these were richly ornamented and bulged in the middle to allow for larger loft shutters. A typical example of this is to be found at Singel 56.

Most of the old houses in Amsterdam are a hotch-potch of styles, the products of centuries of renovations and additions. It's often quite easy, though, to puzzle out the jigsaw.

Stoops, pothouses, and **gable stones** indicate 17th-century buildings. Common 17th-century ornamentations are **fruit and flower motifs, frontons on top** and **festoons**. Houses with **more than two floors above the bel-etage** date from the end of the 17th century. **Sandstone ornamentation** along the tops of façades began in the 17th century and stopped after about 1800.

Leaning façades don't always mean subsidence. Until 1850 houses were built like that to stop goods that were being hauled up on the hoist beam from banging into the wall.

Windows were usually the first things to be replaced or modernized. The oldest windows have cross-frames. The general rule is the smaller the panes, the older the window. Before 1800 upper windows would get progressively smaller in each floor towards the roof. Sash windows were introduced around 1700, and T-windows around 1870.

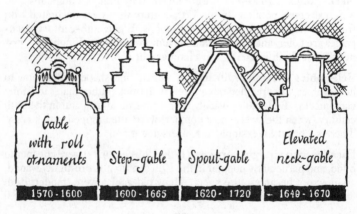

Gable with roll ornaments	Step~gable	Spout~gable	Elevated neck~gable
1570 - 1600	1600 - 1665	1620 - 1720	1640 - 1670

A Short Glossary of Architectural Terms

attiek: (stress the second syllable—'teak'), not the same as English 'attic', but the line of ornaments above a cornice (q.v.) that hides the roof from the street.

bel-etage: (rhymes with massage), the floor above the souterrain (q.v.), reached by a short flight of steps, but functionally the ground floor.

cartouche: elaborate sandstone ornamentation often seen around small oval windows or hoist beams (q.v.).

claw-piece: the ornamentation that fills in the right-angled step made by the side of a neck-gable and the wall below.

console: a supporting bracket (rather like a shelf bracket), often ornamented and supporting a cornice (q.v.).

cornice: a moulded projection which crowns a façade and runs the width of the building. It may be simple and flat, or ornamented.

festoon: ornament in the form of a garland—usually with fruit or flower motifs.

fronton: triangular (though sometimes rounded) piece that crowns façade. It runs the width of the gable only (not the whole building, like a cornice). In some classical designs the fronton is very large, often supported by pillars and running almost the full width of the building—this is called a **tympan**.

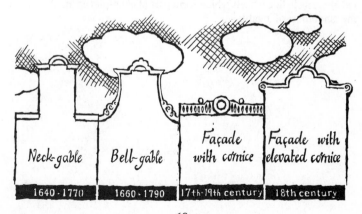

| Neck-gable | Bell-gable | Façade with cornice | Façade with elevated cornice |
| 1640-1770 | 1660-1790 | 17th-19th century | 18th century |

gable: the Dutch word *gevel* refers to the whole façade, but technically this is just the part of the wall that covers the triangular end of the roof.

gable stone: stone tablet, with a picture or symbol carved on it, embedded in the façade. In the 17th century it acted as a house number.

hoist beam: beam sticking out from the top of a façade. It has a hook on the end through which a block and tackle can be hung to hoist goods to the upper floors.

oeil-de-boeuf: ('bull's eye') small oval windows, often with an elaborate sandstone framing, seen in the tops of façades.

pilaster: flattened pillar that projects slightly from a façade. May be decorative or have a structural function.

pothouse: an extension of the kitchen with a separate entrance slightly below street level. (Originally used to store pots, later as workshops for craftsmen.)

souterrain: the part of the house below street level. Because of Amsterdam's high ground water level, the souterrain is not as low as a conventional cellar, and is usually reached by a door under the stoop (q.v.).

stoop: the steps leading up the front of a building to the front door (which is usually a little above street level). In most houses the steps rise across the façade, rather than extending frontally from the door down to the street. The landing is sometimes big enough for a few chairs, and there is occasionally a small bench built into the railings.

volute: scroll-like whorls which form part of claw-pieces (q.v.), or fill in the 'shoulder' of a gable.

Topics

Riot-control police with wicker shields

Cleanness

Seventeenth-century travellers used to slopping through the ordure and dodging flying sewage in other European cities were impressed—if not a little embarrassed—by Amsterdam's pristine pathways. 'The beauty and cleanliness of the streets', marvelled one passing Englishman, 'are so extraordinary, that Persons of all ranks do not scruple, but seem to take pleasure in walking them.' Jets of water from special spray devices regularly washed down the houses, roads were 'paved with brick and as clean as any chamber floor' and flotillas of maids and housewives scrubbed, buffed, swept and polished until (in the words of an astonished Owen Felltham, Cromwell's propagandist, and so no great lover of the Dutch) 'every door seems studded with diamonds. The nails and hinges keep a constant brightness as if there were not a quality incident to iron.' As early as the 15th century, Emperor Charles V's quartermaster—who had plundered the kitchens of Europe—thought that there was none to equal the neatness of Dutch housekeeping.

As time wore on, the Dutch became even more scrupulous. By the end of the 19th century canny Dr Samuel Sarphati was sealing up household waste in barges, shipping it out to the countryside and selling it to farmers as compost. In 1874 the writer Henry James was riveted by the

71

sight of an Amsterdam housemaid compulsively scouring an apparently spotless stoop:

> Where could the speck or two possibly have come from unless produced by spontaneous generation: there are no specks on the road ... nor on the trees whose trunks are to all appearance carefully sponged every morning. The speck exists evidently only as a sort of mathematical point, capable only of extension in the good woman's Batavian brain.... It is a necessity, not as regards the house, but as regards her own temperament.

This ablutionary temperament was not to the liking of all. Some visitors complained of the excessive neatness, of trees all clipped to look the same and of 'the endless avenues and stiff parterres' which seemed like 'the embroidery of an old-maid's work-bag'. A supperless Abbé Sartre opined that the Dutch would die of hunger surrounded by their glittering cauldrons and sparkling crockery 'rather than prepare any dish that might conceivably disarrange this perfect symmetry'. Sir William Temple, British ambassador to the Netherlands in the 17th century, was much tickled by the story of an English magistrate who dared go visiting in muddy shoes. A forthright Amsterdam housemaid plonked him down on the stoop, plucked off the offending footwear, and carried him across the shining hall floor to her mistress's parlour.

Nowadays you're in little danger of being manhandled, but the scrubbing and polishing go on. Windows have a transparency rare in big cities, the humblest bed-and-breakfast (if it's owned by a Hollander) will be spotless, and battalions of street-sweepers work right through the day (joined in the early hours of the morning by spraying and scrubbing machines). On the morning after Queen's Day—when up to three million people party on the streets—Amsterdam is as spruce as ever. As a 20th-century tourist used to the grime of London, Rome or New York, you'll be just as impressed, and embarrassed, by immaculate Amsterdam as were your counterparts three hundred years ago.

Opera and Stopera

The early Calvinist Church regarded opera with horror. It was not only most certainly an invention of the devil, but (perhaps even more damning) was most extravagantly un-Dutch. Conventional drama was bad enough. In 1655 one Revd Wittewrongel railed against stage performances 'because they are generally lecherous and wanton, full of indecency, cruel, bloody, usually taken from the heathen comedies and tragedies which are filled with superstitions, shameful idolatry, blasphemy and embellished fables and lies'. Anything so solely committed to entertainment as the *opera*, which added profane music and 'enjoyable dancing' to this list of wrongs, was intolerable. Amsterdam's first opera house survived just 53 weeks.

Dirk Strijker was the son of the Consul of Holland in Venice. He grew up feeling more Italian than Dutch, changed his name to Theodoro, and returned to Amsterdam around 1679 filled with a missionary's zeal. Opera was the driving passion of his life, and he was determined that his fellow Hollanders should see the light. Despite the disapproval of the Church elders, the general populace of Amsterdam was already developing a taste for opera. Amsterdam did have a theatre—on the Keizersgracht. The Calvinist Church (which seemed to have learned accounting practices from its Roman Catholic predecessor) was willing to turn a blind eye to the existence of this house of sin, provided that certain 'charity levies' were made to Church concerns. Almost the entire box-office receipts from the theatre on the Keizersgracht went to the Orphans' Home and the Men's Home for the Aged. On the evenings when nothing was scheduled, itinerant Italian and French opera companies would sometimes stage performances. These met with wild success—they were even more popular than the theatre's conventional fare.

Strijker, however, was determined that the city should have a purpose-built opera house. In 1680, after complex negotiations with the Church and the city fathers, and substantial donations to the orphans and aged men, he was finally granted permission to build a theatre on the Leidsegracht for (in the words of the uninitiated council secretary) 'silent performances and fine music'. But this was the beginning rather than the end of the battle. The building of the new theatre took longer and proved more expensive than Strijker had anticipated. The musicians he had contracted sat around, twiddled their thumbs, and collected their pay packets. When he finally set the opening night for Saturday 28 December 1680, the Church objected that it was the night before a Holy Communion celebration and would brook no competition. The opera house eventually opened on New Year's Eve. Over the next few months, audiences flocked over from the theatre on the Keizersgracht, and its box office takings dropped to such a sad level that the Orphans' Home and

Men's Home for the Aged began to complain. The large chunk of Strijker's profits that was destined to placate these worthy concerns never materialized. Opera is an expensive business, and his theatre ran at a loss. Deprived of this income, the Church began to exert pressure for the closure of the opera house. Strijker got no help from a blandiloquent city council, and after a year and a week he was forced to abandon his venture and retreat '*in slechten en miserabelen stand*' ('in a sorry and deplorable state') into obscurity. Today there is no sign of the old opera house on Leidsegracht. No-one even knows what happened to it and not a single picture of the building exists. The Church must have been determined to obliterate every trace.

Strijker's audience, however, had had their appetites whetted. They streamed to French and Italian operas given in theatres outside the city's boundaries—in Overtoom and in Buiksloot across the IJ. Gradually the Church's attitude began to soften. The theatre on the Keizersgracht, which had been churning out a steady diet of moralistic dramas, began to stage operas again, and the first *Stadsschouwburg* (Municipal Theatre) opened on Leidseplein in 1774. Here you were subjected to operas of a rather questionable standard—good singers were thin on the ground and all the female leads were taken by the director's wife. Towards the end of the 18th century performances of a rather better quality could be seen at the German Opera House and the French Opera House (now the Kleine Komedie) which opened on the Amstel. The middle years of the 19th century were boom years, with a good local opera company resident at the *Stadsschouwburg*, but by the turn of the century interest had dwindled dismally. A plan in the 1920s to build a national opera house across from the Concertgebouw on Museumplein was vetoed by the city council.

After the Second World War, however, there were murmurings in the corridors of power about the need for a national opera house. Plans for a building on the Museumplein, and for one further to the south on Allebéplein (where a Hilton hotel was later built), were abandoned when someone suggested Frederiksplein. This large site, closer to the city centre than the other two, had been derelict since Amsterdam's Crystal Palace—the glittering *Paleis voor Volksvlijt*, built to house international exhibitions—had burned down in 1929.

At just the same time, the council committee responsible for the building of a new city hall was also attracted to the idea of Frederiksplein. There followed a sort of architectural musical chairs, during which opera house and city hall pursued each other about Amsterdam, claiming for

74

themselves in turn the few choice sites available and preventing each other's plans from materializing.

By 1969 the council had decided to build the new city hall on Waterlooplein. An Austrian architect, Wilhelm Holzbauer, won the competition to design the new *Stadhuis*, but in 1972 the provincial authority vetoed the funding because his building was going to be too expensive to run. One afternoon in 1979, with the authorities still locked in negotiation, Holzbauer was standing on the Blue Bridge, looking glumly over Waterlooplein, when he had the brilliant idea of *combining* the *Stadhuis* and opera house into one complex. This seemed to solve everyone's problems. Within weeks the Prime Minister had approved a 230 million guilder budget and a combined plan by Holzbauer and local architect Cees Dam had been passed. But the idea caused a furore among the burghers of Amsterdam.

Many of the objections seemed to follow the old Calvinist pattern. Opera was unnecessary. Amsterdam didn't need an opera house, especially not in the centre of town. Those who really felt the urge could indulge themselves in theatres on the outskirts. But it was the choice of the site that caused the greatest ill-feeling. Waterlooplein had been the heart of Amsterdam's large Jewish neighbourhood, and had been a sad and derelict scar since the Nazis had all but obliterated the Jewish population. Many people thought an opera house to be an inappropriate building to occupy a location with such poignant associations. The few people still living on Waterlooplein after the war had already been evicted in the 1960s to make way for the proposed *Stadhuis*, they had then looked on as their empty homes were occupied by squatters while the council dithered over the cost of the proposals. When plans for the combined *Stadhuis* and *Muziektheater* were mooted, the by-then-long-established squatter communities had no intention of giving up their homes to what they saw as a temple of élitist entertainment. The complex was nicknamed the Stopera (from *St*adhuis and *opera*) and a vociferous 'Stop the Stopera' campaign erupted. Police attempts to evict squatters met with the strongest public resistance the city had seen since the street fighting of the 1960s and 1970s. Opposition raged, with little success, right up until the day the *Muziektheater* opened in 1986. (At the opening ceremony Queen Beatrix and Prince Claus had to be smuggled in through the stage door to avoid the angry throngs around the main entrance.)

Today the dust has settled, and though few people like the austere, bland *Stadhuis*, most Amsterdammers will admit that the elegant

Muziektheater, with its coliseum of pink marble has become an attractive city landmark.

Flowers and the Great Tulip Mania

Flowers are everywhere in Amsterdam. The tattiest houses sprout windowboxes, you'll see neat little posies on the counters of bars and fetching bouquets on bank clerks' desks. People give flowers for the flimsiest reasons. Bunches hurriedly bought from canal-side barrows pass between friends like pecks on the cheek. Everyone has favourite blooms and nose-curling aversions, and to forget your loved-ones' floral preferences is like neglecting to remember whether they take milk in their coffee.

Flowers are a national obsession. In the 17th century, when the blossoms were stratospherically pricey, painters made a comfortable living churning out floral still lifes as a substitute. Though these cost as much as the blooms themselves, the (at times regrettable) permanence of the paintings justified the expense. More recently, carnations were the vehicle for a subtle national rebellion. In the early months of the Nazi occupation, thousands of Amsterdammers wearing white carnation buttonholes suddenly appeared on the streets one morning. The Germans were taken by surprise and hadn't the faintest idea what was going on, but any Hollander knew: it was the birthday of their exiled Prince Bernhard, who always wore a carnation in his lapel. When the war ended and Queen Wilhelmina returned, people flocked spontaneously to Noordeinde Palace in The Hague and left so many offerings of bouquets that the lawn in front of the palace was completely covered in flowers. Ever since then, the reigning monarch has had to emerge on her birthday to accept thousands of posies and shake the hands of adoring subjects as they file past.

Tulips—homely, suburban and pure—have become a national cliché. Yet behind these apparently innocent blooms lurks a past of envy, greed and intemperance almost unparalleled in Dutch history. Tulips were first spotted in Adrianople, Turkey, by Dutch diplomats at the Ottoman court. In the early 17th century the flowers made a spring debut in some of French and Dutch society's best gardens. Soon, Johan van Hooghelande, a Leiden botanist, had found out how to vary the colour and shape of the blooms. Connoisseurs queued up, money pouches bulging, for the latest varieties and by the 1620s the tulip was *the* flower of fashionable aristocracy. This alchemical combination of scientific research, visual allure and the chance of profit—three great Dutch enthusiasms—incited the Great Tulip Mania.

At first, the bulbs were seen as exotic rarities. The Calvinist Church even regarded them as dangerous—perhaps because the flamed petals reminded them of the ribbons, ruffs and other vanities that ministers railed against from the pulpits. The bulbs were swapped and grown by a handful of aristocratic connoisseurs who, as was their wont, imposed a strict hierarchy on the tulip world. The noblest were the roses (red and pink on white), then came the violets (lilac and purples on white) and finally *bizarden* (red or violet on yellow). Humble plain colours barely merited an estate. It was the irregular, flamed and striped varieties, like the red and white Semper Augustus and the Viceroy, that mattered. (The democratically-minded Dutch, however, preferred to call their nobler varieties 'Admiral' or 'General' followed by the name of the grower.)

Gradually the hoi polloi began to edge in on the scene. Tulips were easily reproducible for a wider market. Delftware, an imitation of rare and expensive Chinese porcelain, was already decorating more modest homes. The Flemish carpet industry had its foundations in copying Turkish rugs. Tulips copied themselves, so by the mid-1630s weavers, blacksmiths and bakers were able to buy the bulbs at village fairs. The fashion spread and a tulip fever gripped the nation. Prices took off, then went into orbit. An Admiral de Maan that sold for *f*15 in 1634, went for *f*175 three years later. At the height of the boom a *f*800 Scipio changed hands after a few weeks for *f*2200. People went to any lengths for a prized bulb. One farmer met the *f*2500 demanded for a single Viceroy by payment in kind: two *last* of wheat, four of rye, four fat oxen, eight pigs, a dozen sheep, two oxheads of wine, four tons of butter, 1000 pounds of cheese, a bed, a suit of fine clothes and a silver beaker.

The rocketing prices were fuelled not only by demand, but by the growth of a futures market. In 1634 one bright dealer had the idea of buying in the winter for future delivery, and then selling to a new buyer before he actually possessed the stock. Soon deals were being done on negotiable pieces of paper, with the time of delivery as an expiry date. A quick turnover meant a quick paper profit. Dealers were selling bulbs they didn't yet possess, for amounts they couldn't possibly raise. As the delivery date drew closer, the danger that you would actually have to pay up increased, but so did the possibility of making an intoxicating profit as prices rose by the hour. At the bottom of the pile, and in danger of ending up with a heap of worthless bulbs if the market collapsed, were the growers. (The actual tulips would be the last thing on the mind of a merchant facing bankruptcy and trying to settle his paper debts.)

And collapse it did. By 1636 this *windhandel* (literally 'trading in the wind') was beginning to worry the city magistrates and outrage the Church. Whether it was the rumour of intervention that caused the panic, or the panic that caused the intervention, is unclear. But on 2 or 3 February 1637 a warning whisper shot round Haarlem and dealers went all out to sell. Prices plummeted, the bubble burst and the magistrates had to intervene with special legislation to rescue the innocent growers from the debris of bankrupts. It wasn't until the spring of 1638 that the market found a normal level, but the passion for tulips was there to stay. As the scandal subsided they quietly assumed their place alongside clogs, cheese and blue-and-white china as part of the nation's iconography.

Provos and Kabouters

If you walk from the Maritime Museum, along the avenue that now links the eastern islands, towards central Amsterdam's last remaining windmill, you'll notice a floating forest of scrap metal and brightly painted wood moored alongside a canalboat in the dock. These crumbling heaps of 1960s flotsam are the vestiges of water-borne sculptures by Robert Jasper Grootveld, one-time window cleaner and self-proclaimed 'anti-smoke sorcerer and medicine man of the Western asphalt jungle'.

Grootveld and his fellow Provos were the fire beneath the cauldron of the Dutch youth revolution; their antics in the mid-1960s were to influence the course of Dutch politics for decades to come. The Provos (from the Dutch *provocatie*—provocation) began as a literary and philosophical group, but soon became a political expression of the youthful rethinking that was going on across Western Europe and the USA. In their chaotic way they captured the attention and sympathy of older Amsterdammers, and shook up the rigid structures of the Establishment. The groundwork done by the Provos, and their successors the Kabouters—especially in such areas as environmental awareness, drugs advice and squatters' housing problems—went far to establishing the liberal attitudes prevalent in Holland today.

On Saturday nights, the Provos would gather around the *Lieverdje* on the Spui for a 'Happening'. In 1960 a tobacco company had donated the *Lieverdje* ('Little Darling'—a diminutive statue of a little boy) to the city, and it was becoming something of a landmark. Grootveld branded the statue a symbol of 'tomorrow's addicted consumer'. He and his band

would subtly provoke the police with faintly ludicrous performances—
like handing out raisins to passers-by while shouting out anti-smoking
slogans. The police invariably rose to the bait and would bash a few
heads with truncheons and make some arrests. But the Provos were
nothing if not master showmen. By the time the police took action, the
protesters would have a sympathetic audience on the café terraces
around the Spui. At best the police appeared fools, at worst bullies.

The campaign wasn't confined to Saturday nights at the Spui. The
Provos frequently met at the 'K-temple', a derelict garage near the
Leidseplein, to sing the *Ugge-ugge-song* (a 'psalm to the smoker's cough'),
listen to cryptic addresses on the cigarette industry and submerge themselves in the 'post-sexual electric jesus pandemonium-language' of
Arnhem poet Johnny the Selfkicker. They also daubed the letter *K* (for
kanker—'cancer') on cigarette advertisements all over town. Later the
words *Gnot* and *Klaas kom* ('Klaas is coming') also appeared. *Gnot* was an
amalgam of *God* and *genot* ('delight')—nobody was ever really able to
fathom out what it meant. Nor was anyone sure just who Klaas was.
Perhaps it was Sint Nicolaas, Amsterdam's patron saint. Perhaps it was
an oblique reference to Nicolaas Kroese, restaurateur of the famous De
Vijff Vlieghen, who wanted to link the towers of Amsterdam's churches
with gold chains to form a shield against the destructive forces of the
universe.

But the Provos also had a serious side. It was they who fomented the
street riots of the mid 1960s and produced the famous White Plans for a
better city. Many of these were frivolous or naïve, but some—like the
provision of 20,000 free White Bicycles to replace cars in the city
centre—were seriously considered by the sitting city council. In the 1966
council elections, the Provos polled 2.5 per cent of the vote and won a
seat on the council. By 1967, however, the Provos had lost impetus and
disbanded.

In 1970 they emerged again as the Kabouters ('Gnomes'—named
after a helpful character in Dutch folklore). The leading light this time
was sociologist Roel van Duyn, who held the Provo (or ex-Provo) seat on
the city council. The Kabouters had a lot of the playful pottiness of the
Provos, but with a jot more common sense and pragmatism. In a ceremony on the Dam they proclaimed an Orange Free State, and inaugu-
rated their own ministers. The Minister of Public Works, for example
was to preside over the planting of more vegetables and the breaking up
of motorways; the Minister of Environment and Hygiene would battle
against pollution and for 'biological balance'. The White Bicycles idea

became a plan for White Cars that was later (unsuccessfully) piloted. They expressed widespread concern that information gathered in a forthcoming census would be correlated on computer, and were chary of the growing powers of corporate industry. The movement caught on around the country, and in the 1970 June elections the Kabouters polled 11 per cent of Amsterdammers' votes, and sent five members to the city council.

Although they have now also largely faded from view (they were officially disbanded in 1981), you can still find the odd ex-Kabouter on neighbourhood committees, or in groups agitating against yet another Amsterdam architectural ravishment. The Provos and Kabouters have had their day, but the effects of the shake-up that they gave post-war Dutch politics still remain. 'Amsterdam is known as a difficult city, and Amsterdammers are difficult people,' said the *burgemeester* in the midst of the 1965 riots. The Provos were the essence of Amsterdam: at once tolerant and far-sighted, cheeky and difficult.

Gezelligheid

Dictionaries translate the Dutch word *gezellig* as 'convivial' or 'cosy'. A 1970s historian defined it, in the idiom of his time, as 'partly a sort of cosiness and partly a living togetherness'. *Gezelligheid* is the stuff of the Dutch temperament, and Amsterdammers pride themselves that their town bulges with it.

A café with nicotine-stained walls and scuffed leather chairs is *gezellig*; when you move into a new apartment you hang a few pictures, buy in some pot plants, adjust the lighting and make the flat *gezellig*; the mood in a neighbourhood bar on a cold winter's afternoon is *gezellig*; the behaviour of British lager louts in the bars of Leidseplein is definitely not. Sometimes *gezelligheid* seems subconscious. During the street riots of the 1960s the police were equipped, not with aggressive-looking anti-riot gear, but with large round wicker shields. It must have been almost impossible to hurl a missile at a policeman who was sheltering behind something resembling a dog basket. In its extreme forms *gezelligheid* becomes oppressive—the lace window screens, shelves of knick-knacks and safe respectability of a stolid burgher sitting-room. At worst *gezelligheid* inhabits a trim, embroidered world somewhere between kitsch and twee. A nice, *gezellig* family hotel in a small seaside town would probably be the *last* place you'd choose to spend your summer holiday.

The up-side of *gezelligheid* is to be felt in the warm conviviality that suffuses Amsterdam cafés, and even markets and town squares. Living in cramped houses in a small-scale city has honed Amsterdammers' social behaviour to a fine edge. They seem to have discovered that the best way of getting on when your neighbours are at such close quarters is by developing a frank, easy-going tolerance—a subtle decorum. Rules are clear, universally understood and sometimes broken if the occasion demands. In 17th-century Calvinist Amsterdam, Roman Catholics were allowed to worship freely, provided that their churches were discreetly hidden behind domestic house-fronts. Today Amsterdam authorities turn a blind eye to the sale and smoking of marijuana (technically still illegal) in certain cafés. Centuries of reasonableness have produced a culture that, perhaps more than any other in Europe, deserves the epithet 'civilized', and at its core are the virtues of *gezelligheid*.

Tesselschade

One rough night, towards the end of the 16th century, a small trading ship ran aground on one of the treacherous sandbanks that line the shores of the island of Texel off the coast of North Holland. The young Dutch merchant and man of letters, Roemer Visscher, was one of the few survivors. That very night his wife (snug in their house on the Engelse-kaai in Amsterdam) gave birth to a baby daughter. Although she was christened Maria, her father felt compelled to mark the coincidence and celebrate his survival by burdening her with the sobriquet 'Tessel-schade' (literally Tessel/Texel damage, but with gentler connotations of mischief).

Despite her nickname (and an accident involving a spark from a blacksmith's anvil) Tesselschade went on to become the one-eyed doyenne of Amsterdam salon culture. Her father made sure that Maria and her sister Anne got a sound classical education (a younger daughter, Geertruid, seemed content with her embroidery) and that they picked up all the subsidiary skills required to sparkle in erudite society. By the time she was a young woman the handsome (if slightly imperfect) Tessel-schade could supply fluent translations of the most complex Latin, Greek or Italian texts, was a prolific and accomplished poetess, would entertain delightfully on harpsichord, lute and viol and had a singing voice of high repute. When some of the older Chambers of Rhetoric (medieval literary societies) joined forces in 1630, it was Tesselschade who won the competition to write a poem celebrating the union.

In the first two decades of the 17th century, the house on the Engelse-kaai became Amsterdam's foremost literary and philosophical salon. When their father died, the daughters were snapped up by the poet Pieter Cornelisz. Hooft to join his famous literary circle at Muiden castle, just outside Amsterdam, where they held court until their respective marriages. The list of Tesselschade's suitors had read like a *Who's Who* of Dutch letters—men like Vondel, Bredero, Constantijn Huygens and P. C. Hooft plied her with eulogistic verses. But she finally married a sea captain from Alkmaar. Anne fulfilled her merchant family's social ambitions by marrying a minor nobleman.

Tesselschade returned to Amsterdam as a widow in 1640 to resume her position as a literary *Grande Dame* and when she died in 1649, Huygens compared her to the sun. Yet despite their obvious attributes and the frantic praises heaped upon them, the sisters never appear in any of the group portraits of the Muiden circle, and seem to have been regarded as prodigious ornaments, and not taken seriously in their own right. It took a 19th-century painter, J. C. Kruseman, to give the Visscher sisters pride of place among the male luminaries of the *Muidenkring* and today (if the painting's not in storage in the cellars) you can see the portrait hanging in the Rijksmuseum.

Water

Oliver Cromwell's caustic sidekick, Owen Felltham, was well known for his pronouncements that Holland was 'an universal quagmire' and 'the buttock of the world', yet even he had to admit that the Dutch were 'in some sort Gods, for they set bounds to the ocean and allow it to come and go as they list'. The Dutch had pretty much the same opinion of themselves. 'The making of new land belongs to God alone,' wrote Andries Vierlingh, the great 16th-century dike-master, '[though] He gives to some people the wit and strength to do it.'

Living alongside, on and even (but for the grace of God and the cunning of His servants) under the water had a deep effect on the national psyche. The Dutch responded to sudden inundations rather as other countries regarded visitations of the Black Death—as evidence of the wrath of God. It was but a short step to seeing the survivors and diligent battlers against the tide as a Chosen People. The Almighty would also come to their rescue, washing away the enemies of the righteous in a flood of water—as He did with the Duke of Alva's troops who were besieging Leiden in 1574. William of Orange broke the dikes to try to paralyse Spanish troop movements; this checked further advances, but was still not enough to relieve the town. However, a storm of such ferocity swept in from the sea that William was able to sail the Dutch navy right up to the city walls and put the terrified Spanish to flight.

Most of Amsterdam is below sea level. The land around Schiphol airport was, until the last century, a 5-metre deep inland sea. The early inhabitants of Amsterdam built their huts on little mudbanks or 'terps'. They had an uneasy relationship with the surrounding *meer*. It kept them well supplied with fish, but periodically rose up and turned their mud houses to mush. So they built two strong dikes to protect themselves— the Zeedijk and the Nieuwendijk still exist as street names in modern Amsterdam.

The invention of the windmill locked the marsh-dwellers into a Sisyphean struggle. As the mills pumped the land dry, the peat dried up, the ground level sank even further, and more dikes and windmills had to be built to prevent inundation. The new stretches of drained land became known as *polders* (a word introduced to the English language by Dutch hydraulic engineers brought over to England to drain the East Anglian fens).

Canals were initially also a means of drainage, but as the city grew, they afforded useful door-to-door transport links, and ducts for sewage. A German pastor who visited Amsterdam in 1838 was quite overcome. He noted in his diary that 'The stranger who views the city wrapped in a blue mist, and in the autumn breathes its unpleasant odours, will conclude with no second thoughts, that it is the least healthy place in the world.' These days, the city tourist authority—with its penchant for statistics—tell us that there are 160 canals in Amsterdam covering some 75.5 km. They are sluiced out daily by a huge pumping station east of the city and sewage is disposed of more subtly than of yore—though algae can turn the waters an alarming green, and in the summer you can still catch the odd whiff of the past in stagnating water in various dank corners of town.

Some Opinions of Holland

> Holland, that scarce deserves the name of land,
> As but the off-scouring of the British sand...
> This indigested vomit of the sea
> Fell to the Dutch by just propriety.
>
> *—Andrew Marvell, 1653*

Holland ... lies so low, they're only saved by being damned.
    —*Thomas Hood, 19th-century British poet*

Holland is a dream. A dream in a haze of smoke and gold,
in the daylight more of smoke, but golden in the evening.
    —*Albert Camus, 1956*

If you look at the manners of everyday life, there is no race
more open to humanity and kindness or less given to
wildness or ferocious behaviour.
    —*Erasmus, 16th-century Dutch humanist*

A Dutchman is a lusty Fat, Two-Legged Cheeseworm. A
Creature that is so addicted to eating Butter, Drinking Fat
Drink and Sliding [skating] that all the world knows him for
a slippery fellow.
    —*Dutch Boare dissected; or, a Description of Hogg-land*
        (1664 English pamphlet)

The women are not particularly engaging. One sees few slim
waists, they do have pale complexion, but are devoid of
personality. Excessive coffee and tea drinking ruins their
teeth completely.
    —*Marquis de Sade, 1769*

A Hollander without a pipe is a national impossibility.... If
a Hollander should be bereft of his pipe of tobacco he could
not blissfully enter heaven.
    —*An old Dutch commonplace*

Physically, even spiritually [the Dutch] are nearer to the
English than any other nation.... Calais Pier is a hundred
times more remote from our shores than the Hook of
Holland.
    —*Sacheverell Sitwell*

It is the peculiar genius of the Dutch to seem, at the same time, familiar and incomprehensible.

—*Simon Schama, Historian, 1986*

If I knew that the end of the world was imminent, I would take myself to Holland; for everything there happens ten minutes later.

—*Attributed both to Dr Johnson and Heinrich Heine*

The Walks

Gable stones set into a wall

Amsterdam is a practised, but subtle, temptress. Her gentle charms begin to work the moment you arrive, as they have for generations of travellers before you. These walks help you to succumb. They draw you along to nooks of curious architecture, reveal secrets which the city would rather keep from you, and entice you in to far more tantalizing cafés than could possibly be good for your health. You are lured down alleyways to glimpse the rough underside of town, then whisked back to the trim respectability of leafy canals. At various times you will find yourself spellbound by some of the greatest art in the world, jostling in a fleamarket with other bargain-hunters and poking about in the maw of a 17th-century trading ship.

Amsterdam is small. If you were single-minded about it, it would take only 40 minutes to traverse its spider's web of canals all the way from Centraal Station to the Rijksmuseum on the other side of town. Along the way, however, you'd be constantly surprised by the changes in pace and atmosphere of the *kwartiers* you passed through. The walks thread through numbers of these neighbourhoods, some no bigger than a courtyard and a few gabled houses, yet every one of them has a distinctive, quite particular, character of its own.

There are six walks, each with a dominant motif. The first two are biased towards the Golden Age, taking in the best 17th-century

86

architecture, rooms of Old Masters and grand stretches of canal. If your time is limited, Walks I and II, with a quick visit to the Van Gogh Museum, will reveal the essential Amsterdam. Walk III takes its cue from the Anne Frank House, and shows you through what remains of Jewish Amsterdam, then introduces you to the vibrant city sub-culture of the Jordaan. Amsterdam's maritime past, and the all-but-forgotten old port are the main focus of Walk IV. Walk V bounces you into the 20th century with modern art at the Stedelijk Museum and a visit to some intriguing architecture, and Walk VI starts at the Van Gogh Museum, then takes you through Amsterdam's antique markets and to some of its quirkier shops. Walks I and II cover the northern and central parts of town, Walks III and IV traverse east and west, and Walks V and VI are largely in the south.

The walks are liberally strewn with cafés where you can rest and take refuge from Amsterdam showers. If the weather is dire each walk has enough of interest inside dry, warm museums to justify the intermittent forays into the elements. You can often cheat a little and ride part of the way on a tram.

At the beginning of each walk there's a list of the main sights, followed by some advice on where to start, how to get there, where to eat and when to go. Walk II, for example, is a good walk for the late afternoon and early evening, especially in summer when the bridges and canal houses are lit up and look their best. Walk IV is most enjoyable on a Sunday, when much of Amsterdam is closed. You can go to a morning coffee-concert then wander about evocatively deserted shipyards.

Take an umbrella: even on heavenly summer and spring days you can be surprised by sudden showers of rain. Watch out for trams and bicycles. Amsterdam's motorists have been intimidated into submission by the hordes of pedestrians and cyclists, but walkers, bike-riders and trams vie for dominance of the narrower streets. Jay-walking will make you very unpopular with the locals. (Beware the busier roads like Prins Hendrikkade and Vijzelstraat—this is where drivers take their revenge.)

Pick of Amsterdam

Canals: Brouwersgracht (Walk II, Walk IV); Egelantiersgracht (Walk III); Reguliersgracht (Walk V); Prinsengracht between Amstelveld and the Amstel (Walk II, Walk V).

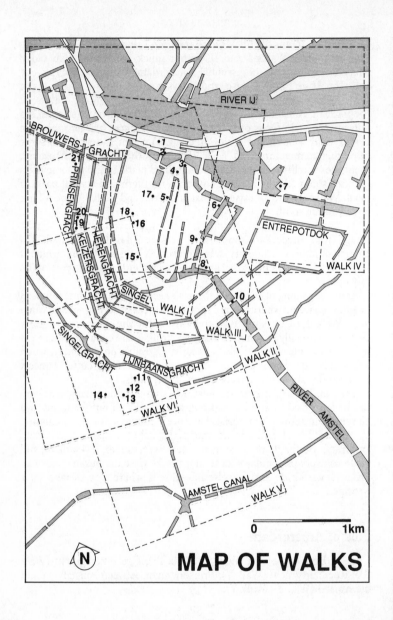

RIVER IJ

BROUWERS GRACHT

• 1
3
21 • 4 • 3
PRINSENGRACHT • 4
17 • 5 •
20 • • 6
19 18 • • 7
• 16
KEIZERSGRACHT ENTREPOTDOK
• 9
15 • • 8
SINGEL
WALK IV
• 10
WALK
SINGELGRACHT WALK III
LIJNBAANSGRACHT WALK II
• 11 RIVER AMSTEL
• 12
14 • • 13
WALK VI

AMSTEL CANAL WALK V

0   1km

N

MAP OF WALKS

Secrets and surprises: The Hollandse Manege (Walk VI); the Amstelkring (Walk I); Buiksloterweg—a little patch of country life across the IJ (Walk IV).

Oases of calm: Begijnhof (Walk I); Koepelkwartier (Walk IV); Amstelveld (Walk V).

Architectural eccentricities: The Scheepvaarthuis (Walk IV); De Dageraad (Walk V); Roemer Visscherstraat (Walk VI).

Stunning interiors: The Royal Palace (Walk I); the glass-box concert hall at the Beurs (Walk I); Museum Van Loon (Walk II).

Views: From the glass dome of the Metz (Walk VI); from the Westertoren (Walk III); across the Amstel to the Muziektheater at night (Walk V).

Rides: Under your own steam on the canals (see Travel); on an antique tram to the Amsterdamse Bos (see Day Trips).

Undeservedly neglected painters: Jan Steen (17th century, Rijksmuseum); Pyke Koch (20th century, Stedelijk Museum).

Neighbourhoods: The Jordaan (Walk III); Western Islands (Walk IV); Spiegelkwartier (Walk VI).

Museum interludes: Cafés at the Stedelijk (Walk V) and Film Museum (Walk VI); gardens at the Theatre Museum (Walk III) and Fodor Gallery (Walk V).

KEY TO MAP OF WALKS

1. Centraal Station
2. Main VVV Tourist Office
3. Schreierstoren
4. Sint Nicolaaskerk
5. Oude Kerk
6. Montelbaanstoren
7. Maritime Museum
8. 'Stopera'
   (Stadhuis and Muziektheater)
9. Zuiderkerk
10. Magere Brug
11. Rijksmuseum
12. Van Gogh Museum
13. Stedelijk Museum
14. Vondelpark
15. Amsterdam Historical Museum
16. Koninklijk Paleis
17. Beurs van Berlage
18. Nieuwe Kerk
19. Westerkerk
20. Anne Frank Huis
21. Noorderkerk

Walk I

Central Amsterdam

Allegory of Amsterdam

Centraal Station—Damrak—Beursplein—Red-Light District—Oude Kerk—Amstelkring—Bank van Lening—Spinhuis—De Dam—Nieuwe Kerk—Royal Palace—Amsterdam Historical Museum—Begijnhof—Spui

This is a short walk, yet it takes in the major landmarks of the city's Golden Age and gives you a taste of the variety and piquancy of modern Amsterdam life. Here is quintessential Amsterdam: compact, vibrant and full of contradictions. Turn the corner of a dark alley and you're blinded by the light reflected off a canal. Slip through a stone gateway, and the fluorescent glitz of a crowded shopping mall yields to a quiet 17th-century courtyard. Brothels surround the city's oldest church; sweaty nightclubs thump away beside the gliding waiters and clinking champagne glasses of the Hotel Krasnapolsky Winter Garden. The railway station is palatial; the Palace looks like a post office.

You can start off with a slap-up breakfast in the sombre elegance of the Centraal Station's First Class Restaurant, then whizz past the tourist razzmatazz of the Damrak and into the red-light district. Here, apart from the expected allures, you can visit a secret church in an attic and potter about canals and alleys little changed since the 17th century. After braving the crush and lethal traffic on the Dam, you can visit the Royal Palace, then ring one of the city's oldest carillons before finishing up with a coffee in a trendy café on the Spui.

It's best start early (in Amsterdam this means 10 am) to avoid the crowds. On Mondays the museums are closed, and you'll have to be in Amsterdam at the height of the season to get into the Palace without an appointment.

Start: Metro or tram to Centraal Station (nos. 1, 2, 4, 5, 9, 13, 16, 17, 24, 25).

Walking Time: 1½ –2 hours. Allow another two hours for visiting the churches and museums.

LUNCH/CAFÉS

Grand Café Restaurant 1e Klas, Platform 2b, Centraal Station. Recently restored First Class dining room, now open to all. It's timeless railway camp. You wouldn't bat an eyelid if you saw women in cloche hats whispering in the corner or an Edwardian touring party march through the door. Coffee f2.50, snacks and much grander meals.

Beurs van Berlage, Beursplein 3. Best place to get a glimpse of the coloured brickwork and murals of the old Exchange. In summer the tables spill out right across the square. Coffee f2.75, beer f2.50.

Het Karbeel, Warmoesstraat 58. An up-market café on the edge of the red-light district. It started life in 1534 as an inn and is still connected to the Damrak by a secret smugglers' passage. Coffee/beer f2.25, good sandwiches, snacks and fondues.

Lunchroom 52, Oudekerksplein. Coffee and sandwiches in the shadow of the Old Church. Coffee f1.75.

Ricky's Koffiehuis, Oudezijds Voorburgwal 206, in the red-light district. Starts early as a workers' café and changes clientele as the day progresses. Accordions hang from the walls, sugar is served from small zinc buckets and there's a large, cheery communal table in a nook at the back. Coffee f1.75, sandwiches.

Crea Café, Grimburgwal, at the end of Oudezijds Voorburgwal. Spacious student café with tatty pool tables, earnest groups arguing in corners and tired-eyed academics. Coffee f1.50, beer f2.00.

Upstairs Pannekoekhuis, Grimburgwal 2 (open Tue–Sun 11–7). Home-made pancakes up an almost vertical stairway, in a tiny room overhanging the street, with space for about ten customers. The owner's collection of teapots outnumbers clients 10:1. Pancakes around f10.

Kaptein Zeppos, Gebed Zonder End 5, (open Mon–Fri 11 am–1 am, Sat and Sun 4 pm–2 am). The street-name means 'Prayer without end'—the narrow alley used to wind through ten different cloisters and

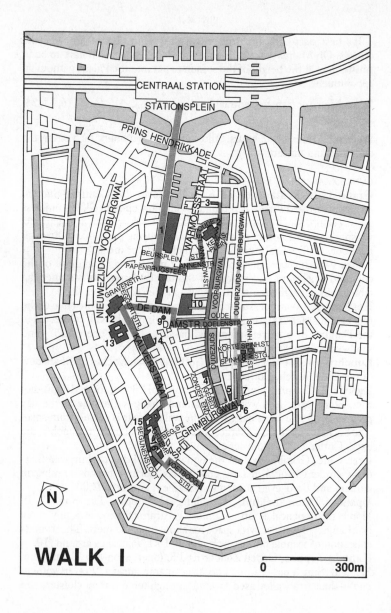

CENTRAAL STATION

STATIONSPLEIN

PRINS HENDRIKKADE

WARMOESSTRAAT

NIEUWEZIJDS VOORBURGWAL

OUDEZIJDS VOORBURGWAL

OUDEZIJDS ACHTERBURGWAL

BEURSPLEIN

PAPENBRUGSTEEG

ST. ANNENSTR.

ST. JACOBSTR.

3

2

OUDE KERKSPLEIN

11

10

OUDE

DE DAM

GRAVENSTR.

DAMSTR. DOELENSTR.

9

12

KALVERSTRAAT

13

14

KORTE SPINH.ST.

SPINH.ST.

SPINH.STG

SPINH.ST.

8

4

OUDEZIJDS VOORBURGWAL

GEBED

ZONDER END

5

7

6

GRIMBURGWAL

15

BEGIJNENSLOOT

NZ.BEG.ST.

SPUI

VOETBOOG

STR.

17

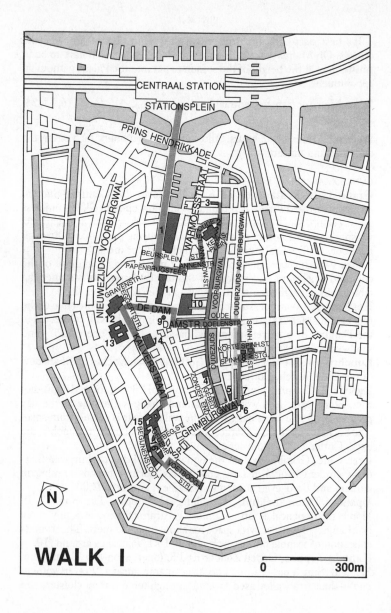

N

WALK I

0   300m

was always crammed with muttering clerics. The restaurant serves simple, well prepared food in an airy, relaxed environment. On some afternoons you'll find a gipsy violinist or jazz band. Lunches around *f*15.

Hotel Krasnapolsky Winter Garden, De Dam. Insensitive moderniz-ation has taken the edge off the old elegance, but you can still sit surrounded by palms and flattering mirrors and enjoy a genteel lunch or breakfast. Breakfast (6.30 am–10.30 am) *f*24, buffet lunch (12–2 pm) *f*42.50.

't Nieuwe Café Restaurant, Eggertstraat 8, next door to the Nieuwe Kerk. A noisy terrace, but quieter interior. Beer/coffee *f*2.50, set break-fasts, snacks and fuller meals.

De Drie Fleschies, Gravenstraat 18. *Proeflokaal* behind the Nieuwe Kerk that dates from 1650.

David and Goliath, Kalverstraat 92, at the entrance to the Amsterdam Historical Museum. The best place to relax after visiting the museum is at the feet of a life-sized wooden David and an enormous Goliath, rescued from a 17th-century pleasure garden. Coffee *f*2.50, beer *f*2.35.

Café Esprit, Spui 10. Trendy aluminium-box café on the Spui (closed Sunday). Beer *f*2.75, coffee *f*2.50.

Café Luxembourg, Spui 22–24. Grand café that becomes crammed with young professionals on the way home from work. Beer/coffee *f*2.50.

Café Hoppe, Spui 18–20. Dates from 1670, also popular with local office workers. On summer evenings there's standing room only on the terrace, and it looks a bit like a cocktail party. Coffee *f*2.00, beer *f*2.25.

☆　　☆　　☆　　☆　　☆

The **Centraal Station**, built between 1884 and 1889 atop thousands of wooden piles on an artificial island, is such an elaborate and sustained exercise in 19th-century ornament that it can almost be forgiven for

---

KEY TO MAP OF WALK I

1. Beurs van Berlage
2. Oude Kerk
3. Amstelkring Museum
4. Bank van Lening
5. Huis op de Drie Grachten
6. Gate to Gastenhuis
7. Gate to Oudemanhuis
8. Gate to Spinhuis
9. National Monument
10. Hotel Krasnapolsky
11. De Bijenkorf
12. Nieuwe Kerk
13. Koninklijk Paleis (Stadhuis)
14. Madame Tussauds
15. Amsterdam Historical Museum
16. Begijnhof
17. Gate to Rasphuis

screening off Amsterdam's view of the old harbour. The architect, P.J.H Cuypers (also responsible for the Rijksmuseum) succumbed to every temptation to gild bits of his red-brick extravaganza, so that it sparkles in the sunlight like a Walt Disney palace. Its twin towers are adorned not only by a clock, but also by a wind-rose, a delightfully superfluous instrument that rotates languidly showing the frequency of winds blowing from the various leading points of the compass. The roof bristles with stone and iron spikes and the central section sports classically inspired reliefs showing allegories of sailing, trade and industry. There's a large section over the entrance depicting the peoples of the world paying homage to the maiden Amsterdam. The building seems very much in the tradition of the triumphal arch or elaborate city gate and is indeed a grand place to arrive in Amsterdam. The city is laid out like a semi-circular spider's web with the Centraal Station in the middle. As you step out of the main entrance you get the full impression, across the shapeless open space of **Stationsplein**, of the spires, gables and cupolas of Amsterdam's delicate skyline.

Stationsplein itself is wildly and happily chaotic. Traditional Dutch barrel organs compete bravely with ten-piece South American bands and the 1970s rock music repertoires of buskers with portable amplifiers. Pedestrians stream in all directions, oblivious of the battalions of trams which, bells clanging, seem intent on converging on one particular spot in the centre. Rent-boys eye you from the arches, junkies and alcoholics lie up against the walls, smart businessmen and paradigms of fashion stride purposefully past and backpackers picnic on the concrete, propped up against their rucksacks.

Head straight across the square for **Damrak**, *once a busy port built along the Amstel, but these days a street lined with the fast food joints, rip-off bureaux de change, tacky restaurants and tackier hotels that usually cluster around tourist inlets. The only remaining patch of water is a tiny dock filled with the glass-covered boats that bus you around on hour-long canal trips (for details, see p. 27).*

The original settlement of Amsterdam grew up in the early 13th century along Kerkstraat (Church Street, later renamed Warmoesstraat) on the left side of the river. Towards the end of the century the village expanded along Windmolenstraat (Windmill Street) on the right bank. The Church Side and the Windmill Side soon became known as Oude Zijd (Old Side) and Nieuwe Zijd (New Side) and the corresponding sides of Damrak are still called that today.

*Hurry past the gaudy signboards and flashing neon lights, but keep
an eye open for the four baboons and twenty-two owls that stare
down at you from the façade of nos. 28–30. They're the work of
expressionist sculptor J. Mendes da Costa. He was lodging opposite
the zoo when he submitted the design. At no. 62 is Albert de Lange,
one of Amsterdam's best bookshops and the outlet for German
refugee writers like Max Brod and Bertolt Brecht during the 1930s.
Halfway up Damrak, on the left hand side, you come to the* **Beurs
van Berlage**. *(Tours of the building can be arranged by Archivisie—see Practical A–Z: Tours.)*

The first Beurs (Exchange) was built by the prolific 17th-century architect Hendrik de Keyser in 1608. The city council thought it necessary to
confine all the outdoor wheeling and dealing that took place along
Damrak and around the Oude Kerk to one (warmer and drier) venue.
The result was deafening. As international trade expanded, such exotica
as Turks, Indians and Hungarians joined the locals packed around the
pillars and arcades of the small hall on the Rokin, bargaining madly for
silks, shares, tobacco and tulips—or anything the boats brought in. De
Keyser's Beurs held out for two hundred years. The building that
replaced it (on the site of the present Bijenkorf department store) was
universally unpopular and in 1874 the city held a competition for a new
design. When it was revealed that the winner had cribbed the façade
from a French town hall, H.P. Berlage (who had come third) smartened
up his original plans and landed the prize. Many revisions later (he was
still at the drawing board while the builders were at work), he came up
with a building that has become an Amsterdam landmark and earned
him the reputation of being the father of modern Dutch architecture.

The Beurs van Berlage (completed in 1903) is all clean lines and
functional shapes. Berlage allows himself some gently patterned brickwork, but there's not one extraneous twirly bit nor a glimmer of 19th-
century gothic fantasy. The pillars and arcades inside are an echo of the
original Beurs. The clock tower (also a quote from De Keyser's building)
displays the mottoes 'Duur uw uur' and 'Beidt uw tijd' ('Last your hour'
and 'Bide your time'), apt maxims given the seven years Berlage took to
come up with a final design. These days the Beurs is used for concerts. In
the smaller of two halls you sit and listen to the music in an enormous
glass box which has solved the problem of abysmal acoustics without
defacing the original interior. You can get a glimpse inside without
buying a concert ticket by popping into the café at the south end.

The café opens out onto **Beursplein**. To the right the traffic on Damrak hurtles past. The dainty neo-classical **Effectenbeurs** (Commodities Exchange) on the left is the place where the real trading now happens. Across the square, a row of silently chewing, blank faces stare out at you from behind a sheet of plate-glass. These are exhausted shoppers propped up along a snackbar in the back window of De Bijenkorf, though they look as if they're for sale.

Leave Beursplein by Papenbrugsteeg at the far left-hand corner. In the days before telex, runners bearing the latest prices from the Beurs would thunder down this narrow alley to the press agency building on Warmoesstraat where, to save time, the despatch would be reeled up to the relevant floor using a fishing rod. At the end of Papenbrugsteeg, turn left into **Warmoesstraat**.

Warmoesstraat is Amsterdam's oldest street. Originally a cluster of wattle and daub cottages, it was by the 16th century a row of prosperous merchants' houses and powerful banks. The Duke of Alva lived here in 1574 during his reign of terror (the rest of the street was understandably empty at the time) and left without paying his rent. Vondel (the 'Dutch Shakespeare') had a small hosiery business at the Dam end before he became a famous poet (see p. 188); and Sir Thomas Nugent, a seasoned 17th-century traveller, recommended it as the only street where you'd find English inns and so avoid being cheated by wily Dutchmen. In 1766 Mozart senior held court in the tavern of De Goude Leeuw and sold tickets for his son's recitals at *f*2 apiece; and a century later Karl Marx pondered and scribbled away in the inn next door.

These days Warmoestraat is the first layer of the red-light district, and a strange mixture of past respectability and the seediness which lies beyond. You arrive directly opposite the Condomerie (condom as consumer item—everything you could imagine). Next door is W139, an enormous gallery, set up by squatters, where you're sure to catch the very latest (though not always the best) of what's going on in Amsterdam art. Further up, past a string of leather fetish bars, you'll find Amsterdam's best tea and coffee specialists (Geels & Co at no. 67). Just around the corner a butcher's shop lays out its trays of chops and drumsticks right next door to a display of enormous dildos and little plain-covered books with titles like 'Pent up Pleasure' and 'Mom's Donkey Urge'. It's a grubby, dishevelled street, but no one seems to take it seriously enough for it to be sordid.

When you've seen what you want to in Warmoesstraat, turn off into St Annenstraat, past the Hotel Winston where the drab bar comes to life after midnight as a favourite drinking spot for local scruffs and artists. St Annenstraat takes you right into the **red-light district**, *known to Amsterdammers as 'de walletjes' (the little walls).*

A 1629 law closed all taverns between St Annenstraat and the Oude Kerk because of the 'great acts of insolence and wantonness' going on there. The taverns have since reopened, though little else has changed. In those days the women nailed up romanticized portraits of themselves outside the doors. Nowadays they display themselves live, barely clad and deeply bored, perched on bar stools in the windows. Catch some-one's eye and immediately there's a bright smile and a sparkle which disappears the moment you look away. If business is bad, or if you walk with eyes downcast, you'll hear the windows being rapped noisily. The rooms are functional cubicles, though from time to time you'll see one decked out in lace, knick-knacks and potted plants—a quaint parody of a Dutch bourgeois sitting-room. In the mornings the little alleys, some narrower than a doorway, are inhabited only by the desperate (on both sides of the glass) and the area has a feeling of secrecy and expectancy, rather like an empty theatre. Off-duty prostitutes join friends to go out shopping, or wander off in groups to the clinic for a check-up. In the afternoons it all seems too blatant and seedy, but later a wild festivity sets in as the lanes fill with the merry, the lecherous and the plain curious. Phalanxes of Japanese businessmen troop about aching to take photo-graphs, drunken schoolboys gawp and try to pluck up courage, tight clutches of Dutch families from the provinces ooh and aah and snicker at all the wickedness.

A left turn down St Annendwarsstraat takes you to the Oudekerks-plein, a peaceful square almost entirely taken up by Amsterdam's oldest building, the **Oude Kerk** *(Old Church; open summer Mon–Sat 11–5, winter 1–3 pm; tower open June–Sept Mon and Thurs 2–5 pm, Tues and Wed 11–2; entrance f1).*

Only the tower of the Oude Kerk actually dates from 1300. The original basilica disappeared behind an increasingly haphazard outgrowth of side chapels, transepts and clerestories. Most of what you see today is lofty early 16th-century Renaissance, but even that has a crust of warden's offices, choir rooms and houses, built over a period of three centuries. The interior has survived frequent bouts of heavy-handed restoration, an engulfing coat of Prussian Blue paint in the 18th century and violent attacks by iconoclasts. In August 1566, roused by the sight of fragments of statuary from smashed-up churches in Antwerp, Protestant mobs stormed the church, breaking windows and destroying all graven images. A local girl, Lange Weyn, threw her shoe at a picture of the Virgin Mary in the excitement, and was later drowned in a barrel on the Dam for the outrage.

After what is discreetly called the 'Alteration' of 1578, when the Protestants finally took control of the city, the new Calvinist city fathers stripped the church of its dedication to St Nicholas (patron saint of sailors and so, aptly, of Amsterdam) and the popular title of Oude Kerk became official. They also set about turning it into a more sombre place of worship. It had become a hearty communal gathering place. Dossers and travellers slept in the corners, pedlars set up stalls in the aisles, merchants clinched deals on the square outside and dog-owners crowded the entrance. (Only certain classes of Amsterdam society were allowed big dogs, and if your mutt couldn't squeeze through the special iron hoop at the church door, its days were numbered.) These days the church plays host to travelling exhibitions and the occasional concert. Inside you can see the tomb of Rembrandt's wife, Saskia van Uylenburgh (near the Weitkoperskapel on the north side); some beautifully restored and remade stained glass (especially the windows depicting the Annunciation in the Mariakapel); and the secret door (once covered by plaster, 5 m above the ground in St Sebastiaanskapel) to the Ijzerenkapel (Iron Chapel), a hiding place for important city documents until 1892.

Walk around the Oude Kerk to the other side of the square and turn left up the nearside of Oudezijds Voorburgwal. You come almost immediately to the **Amstelkring Museum** *(Oudezijds Voorburgwal 40), one of Amsterdam's most charming small museums (open Mon–Sat 10–5, Sun 1–5; entrance f3.50).*

The Amstelkring Museum, also known as *Ons Lieve Heer op Solder* (Our Lord in the Attic), was a 'schuilkerk'—a clandestine church. During the 17th and 18th centuries Roman Catholic services were illegal, but ever-tolerant Amsterdam turned a blind eye to what was going on behind domestic façades. The attic of the little spout-gabled house joins up with two others in the houses behind and was consecrated as a church in 1663. Inside the museum you can wander about an 18th-century reception room, into a classic 17th-century Dutch 'sael' (living-room) with symmetrical black and white marble flooring and a monumentally grand walnut fireplace, up through bedrooms with quaint box-shaped cupboard beds, higher and higher to a small wooden staircase. Turn the corner at the top of the stairs and suddenly you're in what seems an enormous church with two galleries, light streaming in, an abundance of carving and painting and a voluptuous organ that *must* have been audible throughout the neighbourhood. The church is filled with treasures and mementoes of oppressed Catholicism (you can get an explanatory pamphlet downstairs). Try to get there early in the day, when you can appreciate the dream-like atmosphere in relative solitude.

Turn right out of the museum and double back along the right-hand side of **Oudezijds Voorburgwal**.

Oudezijds Voorburgwal was the canal immediately inside (*voor*, 'in front of') the first city wall. Today it's a brash, brazen strip of porn shops, video booths and peep-shows, though some stylish gables and façades poke out above the lurid layer at street-level. Look out for: the diving dolphins opposite the Amstelkring; a mask and bust encrusted house opposite the Oude Kerk; Africans and Indians relaxing on tobacco bales on the neck-gable at no. 187; and an elegant neo-classical building by one of the three great 17th-century domestic architects, Philips Vingboons, at no. 316.

Halfway down the canal the sleaze shops suddenly come to an end and you find yourself in a leafy nook of old Amstersdam. At no. 300 is the Municipal Pawn Broker—the **Bank van Lening**, euphemized as 'ome Jan' (Uncle John's). For the past three hundred years it has been a more sympathetic alternative to professional moneylenders—interest is fixed at a rate that corresponds to your ability to pay. Vondel, bankrupted by his playboy son, spent his septuagenarian years here as a clerk, going to work each day through a gateway that had one of his own poems inscribed in the arch. (It's still there, advising the rich to hurry past, as they have no business inside). On the opposite side of the canal is the **Agnietenkapel**, (open Mon–Fri 9–5; entrance free, but by appointment: tel 525 3341), a 15th-century convent church that houses a specialized and not particularly captivating collection of prints, photographs and ephemera centring on academic life.

Turn left into Grimburgwal, past the **Huis op de Drie Grachten** *(House on the Three Canals—the only one in the city with this qualification), and left again up the right-hand side of Oudezijds Achterburgwal, the canal that was just outside (*achter, *'behind') the first city boundary.*

Most of the buildings in this area are now part of the University of Amsterdam, but they were once (in the words of a 17th-century visitor) a collection of 'almshouses which look like princes' houses, hospitals for fools and houses where beggars, frequenters of taphouses, women who feign great bellies and men who pretend they have been taken by Turks' were confined and set to hard work. These institutions, a product of prosperous and Calvinistic Amsterdam, were considered far-sighted and revolutionary by the rest of Europe. The gateway on the corner, copied from a Michelangelo design, led to the **Gastenhuis** (hospital). A little further down you come to another elaborate arch, the entrance to the **Oudemanhuis**, an old men's almshouse. These days glass doors slide back as you approach and you find yourself in a dim arcade of second-hand bookstalls with medieval-looking proprietors. A shaft of light halfway along comes from a door that leads to the elegant almshouse courtyard. It's a private court belonging to the university, but nobody will stop you if you want to have a look.

> *Continue down Oudezijds Achterburgwal and turn right into Spinhuissteeg. On the left you'll see the entrance to the* **Spinhuis**.

The **Spinhuis** was a place where 'incorrigible and lewd women' were made to spin cloth for the poor. A rather alarming relief above the door shows women being whipped with a cat-o'-nine-tails. Underneath is the not entirely convincing inscription:

> *Schrik niet, ik wreek geen quaat maar dwing tot goet.*
> *Straf is mijn hand, maar Lieflijk mijn gemoed.*
> Cry not for I exact no vengeance for wrong, but force you to be good.
> My hand is stern but my heart is kind.

The altruism of successive custodians seems to have been directed more towards passing gentlemen. For a small fee they were given access to the wicked inmates.

> *Turn left into Spinhuisdwarsstraat and back along Korte Spinhuissteeg to Oudezijds Achterburgwal. Turn right and walk up to Oude Doelenstraat, where you turn left again. As you cross the canal you'll see the* **Hash Info Museum** *on the corner (see p. 199). Ahead of you on Damstraat is an enormous blue neon sign asserting* 'GOD is er' *(in fact it means 'God exists'). At the end of Damstraat you come to* **De Dam**.

Riots, garrottings, camping hippies—**De Dam** has seen it all. Reputedly the site of the original dam across the Amstel, it hit its zenith as city centre in the 17th century. Pragmatic Amsterdam merchants wouldn't stand for any decorative open space at the heart of the city and the Dam bustled with a fishmarket, a public weighing house, a communal crane and a dock that allowed ships to sail right up into the middle of town to offload. Popular tunes rang out from the Stadhuis carillon and, above all the racket, the town crier's horn would from time to time blast out (once for good news, twice for bad). When you needed to go home, you could ring a bell to summon a taxi. After a brief wait for the drivers to throw dice to decide who should take you, you'd set off at reckless speed in a slide carriage (wheels presented a problem on the hump-backed bridges), accompanied by packs of sprinting boys throwing water and greased rags under the runners to make the carriage go faster, or straw to make it stop. You'd have to drop out coins at intervals to ensure your rapid progress, and a few more at the humpy bridges to the stalwart lads who hung around to give a much needed extra push.

Traffic on the Dam these days is just as frantic, but the square has lost all its verve. It's still the city centre and the carillon still peals out pop tunes, but the Dam is soulless, fumid and dull. The eastern end is dominated by the towering, phallic **National Monument**, erected in 1956 as a memorial to the people killed in the Second World War. In the 1960s it became a sort of hippie totem pole and hundreds of people would sleep around it in the summer. Police attempts to put a stop to this (such as washing it down with firehoses) led to protest riots, but in 1970 a marauding group of off-duty marines chased away the campers forever.

*Walking anti-clockwise around the Dam you pass the **Grand Hotel Krasnapolsky**, where the Winter Garden has been a chic gathering place for over a century, and **De Bijenkorf**, a run-of-the-mill department store with a grand reputation and arty window displays. On the other side of the square you reach the **Nieuwe Kerk** (New Church; open Mon–Sat 11–4, Sun noon–2 and 4–5).*

The construction of the Nieuwe Kerk actually began nearly six hundred years ago. It's a soaring Gothic heap without a steeple. (In the 17th century, Oude Kerk parishioners, who had always been jealous of the flash rival church, were delighted when the city council stopped construction of the tower because it was going to be higher than the town hall). Until 1890 all the city's clocks were set weekly by the church's sundial. Like most of Amsterdam's large churches, the Nieuwe Kerk is now used mainly for exhibitions and concerts. Even if you can't catch a recital on the sumptuous Great Organ, the instrument itself, fluttering with angels and cherubs and surrounded by soft-painted shutters, is worth a visit. Admiral de Ruyter, the Dutch naval hero, is buried in the choir. (His invasion of the River Medway in England caused Sir William Batten, Surveyor of the British Navy, to explode to Samuel Pepys: 'I think the devil shits Dutchmen.') There's a memorial to the poet Vondel near the west door. Before you leave, have a look also at the richly carved pulpit and ornate copper choir screen.

Next door to the Nieuwe Kerk, taking up the entire western end of the square is the **Koninklijk Paleis** *(Royal Palace; open July–Aug daily 12.30–4, Sept–June guided tours Wed 1.30 pm, sometimes closed for state functions).*

The Koninklijk Paleis was the Stadhuis (City Hall) until Louis Bonaparte decided he wanted to live there in 1808. It's been a royal palace ever since, though Queen Beatrix prefers the leafier groves of Huis ten Bosch in The Hague and never spends the night here. The area in front of the Stadhuis was a favourite spot for theatrical public executions. On the right, above the entrance arches, you can still see the blocks where the scaffold slotted into the wall. The ornate street lamps along the front were commissioned by King Willem Frederik in 1840. They were the city's first gas lamps, but were so expensive to run that the council secretly turned them off whenever the king was out of town.

When the Stadhuis was built in the mid-17th century, only St Peter's, the Escorial and Venice's Palazzo Ducale rivalled it in grandeur. The poet Constantijn Huygens dubbed it 'the eighth wonder of the world', and a passing Englishman wrote of 'a most neat and splendid pile of a building'. But Sir William Temple, the British Ambassador to the Netherlands harrumphed that it was *una gran piccola cosa* ('a big little thing'—he was quoting someone else's remark about the Louvre).

The architect, Jacob van Campen (designer of the ill-fated Nieuwe Kerk tower), had produced a grandiose celebration of Amsterdam's mercantile supremacy and civic might—a neo-classical heap of windows, pilasters and relief carving. On the front pediment collected water deities worship an allegorical Maid of Amsterdam; at the back of the building the trading nations of the world grovel to her. Peace stands high under the dumpy dome (a cornucopia overflowing at her feet) holding not only an olive branch, but also Mercury's staff (a symbol of commerce). Atlas buckles under a copper globe so heavy that it needs iron rods to prop it up. Despite all this confident symbolism, there's no grand entrance (the eight little arches along the front look more like tradesmen's gates or the way in to the stables) and nowadays you are more likely to agree with Sir William Temple than Constantijn Huygens: the rather grimy palace in a busy city centre has as much architectural impact as a main post office or magistrates court. However, if you're passing during the rather restricted opening hours, don't miss the chance of popping inside to be dazzled by the *Burgerzaal* (Citizens' Hall). It's a vast space encrusted with marble carving that glints in the light pouring in from all sides. Rows of chandeliers drip from the distant ceiling, and brass inlaid maps on the floor show the heavenly and terrestrial worlds (with Amsterdam very much at the centre of things and the enthroned maid of Amsterdam proudly surveying it all). The few chairs around the edges, even a grand piano for the inevitable recital, look like doll's house furniture. Scattered throughout the building are delicate and often witty marble reliefs (Icarus takes a tumble outside the Bankrupts' Court, caryatids look bored with holding up the cross-beams). Most of them are by Artus Quellinus, the noted Golden Age sculptor who also carved the pediments outside. The city fathers, however, blundered when it came to commissioning the wall paintings: they sent Rembrandt packing after he had presented his preliminary sketches.

The Empire furniture dispersed around the building was left behind by Louis Bonaparte. When he took over the Stadhuis he carpeted the marble floors, boarded up the galleries, turned the virtually empty upper storey into living accommodation and also had the weighing house on the Dam demolished because it spoiled his view. When the bored and wayward Queen Hortens granted a royal pension to a foundling abandoned at the palace door, he forestalled an inundation of hapless infants by surrounding the entrance with cobble stones and appointing guards to prevent anyone from stepping on them. His wooden-partitioned upstairs apartments lasted well into this century and were such a fire risk that whenever Queen Wilhelmina used the palace everyone was instructed not to smoke and to sleep with the doors open. A fireman in gym shoes would creep about at night to catch offenders.

*Carry on in an anti-clockwise direction around the square. Before leaving the Dam you might like to visit **Madame Tussaud's** waxwork museum in the Peek & Cloppenburg department store.*

Here you can see some rather good reconstructions of 17th-century life and a perfectly horrible personified Europe (in a frock made of national flags) who rises from the centre of a tulip to the strains of Beethoven's 'Ode to Joy'. Madame Tussaud disdainfully floats away from it all on a painted cloud.

> *To leave the Dam, turn down Kalverstraat, a pedestrianized shopping street where shoulder-to-shoulder consumers push in and out of Euro-High Street stores, scrabble about in the sales baskets and devour pungent fast food. A little way down, on the right, you can seek sanctuary behind the lost-looking Gothic door of* **De Pappegaai** *(the Parrot), a 19th-century Catholic church which gets its name from the fierce looking polly carved into the archway. Walk on down to no. 92 and up the yellow cobbled path to a rather lopsided gateway. At one time all houses on public roads had such cobbles in front of them to stop night-time travellers veering off the highway into the gutter. The gate, by Joost Jansz. Bilhamer (who designed the main extensions to the Oude Kerk) leads you in to the old* **Burgerweeshuis,** *a home founded in 1520 for orphans from the top ranks of Amsterdam society.*

You find yourself immediately in the quiet loggia and courtyard of the boys' section, now the terrace of In de Oude Goliath café, but with the boys' wooden lockers still visible in the wall. Through the next arch, the girls' courtyard is even quieter and emptier. It's a sober red brick court with sensible Ionic pilasters. Occasionally an itinerant lutist or string quartet plays something suitably restrained in one corner, while beyond the walls the crush in Kalverstraat pushes past oblivious. The girls had their own gate, on the right side of the courtyard. The thrifty governors transferred it stone by stone from a building that was being demolished nearby and had a mason carefully alter the date stone from 1571 to 1634. Boys and girls were effectively kept separate by an open sewer that ran between their respective dormitories. The sewer has been covered and the resulting passageway converted into a promenade gallery for civic guard portraits which are too big to hang anywhere else, but they don't make particularly riveting viewing.

> *On the far side of the court is the door to the* **Amsterdam Historical Museum** *(open daily 11–5; entrance f5), a compact and accessible introduction to the city's history.*

The exhibition is arranged chronologically from Amsterdam's foundation right up to the 20th century and, armed with a file of English explanations of all the exhibits (free from the ticket desk), you can skim round quickly or stop to pick up details about periods that interest you. A map on the ground floor lights up in sections showing different phases of Amsterdam's growth. There's a sudden expansion in the Golden Age and an even bigger one in the late 20th century, after which all the lights go out with an alarming thud. You can get a bird's eye view of early Amsterdam from a medieval painting (quite a feat of imagination for an artist who had never been higher than the top of the Oude Kerk tower); see a collection of the surprisingly basic navigational instruments that guided the Dutch East Indiamen all over the world; and push buttons that make period music come out from behind models and paintings. There's a whole room of paintings, banners and relics connected with Amsterdam's 'miracle' (see p. 31). Up a spiral staircase at the top of the building you can listen to recordings of the city's various carillons, and even have a go at playing the one taken from the medieval Munttoren (see p. 136)—though if you get too carried away an attendant clambers up to glower at you.

*Turn right out of the museum and leave the girls' court by the door in the far corner. Turn left and walk through the gates to Gedempte Begijnensloot, where you turn right. Where this alley is joined by Begijnsteeg, you'll see a stone gateway on your right. This opens into the **Begijnhof**.*

The Begijnhof has the atmosphere of a quiet village square. You can hardly believe, in the leafy calm walled in by its neat gables, that the busiest parts of the city are only a few metres away. The Beguines were an order of lay nuns, founded in the 15th century, who, through self-effacement and powerful family connections, remained undisturbed by the religious upheavals of the following centuries. Sister Antonia, the last of the order, died in the house at no. 26 in 1971. The small mound near the gate (covered by flowers in the spring) is the grave of another Beguine, Sister Cornelia Arens. When she died in 1654 she was buried, at her own request, in the gutter. Most of the houses were rebuilt in the 17th and 18th centuries, but at no. 34 you can see the last remaining original façade, one of only two medieval wooden houses left in Amsterdam. Next door is an old clandestine church which still holds weekly mass. The church across the pathway was the original **Begijnkerk**, consecrated in 1419 and the only medieval church in the city with the tower in its original state. After a period of disuse during the Reformation, it was offered to Protestant dissenters fleeing England in 1607 and became known as the English Church. A plaque on the tower and stained glass in the chancel commemorate the fact that this group formed the core of the Pilgrim Fathers who sailed for America in 1620.

> *Leave the Begijnhof through an arch in the red brick house on the far left of the courtyard, along a short passage lined with Delft wall tiles, and out onto the* **Spui**.

Some of Amsterdam's trendiest cafés skirt the **Spui**. At the southern end, the diminutive statue of *Het Lieverdje* ('The Little Darling', an impish Amsterdam rascal) was the focal point of provocative 'happenings' in the 1960s (see p. 78). You can end your walk with a quiet coffee, or nip down Voetboogstraat for a look at the outrageous gate of the old **Rasphuis**, the male equivalent of the Spinhuis, where men had to saw wood into a fine powder used for dye. Carved figures are tied down by real chains. A castigating Amsterdam raises her hand high, but someone has pinched her flail. The Calvinist custodians of the Rasphuis thought up a most ingenius method of compelling the inmates to good soul-saving work. A 17th-century British consul in Amsterdam was much impressed: 'They are beaten with a bull's pissel [penis] and if yet they rebel and won't work, are set in a tub, where if they do not pump, the water will swell over their heads.'

> *When it's time to go home, trams 1, 2 and 5 will set you on your way.*

Walk II

Essential Amsterdam: The Rijksmuseum and the Herengracht

Magere Brug

Rijksmuseum—Prinsengracht—Carré—Magere Brug—Amstelhof—Museum Willet-Holthuysen—Herengracht—Brouwersgracht

For most people, Amsterdam means old paintings and charming canals. The most hallowed artworks are in the Rijksmuseum, and the Herengracht is the most splendid of the waterways. This walk guides you through the warren of Old Masters, reveals treasure-troves of antiquities and then leads you out for a leisurely stroll around the Golden Bend, a curve of Amsterdam's smartest canal-houses. You'll see Rembrandt's *Night Watch*, Vermeer's exquisitely poised interiors and Jan Steen's riotous family scenes. There's a Delft-china violin and a portable altar, jewellery to make your knees weak and four-poster beds that will make you want to collapse entirely. Back in the open air, you can visit one of the city's most eccentric coffee shops, wander around a Golden Age mansion and, if you're not careful, become undone by some curiously named local liqueurs.

The canals look their best in the early evening. On summer nights the stateliest stretches are floodlit, and the bridges twinkle with fairy-lights. You might like to set off on this walk in the mid-afternoon, then take your time walking along the Herengracht once the museums have closed.

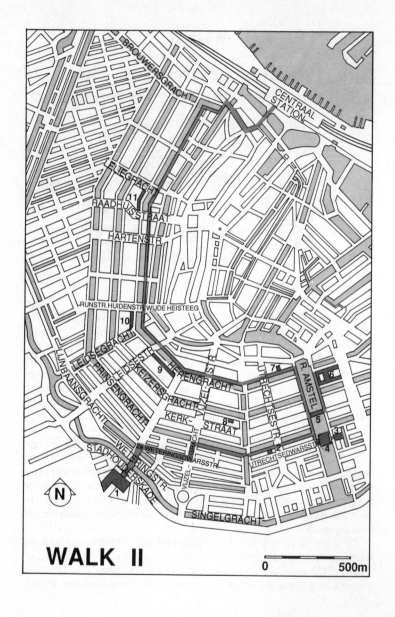

BROUWERSGRACHT

CENTRAAL STATION

VLIEGRACH

11

RAADHUISSTRAA

HARTENSTR.

RUNSTR. HUIDENSTR. WIJDE HEISTEEG

10

LEIDSEGRACHT

PRINSENGRACHT

LEIDSESTR.

KEIZERSGRACHT

LIJNBAANSGRACHT

9   HERENGRACHT

7

R. AMSTEL

6

VIJZELSTR.

UTRECHTSESTR.

5

KERK-   8   STRAAT

GRACHT

VIJZEL-

2e WETERINGSDWARSSTR.

12   UTRECHTSEDWARSSTR.

3

4

STADHOUDERSKADE

WETERINGSTR.

N

1

SINGELGRACHT

WALK II

0   500m

You'll pass some of Amsterdam's best restaurants, so you could stop for an early dinner or choose somewhere and make a reservation for later.

Start: Take Tram 6, 7 or 10 to Weteringschans.

Time: $1\frac{1}{2}$ hours, though this depends on the amount of time you want to spend eating, drinking or in museums. You're unlikely to need more than half an hour for the Willet-Holthuysen Museum, but the Rijksmuseum is the sort of place where you could spend the whole day. Allow at least an hour for the Dutch collection, and another to skim through the rest of the museum and whet your appetite for a return visit. Both museums close on Mondays.

LUNCH/CAFÉS

The Rijksmuseum Café has got you where it wants you. It's the only convenient place for a coffee, and they know it. Use it for a (vital) break, but have your lunch somewhere else.

Morita-Ya, Weteringstraat 29. A homely and rather haphazard Japanese fast-food bar. Good for a warming soup or between-meals *sushi*. Snacks under ƒ10.

Backstage Boutique, a.k.a. 'The Twins', Utrechtsedwarsstraat 65–67. Boston twins Greg and Gary Christmas (they swear the names are real) serve up teas, coffee and home-made cakes in a coffeeshop that doubles as a boutique for their fluorescent knitwear (only the English ever buy anything, Gary remarks sadly). Sit among the gaudy jerseys, tea-cosy hats and photographs from the brother's heyday as cabaret stars and enjoy your tea with the transvestites, busy mums, pretty young men and local lads who come in for the infectious humour and good food. Closes 6 pm. Coffee ƒ2.25.

Huyschkamer, Utrechtsestraat 137. The name means 'living-room', but there's little sign of comfy sofas or cosy firesides here, nor of the building's dubious past as a male brothel. Instead you find a tastefully designed and studiously hip café that sells good food. Beer ƒ2.25.

KEY TO MAP OF WALK II

1. Rijksmuseum
2. Backstage Boutique
3. Carré Theatre
4. Sluice gates
5. Magere Brug
6. Amstelhof
7. Willet-Holthuysen Museum
8. Van Loon Museum
9. Golden Bend
10. Fine houses
11. Fine houses

De Magere Brug, Amstel 81. On the banks of the Amstel near the 'Skinny Bridge', hence the name. One of the few traditional brown cafés on the walk. Coffee/beer *f*2.25.

De Knipoog, Wijde Heisteeg 1, off the Herengracht. Tasty cakes, complicated salads and out-of-the-ordinary sandwiches. Closes 6 pm. Coffee *f*2.25

De Admiraal, Herengracht 319. *Proeflokaal* for Amsterdam's last remaining independent distillery, De Ooiyevaar. Here you *will* find soft sofas, and also potent liqueurs like 'Hempje ligt op' and 'Pruimpje prik in' (the names translate obscenely).

Beiaard, Herengracht 90. Reproduction Art-Deco lamps, snooker tables and numerous varieties of Belgian beer.

De Belhamel, Brouwersgracht 60. Art-Nouveau café/restaurant on Amsterdam's most photographed canal. A relaxed, arty crowd eat snacks from *f*8.50 or meals with imaginative sauces (like Saffron Tagliatelle with oysters, cream, blue cheese, wine and sunflower seeds). Open daily 12–12. Lunch served 12–2.30 pm. Coffee/beer *f*2.50. Full menu with wine *f*50.

The best restaurants for an evening meal are in **Utrechtsestraat**, **Leliegracht**, or **Huidenstraat**, **Runstraat** and **Hartenstraat** (a cluster of side-streets halfway along the Herengracht) (see p. 108).

☆   ☆   ☆   ☆   ☆

The tram stops right at the bridge which takes you over the Singelgracht. Across the canal, and the busy Stadhouderskade, you'll see the **Rijksmuseum** *(National Museum, pronounced 'reyksmuseum'; open Tues–Sat 10–5, Sun 1–5 entrance* f6.50*).*

The Rijksmuseum was completed in 1885 to house the national collection of paintings and sculpture. The collection had evolved from a hoard of two hundred paintings confiscated from the exiled Prince William V in 1798. First they had been gathered in the Huis ten Bosch palace in The Hague, and later were brought to the Trip brothers' 17th-century mansion in Amsterdam (see p. 155). By the 1860s it was clear that the Trippenhuis was going to be too small for the growing collection. The quest for a new temple for the nation's art sparked off a conflagration of chauvinism, in-fighting and intrigue that would have impressed the Borgias. When the winners of an anonymous competition for a new museum design turned out to be German, the plan was rejected as 'non-Dutch'. Once a suitable Dutch architect was found in P.J.H

Cuypers (of Centraal Station fame) a new scandal emerged. The architect, project co-ordinator, government adviser *and* decorator were all Roman Catholics. Protestant Holland scented nepotism and popery. The building Cuypers produced was thought altogether too extravagant, too churchy and too foreign to house the treasures of Dutch culture. What made it worse was that Cuypers, having had a more sober Romanesque plan accepted, managed, while building was in progress, to slip in more fantastical bits of a previously rejected Gothic plan. Good patriotic Calvinists found this mish-mash of foreign styles deplorable. One critic railed: 'For two million guilders we now have the most sorry spectacle of a building that anyone could have thought to call a museum.' In response to the gilding and plethora of sculptures, portraits and tiling depicting Dutch artists that adorns the outside walls, another critic compared the museum to 'a garishly decorated house of a rich parvenu'. Even the king pleaded a prior engagement on the day of the opening ceremony. Ironically, Cuypers thought his red-brick and wood building with its clean, simple lines to be quintessentially Dutch, and today one would be inclined to agree with him. Though not as magical as the Centraal Station, 'De Rijks' is one of Amsterdam's most conspicuous landmarks, and has become a cultural icon. When it re-opened after the Second World War the waiting queue of pallid, underfed Amsterdammers in slightly shabby formal dress stretched right down Stadhouderskade.

In the years following the completion of the Rijksmuseum in 1885 so many people left their complete collections to the museum that it had, almost immediately, to embark on a programme of expansion. Not all the additions have been happy ones. In 1906 a committee of artists and architects spent months fiddling about in a life-sized model of a hall intended to show off Rembrandt's *Night Watch*. They finally decided that light from the left, tempered by carefully placed curtains would be ideal. It wasn't. The room was a disaster, ended up being used for minor exhibitions and earned the monicker 'De Puist' (the pimple). All of Cuypers' ornate interior decorations have been removed and today the museum is a maze of whitewashed rooms. Prince William V's modest collection has become: 5000 paintings, 30,000 sculptures and works of applied art, 17,000 historical objects, 3000 works of Asiatic art and a million prints and drawings.

Like the Centraal Station on the other side of town, the Rijksmuseum was designed as a grand entrance to the city. (When it was built there were only fields beyond it.) A walkway through the middle of

111

the building has bright bathroom acoustics that attract anything from opera-singing accordionists to steel bands. Because of this tunnel, the museum's important halls are on the first floor. There's a ground-plan at the entrance, but if you climb the stairs to the museum shop you can buy your own plan for f1.50 or a comprehensive pocket-sized guide to the collection for f7.50. An archway in the middle of this top-floor entrance hall leads to the **Gallery of Honour.** *If your time is really tight, this is the one place to visit. It gives a good introduction to Golden Age painting, and houses the Rembrandts for which the museum is famous. At the far end, taking up the full wall, is Rembrandt's* Night Watch.

Rembrandt Harmensz. van Rijn (1606–69) was the son of a Leiden miller. When the poet Constantijn Huygens, who was also something of an art critic, visited Leiden in 1628, he went into raptures over Rembrandt's paintings (though he reprimanded the then unknown youth for his puniness and lack of manly exercise). A few years later Rembrandt upped sticks for the big city. He had made his mark in Leiden, and as the *burgemeester* wryly remarked: 'His portraits and other pictures pleased the citizens of Amsterdam, who paid him well for them.' And indeed they did. Wealthy burghers, trades guilds and companies of the civic guard all spent handsome sums to be painted by the fashionable young artist. His unromanticized portraits hit just the right note in rationalistic, post-reformation Holland. Even his biblical and historical paintings have a truth and psychological rigour, especially in the faces, that seem to suggest direct experience of the world he's depicting. In 1634, already a rich and celebrated painter, he married heiress Saskia van Uylenburgh and five years later felt confident about paying a swingeing *f*13 000 for a house in the Jewish quarter (see p. 134). (This was where he had always wanted to live—he found Hebrew culture fascinating and preferred Jewish models for his religious painting). Saskia died in 1642, having just changed her will to leave everything to their infant son Titus, with the estate to be held in usufruct by Rembrandt for as long as he didn't remarry. The painter got round this by having a clandestine affair with Titus' nurse, Geertghe Dircx. Then, in 1649, he fell in love with a younger servant, Hendrickje Stoffels. Geertghe sued successfully for breach of contract. This came at a bad time. Rembrandt was receiving fewer commissions now—perhaps because of gossip about his domestic affairs, perhaps because he was becoming increasingly uncompromising in his work, or maybe he was just going out of fashion. He'd also spent far too much on paintings and the house. In 1656 he was declared bankrupt. The property that had been his home for some 20 years was sold, and he moved out to live on the Rozengracht with Hendrickje and Titus. They were going to try to revive his flagging fortune by working as his agents, but Hendrickje died within two years, followed by Titus in 1669, only months after he had married. Rembrandt was so hard up that he had to sell Saskia's tomb to pay for Hendrickje's funeral. When he himself died, he was buried in an unmarked grave in the Westerkerk.

The *Night Watch* was commissioned in 1642 by the militiamen of the Kloveniersdoelen (the Arquebusiers' Guildhall) to hang in their banqueting room alongside five other portraits of companies of the civic guard. It's officially called *The Company of Captain Frans Banning Cocq and Lieutenant Willem van Ruytenburch* and got its present title in the 19th century because aging layers of varnish made it dim and murky. For years it's had the reputation of being the work that signalled Rembrandt's decline. This is ill-deserved—he still had some of his most important commissions ahead of him. It is true, though, that the 17th-century public didn't like it very much and when it was moved to the Town Hall in 1715 the city fathers thought nothing of lopping a bit off the right-hand side so that it would fit on the wall. Two of Captain Cocq's militiamen disappeared forever. Today, together with *The Syndics*, it's considered the prize of the Rijksmuseum's collection. It was usual to paint group portraits in fairly static compositions, giving each member equal prominence. Rembrandt, however, paints the company in a flurry of movement, as if about to set off on a march. Rich clothes and a wonderful collection of plumed and pointed hats all add to the sense of grandeur and motion (this is all pure invention—the guards' uniforms were in reality rather dull, and they never marched). A little girl in a luminous gold dress, possibly the company mascot, looks bewildered by all the activity. (The rather surreal touch of a dead chicken tied to her waist is an allusion to the militia's coat of arms.) The captain and his lieutenant, in fine clothes, dominate the scene. The rest of the company look far less important—which is possibly why the painting was initially unpopular: they had after all each paid their ƒ100, and deserved the same billing.

When the controllers of the Drapers' Guild (the *'Staalmeesters'*, or 'Syndics') commissioned Rembrandt to paint their portrait in 1662, they were determined not to make a similar mistake, and stipulated a more traditional composition. Rembrandt obeyed, yet still managed to create a work that brims with life. The Syndics look up from their table, and the viewer has the odd sensation of having just walked into the room and disturbed them at work. It's one of the finest group portraits ever painted—Kenneth Clark goes as far as acclaiming it 'one of the summits of European painting'—and seems to be the image picture librarians most reach for to evoke old Holland.

As you wander through the Gallery of Honour, look out for three more of Rembrandt's paintings: *The Jewish Bride* (1667), a glowing, tender portrait of a couple, no longer all that youthful, but very much in love; a rather depressed, world-weary *Self-portrait as the Apostle Paul* (1661); and *St Peter's Denial* (1660), showing a very troubled, down-to-earth apostle. You can also see Nicholaes Maes's delicately detailed *Old Woman at Prayer* and Albert Cuyp's sun-drenched Italian landscapes (which he managed to paint without having set foot in the country). Work by Rembrandt's better-known pupils—such as Govert Flinck and Ferdinand Bol—is also on view.

> *Make your way back to the entrance hall where, if you turn through the door on the right, you can set off on a chronological journey through Dutch painting. In Rooms 201–6 you'll find works from the Middle Ages and Renaissance (which reached the Netherlands a century later than Italy).*

You'll probably want to save your energy for the Golden Age, but as you pass through the early rooms have a look at Geertgen tot Sint Jans' brightly detailed *Holy Kinship* (1485), crammed with emblems and symbolic references and his *Adoration of the Magi* (1490), set against an intricate backdrop of ruined landscapes, processions and misty forests. *The Seven Works of Charity* (1504), instructive panels by the Master of Alkmaar, have survived attacks by iconoclasts and creeping damp, and still preach their catalogue of worthy acts. Lucas van Leyden's *Adoration of the Golden Calf* (1530) is suitably riotous and a good example of the way Dutch Renaissance painters introduced realistic landscape settings for mythological scenes. The youth trying hard not to break the egg on the tavern floor in Pieter Aertsen's *Egg Dance* (1557) prefigures the scenes of everyday life that were to be such a feature of the Golden Age. The Dutch Mannerists, who worked in Haarlem between 1580 and the 1620s, get a good showing. Cornelis Cornelisz.'s enormous *Fall of Man* (1592) teems with animals mythical and domestic. In Karel van Mander's *The Magnanimity of Scipio* (1600), the 3rd-century BC Roman hero nobly refuses the offer of a beautiful captive for his slave and returns her to her betrothed.

Rooms 207–223 are filled with paintings from the 17th century, the 'Golden Age' not only of Dutch art but of the Netherlands' political and economic might.

Intense realism and the naturalistic rendering of domestic and everyday life are the hallmarks of the Golden Age. There are precise, calm interiors, minutely detailed still lifes, wild taverns and salacious brothel scenes. Homely Dutch mothers and their *onnozele schaapjes* (innocent lambs) take the place of the Madonna and Child, and you'll see businessmen and civic guards rather than generals and fantastical battle scenes. As you walk around the collection you'll see more of Rembrandt and his pupils, but there are a number of other artists particularly worth searching out.

Frans Hals's happy and rather cheeky looking *Wedding Portrait of Isaac Abrahamsz. Massa and Beatrix van der Laen* (1622), and the florid *Merry Drinker* (1628–30)—seemingly dashed off with swift brushstrokes and scratches in the wet paint—testify to his greatness as a portrait painter. Pieter Saenredam's church interiors are so still, and he pays such close attention to architectural shapes, that they seem almost abstract. Pieter de Hooch—especially in *Woman and Child in a Pantry* (1658) and *Women beside a Linen Chest* (1663)—is a master of quiet family scenes. Light from the busy outside world streams in through a door or window in the background, while in the spotless rooms with their symmetrical black and white floor tiles, all is order and calm—though the impish children seem just on the verge of disrupting it. A somewhat sadder *schaapje* can be seen in Gabriel Metsu's touching, yet unsentimental *Sick Child*. Jan Steen gives quite another idea of family life. He used his experiences as a tavern keeper to create scenes of such jolly domestic upheaval—as in *The Merry Family* (1670)—that the Dutch still use the expression 'a Jan Steen household' for any chaotic but cheerful home. You'll also find still lifes which, at the beginning of the century are sober arrangements of herring, bread and cheese, but later overflow with ornate tableware, full-blown flowers and juicy fruit at its *toppunt* (literally: top-point)—the last moment of perfection before decay. Abraham van Beyeren's 1665 painting shows fat peaches, seafood, leaking melons and a toppled silver candlestick in meticulous detail. Look out also for Gerard ter Borch's exquisite fabrics—poor little *Helena van der Schalke* (1648) is weighed down by her fine silk dress and in *Gallant Conversation* the young woman's silver gown shimmers. (The conversation wasn't really that gallant—the man holding up his hand in gentle admonition was originally offering her a coin. A pious owner painted it out.)

Skim as fast as you like through the rest of the collection, but don't miss the **Vermeers** (Room 222). Only thirty works by Johannes Vermeer (1632–75) exist; the Rijksmuseum has four of them. He had a passion for light and his paintings seem translucent. Light from a window reflects off a white wall, a jug, or softly glowing fabric. The tranquil *Kitchen Maid* (1658) and *Woman Reading a Letter* (1662/3) are totally without stylistic artifice, yet come close to perfection. In quiet, everyday scenes, Vermeer captures a sense of eternity.

If you walk through the rooms in numerical order you'll end up back in the Gallery of Honour. From here you can totter downstairs for a coffee. Before you do, have a look in Room 225, tucked away behind the Night Watch. *Here you'll find the small* **Foreign Collection** *with some chubby pink Rubens, Carlo Crivelli's elegant tempera* Mary Magdalene *(1485/90) and Piero di Cosimo's warts-and-all portraits of a Florentine architect and his cauliflower-eared father (1485).*

It's probably a better idea to come back another day to see the rest of the museum, but if time is short refresh yourself as best you can in the museum café and head back up the stairs, this time to the right wing of the building, devoted to **sculpture and applied art.**

The museum's collection of sculpture and applied art includes ceramics, china, glass furniture, costumes, lace, tapestries, jewellery and silver from the Middle Ages to the 20th century, and can be utterly overwhelming. On a first visit the best idea is to give yourself a gentle overview. In the rooms leading off the entrance hall (Rooms 238–42), you'll find some of the best pieces in the collection. Ten 15th-century bronze figures, poised in graceful attitudes of mourning, have been filched from the tomb of Isabella de Bourbon in Antwerp. There's a tiny portable altar, carved in gold and encrusted with enamel, that some lucky nun used for her private devotion in the Abbey de Chocques in France in the 16th century. Look out also for Adriaen van Wesel's busy and energetic oak carving of *The Meeting of the Three Magi* (1475–7). A little further on, in Room 245, you can see Late Gothic German carvings of Christ and the Last Supper, still with some original polychrome and gilding.

If you have a taste for camp, head straight for Room 251A and Wenzel Jamnitzer's extraordinary *Table Ornament*, made for the City of Nuremburg in 1549. Mother Earth stands, one hip cocked, in a rockery of flowers, lizards and shrimps (all silver casts of real specimens) and supports on her head an enormous birdbath of cherubs rampant, scrolls, snakes and more flowers. All this is surmounted by yet another posy of enamelled silver foliage. Its ornate gilded wood and leather carrying-case is displayed alongside.

The collection of **Delftware** (rooms 255–57) has some prize poly-chrome as well as more traditional blue and white pieces. The people of Delft first started making cheaper imitations of the Chinese porcelain brought back by the Dutch East India Company in the 17th century. (Things have turned a full circle. Now souvenir shops sell imitation Delftware made in Taiwan.) Among the usual plates and cups you can see a functioning Delftware violin and towering tulip pagodas with space for forty stems (which, in the 17th century, would have cost a fortune to fill).

A blue staircase off Room 261 will take you back to the ground floor.

Back downstairs you can see two exquisite early 18th-century dolls' houses—collectors' pieces assembled by the lady of the house, rather than toys—and an ornate oak table-leaf veneered with tortoiseshell and inlaid with a mass of birds, monkeys, fruit and *putti* worked in copper, brass and mother-of-pearl. There's more choice furniture in the museum, but it's rather coldly presented and unless you have a specialist interest, the canal-house museums later in the walk will probably appeal to you more. If you appreciate good porcelain, however, the Meissen collection (Rooms 170–71) is one of the best in the world. An alchemist in the German town of Meissen, near Dresden, discovered the secret of Chinese porcelain manufacture while trying to make gold for the king, and the pieces subsequently produced in the area have been collectors' items for centuries.

*As you work your way back to the central staircase you pass a series of four-poster beds: the first is peppermint green with embroidered birds, the second hung with rich tapestries, the third sparkling gold and silver—each is more alluring and sumptuous than the last, like the temptations in a fairy-tale. A door off the staircase (near the café entrance) leads to the **Rijksprentenkabinet** (Printroom) exhibition hall where you can see temporary exhibitions from a vast collection of prints, drawings and watercolours by the likes of Rembrandt, Dürer, Goya and Canaletto. The printroom itself has a separate entrance around the side of the museum and you need written permission (from The Director, Jan Luykenstraat 1A) to see*

117

works not on open view. At the end of the print exhibition you pass through a room of Islamic art and some bright, ethereal pastels by the Swiss artist Jean-Etienne Liotard (1702–89)—mostly of aristocrats and socialites. This takes you to the Drucker wing, an extension which houses 19th-century Dutch art and the Asiatic Collection.

The **19th-century art** is on the upper floor. Here the best work is by painters of two movements from the second half of the century. The three Maris brothers were leading artists of the Hague School (nicknamed the 'grey' school after its heavy, cloudy skies). Jacob painted beaches and townscapes, Matthijs portrayed romantic fairy-tale scenes and Willem seemed preoccupied with ducks. Anton Mauve's pearly grey *Morning Ride along a Beach* (1876) is characteristic of the movement. The Amsterdam Impressionists are well represented by George Breitner, who liked to paint Amsterdam in the rain, and Isaac Israëls, whose brighter pictures are closer to the work of the French Impressionists.

The Asiatic Art Collection is in the basement. Three hundred years of Dutch trade connections have resulted in a glittering stash of treasures from the East. You can see lacquerwork, ceramics and textiles from Japan, Javanese sculptures, and religious works from China and India. A small, bronze dancing Lord Shiva (the Hindu god of creation) from the 12th century and an elegantly relaxed Chinese Buddhist saint, the **Bodhisattva Avalokitesharva**, from the same period, make the trip downstairs worthwhile.

On the ground floor of the left wing of the main building, you'll find the Dutch History Collection.

The history collection comprises paintings, documents and memorabilia dating from the Middle Ages to the Second World War. There's an understandable emphasis on ships and sea battles. The presentation is not very exciting, and most explanations tend to be in Dutch only. The Amsterdam Historical Museum (see p. 104) will give you a far more interesting and accessible introduction to Dutch History. If you have the time, pop in for a look at some of the more amusing curiosities—like a deceptively gorgeous copper crown with glass jewels sent as a trade bribe to an African king by the 17th-century Duke of York (via the Dutch naval hero Admiral de Ruyter), or the grand but diminutive jackets worn by the toddler Prince William V.

*Before leaving the museum, have a quick look at the divinely nonchalant statue of Apollo in the small sculpture garden at the back. Then cross the busy Stadhouderskade, which runs in front of the building, and go over the Singelgracht and Lijnbaansgracht. Turn right along Tweede Weteringsdwarsstraat, where at no. 40 you can peek into the 78 rpm Society's den. Old horned gramophones are stacked up against the walls and a row of enthusiasts concentrate intensely under their headphones. At the end of the street turn left into Vijzelgracht, then right up the right-hand side of Prinsen-gracht. This brings you to the **River Amstel**. On your way you'll cross Utrechtsestraat. This is a good street for restaurants, and your chance to duck down to Utrechtsedwarsstraat and visit Greg and Gary Christmas (see 'Lunch/Cafés' above).*

Across the river is a lively classical building with a cornice of jesters and grinning clowns. This is the **Carré** theatre, built as a circus for Oscar Carré in 1887. Now it hosts mainly musicals, but the best time to see its circular plush interior is when it reverts to being a circus over the Christmas holiday.

In the river is a barrier of **sluice gates**. Every night between 7 and 8.30 two hefty men turn the wooden wheels that close them. Far to the east of the city, on the island of Zeeburg, a pumping station starts up and forces 600,000 cubic metres of water into the canals, forcing the old water out through sluices in the west. This helps stop the pong, which at one time was quite overpowering. Even when Amsterdammers stopped tipping their sewage into the canals and sent it off in covered wagons to be sold as field manure, the stagnating water still presented a problem. Not everyone seemed to mind. When in 1765 plans for better water circu-lation were proposed, 33,000 domestic maids petitioned against the idea as they felt that a reduction in the vile emanations from the canal would lose them cleaning work.

A little way up the river you can see the **Magere Brug** ('Skinny Bridge'). It was built in the 17th century for two spoilt young maidens who were too lazy to walk the long way round from their house in Kerkstraat to their stables across the river. A public outcry prevented its being replaced by a steel bridge in 1929, but the old structure was rotting and today's delicate white wooden swing bridge is a replica. The long, rather austere two-storey brick building on the far side of the river, just beyond the Magere Brug is the **Amstelhof**, a 17th-century almshouse.

The severe walls enclose a luscious garden courtyard with fountains, arbours and choruses of birds, where you can sit and rest if you're discreet.

*Walk up the Amstel and turn left onto the **Herengracht**, keeping to the right-hand side.*

Amsterdam's population increased tenfold between 1550 and 1650. In the early 17th century the far-sighted city fathers were already planning to push the city boundaries outwards with three grand concentric canals. The Prinsengracht (Prince's Canal), Keizersgracht (Emperor's Canal) and Herengracht (Gentleman's Canal—rather than 'King's', a nice move by bourgeois Amsterdam) were intended for *rentiers* and rich merchants who wanted to live away from the smells and noise of the harbour. The shops and industries there were banished to poorer parts of town. The city hall parcelled out the land in 30-ft, rather than the usual 20-ft lots (though wily speculators would buy up two adjacent plots and split them into three and the really opulent merchants would combine two into a single house). Fashion has claimed each canal, at one time or another, as Amsterdam's best address, but it was the Herengracht that was *really* built to impress. It's more grand than pretty, a little ravaged by centuries of ostentation. Subsequent occupiers have (until recently) thought nothing of pulling down old buildings to make way for bigger and better displays of wealth, but the survivors have an endearing, if worn, panache. Some extraordinary gables poke up out of the trees that line the canal.

Space was at a premium in Amsterdam and you were taxed on the width of your house, so *height* often became an expression of wealth and the boastful decoration was applied to the inside, or to the gables. Even the rear façades got special attention. ('Our Lord finished off a canary's behind as neatly as its front,' remarked one contemporary architect.) Narrow houses mean winding stairways, uncongenial to four-poster beds and heavy carved dressers, hence most Amsterdam buildings have a hoist beam poking out from the gable so you can winch your furniture up the outside. Many lean dangerously over the street, not necessarily because they're about to subside into the city's soggy soil, but because this shows off the gables to passing pedestrians and makes the building more imposing. It also stops rising furniture from crashing into the wall. Angles became so alarming that a bye-law was introduced in 1565 to put a stop to the more adventurous tilts.

A short way along the Herengracht, at no. 605, you'll come to the **Willet-Holthuysen Museum** *(open daily 11–5; entrance f2.50).*

The Willet-Holthuysen Museum is a 17th-century canal house. For two centuries it was occupied by a succession of Amsterdam glitterati. The last, Sandrina Holthuysen, had spent most of her life married to Abraham Willet, an avid collector of paintings, art books, glass, ceramics and silver. When she died in 1895, alone, ridden with cancer and surrounded by cats, she left the house and contents to Amsterdam as a museum. The city then filled it with pickings from a number of similar bequests. Most of the rooms are now reconstructed as 18th-century period pieces, with the different collections scattered about the house, mainly in rather stiff salons and boudoirs; there's also a crisp formal garden. Everything seems in its Sunday best—including the surreal headless mannequins that stand strategically about, sporting 18th-century costume. It's a good place to get an insider's view of one of the more stately canal houses, but if you'd prefer something that feels a little more lived in, try to get to the Van Loon Museum just around the corner in Keizersgracht (unfortunately open only on Mondays—see p. 199).

Turn right out of the museum to begin a stroll along the canal. You'll probably want to criss-cross it as you walk, but the best views are generally to be had from the right-hand side.

Monumental sandstone frontages seem to push aside the traditional dainty gabled brick façades. Cornices curled with acanthus leaves, strung with garlands and surmounted by urns lord it over the modest step-gables, though the odd defiant bell or neck-gable might reply with an extravagant claw-piece. At no. 502, though, you'll find an austere, late 18th-century building with only the slightest flutter of exuberance in the three raised *oeils-de-boeuf* along the roof-line. This has been the official residence of Amsterdam *burgemeesters* since 1927 (see p. 174–5). Nearby (nos. 504–10) is a little stretch of wildly decorative claw-pieces. Tigers, dolphins and seagods curl about the gables and for once upstage the grander buildings.

The bit of the canal between Vijzelstraat and Leidsestraat is known as the **Golden Bend**, *perhaps more for the wealth of the inhabitants than the refinement of the architecture. There are two clusters of more gorgeous and more graceful dwellings further up the canal that* *better deserve the epithet, though the elegant Louis XIV building with curved balustrades at no. 475, does have the reputation of being Amsterdam's most beautiful house. You'll find the first of these more impressive constellations on the corner just beyond the Leidsegracht.*

On the right-hand side of the canal, no. 401 manages to lean in three different directions at once. Across the canal is a pretty little 17th-century house with a simple festooned neck-gable (no. 394). The outrageous confection at no. 380–2 is a late 19th-century imitation of a French Renaissance château scrunched down to city mansion size. The more dignified row of four houses (nos. 364–70) with clean lines, stately neck-gables and quieter decoration are by the famous 17th-century domestic architect, Philips Vingboons. The house at no. 366 is now the **Bijbels Museum** (Bible Museum, open Tue–Sat 10–5, Sun 1–5; entrance *f*3) worth a visit only if you are interested in models of Solomon's temple and the history of the Dutch Bible over the past millennium.

The next notable group of houses is on the sharp curve in the canal, just after you cross Raadhuisstraat.

The Barlotti House at nos. 170–2 was built in 1617 by Hendrick de Keyser (who designed most of Amsterdam's spiky towers) for West India Company director Van den Heuval. (It was paid for by Van den Heuval's mother-in-law who stipulated the house be called after her late husband). Its enormous neck-gable is all but invisible under the encrustation of pilasters, pinnacles and decorative reliefs. These days it houses the Theatre Museum (see p. 137). The white sandstone house next door (known as the White House), built in 1668, was Philips Vingboons's first.

As you walk up to the end of the Herengracht, you'll pass (at no. 120) one of the few smaller 17th-century houses to have kept its façade free of later additions and amendments. The Herengracht flows into the Brouwersgracht, a quiet, pretty, picture-book canal (see p. 147).

You could end your walk with coffee or a meal at the Belhamel (see Lunch/Cafés above), or wander back along the other side of the Herengracht (quite a different experience) or along one of the other canals to a restaurant you might have found earlier. If you'd prefer to head home, cut across to Centraal Station, where you'll find trams to take you to virtually any part of the city.

Walk III

Jewish Amsterdam and the Jordaan

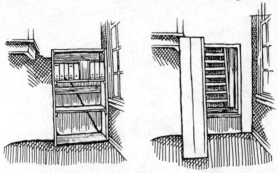

The false bookcase in the 'Anne Frank Huis'

Hollandse Schouwburg—Hortus Botanicus—Portuguese Synagogue—
Jewish Historical Museum—Waterlooplein Fleamarket—Rembrandthuis—
Munttoren—Flowermarket—Singel—Money Box Museum—Theatre
Museum—Westerkerk—Anne Frank Huis—The Jordaan—Noorderkerk

Amsterdam has dinky architecture, immaculate streets and pretty canals, but no-one would call it precious. It gets its edge and vigour from the people who live there, and this walk gives you a glimpse of that life. It begins in the old Jewish quarter and ends in the neighbourhood that gave birth to the Amsterdam cockneys. On the way you take in two famous markets, climb the highest tower in town and visit the secret rooms where the Frank family hid from the Nazis. You'll find a bar that sells banana beer, some quirky museums and cosy artists' cafés.

It's a good walk to take children on. It begins right opposite the zoo (see p. 14) and near the TM Junior Museum (see p. 14). There's a lot to do along the way and a tiny, but magical, toyshop at the end. Bear in mind, though, that the Spaarpotten Museum (Money Box Museum) is closed over the weekend.

Start: Take Tram 7, 9, 14 to Plantage Kerklaan.

Walking Time: 1½–2 hours. The museums are all fairly small. Another two hours should be quite enough browsing and shopping time

123

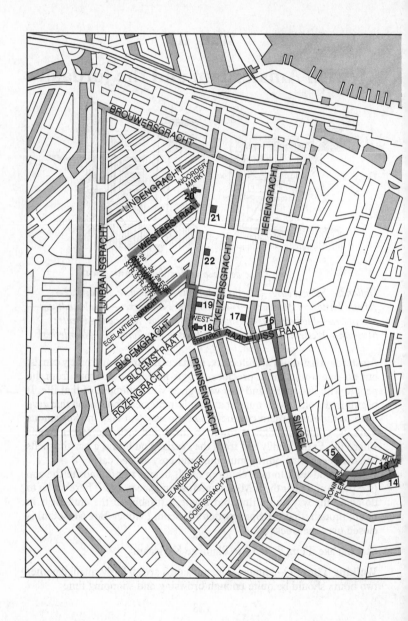

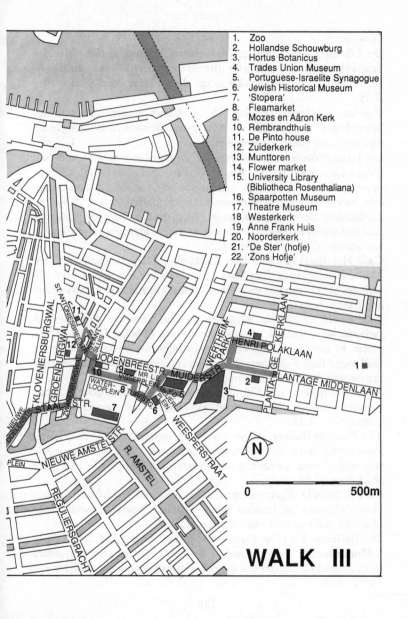

1. Zoo
2. Hollandse Schouwburg
3. Hortus Botanicus
4. Trades Union Museum
5. Portuguese-Israelite Synagogue
6. Jewish Historical Museum
7. 'Stopera'
8. Fleamarket
9. Mozes en Aäron Kerk
10. Rembrandthuis
11. De Pinto house
12. Zuiderkerk
13. Munttoren
14. Flower market
15. University Library
    (Bibliotheca Rosenthaliana)
16. Spaarpotten Museum
17. Theatre Museum
18 Westerkerk
19. Anne Frank Huis
20. Noorderkerk
21. 'De Ster' (hofje)
22. 'Zons Hofje'

WALK III

LUNCH/CAFÉS

De Eik en Linde, Plantage Middenlaan 22, next to the Hollandse Schouwburg. Brown café with diverse local crowd. It was once connected by an upstairs corridor to the theatre next door. Coffee/beer *f*1.75.

Puccini, Staalstraat 21 (closed Mon). Classy modern café with delicious cakes. The air is filled with the aroma of chocolate steaming in the vats of the adjoining 'Dessert Shop'.

De Jaren, Nieuwe Doelenstraat 20. Amsterdam's newest and best Grand Café, right on the Amstel. Comfortable chairs, high ceilings, newspapers in all languages, and anyone who's anyone in Amsterdam arts. Sandwiches and light meals *f*4.50–*f*15. Coffee *f*2, beer *f*2.50.

Coffeeshop Divertimento, Singel 480, in the flowermarket. A fragrant café that serves enormous icecreams as well as inexpensive sandwiches and snacks. Coffee *f*2.25, beer *f*2.50.

Café Het Biervat a.k.a. 'Bier Akadamie', Raadhuisstraat 17. Open Mon–Sat from 3 pm, Sun from 4 pm. Poky bar that serves over 150 varieties of beer ranging from classic award winners to sickly strawberry and banana brews.

Café Chris, Bloemstraat 42, across the canal from the Westerkerk. A taphouse since 1624, it predates the bar that calls itself 'Amsterdam's oldest' by five years. The workers who built the Westerkerk received (and spent) their wages here. It's so small there's no room for a cistern in the loo; you flush it from behind the pool table in the bar.

Zemmel Prinsengracht 126, open from noon. Trendy café with a sunny canalside terrace. Serves good sandwiches and snacks (*f*4–*f*15). Coffee/beer *f*2.25.

The Pancake Bakery, Prinsengracht 191, near the Anne Frank Huis. A low-beamed cellar that boasts the best pancakes in town. They could very well be right. Sweet and savoury pancakes from *f*6.50–*f*16. Coffee *f*2.25, beer *f*2.50.

Café 't Smalle, Egelantiersgracht 12. Restored *proeflokaal* of Pieter Hoppe's famous 18th-century liqueur distillery. Now sells a wider range of drinks and snacks. Coffee *f*2, beer *f*2.25.

De Blaffende Vis (The Barking Fish), Westerstraat 118, and **'t Monumentje**, Westerstraat 120. Two busy Jordaan cafés frequented by traditional Jordaaners and the new generation of music students and young artists.

Café 't Papeneiland, Prinsengracht 2, just up from the Noorderkerk. Full of pink-faced old men. A 17th-century café with a shady past. It was originally a funeral parlour that sold beer on the side. There's an unexplained secret passage running from the cellar to the house over the canal.

Winkel Lunchcafé, Noordermarkt 43, opposite Noorderkerk. Splendid salads. Gets its produce (much of it organic) fresh from the farm.

☆   ☆   ☆   ☆   ☆

If you've arrived on Tram 7, double back a few yards along Plantage Kerklaan and turn right into Plantage Middenlaan. The other trams drop you off right on Plantage Middenlaan, which, if you follow it westwards, takes you into what was the heart of Jewish Amsterdam.

Amsterdammers nickname their city 'Mokum', from the Yiddish 'Mokum aleph', 'the best city of all', and they'll often leave you with a cheery 'de mazzel'—'good luck'. As early as the 16th century, Amsterdam's religious tolerance was attracting Jews fleeing persecution in other European countries. This tolerance stemmed less from the milk of Christian kindness than from sound commercial reasoning. The Sephardic Jews, who came from Spain and Portugal in the 16th and 17th centuries, brought good inside information on the opposition's colonies and trade routes. Even the poorer Ashkenazim (from central and eastern Europe) had skills that fuelled the Golden Age boom. The city's trade guilds, however, refused to admit Jews and so Jews could only find work in fields that did not present direct competition to locals. Many were physicians or apothecaries, or worked in high-risk finance and in the new trades associated with the cotton or diamond industries. But they could retain their religion and didn't have to live in ghettoes or wear distinguishing badges. The city soon became known as the 'Jerusalem of the West'. Jewish prayers rang out above the clamour of the market and lumber yards around Waterlooplein, where most Jews settled. There was hardly a more crowded or busier place in town. The Nazi occupation put an end to that. Of the 130,000 Jews living in Amsterdam in 1938 (10 per cent of the total population), 100,000 did not survive the war. For a long time the old Jewish quarter lay empty and derelict, as if the buildings themselves were in a state of shock. Recovery took decades, but the market is now back in place and the area is as lively as ever, though the Jewish community itself is all but invisible.

The walk begins on the edge of the original Jewish quarter, in the elegant, wide streets of the **Plantage** district. The 'Plantation' was a bushy parkland where Amsterdammers would lounge about on feast days, or go on long evening walks. At the end of the 19th century it was flattened by rows of showy neo-classical houses with outrageous colonial embellishments (pineapple pinnacles, exotic festoons, negro figurines propping up the beam ends). Many of the wealthier Jews moved into the grand new houses and by the 1920s it was the suburb of the Jewish élite. In 1897 the **Hollandse Schouwburg** (Holland Theatre) at Plantage Middenlaan 24, after a false start as an operetta theatre, became the home of the Nederlandsche Toneelvereeniging (Dutch Drama Society)—the company that propelled Dutch theatre into the 20th century. Because of the large number of Jews in both the audience and the theatre group itself, the occupying forces during the Second World War renamed it the Joodsche Schouwburg (Jewish Theatre). In 1942 it was designated an assembly point for Jews waiting to be deported. People were kept in the darkened building for days and then (apart from a few children who had managed to escape through the crèche across the road) were herded onto trains bound for Westerbork, a transit camp in the Dutch province of Drenthe. In Amsterdam, Jews spoke of Westerbork as 'the first circle of Hell'. From there trains left weekly for the deathcamps at Auschwitz and Sobibor. Understandably, after the war no-one much wanted to use the Hollandse Schouwburg as a theatre again. In the 1960s it was declared a memorial to the deported Jews who never returned. Today only a secluded memorial garden lies behind the façade. Every year on 4 May (Remembrance Day) the city keeps a two-minute silence to commemorate those who died in the war. Just before 8 pm people from the neighbourhood start to arrive at the Hollandse Schouwburg (as they do at similar monuments all over the city). Trendy young things, children, people old enough to have lived through the war all quietly join the swelling groups converging on the theatre. Most carry small posies of flowers. At 8 o'clock the trams stop, cars switch off their engines, people still in cafés put down their drinks and the whole city goes quiet.

Walk down Plantage Middenlaan past the **Desmet Cinema**. *During the war, German Jewish refugees staged theatre and cabaret here. The shows were so good that even the Nazi officer in charge of deportation would slip in at the back to watch. At the end of Plantage Middenlaan you come, on the right-hand side, to* **Wertheimpark**, *and, on the left, to the Hortus Botanicus.*

The tiny Wertheimpark is the last remaining patch of the old Plantage gardens. At the entrance, two sphinxes with lanterns on their heads glower from the top of disproportionately large gateposts. Most of the park seems taken up by a fountain in memory of A.C. Wertheim (1832–97), a philanthropic banker who lived out his motto: 'Be a Jew in the synagogue and a human being in society', by being available in his office for an hour every morning to anyone who needed to appeal to his charity.

The **Hortus Botanicus** (Botanical Gardens; open 1 April–1 Oct 9–5 on workdays and 11–5 other days; from 1 Oct–1 April it closes at 4 pm; entrance ƒ5), was originally an apothecaries' herb garden in a marshy corner of the Plantage. It was later inundated by tropical plants pillaged by the Dutch East India Company, and has ended up with one of the biggest botanical collections in the world. A coffee shrub cultivated at the Hortus was presented to Louis XIV in 1714. Its seeds were used to initiate the cultivation of coffee in South America. A century later the gardens narrowly survived Louis Bonaparte's attempt to turn them into a zoo. The animals arrived before any cages had been built and the orangery became a volatile dormitory for wolves, lions, monkeys and porcupines. Tranquillity was restored when, after the king's untimely departure from the Netherlands, a relieved directorate put the animals up for auction. During the first half of this century, the gardens' biggest attraction was the massive *Victoria Regia* water lily. People would sometimes stand, three at a time, on the broad lily pads and queue for hours on the one night of the year when it flowered, to see the gorgeous blossom. The sturdy plant survived this abuse, but not the demolition of its greenhouse in the 1960s (though there are plans to cultivate it again).

These days the Hortus is a quieter place, a pocket-sized patch of green that's not really part of the tourist circuit. It won't take you long to nip in and see the ancient varieties of tulip, visit the world's oldest pot plant, enjoy the tropical climes of the glass-domed palm house or the sticky confines of a hut full of flesh-eating plants, and in the summer you can cool off with a fruit juice in the Orangery. There are plans for an indoor mangrove swamp, complete with live animals.

*The **Nationaal Vakbondsmuseum** (Trades Union Museum) at Henri Polaklaan 9, just around the corner from the entrance to the Wertheimpark, is worth a diversion for the building alone (open Tues–Fri 11–5 and Sun 1–5; entrance ƒ5).*

The father of modern Dutch architecture, H.P. Berlage, designed the building in 1900 for Holland's first trade union, the mainly Jewish

General Netherlands Diamond Workers' Union (ANDB). Wedding-cake layers of brick arches create a light and airy entrance hall. An ornate *Jugendstil* lamp hangs through the depth of two storeys in the centre of the room. Upstairs there is a cosy panelled boardroom with more metal lanterns, and murals by the Dutch Impressionist Roland Holst. However, you'll have to be severely interested in the Dutch labour movement to appreciate the small exhibitions of photographs, clippings and documents (all in Dutch) in the other rooms.

At the end of Plantage Middenlaan you cross the canal to **Muider-straat**, *part of the original Jewish quarter.*

Collectors, on the corner of Muiderstraat, looks more like a museum of 20th-century design classics than a shop. One wall is lined with pinball machines, another with Coca-Cola dispensers. If you have the ready cash, you can pick up a gleaming Maserati or a comfy little Morris Minor Traveller. The **Apotheek De Castro** (De Castro Pharmacy) at nos. 14–16 was established in 1832 during a cholera epidemic. It had a successsion of art-loving owners, one of which—E.M. Vita Israel—exhibited his collection in the rooms above the shop and became the first curator of the Jewish Historical Museum. De Castro's is still a pharmacy, though all that remains of the original shop is the façade.

Keep to the left side of Muiderstraat. At the end of the street you come to the **Portuguese-Israelite Synagogue**.

There was little love lost between the Sephardim and Ashkenazim. Even today old Sephardic Jews can remember being warned off '*vrotte Tedescos*' (filthy Germans) with: '*Je kan nog beter met een Goya trouwen dan met een Tedesco*' (Rather marry a gentile than an Ashkenazi). The Sephar-dim were a smaller, but more powerful community with a class of wealthy professionals, and were happily welcomed into Dutch society. Their Portuguese-Israelite Synagogue (or 'Snoge' after the Spanish *esnoga*) was built between 1671 and 1675 as a showpiece. It was more than twice the size of the Ashkenazi temple completed the year before on the site next door. Only in Amsterdam could Jews make such an open display of their place of worship. There was no established building style for synagogues, and the architect, Elias Bouman (who had also designed the Ashkenazi building) claimed he was creating an imitation of Solomon's temple following descriptions in the Old Testament. However, the building he produced, with its mahogany pews and brass chandeliers, bears a remarkable resemblance to the larger Christian churches of the period. It's an imposing brick block that dwarfs the buildings around it. The Hebrew letters of the name 'Aboab' are worked into the text above the door (which translates as 'And I—in Thy great love—shall enter Thy House') in acknowledgement of Rabbi Isaac Aboab de Fonseca's efforts to get the synagogue built.

> *Turn left, along the front of the synagogue, into* **Mr L.E. Visserplein** *('Meester' is the Dutch title for a lawyer), named after the Jewish Dutch President of the Supreme court dismissed in 1940 for refusing to co-operate with the occupying forces. He later refused to wear a Star of David and worked for* Het Parool, *the illegal Resistance newspaper that developed into a popular Amsterdam daily. The square is a turmoil of traffic hurtling in and out of the IJ Tunnel. Hurry down the other side of the synagogue to the relative peace of* **Jonas Daniël Meijerplein***.*

Jonas Daniël Meijer (1780–1834) whizzed through his school years and was a Doctor of Law by the time he was sixteen. He was the first Jew admitted to the Bar and one of the first to fight for and get full Dutch citizenship. As a favourite of the potty but enlightened Louis Bonaparte and under William I, Meijer did a lot to improve the legal position of the Jews.

In the middle of the square, standing stalwartly, his sleeves rolled up and chin cocked defiantly—ready for a fight—is Mari Andriessen's bronze statue **De Dokwerker** (The Dockworker, 1952). Every year on 25 February people lay flowers at its feet to commemorate the resistance to Nazi occupation. This is the anniversary of the general strike which swept through a shocked Amsterdam in a matter of hours as an expression of solidarity with the Jews after the first Nazi round-ups. During his brief spell as a theology student in Amsterdam, Van Gogh could be seen 'with his books clamped under his arm, holding snowdrops in his left hand in front of his chest, his head stooped forward slightly', making his way across this square to the third floor of the house at no. 13, where he studied classics with Mendes da Costa for ƒ1.50 a lesson. (The original house has been demolished).

> *During one of the brief moments that traffic lights halt the flow on Weesperstraat, you can shoot across to Nieuwe Amstelstraat, once called Shulgas (Synagogue Alley). A complex of four old Ashkenazi synagogues now houses the* **Jewish Historical Museum** *(open daily 11–5 except Yom Kippur and Day of Atonement; entrance ƒ7).*

The Ashkenazim, fleeing pogroms in Poland and massacres in Germany, arrived in Amsterdam in the mid-17th century. They soon outnumbered the Sephardim (who had begun arriving half a century earlier) by ten to one, but were pitifully poorer. They really had to struggle to get together enough money to build themselves a synagogue. Just as they were about to begin their attention was diverted by Sabbatai Zvi, a false Messiah who claimed he would lead them back to the Holy Land. They waited for four years before giving up on him and building the Grote Sjoel (Grand Synagogue) in 1671. As the congregation expanded, more temples were built on adjacent plots. The Obbene Sjoel (Upstairs Synagogue, 1686) was followed by the Dritt Sjoel (Third Synagogue, 1700). The Neie Sjoel (New Synagogue, 1752) opened with great ceremony. Tickets were sold at an outrageous *f*10 (though crowds of poor were let in for free). Ashkenazi Congregation records revel in the pomp of the occasion and bristle with anti-Sephardic rivalry: 'An orchestra pit has been placed next to the bima [raised central platform], where the musicians took their places with their music. Below that there was an *uncircumcised* musician playing a contrabass and for the rest only Jews who played for free *and even one Portuguese Jew*'. The complex was gutted during the Second World War and remained empty and dilapidated until the 1980s, when the temples were restored, linked by glass and metal stairways and reopened as the Jewish Historical Museum.

The Museum's displays do not dwell on gruesome images of the Holocaust and tales of woe, but are a combination of works of art, memorabilia and artefacts aimed at explaining Jewish life. Naturally, it is moving to see one of the yellow stars Jews had to wear during the war, but the museum also diffuses a positive energy from the delicately embroidered prayershawls, photographs of barmitzvahs and overwhelmingly extravagant silverware also on show. The 'Jewish identity' displays in the New Synagogue explain aspects of tradition, Zionism and the reaction to persecution. Most of the Great Synagogue is given over to expositions of the religion itself—the rituals, festivals and rites of passage. You can see the original Mikveh (ritual bath) unearthed during the renovations, a rather cute circumcision set and some stylish modern temple silverware. In the galleries of the Great Synagogue paintings and old documents illustrate the history of Jews in Amsterdam. The connecting walkways house temporary exhibitions and work by Jewish artists (Jaap Kaas's fierce and funny bronze monkeys are worth looking out for). The museum also has a library and media centre, a kosher café and a good bookshop.

Across the alley from the museum is the **Oudezijds Huiszitten-huis** *(the rather Dickensian sounding 'Old Side Home for the Domiciled Poor', built in 1654). The Alms Board Wardens would enter through a rather grand public staircase on the other side of the building. Paupers could come in through a gate opposite the Dritte Synagogue and huddle for hours in the courtyard waiting for handouts of bread, cheese and peat. The peat was stored next door in the Arsenaal (built 1610). The road down the side of this warehouse is still called Turfsteeg (Peat Alley).*

Walk down the narrow Turfsteeg. At the end you pop out into the cheerful din and architectural hotchpotch of Waterlooplein. On your left is the giant pink **Stopera**, *the City Hall/Opera House complex that has caused the biggest public row in recent years (see pp. 72–6). Bang up against its back wall, and creeping round the edges, reclaiming the space it has occupied for over a century, is the famous* **Waterlooplein Fleamarket** *(open Mon–Sat approx. 9–5).*

Waterlooplein was originally the manmade island of Vlooyenburg, so named because the Amstel flooded it with monotonous regularity. (*Vlooyen* means 'flow', and also 'fleas', which seems rather more appropriate these days.) Vlooyenburg was built on a sandbank in the Amstel in 1593, and soon became a popular neighbourhood for Jews arriving from Portugal. In the mid-17th century they were joined by the Ashkenazim, and Vlooyenburg became the heart of the Jewish quarter. Despite its sogginess, it was at first quite well-to-do. Prosperous Sephardim lived along the water's edge but, with the great influx of Ashkenazim, buildings were constantly subdivided and more and more people were crammed into less and less space. The economic decline of the 18th and 19th centuries made conditions even worse. A contemporary traveller complained that everywhere there were 'horrible piles of excrement and offal, the walls around drenched with urine'. Later in the 19th century, however, the economy boomed and conditions improved. In 1882 the council reclaimed more land, and filled up two canals to create a large market square to replace the squalid, crowded network of alleys. In 1886 the clusters of market traders who had overrun the side streets were moved to the newly created Waterlooplein. There was much grizzling because it was so open and windy (an objection you're sure to sympathize with if the weather is bad) but soon the market had the reputation of being the busiest and most cheerful in Amsterdam.

The district was devastated during the Nazi occupation. Convoys of trucks would rumble into the market and cart away hundreds of people at a time. The empty houses they left behind were stripped of anything burnable during the freezing winters. For decades after the war the square was silent and deserted. A few squatters in the 1960s began to revive the old spirit, but they were evicted to make way for the Stopera, and Waterlooplein ceased to be a residential square.

It's only recently, since the Stopera builders' rubble has been cleared away, that the market has regained anything like its old liveliness. There's a wonderful lack of logic in its layout and a pervasive air of bargain-hunting and money-making. Antiquarian booksellers rub shoulders with purveyors of used porn. Lines of Peruvians, Balinese and Indonesians sell bright national clothing and jewellery. There are heaps of mildewy second-hand overcoats and racks of precision selected designer classics, tables of used kitchenware and haphazard conglomer-ations of expensive antiques. The rows of oddities and exotica are punctuated by more down to earth stalls selling bicycle parts, underwear or cleaning equipment. A fringe of derelicts gathers around the edge of the market, returning day after day with little spreads of unwanted (and sometimes unidentifiable) bric-a-brac. In one corner a muttering clump of old men surreptitiously flash watches and bits of gold to each other and transfer little wads of notes. A relentless stream of collectors, tourists, Amsterdammers looking for bargains, and the openly curious flows up and down between the stalls.

The near end of the market is dominated by the **Mozes en Aäron Kerk**. In 1649 it was a clandestine Roman Catholic church, named after the gable stones (one depicting Moses and the other, Aaron) on the two house fronts that hid it. The present rather heavy looking neo-classical church (with wooden towers painted to look like sandstone) was built in the 19th century, but you can still see the original gable stones set into the wall round the back. The church was famous for its choir and even the local Jews would come in for the music on Christmas night. The Jewish philosopher Spinoza lived in the house next door to the original church. The Sephardic community excommunicated him for his secular beliefs, but regretted their haste when he went on to become one of the most lauded intellectuals of his time.

Make your way to the far end of the market. Turn right and walk up to Jodenbreestraat. Turn right again. The second house on your right is the **Rembrandthuis** *(open Mon–Sat 10–5, Sun and holidays 1–5; entrance f4).*

Rembrandt lived at Jodenbreestraat 4–6 for nearly twenty years (see p. 112) and his old house is now a museum. The rooms are bare of period furniture and there is none of the atmosphere of Rembrandt's rather chaotic household. Rather, you wander through room after dimly lit room of the Master's etchings—245 in all, virtually a complete collection. Etchings, despite their reputation as tools of seduction, are simply indigestible at this level of concentration—but there's a series of tiny self-portraits of the painter pulling funny faces that's worth seeking out. Rembrandt used himself as a model more than any other 17th-century painter. He even slips into crowd scenes on some of his larger canvases. You can also see the famous *Hundred-guilder Print* (so-called because that's what Rembrandt, who'd lost his own copy, had to bid for it at an auction). The various versions, as well as the touching-up done on the original plate by an Englishman, William Baillie, in the 18th century, are an intriguing illustration of how etching and drypoint work. The museum sells a short explanatory booklet (f2.50) and there's a slide-show on Rembrandt's life, in English, in the basement (hourly on the hour until 3 pm).

*Turn left out of the Rembrandthuis. Across the road is Amsterdam's ugliest 1960s concrete box, nicknamed the 'Maupoleum' after its builder, Maurits 'Maup' Caransa. You cross the canal at St **Antoniessluis** (St Antony's Sluice). Before the move to Waterlooplein, this was the site of a busy second-hand clothes market. The common Dutch surname 'Sluis' or 'Sluys' can often be traced back to Ashkenazi families who worked here. On the other side of the bridge you come to St **Antoniesbreestraat**.*

The great slab of a house at no. 69 belonged to the wealthy 17th-century banker, Isaac de Pinto, and was the envy of the neighbourhood. The poorer inhabitants of the surrounding alleys would mutter that someone was 'As rich as De Pinto'. These days it's a public library, so you can nip in for a look at the odd bits of gilding and the brightly painted birds and cherubs which fly all over the ceiling.

*Opposite the entrance to the De Pinto House is a sculpted gateway embellished with a macabre skull motif, which leads you through to the **Zuiderkerk** (open Mon–Fri 12.30–4.30, Thurs 6–9).*

The Zuiderkerk built between 1603 and 1614 was the first Protestant church to be built after the Reformation, and is a triumph of Amsterdam's great steeple designer, Hendrick de Keyser. The soaring spire with its decorative ionic columns and its clusters of slightly oriental pinnacles was much admired by Christopher Wren, and inspired the designs of his city of London churches. During the harsh winter of 1944–5 more people died in the neighbourhood than the authorities were able to bury, and the church had to be used as a temporary mortuary. Today it's a deeply uninteresting information centre for urban development.

> *Walk back through the gateway and turn right, doubling back towards St Antoniessluis, then right again down the stairs before the bridge at the beginning of St Antoniesbreestraat. Follow the canal back along the Zwanenburgwal. Turn right into Staalstraat, a quiet lane of second-hand book dealers. As you cross Groenburgwal, you get a clear view of the elegant Zuiderkerk spire at the end of the canal. Walk on across Kloveniersburgwal and left into Nieuwe Doelenstraat, the address of some of Amsterdam's grander hotels. At the end of Nieuwe Doelenstraat you come to Muntplein and the* **Munttoren** *(Mint Tower).*

The Munttoren, a solitary clock tower with a polygonal base, is yet another steeple by Hendrick de Keyser—a verticomaniac responsible for nearly every spike on Amsterdam's skyline. The base dates from 1490 and was part of Regulierspoort, one of the gates in the old city wall. The structure gets its name because the guard house was briefly used as a mint in 1672–3, when the French were occupying much of the rest of the Netherlands and the Amsterdam merchants couldn't get at their usual source of Rijksdollars and ducatoons.

> *Pass the Munttoren and turn right into the* **flower market.**

After all the fuss that's made about it in the brochures, Amsterdam's floating flower market can be a bit of a disappointment. It's not very long, not all that cheap, you can't tell from the street that it's floating, and it's full of confused tourists clutching maps and asking each other: 'Is this it?' But the buckets of cut flowers and rows of potted plants are pretty to look at, and on hot days the mingled scents of the flowers fill the whole passage. If you're a keen gardener there's a tempting variety of seeds and bulbs that can be posted home (but see Travel: Customs).

> *At the other end of the flower market, cross Koningsplein onto the left-hand side of the Singel. In the 15th century the Singel was the city's first line of defence ('singel' means 'moat'). These days it's a*

*sober business and residential canal. Amsterdam's smallest house is
at no. 312.*

*If you're interested in Judaica you may want to visit the **Bibli-
otheca Rosenthaliana**, housed in the University Library, the
modern building on the other side of the canal (open Mon–Thurs
9.30–5, Fri 9.30–1, closed public and Jewish holidays).*

This priceless collection of over 100,000 volumes, dating from the 15th
century, disappeared during the Second World War, but was later
tracked down to a village near Frankfurt. As well as old Hebrew manu-
scripts, there's a large collection of Spinoza, old broadsheets, engravings
and photographs.

*Walk on up to **Raadhuisstraat**, one of the city's busiest thorough-
fares, and turn left.*

At Raadhuisstraat 12 you'll find the **Spaarpotten Museum** (open
Mon–Fri 1–4; entrance *f*1), three tiny rooms crammed with over 2000
money boxes. There are musical ones, precious gold and silver caskets,
flimsy cardboard canisters, famous faces and clockwork figurines. The
oldest is a clay pot from 500 BC and there's a Javanese pig that looks just
like Churchill. The collection was started by a bank manager in the
1950s, and there are 10,000 more boxes in the cellar waiting for exhibition space.

Just off Raadhuisstraat, at Herengracht 168, you'll find the **Theatre
Museum** (open Tues–Sun 11–5; entrance *f*2.50) which always has good
exhibitions, usually of the sort where you push buttons or pull levers and
make things happen. If there are three of you, you can raise a storm with
the wind, thunder and lightning machines on the ground floor.

*Carry on along Raadhuisstraat. An elaborate Art-Nouveau shop-
ping arcade takes up much of the left-hand side of the street. It was
built for a life insurance company, which might explain the frightening crocodiles and other dangerous creatures which adorn the canopy.
At the end of Raadhuisstraat you come to Westermarkt and the
towering spire of the **Westerkerk**.*

The Westerkerk was consecrated in 1631. Its sober Protestant interior is
brightened by large painted organ shutters showing a dancing King
David and a voluptuous Queen of Sheba laden with gifts for Solomon.
Rembrandt was buried here, but no-one knows where the body is.
There's a flutter of academic excitement every time old bones are found,

but it's most likely that he was crunched up during the digging of an underground car park. A memorial plaque has been put up near his son Titus's grave. The church tower, known as the **Westertoren**, built by (you guessed it) Hendrick de Keyser, is Amsterdam's highest (85 m) and contains its heaviest bell (7500 kg). In the 1940s a fervent engineer climbed out onto the top of the tower during a violent storm and, with the help of a theodolite, worked out that it swayed all of 3 cm. During the summer months you can climb up rather more sedately for a rare view of Amsterdam from high up (open 1 June–15 Sept, 2–5; entrance *f*1). At the top is the gaudily painted imperial crown of Maximilian of Austria. Amsterdam's merchants gained considerable international clout when, out of gratitude for support given to the Austro-Burgundian Princes, he granted them the right to use the crown in the city coat of arms.

If you walk around the outside of the church you can see the house where Descartes lived when he was in Amsterdam (Westermarkt 6); the pink marble triangles of the **Homomonument** which commemorates gays killed in the concentration camps; and a sad little statue of Anne Frank, who wrote her diary just around the corner.

*At the far end of Westermarkt, turn right and walk down the right-hand side of the Prinsengracht. The **Anne Frank Huis** is at no. 263 (open daily 9–5, Sun and public holidays 10–5; entrance f6).*

Anne Frank, the second daughter of German-Jewish immigrants living in Amsterdam, got her diary for her thirteenth birthday on 12 June 1942. Three weeks later her family were 'onderduikers' ('divers')—in hiding from the Nazi occupying forces. They lived for two years in a small suite of rooms at the back of Anne's father's herb and spice business on the Prinsengracht. The windows had always been painted over to protect the herbs previously stored there, the entrance was hidden behind a hinged bookcase and, apart from four trusted office workers who supplied them with food, nobody knew they were there. Later they were joined by a dentist called Dussel and the Van Daans and their son Peter. For two years they were cooped up in what became known as the Annexe, and Anne wrote in her diaries about life with the petulant and demanding Mrs Van Daan and her hen-pecked spouse, of the tiresomely childish Dussel, and of moments of joy and desperation within her own family.

No-one knows who betrayed them, but in August 1944 German police barged into the offices, walked straight up to the bookcase and demanded entry. All the hideaways, except Anne's father, died in concentration camps in Germany. The office cleaner found the diary in which Anne had written with astonishing lucidity about life in the 'Annexe' and about growing up. When it was given to her father, he found that she'd already begun to edit it for publication. It appeared in 1947 with the title *The Annexe*, the one Anne herself had chosen. Now it's printed in over fifty languages and an estimated thirteen million copies have been sold.

At the Anne Frank Huis , you can wander around the Annexe, but it's completely empty of furniture, filled with tourists and lacks the atmosphere you might have built up for it by reading the diary. The exhibition in the rest of the building—on Anne, the diary and Jews in Amsterdam—ends up being the more moving experience of the visit.

Turn right out of the Anne Frank Huis, walk up the Prinsengracht and cross it at the first bridge you come to. You are now in the **Jordaan.**

The inviting side streets, alleys and intimate canals of the Jordaan are lined with cosy cafés, curious shops and good restaurants, all luring you to ferret about in your own way. The last part of this walk leads you quickly through the quarter and gives you just enough of an idea of what you might like to come back and explore later. Jordaan comes from the French 'jardin', but during the housing crisis in the 19th century this 'garden' on the outskirts of the city disappeared under rows of working-class housing. The houses were small, dark and close together and all the smellier industries (such as tanning) were banished to the Jordaan from the posher areas of town. Naming the streets after flowers didn't cheer things up much. Conditions were appalling, but the Jordaaners developed a pride and a culture akin to London's cockneys. The true Jordaaner is born in the small patch bound by Prinsengracht, Brouwersgracht, Lijnbaansgracht and Looiersgracht, in the shadow of the Westertoren. The church tower is the symbol of the Jordaan. Jordaaners have their own accent and are renowned for a wry sense of humour and for being adept pigeon-fanciers. Everyone over the age of forty is known as 'ome' or 'tante'—uncle or aunt. (Until a few years ago, you could still be woken by Ome Hein, a professional 'waker-up', as he made his early morning rounds with a pet goat.) They're a rebellious lot. There have been a number of historical riots, including one in 1886 when police tried to put a stop to the gory-sounding pastime of 'eel-jerking'; and another when the council threatened to reduce the dole in 1934. Recently traditional Jordaan life has been given a new edge by an influx of artists and music students. You're quite likely to be accompanied on your walk by strains of Mozart and will probably encounter odd art objects suspended over the street.

Turn right up Prinsengracht, and almost immediately left down Egelantiersgracht. Keep to the left side of the canal. At no. 107–114 you'll find one of several **hofjes** *in the district, St Andrieshofje.*

Hofjes, the courts of almshouses, are magically quiet garden courts, often completely hidden from the street. You reach this one (built 1616) through a door that looks like any other front door along the canal and down a passage lined with Delft tiles. Most *hofjes* are private residences, but as long as you're sensitive to that, residents don't mind you popping in for a few calming moments.

Outside St Andrieshofje, double back a little and cross over to the other side of the canal. Walk back up towards Prinsengracht and turn left into Tweede Egelantiersdwarsstraat, a narrow road of shops and cafés typical of the Jordaan's quirky charm. It changes its name to Tweede Tuindwarsstraat and then Tweede Anjeliersdwarsstraat before spilling out into **Westerstraat***, where you turn right.*

Westerstraat (once a canal) is too wide to be really attractive, but at no. 67 there's a tiny shop full of good, old-fashioned, low-tech toys. Skipping ropes, bright-coloured balls, red wooden buses, pretty paper cut-outs are stacked on shelves and hanging from the walls and ceiling. There are boxes and boxes of all sorts of little things that will keep parents and kids digging about for ages.

Westerstraat, and the walk, end at **Noordermarkt***.*

The square is quiet, and usually empty, but if you come back early on a Monday morning you'll find a crush of trendies, students and down-and-outs at Amsterdam's cheapest clothes market. The **Noorderkerk** was Hendrick de Keyser's last church and, as befits an old man, is solemn and austere with only the teeniest of spires. You could end the walk with a quiet coffee in one of the cafés around the square, plunge back into the Jordaan (Bloemgracht and Lindengracht are both very much worth a look) or cross the canal to two more *hofjes* ('De Ster' at Prinsengracht 89–133—one of the best—and 'Zons Hofje' at no. 173).

When you've had enough, wander back up Prinsengracht towards the omnipresent Westertoren. One of the trams from here (13, 14, 17 or 21) will probably be able to take you home.

Walk IV

The Port of Amsterdam

The Dutch East India Company (V·O·C) emblem

Koepelkwartier—Brouwersgracht—Westindische Huis—Western Islands—
Centraal Station—Sint Nicolaaskerk—Zeedijk—Schreierstoren—
Nieuwmarkt—Scheepvaarthuis— Montelbaanstoren— Entrepotdok—
Kromhout Shipyard Museum—Eastern Islands—Maritime Museum

Amsterdam's harbour hides behind the massive Centraal Station. Few
visitors even know it's there. This walk takes you around the old port and
through island neighbourhoods redolent of the days when wooden ships
bulging with corn, spices, silks and gold came from all over the world to
fill the city's warehouses. It starts in the shadow of the imposing copper
dome of an old Lutheran church, touches briefly on Amsterdam's
prettiest canal, then ducks under the tracks to a secluded area of crumbling warehouses, startling new apartment blocks and colourful houseboats. You cross town to fortify yourself in the city's oldest bar. Then you
skirt the red-light district and follow the course of the old city wall,
passing the tower where weeping sailors' wives waved their farewells and
the market square where 'poor sinners' were branded, flogged, hanged
and/or cut into bits. Then it's through the old shipyards, past the
centre's one remaining windmill and into the bowels of a 17th-century
sailing ship at the Maritime Museum.

It's a good walk for a Sunday. It taxes the legs rather than the mind. If
you get up early enough you can start gently with a *Koffieconcert* (coffee

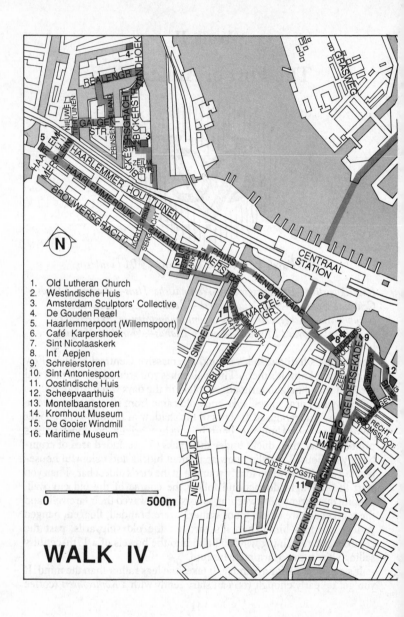

1. Old Lutheran Church
2. Westindische Huis
3. Amsterdam Sculptors' Collective
4. De Gouden Reael
5. Haarlemmerpoort (Willemspoort)
6. Café Karpershoek
7. Sint Nicolaaskerk
8. Int Aepjen
9. Schreierstoren
10. Sint Antoniespoort
11. Oostindische Huis
12. Scheepvaarthuis
13. Montelbaanstoren
14. Kromhout Museum
15. De Gooier Windmill
16. Maritime Museum

0   500m

WALK IV

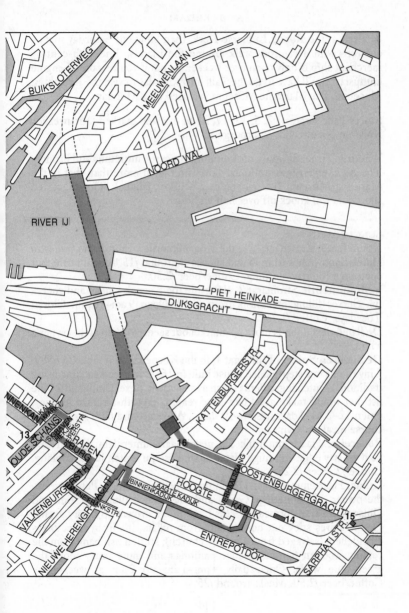

concert) at the Ronde Lutherse Kerk, then blow out Saturday night's cobwebs with a vigorous walk around the islands. The 17th-century merchant ship is only open over weekends, but if you're a diesel engine enthusiast you'll have to do the walk on a weekday to visit the Kromhout Museum. The Maritime Museum is closed on a Monday.

Start: Take Tram 1, 2, 5, 13, 17, 21 to the stop marked 'Nieuwezijds Kolk' on Nieuwezijds Voorburgwal.

Walking Time: 3½ hours not counting concerts, museums and brunch. The *Koffieconcert* lasts an hour. You won't need more than that in the Maritime Museum (unless you're a sailboat fanatic). The suggested short cuts will knock off over half an hour.

LUNCH/CAFÉS
Koepelcafé, Kattengat 1, in the Koepelkwartier. Part of the Sonestra Hotel. Sandwiches from ƒ6 and snacks at around ƒ15. A bland café, but open on a Sunday morning. Coffee/beer ƒ2.50.
't Monumentje Stromarkt 2, alongside the Koepel. Cheap and cheerful. Serves filling breakfasts from ƒ8.50. Open 9 am–10 pm. Closed Tuesdays. Coffee ƒ1.75.
De Roef, next door, is more up-market but seems to open at the owner's whim.
De Silveren Spiegel Kattengat 4, in the Koepelkwartier, tel 624 6589. Tiny rooms in a step-gabled house built in 1614. Inspired cooking using traditional Dutch ingredients (such as succulent Texel lamb) and a wine list that would make good bed-time reading. Worth a return journey. Open 12–2 weekdays, also 6–10 daily . Allow around ƒ100 for a three-course meal with wine.
Rosereijn, Haarlemmerdijk 52, near Haarlemmerplein. Brown café with an arty edge and huge plates of wholesome Dutch home cooking. Coffee ƒ2, beer ƒ2.25.
Dulac, Haarlemmerstraat 118, in the Scheepvaartbuurt. Peter Barent, the owner, is inspired by Gaudi and the French illustrator Edmund Dulac. He's transformed a 1920s bank into a grown-up's fairy grotto. Gothic spires stick out horizontally from pillars; it's lit by huge brass chandeliers (salvaged from a nearby church); stuffed fish hang from the ceiling; wooden figures, strange paintings and more brass adorn the green-blue walls. Open daily 4 pm–1 am (to 2 am at weekends). Coffee/beer ƒ2.50. Meals around ƒ25.

De Gouden Reael, Zandhoek 14, Realeneiland, tel 623 3883. Situated in a 17th-century house in the heart of the Western Islands. You can pop in for just a drink or sample French provincial cuisine (from a different region every three months). Open Mon–Fri noon–1 am; Sat and Sun 5 pm–1 am. Coffee/beer *f*2.50. Full menu and wine around *f*100.

Café Karpershoek, Martelaarsgracht 2, opposite Centraal Station. Claims to be Amsterdam's oldest bar (dating from 1629—but see Café Chris, Walk III Lunch/Cafés). Once right on the waterfront, it was a popular seaman's tavern. It still has sand on the floor, as it would have had in the 17th century.

Café Ot en Sien, Buiksloterweg 27, across the water from Centraal Station. A friendly, family-run café in a lane of country gardens and old wooden houses. Open 12–9 pm. Closed Saturdays. Coffee *f*2; beer *f*2.50; pancakes from *f*6.50.

Int Aepjen, Zeedijk 1, fills the tiny ground floor of a 15th-century seaman's lodging house. It's a 'rariteitencafé' crammed with antiques, leather armchairs and barrels. The painted wall-panels were rescued from a 1920s travelling dance hall. Open daily from noon. Coffee *f*2.25, beer *f*2.50.

De Druif, Rapenburgstraat 83, at the gate to the Entrepotdok. Opened in 1631. A brown café with barrels to the ceiling and a rare antique *jenever* pump on the counter. Locals maintain that naval hero Piet Heyn was a regular visitor. His entrance would have caused a stir, as Heyn died in 1629. Coffee *f*2.00, beer *f*2.25.

In Dubio, Entrepotdok 36. Well managed café/restaurant with a large canalside terrace and good food. Coffee/beer *f*2.25. Meals from *f*30.

Maritime Museum Café is a good place to sip a coffee and look out over the harbour, but the tired sandwiches and plastic cheesecake are to be avoided. Coffee *f*2.50.

☆　　☆　　☆　　☆　　☆

The walk begins in the Koepelkwartier, but nearest tram stop is on the busy Nieuwezijds Voorburgwal. To get to the Koepelkwartier you can walk up Nieuwezijds Voorburgwal and duck down Klimop-straat, a rather dull alley. A more intriguing route is through **De Klompenboer** *(Nieuwezijds Voorburgwal 20; open daily 10–6).*

From the outside, De Klompenboer looks like an ordinary souvenir shop. Inside, however, live chickens and guinea fowl peck their way between rocking-horses, wood carvings and piles of pewter. The shop assistant sits burning patterns into freshly carved clogs. Through a door at the back you can see craftsmen working hard to keep up the supply.

Leave through the small workshop at the back of the shop. You emerge into the quiet and leafy **Koepelkwartier** *(Dome Quarter), aptly nicknamed the Montmartre of Amsterdam.*

It's easy to see where the Koepelkwartier gets its name. The enormous copper dome of the old **Lutherse Kerk** (Lutheran Church) towers over the narrow lanes and pavement cafés. The church (also known as the Ronde Lutherse Kerk—Round Lutheran Church) was built in 1668 by Adriaan Dortsman, a leading light of the appropriately named Restrained Dutch Classicists. A careless plumber caused a fire which burnt it down in 1822; it was rebuilt the following year and, after some years of disuse, was recently converted into a conference hall for the hotel across the road—and gained yet another name: the Sonesta Koepelzaal. The round brick walls look impenetrable (conference delegates reach it through an underground tunnel). On Sunday mornings, however, you can get in through a small green door on the Kattengat side for a *Koffieconcert* (11 am; doors open 10.30 am; entrance *f7*, including coffee; booking possible through the VVV or AUB Ticketshop). You sit under the dome, encircled by Ionic pillars, lots of sandstone and white paint and sip cups of free coffee while listening to the music—anything from Bartok to Jacques Brel (the VVV and listings magazines publish a programme). It's a marvellously restorative way to begin the day if you've been carousing the night before.

In 1614 Laurens Spiegel, a wealthy soap-manufacturer, built the dainty twin step-gable houses next door to the Koepel as an investment. He seemed to rather enjoy punning on his surname (which means mirror). He called his own house (in a classier part of town) 'De Drie Spiegels' (The Three Mirrors), and the two houses on the Kattengat (possibly in view of the profits he hoped to make by letting them out) were called 'De Goude Spiegel' (Golden Mirror) and 'De Silveren Spiegel' (Silver Mirror).

Walk past the Koepel, up Kattengat ('Cat-hole'—it was once a narrow ditch), along Stromarkt and left over the bridge. A brass propeller and black anchor on the street corners mark the beginning of the **Scheepvaartsbuurt** *(Shipping Neighbourhood).*

For centuries, most travellers arrived in Amsterdam by boat. Their first view of the spikes and spires of the city was through a forest of wooden masts. From the shore you looked out at a floating extension of the town. Large sea-going ships made up the horizon. Small boats scuttled between the larger craft. Flat barges plied to and fro carrying fresh water and other supplies. Offices, warehouses and inns were built on timber platforms far out in the water. Amsterdam was the nexus between extensive inland waterways and the open seas, and its port provided welcome protection from the elements for the tiny, rather clumsy, sea-going trade ships on their journey 'within the dunes' across the Wadden Sea, the Zuider Zee and the river IJ.

Under the auspices of the famous Dutch East Indies Company (founded in 1602, see pp. 36–7) and the smaller West India Company (founded 1624), shipbuilding and navigational skills quickly improved, and Dutch ships were soon travelling all over the world. But the Napoleonic wars completely disrupted the Netherlands' trade and the newer, larger ships built in the 19th century had trouble reaching Amsterdam. By 1882 sea trade had declined to such an extent that P.J.H. Cuypers was happy to curtain off the harbour with his palatial Centraal Station. The docks have all but disappeared from view, but there are still corners of Amsterdam where you can find vivid reminders of the bustling, prosperous old port.

To begin an exploration of the Scheepvaartsbuurt, turn left and double back along Singel. Cat-lovers might like to nip down to De Poezenboot ('The Cat Boat'), a houseboat full of stray cats (opposite Singel 40; open 1 pm–2 pm daily). Fat moggies pad nonchalantly around their own terrace, or stare complacently from baskets and wait for you to go away. Lean days of alley fights and tough living seem a dim memory. An enormous platter of very dead day-old chicks lies untouched in the corner. A leaflet assures you that all strays are neutered so that the 'problem is dealt with by its roots'. If the idea of 101 floating felines doesn't take your fancy, then turn right onto Brouwersgracht, keeping on the right-hand side of the canal.

The **Brouwersgracht** (Brewers' Canal) is quintessential Amsterdam. Its neat, gabled houses, humped bridges and shady towpaths feature in almost every brochure intended to lure you to the city. Yet the crowds that tramp up and down the grand canals seem to pass it by. There are no neon lights or noisy cafés. It's a quiet, residential canal for the hopelessly romantic. Most of the houses are converted warehouses. In the 17th century the Brouwersgracht, right at the harbour's edge, seethed with traders and reeked of fish and beer. Stockfish warehouses and no fewer than twenty-four breweries crowded its banks. Amsterdam had to import fresh water from the surrounding countryside to feed its industries and populace. Most of the long flat boats carrying this water entered the city along the Brouwersgracht, so breweries sprang up along the canal that afforded them the pick of the incoming supplies.

Walk up Brouwersgracht and turn right into Herenmarkt, a small square dominated by **Westindische Huis** *(West India House).*

The dumpy red-brick exterior of Westindische Huis (West India House) dates from the 19th century, when it was rebuilt as a Lutheran orphanage. Nowadays it's an adult education college, but you can usually nip in for a glimpse of the 17th-century courtyard—the only remnant of the building's romantic past as headquarters of the West India Company. In the courtyard there's a memorial to Peter Stuyvesant, the notoriously grouchy, peg-legged Governor of Nieuw Amsterdam—the Company's chief American trading post. In 1664 he surrendered the settlement to the British, who renamed it New York.

Turn left, in front of Westindische Huis, along Haarlemmerstraat. Cross the bridge and turn right into Korte Prinsengracht. Follow the pedestrian walkway under the railway bridge to Bickerseiland, the first of the **Western Islands**.

The Western Islands are man-made. They're close together, crisscrossed by canals and connected by little wooden bridges. There's an eerie sense of isolation, even though they are nowadays very much part of the mainland. In the 17th century Amsterdam burst beyond the boundaries that had contained it for generations. More and more land was created by draining off water into new canals. The area of the city increased by nearly 40 per cent. The poet Vondel wrote some histrionic verse in praise of the achievement (as was very much his wont), using the sort of hyperbole usually reserved for military victories. Travellers marvelled at the size and number of the warehouses. Buildings shot up all over the new islands, and were immediately filled with tobacco, salt, tin, wine, draperies, spices, copper, furs, gold—almost any commodity that could realize a profit.

On **Bickerseiland** (Bicker's Island, named after the original developer), modern concrete apartment blocks with bright red and blue window frames line one side of the narrow walkway. The other side is a jumble of houseboats. Rafts, tugs, canal boats, barges—anything that floats (and some things that almost don't), have been commandeered to solve Amsterdam's chronic housing problem. In the 1950s, when the canal transport industry went into an almost terminal decline, skippers were only too pleased to off-load their craft on the oddballs who wanted to live on the water. By the 1970s there were around 800 legally licensed moorings and countless illegal ones. The council outlawed all new-comers and granted an amnesty to over a thousand of the unlicensed boats that were already occupied. Their occupants were allowed (like those on the legal boats) to connect up to the water and electricity supplies. Arrangements for the latter are alarmingly Heath Robinson. Wonky home-made poles hold up yards of black flex as it snakes along the canalside and between boats. Wet washing flutters from these impro-vised clothes lines. The electricity supply is temperamental. Anyone who wants to use a washing machine has to check that the neighbours aren't watching TV, or everyone could be plunged into darkness. There are other drawbacks to boat life—like having to get up in the middle of the night to check your moorings in a storm, or chase off drunk men who pee over the edge of the canal onto your bedroom roof. Despite the hazards, houseboats are popular. Originally they were the domain of the weird and rebellious, but now lawyers and stockbrokers sun themselves on deck and talk for hours about waterproofing techniques. One boat even houses a community of nuns. But the old eccentrics are still there. From Bickerseiland you can see the boat of a 'collector', piled high with scrap metal, rusting machines and bits of wood.

Carry on along the pedestrian walkway, then turn left into **Zeil-makerstraat***.*

Streetnames like 'Sailmaker's Street' and 'Blockmaker's Street' are all that's left of the shipbuilding yards for which Bickerseiland was re-nowned. (It was also famous for its dogs. There were so many that the local church had to employ two dog-chasers to keep the aisles free during services.) Most of the island is taken up by soulless 1970s housing estates. At Zeilmakerstraat 15, in one of the few buildings to escape post-war redevelopment, you'll find the **Amsterdams Beeldhouwers Kollektief** (Amsterdam Sculptors' Collective; open Wed–Sun 1–6). The sixty members (some of the city's best young sculptors among them) keep the gallery well supplied. Exhibitions change frequently. Most work is on sale, and not all of it is of a size to preclude taking it home in your overnight bag.

At the end of Zeilmakerstraat turn right, then immediately left into Minnemoersstraat. Turn right again into Bickersgracht where there's a tiny urban farmyard. Fat rabbits lie stretched out in the sun next to curly-horned goats. Various fowl peck about the edge of the concrete. If you find the pong a bit much, hurry on around the corner and over the white wooden bridge to **Realeneiland.**

Realeneiland is named after Jacob Real, the original owner. Ahead of you as you cross the bridge is a neat little row of 17th-century houses. Jacob Real's own, rather modest, house (now a restaurant) is at the end. He was a fervent Catholic. The gold painted coin on the gable stone commemorates the treasures he saved from the iconoclasts by smuggling them out of a monastery in the nick of time. Real's surname (also the name of a coin) afforded an appropriate pun, and the house became known as 'De Gouden Reael'. There's a tang of tar and varnish in the air. The diligent occupants of the rather stately row of boats on the dockside seem perpetually involved in maintenance.

After you've nosed about a bit, make your way left from the bridge along Realengracht, past the floating police station. Across the bridge at the end of Realengracht is **Prinseneiland.**

Hidden in the middle of the Western Islands, Prinseneiland is the best of all. Its little lanes are a mish-mash of architectural styles. Tumbledown warehouses crumble quietly next to smart, sharp-edged new apartments. Tall, carefully restored façades grace the canal. The island is perfumed by freshly sawn timber from the working boatyard. There's seldom any traffic. All you hear is the sound of sawing, workmen calling to each other and (to jolt you back down to earth) pop music from their ghettoblasters.

Turn left, past the Walvis shipyard, and follow the road as far as **Galgenstraat.**

'Galg' means 'gallows'. The bridge at the eastern end of Galgenstraat used to afford a fine prospect of the city's Golgotha. The curious were not always afforded a view of the whole process. Offenders were often executed in the city centre. The heads, sometimes with the heart stuffed into the mouth, were posted on the city wall and only the discarded bits ended up on the grassy mound near the Galgenbrug.

Turn right into Galgenstraat and leave the island over the small white bridge leading to Nieuwe Tiertuinen. Just to the left of the bridge, behind a matching pair of white doors, George Breitner

(1857–1923) had his studio. Breitner's paintings of Amsterdam have made him a local favourite. He loved the low life and, when he went to The Hague, he used to prowl the seedy areas with his good friend Van Gogh, looking for inspiration.

Turn left into Nieuwe Tiertuinen. Walk back under the railway tracks to **Haarlemmer Houttuinen** *on the mainland.*

The gaudy daubings in the arches under the tracks are part of Amsterdam's longest painting. Five hundred metres of bright colour were commissioned of Fabrice Hünd, who seems to have ended up covering up ugly concrete surfaces all over the city. (He's also responsible for the walls of the Stopera carpark).

Haarlemmer Houttuinen opens out into **Haarlemmerplein**. Bewildered old men, looking for all the world like retired sailors, sit in rows on the benches, puffing pipes and staring at the traffic as it whizzes round them.

Willemspoort (a.k.a. Haarlemmerpoort), a neo-classical gatehouse built for the entrance of King William II in 1840, takes up all of one end of the square. The masons botched the rather special *trompe-l'oeil* effect that has to be achieved to keep the perspectives right: the central columns appear to taper rather suddenly at the top. It's never been a popular structure. At a town council meeting at the turn of the century it was saved from demolition by only four votes. If you walk through the gate you'll see four small rectangles set into the second pillar on the left. They mark the position of the old *stokmaat*, the measure by which horses were judged large enough for military service. It was used right up to the First World War.

From Haarlemmerplein you can catch a Tram 18 or 22 to Centraal Station for the second part of the walk. This will save about half an hour. If you have the time and energy you can walk it. Coffee and chocolate cake in the bizarre Café Dulac (see Lunch/Cafés listings above) will reward you for the extra effort. Leave Haarlemmerplein by **Haarlemmerdijk***, which becomes Haarlemmerstraat.*

Haarlemmerdijk is a local shopping street with some curious attractions. If you take your photograph to Beune's confectioners at number 156, they'll reproduce it in icing on the cake of your choice. The result is a white slab with a sombre sepia image, rather like a Portuguese tombstone. There's a chess and go shop (no. 147) and a shop selling wildly coloured hand-woven Tibetan tiger rugs. A church by the 19th-century

151

grandfather of modern Dutch architecture, P.J.H. Cuypers, has (like so many of his others) been converted into offices. Towards the end of the street you'll have to concentrate hard not to miss The Green Lanterns which, at 128 cm wide, claims to be the world's smallest restaurant. (The *Guinness Book of Records* confirms that it's Holland's narrowest).

> *At the end of Haarlemmerstraat, turn left into Prins Hendrikkade. Trains, trams, buses, lorries, cars and phalanxes of cyclists hurtle by. A little Dutch courage may be needed to cross this manic fray. Luckily, Café Karpershoek, Amsterdam's oldest bar, is close at hand (see Lunch/Cafés listings above). Suitably fortified, you can cross to* **Centraal Station***. Walk in the main entrance, right through the concourse, and out the back for a free* **ferry trip across** **the IJ***.*

P.J.H. Cuypers' grand, gilded red-brick Centraal Station (see p. 93) so effectively blocks out the city's view of the water that the harbour on its back doorstep comes as a complete surprise. The IJ is quite narrow at this point, so the modern docks have moved far out to the west. Most of the *steigers* (piers) now provide mooring for tour boats and the water police. A bright red evangelical churchboat at Steiger 14 throbs with rock music. Two (free) ferries that look like floating air traffic control buildings work in tandem, making the journey to the opposite bank (the crossing takes only a few minutes). There, in the shadow of the towering Shell laboratory, you'll find a neat country lane of dapper wooden cottages, cheerful houseboats, gardens and trees. The wide wooden houses in **Buiksloterweg** date back to the 16th century and are examples of a style that has now entirely disappeared from the city centre.

> *Retrace your steps through the station. Diagonally across the inter- section in front of the main entrance you'll see the rose window and spires of Sint Nicolaaskerk (St Nicholas's Church) (open April–Oct, Mon–Fri 11–4; Sat 2–4).*

Sint Nicolaaskerk is a tatty 19th-century neo-Renaissance building with a murky interior. A small ship set above the door at the back is the only reminder that it was a seamen's church. Every March during the *Stille Omgang* (Silent Procession), Roman Catholics walk silently through the streets to the Sint Nicolaaskerk to commemorate Amsterdam's miracle (see p. 31). Paintings in the left-hand transept depict the story.

Turn left out of the church, past the Barbizon Hotel and left again into **Zeedijk**.

In the 14th century Zeedijk marked the city limits. Modern Amsterdammers associate it with the *rode knipoog en witte kick* (the 'red wink' of prostitution and 'white kick' of heroin). A massive clean-up campaign by the council and police has got rid of the drug dealers and is turning Zeedijk into a respectable street of restaurants and galleries. The red wink is still just around the corner.

The timber house at no. 1 is one of the oldest buildings in the city and one of the two remaining wooden buildings in central Amsterdam. It was built in 1550 as a seaman's hostel. The innkeeper allowed sailors who'd drunk or gambled away their wages to leave pet monkeys in payment. The hostel became infested with apes and fleas and became known as 'Int Aepjen': you could always spot the poor scratching seamen who'd slept 'in the monkeys'. (You can still visit Int Aepjen—see Lunch/Café listings above.)

Turn left down Oudezijds Kolk, a canal with doors opening, Venetian style, directly onto the water. Walk down to the **Schreierstoren** *(the 'Weepers' Tower').*

The Schreierstoren (built 1480) is a dwarfish brick tower with a pixie-hat roof. It's one of the few remnants of Amsterdam's first city wall. Romantics maintain the tower gets its name because sailors' wives would gather on the battlements to see the men off to sea. Well might they weep and wave. Voyages could take up to four years and, on average, two thirds of the men who set off never returned. More pedantic linguists point out that 'schreier' comes from the old Dutch word for 'astride' or 'angle' and that the tower straddles two canals. The romantics win: a stone tablet on the wall depicts the wailing wives. Henry Hudson also has a plaque, as it was from here, in 1609, that he set off to discover a new route to the East Indies and found Manhattan instead, giving his name to the Hudson River. The Schreierstoren was originally a solid defence tower. The top storey, windows and doors were all added later. Nowadays it houses a nautical instruments shop.

Double back and walk south along the right-hand side of the **Geldersekade**.

The old city wall ran along the far side of the canal. Along this stretch it was covered in a tangle of herbs and camomile. Centuries later Van

Gogh's Uncle Stricker lived on the site of no. 77. When Vincent was in Amsterdam studying for the priesthood, Uncle Stricker had the fairly hopeless task of supervising his lessons. The drinking houses on the right-hand side of Geldersekade were notorious. A 17th-century British ambassador to the Netherlands was horrified: 'There are tolerated in the city of Amsterdam, amongst other abuses, at least 50 musick-houses where lewd persons of both sexes meet to practise their villainies.' His moral outrage didn't preclude him from having a detailed knowledge of the prices and opening times of the 'Long Seller', a public meeting house where 'rogues and whores make their filthy bargains'. The red-light district has moved fractionally eastward. Geldersekade is now a grimy collection of downmarket Chinese shops and restaurants.

At the end of Geldersekade you come to **Nieuwmarkt** *(New Market).*

Nieuwmarkt is an open, brick-paved square that connects some of the more sinister alleys of the red-light district. Furtive men pop out of side streets, blink uncertainly in the bright light, then slip away. The police have cleared out the junkies and dealers who used to hang about the square, and it's been given a facelift. Now that the underworld is banished, Nieuwmarkt has moved into limbo. It's empty and a little tense—unwilling to assume a new role.

A ring of modern street lamps, like giant mauve praying mantises, seem about to devour the solid medieval **St Antoniespoort** which huddles, flanked by dumpy towers, in the middle of the square. St Antoniespoort began life in 1488 as one of the main gates in the city wall. It was a popular spot for public executions. If you have a look on the south side you can see the rectangular holes (now bricked up) where the support beams of the scaffold slipped in. In one of the octagonal towers was a *galgekamertje* (little gallows room). From here the hapless prisoner got a foretaste of what was to happen to him. A small window looked out on the hangings, brandings and chopping off of bits going on a few feet below. In 1617 the gate was converted into a public weighing house. As all wholesale goods had to be weighed for taxes, '*De Waag*' was the centre of trading activity. Liveried porters carried produce to and fro. Fierce armed guards were posted everywhere to keep an eye on the filling coffers and to arrest defaulters. (The sewer below the square was a highway for smugglers and bandits.) In 1691 St Antoniespoort housed the dissecting room of the Guild of Surgeons (cadavers being so conveniently at hand). You can just make out their inscription above the door in the south tower. On the other side bricklayers decorated the door to *their* guild room with elaborate wreaths of trowels. The building still looks sadly derelict, though it's now been converted into a TV studio.

Nieuwmarkt occasionally regains some of its old liveliness. On Sundays in the summer months there's a bustling antique market and on feast days you can sometimes find a fairground or one of the old Dutch travelling dance halls. Before you leave the square treat your nostrils to the herbalists Jacob Hooy & Co at no. 12. In one half of the shop barrels and boxes of herbs are piled to the ceiling; in the other half it comes right up to date with a range of ecologically sound products.

Cross Nieuwmarkt and walk down the right-hand side of **Kloveniersburgwal***. Walk down as far as the police station.*

Kloveniersburgwal was a fashionable address in the Golden Age. The grand neo-classical house at no. 29 (across from the police station) belonged to the Trip brothers. The brothers were powerful arms dealers: together with their rival, De Geer, they controlled almost all of Europe's munitions supply in the 17th-century. In an ostentatious display of wealth, they clubbed together and built two separate houses behind a vast single façade. The chimney pots were made to look like cannons. When they were moving in, the coachman grumbled that he would be happy with a house the size of their front door. He got what he wanted, across the canal at no. 26.

Walk on up to Oude Hoogstraat. The monumental red brick building on the corner was **Oostindische Huis** *(East India House), the headquarters of the Dutch East India Company.*

It used to fill the whole neighbourhood with the scent of spices. Nowadays it's used as government offices. At first glance it seems rather austere—though if you take a peek into the courtyard (off Oude Hoogstraat) you'll be surprised by the richly decorated entrance. A rather small door is surrounded by wedding-cake embellishments of volutes and scrolls.

The company treated sailors well, but found recruiting seamen to be a problem—the odds on ever returning from a voyage were pretty low. 'Soul merchants', employed by the company, would ensnare Amsterdam's (often foreign) poor by paying their board and lodging. When the drums and trumpets announced enlistment day, the soul merchants stopped paying the rent. For many the only alternative was to sign up. Once at sea sailors were well paid. They were given danger money and supplements for sighting land. Most did a bit of trading on their own count. (Smuggled goods weighed down some ships so much that they sank.) Sailors who got back home found themselves wealthy men—and in relief at having returned safely would often go on a frenzy of spending. A favourite prank was to hire three coaches, in an ostentatious display of their new wealth. The first would contain the sailor's hat and would have to drive fast enough to keep a flag constantly flying. Careering behind would be a coach with the sailor's pipe and tobacco box, and the third contained the sailor himself. These 'six-week masters' were as poor after a few weeks as they had been before the voyage.

> *Cross over the bridge and walk back to Nieuwmarkt along the other side of the canal. Cross Nieuwmarkt and walk down the east side of Geldersekade. Turn right into Recht Boomsloot, a quiet residential canal. Keep to the left-hand side of the canal. Turn left into Lastageweg. Cut through the children's playground and turn left into Kromme Waal. Turn right over the bridge on Prins Hendrikkade.*
>
> *From Kromme Waal you begin to get a view of the ship-shaped* **Scheepvaarthuis** *(Shipping House). By the time you're on the bridge, it's bearing down on you at full steam.*

The house was built in 1916 (on the site of the place where the first Dutch fleet set sail for the East Indies) as the offices for six big shipping companies. Today it's the headquarters of the municipal transport authority. It was the first building designed by the team of architects (Van der Meij, Kramer and De Klerk) who became known as the Amsterdam School, a sort of fantastical Dutch Art Nouveau movement (see p. 169–70). Nothing escapes decoration. The building comes to a prow-like point crowned by a statue of Neptune. He waves his trident while his wife Salicia takes the wheel. Four female figures represent the points of the compass. The walls are encrusted with unflattering reliefs of sea heroes. Doors, stairs, window frames and any wall space left are patterned with appropriate images—wave forms, sea horses, dolphins, anchors, seals and ship's wheels. The roof line is a cheval-de-frise of moulded lead. It's as if you're viewing the building in a distorting mirror: there's hardly a smooth surface in sight. It's not open to the public, but Archivisie (see Practical A–Z: Tours) can organize a tour. It's worth a return journey. The maritime motifs continue inside with filigreed metalwork ornamentation, beautiful stained-glass skylights and windows and much of the original furniture (also designed by the architects). Door-knobs, lamps, wall-panels, floor patterns all reflect the theme. No detail is missed.

Pop across the road for a look at the magnificent moustachios of Prince Hendrik, 'the seaman' (1820–79). (He did a lot to promote sea trade, and the bust was erected in gratitude). Walk down **Binnenkant**, *to the right of the Scheepvaarthuis.*

Binnenkant was created in 1644 to provide more mooring. Its sedate charm is a relief after the traffic on Prins Hendrikkade. It was always a quiet spot in the harbour and a popular place to live. You can still see some fine old merchant houses. At the end of Binnenkant is the **Montel-baanstoren**, a defence tower built in 1512 when the wharves were still outside the city walls. In 1606 (when the tower was no longer used for defence) the builder Hendrick de Keyser added a wonderfully gratuitous spire. This was an activity he apparently enjoyed: he's responsible for much of Amsterdam's spiky skyline. Five years after it was built, the Montelbaanstoren began to tilt over. The good burghers of Amsterdam, unlike their more flamboyant counterparts in Pisa, would have none of it. They attached ropes to the top and pulled it straight again. Rembrandt loved to draw it, and it's still a favourite subject for visiting artists. VOC sailors left from the Montelbaanstoren to join the large seafaring East Indiamen which were too bulky to navigate as far as Amsterdam and were moored far to the north. These days it houses the city water authority. There's a delightful grotto of antiquarian and second-hand books in a shop opposite the tower.

Turn left into Kalkmarkt. right over the bridge, then right again down **'s Gravenhekje.**

On the corner of 's Gravenhekje you can see the old warehouses of the West India Company. Their monogram is on the pediment. In its later years the ailing company gave up its head office in the western docks and moved the administrative sections in here too. The impoverished owner of no. 5, further up the street, had to sell off part of his property to the neighbours, and as they expanded they cut his house in half.

Follow 's Gravenhekje round, across Peperstraat into Rapenburg-straat. Pepper was the most prized commodity of the VOC—enough for a street to be named after it. The Dutch still use the expression 'peperduur'—'pepper-expensive'. Piet Heyn—the admiral who captured the Silver Fleet—lived at Rapenburgstraat 13.

At the end of Rapenburgstraat, cross the main road at the lights to your right and walk up Anne Frankstraat. Turn left along the Nieuwe Herengracht canal and across the middle of three bridges, Scharrenbiersbrug, which gets its name from the cheap beer that used to be sold to smugglers and stowaways.

Whenever boats pass, the low bridges here have to be raised in succession. The operator bicycles swiftly from one to the other, just beating the boat. Across the bridge is the solid neo-classical entrance to the **Entrepotdok**, a customs-free area where goods in transit could be stored. It was once the largest warehouse complex in Europe and recently it was converted into apartments. The architects created an indoor street at first-floor level to combat the gloom.

The weary can cut straight across Prins Hendrikkade to the Maritime Museum. Others can go through the Entrepotdok gates and nose about this district a little more. The stairs marked Binnenkadijk take you up to the internal street. The long row of simple step-gabled warehouses is named in alphabetical order. There's no motor traffic: all you hear is the lap of water and the odd squawk from the zoo on the other side of the dock.

*At the end of the line of warehouses, turn left into Laagtekadijk. Cross the playground and walk up the steps to Hoogtekadijk. Across the bridge to the right is the **Kromhout Museum** (open Mon–Fri 10–4; entrance f2.50).*

The Kromhout Shipyard, one of Amsterdam's oldest, was one of the few to survive the 19th-century decline in shipbuilding. It had a new lease of life in the 20th century when it produced the diesel engine used by most Dutch inland craft. In the 1960s it moved to larger premises and the old yard became a museum. Some boat building and restoration still goes on, but rows of diesel engines form the bulk of the exhibits. It's very much a place for the enthusiast.

*If the smell of oil and tar doesn't excite you, cross Hoogtekadijk, walk down Overhaalsgang and over the brightly painted modern bridge to the **Eastern Islands**.*

To your right as you cross the canal, central Amsterdam's last windmill pokes up out of squat 1960s architecture. The Eastern Islands (Wittenburg, Kattenburg and Oostenburg) are now joined together by a wide

158

boulevard, but were once not only separate, but fiercely isolationist. There are islanders still living who remember neighbours who never once went to central Amsterdam. In 1928 the council built a public bath-house on Wittenburg and a bridge across to Kattenburg. It was a long time before anyone could be persuaded to cross the bridge and bath on 'foreign territory'.

Walk left up the boulevard to the sturdy **Nederlands Scheepvaart Museum** *(Maritime Museum) , built as an admiralty warehouse in 1655 (open Tues–Sat 10–5, Sun 1–5; entrance f7.50).*

It's a wonder the building's still upright: workers were bribed with 'drinkgelt' (drinking money) and finished it in an amazing nine months and fourteen days. The new warehouse had a system of cisterns and sprinklers to put out fires and an army of rat-catching cats with their own office and keeper. The museum's main attraction—a full size replica of the *Amsterdam*, one of the VOC's ships—is moored outside (open weekends only). You can swan about the captain's cabin, have a look at his tiny loo then descend into the ship's murky maw where up to 200 sailors would live for months at a stretch. From the upper deck you can look across to the VOC warehouses on the end of Prins Hendrikkade. Back in the museum you can see a cutaway of an 1840s outrigger and the ostentatiously gilded (and rather uncomfortable) Royal Barge used for state occasions and for paddling visiting dignitaries around the canals. You can also climb up to the Second World War room to peer out at Amsterdam through a periscope. The rest of the museum comprises room after room of maps, navigational equipment, models and pictures of ships. Unless you're really keen, this soon begins to pall. If you're developing an interest, the Explanatory Notes (f2.50 from the museum shop) are a good introduction to the history of Dutch seafaring. In an unmarked room in the cellar a man sells model kits of awesome complexity (Thurs–Sat only).

Bus 22 takes you from outside the museum back to Centraal Station, or you can end the walk more appropriately by making the journey in the Museum Boat (f1.50; departure details from the ticket office).

Walk V

Modern Amsterdam

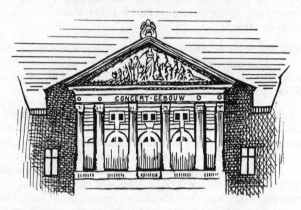

Stedelijk Museum—Concertgebouw—Nieuw Zuid—Albert Cuyp Market—Heineken Brewery Museum—Amstelkerk—Tuschinski Cinema—Rembrandtsplein—Stopera

This is a walk to do once you've explored the canals, seen the main sights and want to escape from the 17th century. It begins at the city's trendiest museum and skirts round the hallowed Concertgebouw to the secluded Nieuw Zuid (New South)—a nook of eccentric modern architecture that few people, even Amsterdammers, know about. Then it's back to the crush of Holland's longest street market. Just when you need it, the Heineken Brewery museum gives you enough free beer to propel you happily through the crowds in Rembrandtsplein, and on to a coffee in Amsterdam's most controversial new building.

It's a good weekday walk. A mid-morning start on a Wednesday will mean that you're in time for a lunch-hour recital at the Concertgebouw. The fancy brickwork of Amsterdam School architecture looks its best in the afternoon sunlight—and if you really want that beer you'll have to make the brewery by 2.30 (earlier in the winter). If you're only in town for the weekend, you'll find the brewery closed, and a deserted market-place on Sunday.

Start: Take Tram 2, 3, 5, 12, 16 to Paulus Potterstraat/Museumplein.

Walking Time: 2 hours—but allow at least another two for museums, markets and relaxing in a café.

Stedelijk Museum Café is the best café on the museum circuit. You can lounge about in basket chairs reading art magazines, or sit in the sun and look out at the sculpture garden. It's not overpriced—you can get a filling salad for ƒ8.

Café Welling, J.W. Brouwersstraat 32, behind the Concertgebouw. A traditional brown café. The main door is always locked—the entrance is around the side. Open daily from 3pm. Coffee/beer ƒ2.25.

Meidi-Ya, Beethovenstraat 18–20, just into the Nieuw Zuid. Japanese Delicatessen. *Sushi* to take down to the canal, or more elaborate dishes to eat there. *Sushi* from ƒ1.75.

Delcavi, Beethovenstraat 40. Haunt of the well-heeled locals. Sandwiches from ƒ3.50 and home-cooked meals at around ƒ30. Coffee/beer ƒ2.50.

Apollo Hotel, Apollolaan 2, Nieuw Zuid, tel 673 5922. It may be ugly and belong to Trusthouse Forte, but it has a terrace right on the water and has poached a chef from the great Gleneagles hotel in Scotland. Snacks from ƒ13.50—or phone and book for a magnificent Sunday brunch (ƒ55).

Café/Restaurant Kort, Amstelveld 2, tucked beneath the Amstelkerk. Sleek and modern with one of the few terraces in central Amsterdam where the traffic doesn't hurtle between you and the canal. Filled baguettes from ƒ5, light meals from ƒ15 and freshly prepared set meals with classic sauces from ƒ50.

Café Schiller, Rembrandtsplein 26. A perfectly preserved Art-Deco interior and a haven from the tourist throngs. Coffee/beer ƒ2.50.

De Kroon Royal Café, Rembrandtsplein 17, (upstairs). All air and light with Louis XV chairs, modern paintings and chandeliers hanging from distant ceilings. Coffee/beer ƒ2.75. Sandwiches from ƒ5. Salads and fuller meals from ƒ10.

Coffeeshop Le Monde, Rembrandtsplein 6. The friendliest of the otherwise indistinguishable pavement cafés. Coffee/beer ƒ2.25.

Café L'Opera, Rembrandtsplein 19. Catches the last patch of afternoon sun. Coffee/beer ƒ2.50.

Café Dantzig, Zwanenburgwal 15, part of the Stopera complex. Deeply trendy, post-modern café. Coffee/beer ƒ2.50.

☆　　　☆　　　☆　　　☆　　　☆

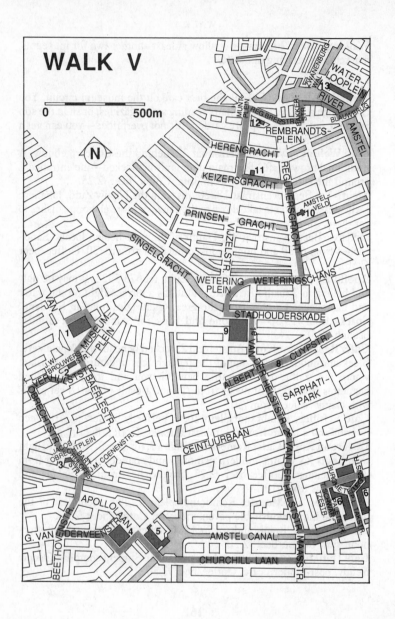

WALK V

0   500m

N

WATER-
LOOPLEIN

ZWANENBURG
WAL

13

RIVER
AMSTEL

BLAUWBRUG

12

MUNT
PLEIN

REG.BREESTR.

REMBRANDTS-
PLEIN

HERENGRACHT

REGULIERSGRACHT

KEIZERSGRACHT

11

PRINSEN-
GRACHT

AMSTEL-
VELD

10

VIJZELSTR.

SINGELGRACHT

WETERING
PLEIN

WETERINGSCHANS

STADHOUDERSKADE

1E VAN DER

9

1

J.W.
BROUWERSSTR.

MUSEUM
PLEIN

CUYPSTR.

8

ALBERT
HELSTSTR.

SARPHATI-
PARK

OVERHULSTSTR.

2

BAERLESTR.

OBRECHTSTR.

JACOB
OBRECHTPLEIN

3

J.M. COENENSTR.

CEINTUURBAAN

2E VAN DER HELSTSTR.

MAASSTR.

7

BURG.TELLGE STR.

P.

6

6

APOLLOLAAN

G. VAN DERVEENSTR.

4

5

AMSTEL CANAL

CHURCHILL-LAAN

BEETHOVENSTR.

Trams 2, 3, 5 and 12 will drop you at the corner of Van Baerlestraat and Paulus Potterstraat, right opposite the **Stedelijk Museum** *(open daily 11–5, adm f7). Tram 16 will drop you near the Concertgebouw, so you'll need to walk westwards up Van Baerlestraat to the museum.*

The Stedelijk Museum is a solid 19th-century red brick building with fussy plaster decorations and spiky gables. A row of rather haughty architects stare down at you from niches on the first floor. The widened entrance and glass box extension at the back were part of a drive in the 1950s to make art more accessible: the guiding principle was that a museum loses its sense of mystery when works can also be viewed from the street. A good idea—if the blinds didn't have to be drawn every afternoon against the damaging sunlight.

Don't be deceived by appearances. It's a bright, lively museum of modern art. You'll find not only conventional paintings, but all sorts of applied art (designer chairs, feather hats and gaudy teapots) and work by less established artists (some of it for sale). As you queue for your ticket the person in front may just as likely be a professor of art history as some painter's proud mother.

The museum owes its existence to two benefactors. Sophia Augusta de Bruyn, the eccentric dowager of Jonkheer (Lord) Lopez Suasso, spent as little as she could on clothes (scandalizing Amsterdam society by wearing the same dress more than once). Instead she amassed as many jewels, trinkets, curios (and especially clocks) as she could. When she died, she left everything to the City of Amsterdam. There was so much that the council felt obliged to build a museum to display it all. At the same time the wealthy Vereeniging tot het Vormen van eene Openbare Verzameling van Heedendaagsche Kunst (Society for the Formation of a Public Collection of Contemporary Art) or VvHK, was looking for a home.

KEY TO MAP OF WALK V

1. Stedelijk Museum
2. Concertgebouw
3. Obrechtplein Synagogue
4. Sociale Vezekeringsbank
5. Apollohal
6. De Dageraad
7. Coöperatiehof
8. Albert Cuyp Market
9. Heineken Brewery Museum
10. Amstelkerk
11. Fodor Museum
12. Tuschinski Cinema
13. 'Stopera'

The city council and the 'society with the long name' (as it was under-standably nicknamed) got together and the museum opened in 1895. It wasn't until the early 1970s that the last of Sophia Augusta's bric-a-brac was dispersed to specialist museums, and the Stedelijk became devoted exclusively to modern art

Successive directors have left their imprint on the collection, but it was the imagination, energy and skill of Willem Sandberg—'part poet, part artist, part designer, part administrator, part magician'—that between 1945 and 1963 established the Stedelijk as one of the world's leading modern art museums. He built up an important collection and held a series of notable, usually controversial, exhibitions. In 1949 there were fisticuffs in the foyer at the opening of the first COBRA exhibition. (COBRA was a group of artists from *Co*penhagen, *Br*ussels and *Am*-sterdam whose colourful, childlike painting was the first to provoke the response that 'a three-year-old could do better'). Though that's not happened again, daring new acquisitions still spark off public uproars.

Space is limited, so only a small portion of the collection is shown at any one time. Every few months a complete change is made (though some paintings surface so often they're more or less on permanent view). Outside the summer months (May–September) you may even find that the whole museum is taken over by a special exhibition and the permanent collection is nowhere to be seen. A plan of what is currently on view is available from the information desk (to the left of the en-trance). The catalogue (a survey of the entire collection, in English) is a bargain at *f*30.

*You'll find whatever is being exhibited of the **permanent collec-tion** up the wide marble staircase, on the top floor.*

In 1972 the large Van Gogh collection, which had been kept at the Stedelijk, moved next door to its own museum (see Walk VI). Because Van Gogh is considered so important to modern art, a few paintings were left behind. *La Berceuse* (The Cradle) was inspired by a story Gauguin told Van Gogh about fishermen who pinned prints of their patron saint—Stella Maris (Maria, Star of the Sea)—to the cabin wall. Van Gogh felt that a portrait of Madame Roulin (a postman's wife), holding a chord for a rocking cradle, would be ideal for such a print. He imagined the seamen '. . . would feel the old sense of being rocked come over them and remember their own lullabys'. It's a pity that the painting isn't hung the way Van Gogh suggested—as a triptych with sunflower paintings on either side. Don't miss the paintings by George Breitner, Van Gogh's contemporary and drinking partner. In *De Dam*, a view of Dam Square, he captures that special Amsterdam light in a way that makes the exact time of year, even the time of day, immediately recognizable. Keep an eye open also for his highly patterned, exotic *Woman in a Red Kimono* (in reality a hat shop assistant).

The museum has a good collection of modern art classics. You'll probably find Manet's picture of a barmaid (staring at you saucily from under a crystal chandelier), a study for his famous *Bar at the Folies-Bergère*. There are some gentle Cézanne landscapes and a whole range of Picassos—from bright early collages to nudes from his Blue Period. One wall is sure to be filled by Matisse's vast paper cut-out *The Parakeet and the Mermaid*, done towards the end of his life when his eyesight was too poor for painting. You'll find at least one of Kandinsky's vivid *Improvisations*—paintings where he used colour to represent the sounds of various musical instruments—and some rather good Chagalls.

The 1960s are well represented by Warhol screen-prints, Roy Lichtenstein's comic strip blow-ups and Bruce Nauman's neon light installations, and the museum comes right up to date with works by some of the best living European and American artists.

The highpoint is the museum's collection of the Russian artist, Kazimir Malevich and the Dutch movement, *De Stijl*. Side by side, these two collections show how abstract art began and we see the gradual disappearance of any reference to outside reality. The visionary director of the museum, Willem Sandberg, was responsible for tracking down the Malevich collection, unearthing a treasury of works that had been forgotten in a cellar in Germany for three decades. Malevich had left the entire contents of an exhibition for safe-keeping with a friend in Beieren, but was subsequently never allowed to leave Russia. He died in 1935, so there the cache remained (under a pile of rubble after the war) until Sandberg swooped down and bought it in the late 1950s. The museum has a complete range of his work, from early impressionist pieces, through a cubist period to the completely abstract—solid shapes of colour (oblongs, squares, triangles) on a white background. Malevich composes these shapes at such angles that the paintings seem full of movement.

At around the same time (1917) the *De Stijl* artists were coming up with very similar work. The best known is that of Piet Mondriaan (he dropped the last 'a' to appear French, but the Dutch prefer the original). His *Compositions* of vertical and horizontal black lines with blocks of primary colours, so shocking at the time, now appear on everything from oven gloves to shampoo bottles. When Theo van Doesberg (co-founder of *De Stijl*) after ten years of rectilinear painting produced a *Contra-composition*, in which he daringly tilted his lines through 45°, Piet left the movement in a huff. They were never reconciled, though Mondriaan later took up the challenge by tilting his *canvas* through 45° and keeping the lines vertical.

Halfway down the staircase you'll find the **Print Room.**

Here you could find anything from a Toulouse-Lautrec poster to Mapplethorpe's startling close-up photographs of male nudes. Keep an eye open for the innovative work of Dutch photographer Cas Oorthuys, and Roland Topor's blackly comic cartoons. Work not on display can be viewed by appointment in the studyroom.

Carry on down to the ground floor, most of which is given over to ***travelling exhibitions and applied art.***

The small door to the left of the ticket office leads to rooms of odd-shaped furniture, gaudy ceramics and lumpy mats. There's a video art room under the stairs, and the glass box extension at the back of the building displays work (often dire) by contemporary Amsterdam artists. Two installations on the ground floor shouldn't be missed. The *Appelbar* (through a door to the right of the information desk)—adorned with murals of colourful birds, fish and children—is the work of the COBRA artist Karel Appel. It was used as a café until the opening of the present restaurant in 1956. The commission was offered to Appel as a palliative after a débâcle at the Town Hall in 1951: a mural in the canteen, commissioned by the Building Department, had to be boarded over when the Catering Department insisted that it would put people off their food. Edward Kienholz's *Beanery* is a near life-sized version of a poky Los Angeles bar. You can wander about in the dim light, examining the bric-a-brac. Rusty music scratches away in the juke-box. There's a murmur of conversation. A couple sit at the bar. Someone has passed out in the corner. A waitress clears the remnants of a disgusting meal. But all the faces of the figures are clock faces, and as you're the only thing that moves it is a surreal and rather disorientating experience. Luckily, the real bar (bright and airy) is just across the corridor.

Leaving the museum, turn right at the main entrance and then right again down the side of the museum. A gate leads into the small

Sculpture Garden. You can't help noticing the American Richard Serra's 12 m high Sight Point. The best place to view these three precariously balanced sheets of steel is from inside the sculpture itself.

There's not much else to detain you in the Sculpture Garden. Walk back out of the gate and turn right into **Museumplein**. *Turn right again and walk up the side of the square to the Concertgebouw.*

The city's greatest cultural institutions border Museumplein—the Rijksmuseum (see Walk II) and Concertgebouw at either end, the Overholland, Van Gogh and Stedelijk Museums up one side—but none of their main entrances opens onto the square. 'Holland's shortest motorway' roars bang through the middle of it. The green patches are all bald and the concrete patches covered with graffiti. In the summer young men thunder around the bits of tarmac playing basketball. Older ones head for the sandier patches to play boules. During the 1990 Van Gogh Centenary Exhibition, Museumplein was the site of the Van Gogh Village, a collection of tents and temporary buildings peddling Vincent paraphernalia and expensive cups of coffee to the hapless crowds waiting to get in. It obliterated the view of the Overholland, an excellent little museum of 'work on paper'. For a whole year hardly anyone went there at all. The owner (it's a private museum) has closed it in protest—permanently, he says.

As you hurry through the square, stop briefly to look at the *Vrouwen van Ravensbrück* memorial, a series of vertical steel slabs erected to commemorate the 92,000 women who died in concentration camps during the Second World War. The text translates as 'For those women who until the bitter end refused to accept fascism'. The flickering light and thumping sound emanating from the sculpture are intended as a beacon to call people to the monument and to continue the fight. Diagonally across the square is Heleen Levano's *Hel van Vuur* (Hell of Fire), a symbol of the persecution of the gypsies. A plaque at the Concertgebouw end commemorates the 400,000 who attended an anti-nuclear rally in 1981. (Museumplein achieves a rare popularity during demonstrations as one of the few places in Amsterdam able to contain a sizeable crowd).

The **Concertgebouw** at the southern end of the square was designed by A.L. van Gendt (one of the collaborators on the Centraal Station design) and completed in 1888. It is solid Dutch neo-Renaissance; no French frivolity here—indeed, the few urns and obelisks he included in the design either never went up for lack of funds, or have fallen off through lack of funds. The twin staircase towers are intended to harmonize with Cuypers' Rijksmuseum across the way (more out of toadyism than artistic integrity—Cuypers headed the committee that chose the design). Busts of Beethoven, Bach and Sweelinck (Holland's one claim to musical fame) grace the façade. The gilded lyre on top is a 1960s replacement of the original (which fell off). The entrance is no longer through the front, but through a shiny glass extension built in 1988 as part of a complete renovation of the building, which had been subsiding dangerously. The portico, classical shapes and colouring of the extension mean that it does fit in reasonably well and it certainly meets the General Manager's stipulation that if there was to be a new front door, he didn't want to have to hang an 'Entrance around the Corner' notice on the old one.

In the 1870s Amsterdam, a city with metropolitan aspirations, found itself without a concert hall and with Brahms's admonition ringing in its ears: '*Ihr seid liebe Leute aber schlechte Musikanten*' (You are lovely people but awful musicians). The government maintained that art was not its business, so it was a committee of private citizens that raised the money, bought some cheap land outside the city limits next to an evil-smelling candle factory and commissioned van Gendt (more for his figures than his design). Van Gendt prided himself on being a salesman rather than an artist and was completely unmusical. It is ironic that he should have produced a concert hall with possibly the best acoustics in the world. The area soon became very fashionable. The candle factory was replaced by ostentatious mansions and every Thursday the streets would be crammed with the carriages of season-ticket holders.

Under the baton of conductors like Mengelberg (who was sacked for his Nazi sympathies in 1945 after 50 years service) and Haitink, the resident Royal Concertgebouw Orchestra has become world famous. If you're passing on a Wednesday pop in for a free 'lunchconcert' (12.30 pm, though it's a good idea to be there by 12). These are usually recitals given in the *Kleine Zaal* (Small Hall—a chamber music room upstairs), but if you're lucky you might catch the RCO itself in open rehearsal in the *Grote Zaal* (Big Hall—the main auditorium).

Walk down the left-hand side of the building following Jan Willem Brouwersstraat and turning left into Johannes Verhulststraat.

At the turn of the century there was a garden behind the Concertgebouw. On summer afternoons it would rustle with silk as Amsterdam's élite gathered for outdoor concerts. Those (literally) outside the charmed circle would have to crush around the railings. In 1922 the garden was sold to developers to raise money for a pension fund for the orchestra, and disappeared behind a housing development. If you walk a short way up J. Verhulststraat and look back you'll get the only view now available of the little gilded mermaid blowing her trumpet on top of the *Kleine Zaal*.

> *Turn left into Jacob Obrechtstraat and carry on down to Jacob Obrechtplein. The block-like* **synagogue** *(1930) on the square isn't usually open to the public, but if you spot an open door, nip in for a look at the vibrant expressionist stained glass windows by W. Bogtman, whose Haarlem studio is responsible for much of Amsterdam's best modern stained glass. Leave the square by Bartholomeus Ruloffsstraat, turn right into Johannes M. Coenenstraat and cross the bridge. On the other side of the Amstel Canal lies the* **Nieuw Zuid** *(New South).*

The Nieuw Zuid was created by the architect H. P. Berlage (1856–1934), the father of modern Dutch architecture (see p. 66), after a new law had revolutionized Amsterdam housing conditions. In 1915–17 he drew up a plan of wide avenues and narrow side streets that reflected the 17th-century canals. He died before he could implement it, and his work was taken on with even greater enthusiasm by Michel de Klerk and Pieter Kramer, architects of what became known as the Amsterdam School. De Klerk was a working-class *wunderkind* headhunted from primary school to begin work with the city's leading architectural firm at the age of 14. He and Kramer set out to design buildings that were, in his words, 'sensationally shocking'. They were successful. When the Nieuw Zuid was finished nobody wanted to live there. The area eventually became a ghetto for Jews fleeing persecution in Germany. (The Frank family lived on Merwedeplein before going into hiding). In the past few years there's been a revival of interest in the Amsterdam School. Houses, bridges and even public lavatories are being declared national monuments.

In reacting against their sober, rational Dutch predecessors, the Amsterdam School produced an idiosyncratic cross between Old Dutch and Art Nouveau, which has led to some quirky and amusing, but also rather beautiful building. You can see why they're sometimes called the 'Gaudis of the North'. As you walk through the New South a checklist of some of their innovations might help you to recognize and enjoy the style.

Shape
Their whimsical brick buildings are instantly recognizable by the curves and bulges of their façades. Entire blocks were seen as one building—waves of roofs and balconies give a delightful sense of horizontal movement. Soaring chimneys and stairways accentuate the vertical lines.

Bricks
Decorative, polychromatic, almost sculptural brickwork is used lavishly. Like Berlage, the new builders used 'honest' Dutch materials of wood and brick, but the buildings are constructed around a reinforced concrete frame, so the bricks can do what they like. The pleats and folds earned the movement's work the nickname *schortjesarchitectuur* (apron architecture). Straight edges are often softened by a frill of vertically placed roofing tiles.

Windows and Doors
Odd parabolic and trapeziform windows and angulated carved doors contrast startlingly with the general symmetry of the buildings.

Sculptures
Stone and brick sculptures are integrated into the building's design, especially at corners and on bridges. In the Nieuw Zuid these are usually the gnome-like mythical figures by Hildo Krop (1884–1970). Krop was the municipal sculptor for many years and his chunky work is all over Amsterdam. Recently it was revealed that for much of that time he was working for the Soviet KGB, and it's even been suggested that he was involved in the recruitment of Anthony Blunt and other famous British spies.

Details
House numbers, letterboxes and hoists are all carefully designed to fit into the larger scheme. Egyptian and oriental influences are especially evident in the metalwork.

> *Having crossed the bridge (by Kramer, sculptures by Krop), cross Apollolaan. In 1969 there was great commotion at the **Amsterdam Hilton** (to the right, up Apollolaan) when John Lennon and Yoko Ono staged a week-long 'Bed-in', the starting point of their world campaign for peace. For f1500 a night you can stay in the same room as the late Beatle, surrounded by John and Yoko memorabilia.*

*The desultory trio on the central island of Apollolaan commemo-
rates the shooting on the spot of 29 people by the Germans in reprisal
for Resistance action in 1944. Walk across to Beethovenstraat, a chic,
but not very imaginative, shopping street mainly frequented by
children of diplomats and bored expatriate housewives. Before turning left into* **Gerrit van der Veenstraat***, look west and you will
see the clocktower marking the schoolbuilding used as the Gestapo
headquarters during the war. It was here that the Frank family were
brought after their capture.*

Gerrit van der Veen—sculptor and Resistance hero—led the raid on the
Amsterdam Registry in 1943 in an attempt to burn all the records. The
mission was only partially successful, but the firemen who were called to
the blaze obligingly drenched what was left. Van der Veen was later shot
in the back while attempting to free some Resistance prisoners, arrested
a few days later and executed in the dunes near Bloemendaal. The
building that rises out of the surrounding domestic architecture at the
end of the street like a huge ocean liner is the **Sociale Vezekeringsbank**
(Social Insurance Bank, built 1937–9). It has an almost magical monu-
mentality, but doesn't seem at all out of place. Its shape is even echoed in
the curved windows of the houses towards the end of the terrace on
either side.

*Walk down the right-hand side of the Sociale Vezekeringsbank and
turn right over the bridge (another by Kramer). The* **Apollohal** *(a
sportshall) on the corner before the bridge is an early example of
Nieuwe Zakelijkheid (the functional concrete-and-glass style that
began in the 1920s, begetter of many 1960s monstrosities). Neglected
and rather sad, it's hard to judge whether it was ever pleasing to look
at. Across the water the* **Amstel Boat Club** *reverberates with the
hearty shouts of boaties. They brave the vilest of weather and seem to
resent the occasional winter freezes when the rest of the world comes
out to skate. Walk on down Churchill-laan—a leafy avenue where
even the trams appear to run over grass. Look out for little sculptures
by Krop set into the walls, expressionist lettering and some bizarre
front doors. Turn left at Maasstraat, then turn right on the canal
and over the white footbridge. Turn right and immediately left into
Pieter Lodewijk Takstraat.*

On the side of the building opposite the footbridge are powerful sculptures of rearing horses and straining figures—*De Geboorte van de Daad*

171

(The Birth of the Deed), some of Krop's best work. Once you turn the corner you're in a patch of streets and squares designed entirely by Kramer and De Klerk. In 1918 the housing association *De Dageraad* (Daybreak) gave the young men free rein to design the neighbourhood. Strikingly curved staircase towers, wavy rooftops, jutting sharp-edged windows and fancy coloured brickwork are the results of this freedom from restriction. The buildings are wonderful to look at, but residents complain that their furniture doesn't fit in the odd-shaped rooms.

Walk anti-clockwise around **Burgemeester Tellegenstraat** *and cut left through Coöperatiehof.*

The two crescents of Burgemeester Tellegenstraat are completely symmetrical. Look at the lettering in the doorways. You'll occasionally even find corresponding lettering on one side reflected in mirror image on the other.

Walk on to Thérèse Schwartzestraat, turn left and walk to the **Thérèse Schwartzeplein.**

De Klerk died in his 30s. The barn-like houses on Thérèse Schwartzeplein are among the last he built. Tiny butterfly-wing windows interrupt vast sheets of yellow brick (it must be dark in there). The houses are linked by bulbous little balconies and tall arrow-shaped chimneys.

Leave the square along Paletstraat, turn right along the canal and walk along as far as Tweede Van der Helststraat where you turn right (behind the towering, blank Hotel Okura). Wander up past (or through) the tiny, but rather pretty Sarphatipark (named after a 19th-century philanthropist who gave Amsterdam an efficient rubbish disposal service, an hygienic bread factory and its own Crystal Palace; see p. 41). Carry on up what is now Eerste Van der Helststraat as far as Albert Cuypstraat. The area between the Amstel Kanaal and the Singelgracht is known as **De Pijp** *(The Pipe) for the long thin passages between the 19th-century tenement houses.*

Once a slum, it's now a lively neighbourhood populated by artists and immigrant communities. The streets seem to get brighter, busier and noisier as you get closer to the **Albert Cuyp Market**, where it all explodes into a cacophony of national musics, a kaleidoscope of colour and a press of eager shoppers that stretches for over a kilometre. Eating seems to be an important reason to be here. Between the piles of silk, gaudy modern clothes and cheap shoes, boxes of dried herbs and teas, people slip raw herrings down their throats, guzzle home-made choco-lates, queue for freshly cooked waffles, taste farm cheeses and stock up on fish, fruit and vegetables for even greater feasting at home. Behind the stalls there's yet another layer of life—tacky clothing shops, ethnic stores and cheap Indian and Surinamese restaurants. An old hippie busker sings *exactly* the same repertoire, on the same corner, every day. To any stall-holder who complains, he points out that their stock doesn't vary much either.

> *After whatever market shopping you might do, leave by Eerste Van der Helststraat (straight across from where you arrived). Walk on up to the canal. The building on the left is the* **Heineken Brewery***, birthplace of Heineken beer.*

The brewery, established here in 1867, stopped production on this site only a few years ago when Amsterdam began to drink more than the brewery could produce. The building is now a **brewery museum** (tel 670 9111; guided tours only: May–Sept Mon–Fri 9, 9.45 and 10 am, 1, 1.45 and 2.30 pm; Oct–April Mon–Fri 9.30 and 11 am, but phone to check; allow 2 hours; adm *f*2, which goes to charity). Smart guides lead you through the stables (old dray horses *in situ*) and past huge copper vats. You learn how beer is made and how the Heineken family made its fortune. The real purpose of the visit for many people, however, seems to be the free beer at end of the tour.

> *If two hours of hops and dray horses doesn't appeal to you, turn left along the front of the brewery and cross the canal to Wetering-plein—a rather hectic traffic intersection. On the left,* De Gevallen Hoornblazer *(The Fallen Trumpeter) is a poignant tribute to a number of people shot by the Germans and left on this spot on 24 March 1945 in a last-minute display of Nazi power as liberation was becoming inevitable. There's also a Krop sculpture (Mother Earth) and a monument erected in appreciation for aid given during the disastrous 1953 Zeeland flood. Leave the square by the corner diagonally opposite the bridge (dodging trams and cyclists that come from all directions) and walk to the right along* **Weteringschans***.*

The concrete and glass monstrosity that looms at the end of Wetering-schans is the **Nederlandse Bank** built in 1968 by M.F. Duintjer (he has a string of unpopular buildings to his name, including the 'coal scuttle church' in Amsterdam West). A cylindrical mirror tower, added in the 1980s, has made it even worse.

Escape left to the quiet gables and humpback bridges of the **Reguliersgracht**.

A little way up Reguliersgracht you pass along the side of **Amstelveld**, a secluded square with a white wooden church and small Monday flower market, tucked away from the surrounding bustle. The recently restored 17th-century **Amstelkerk** has a popular left-wing preacher and is the one of the few churches in central Amsterdam that packs in a congregation. It isn't continuously open to the public, but sometimes stages chamber recitals. Further up Reguliersgracht, at nos. 57–9 and 63, you come across two elaborately carved façades designed by I. Gosschalk in the late 19th-century—rather like two extravagant sisters flanking a maiden aunt. The one is a wild combination of Old Dutch and German, and the other a slightly more modest mingling of Old Dutch with Old English and Queen Anne.

Turn left to follow **Keizersgracht**, *one of the grand 17th-century canals. Keep to the right-hand side of the canal. The wealthy 19th-century art collector, C.J. Fodor, left his collection (housed in a converted warehouse at Keizersgracht 609) to the Stedelijk Museum. They whisked it away to Museumplein and use the* **Fodor Museum** *on Keizersgracht to display contemporary Amsterdam art (open 11–5 daily, adm usually f1).*

Lots of good artists—Dutch and international—live in Amsterdam, so the exhibitions (which change every 3–5 weeks) are good. Watch out especially for the annual summer exhibition of work bought by the city council. If you're beginning to feel like a rest, the museum's tranquil garden will be a welcome surprise. (You're not often able to get into one of these grand old canal houses to see what big gardens they conceal from passers-by).

Turn right into **Vijzelstraat**.

In the 1920s Vijzelstraat was a tiny shopping street, in places only a few metres wide. Over fifty 16th and 17th-century houses were demolished down the west side to turn it into a traffic thoroughfare. The council promised a mixture of housing, businesses and shops in the rebuilding programme. To the Amsterdammers' horror, the first building to go up, on land leased from the council, was the huge brick Nederlandse Handelsmaatschappij (Netherlands Trading Company). Ten days before the opening, the company's president donated his Herengracht mansion to the city as an official home for the mayor. A whole wall of heavyweight commercial buildings has since gone up—all the way down to Muntplein. Each has caused a storm of protest.

Walk down the right hand side of Vijzelstraat towards Muntplein. Before turning right into Reguliersbreestraat pop your nose into the **apothecary** *on the corner. A remnant of the old Vijzelstraat, it's stuffed to the ceiling with scents, spices and cough drops that can cure at twenty paces. At Reguliersbreestraat 26 you'll find the* **Tuschinski Cinema**.

Abraham Tuschinski, a Jewish refugee from Poland, saw his first film in 1910 and immediately wanted to own a cinema. He got a friend to write to Pathé in French, requesting the machinery and rights to show films. His first 'bioscope' opened in 1911 in a disused seamen's church with a converted outside lavatory as the box office. But Tuschinski wanted a cinema where his 'guests' could lose themselves in another world. In 1921 he was wealthy enough to achieve his dream. You walk through a soaring Art-Deco façade with flagpoles, camp statuary and curly iron lamps into an interior that lurches between heady luxury and high kitsch. It's a stylistic cocktail of five different colours of marble, Persian carpets, thousands of electric lights, wall decorations, stained glass and exotic *objets d'art*. You can go on a guided tour (Sun and Mon during July and Aug, 10.30 am, *f*5), or come back later and see a film. Ask for a balcony ticket in the main cinema. It doesn't matter what's showing, the interval will be reward enough.

The concrete and glass **Cineac** (opposite the Tuschinski) seems from another century. It's hard to believe it was built only 13 years later. The architect, J. Duiker, was a movie fanatic. The auditorium opened directly onto the street and the projectionist could be seen from outside through the glass wall on the first floor. Rebuilding in the 1960s and 1980s has all but destroyed the original concept.

Reguliersbreestraat opens onto **Rembrandtsplein**.

Rembrandtsplein was a butter market until the mid 19th-century when a group of worthy burghers plonked a statue (Amsterdam's first) in the middle and grew some grass around it. Cafés sprang up. Variety artistes from the halls along the Amstel would meet their agents at the posh Café Kroon, then retreat across the square to the darker recesses of the Hotel Schiller where they felt more at home among the artists, writers and other friends of proprietor Frits Schiller (whose paintings still decorate the walls). Nowadays the square is a favourite after-work stopover and a magnet to tourists, who come for the relaxed Amsterdam conviviality. You can lie about on the grass (amongst masses of tulips if it's spring) or sit and drink at one of the pavement cafés. Traffic is banished from most of the square but buskers keep the noise level high. When the sun sets, things get even livelier. The cafés change gear as the night staff come on duty. Music systems are turned on full. Jazz from one corner, Dutch sing-a-long from another. Congas of drunken Dutchmen snake out of pubs and around bemused policemen. Spanish schoolgirls move about in wide-eyed groups. At one bar the three barmen break out at intervals into a well rehearsed dance routine. Whether you're carousing with the revellers, or just sitting and watching it all, it's a cheerful place to stop for a drink.

> *Leave the square at Bakkerstraat, turn right and cross the Amstel via the Blauwbrug (and its maritime inspired decorations) to reach* **Waterlooplein**.

Waterlooplein was once the heart of the Jewish neighbourhood. For decades after the war it lay desolate. When the city council announced plans (in 1979) to build a combined city hall and opera house on the site, there was public outrage (see Topics, pp. 72–6). The city hall was ugly, the opera house seemed unnecessary, and the few people still living in the neighbourhood would have to be evicted. The building was nick-named the Stopera—from *Stadhuis* (city hall) and opera. 'Stop the Stopera' campaigns were held all over Amsterdam but, as always, the council won. The new **Muziektheater** (the opera house) opened in 1986, followed two years later by the Stadhuis. The city hall is indeed bland and ugly, but most Amsterdammers grudgingly admit to the beauty of the Muziektheater. Its glass walls, sweeping stairways, soft pink colour scheme and marble coliseum-like shell look their best in the early evening. As the light fades, the whole building seems to glow. The artists themselves are delighted with the state-of-the-art equipment and huge dressing rooms. There are even colour-coded stairways backstage (yellow for opera, pink for ballet and blue for technicians). But acoustics experts from around the world haven't been able to solve the (severe) problems in the auditorium and there have been some massive architectural blunders backstage—the ballet rehearsal rooms have ceilings so low that dancers can't practise lifts, the orchestra doesn't have a rehearsal room at all and the scenery lifts are at the opposite end of the building from the loading entrances. Both the Netherlands Ballet and

Opera are resident, and the programme is varied, with many international visitors (see Entertainment and Nightlife).

In a passageway connecting the Stadhuis and Muziektheater three water columns show the tides at IJmuiden and Vlissingen (below knee-level) and the sobering sight of the level reached during the 1953 Zeeland flood (way above your head). You can walk down a flight of stairs, below sea level, and touch the bronze knob (its position was calculated in the 17th century) which represents the **zero point** from which heights in much of Europe are calculated.

Behind the Stopera, and creeping slowly around it, is the Waterlooplein fleamarket—but that's best saved for Walk III. Pop into the post-modern Café Dantzig which overlooks the river on the Amstel/Zwanenburgwal corner of the Stadhuis, or wander back across the bridge and end the walk café-crawling on Rembrandtsplein.

Walk VI

Van Gogh, Diamonds and Antiques

Art-Nouveau lamps in the Café Américain

Van Gogh Museum—Coster Diamond Factory—Pieter Cornelisz.
Hooftstraat—Vondelpark—Film Museum—Hollandse Manege—
Leidseplein—Spiegelkwartier—Keizersgracht—Rommelmarkt—
De Looier Antiques Market

Few artists have a national museum all to themselves, but there's a sad
irony in the long queue that snakes back under the simple silver lettering
'Vincent van Gogh' to one side of Amsterdam's top tourist attraction.
The lonely artist, who sold just two paintings and got only one good
review in his lifetime, is now the still point in a money-spinning world of
multi-million dollar picture sales, bizarre art theft, pop songs, novels,
films and tacky souvenirs.

This walk gives you a close insight into Van Gogh, then whisks you out
to a more frivolous Amsterdam. You can relax in the park, become party
to the city's best kept secret, and have hashish with your coffee on the
Leidseplein. The walk then takes you to classy antiques shops in the
Spiegelkwartier and to the Keizersgracht's modern galleries. After exploring a network of fanciful shopping alleys, you saunter down a dapper
little canal and end the day looking for bargains in an indoor antiques
market. It's a good walk for a Saturday: the museum is open all day,
Vondelpark is festive and the markets are well-stocked and buzzing.

178

You'll find most shops closed on a Monday, and on Friday the De Looier Antiques Market is shuttered and grim.

Start: Take Tram 2, 3, 5 or 12 to the corner of Van Baerlestraat and Paulus Potterstraat. You can also take Tram 6, 7 or 10 to the Rijksmuseum and cut through to Museumplein.

Walking Time: About 3 hours, though that depends on how long you linger in the shops. Allow at least another hour for the Van Gogh Museum.

LUNCH/CAFÉS

't Ronde Blauwe Theehuis, Vondelpark. 'The Round Blue Teahouse' is an odd piece of 1930s New Functionalist architecture in the middle of the Vondelpark. It's a good place for a coffee or beer and a cheap (if uneventful) sandwich.

Café Vertigo is in the cellar of the Film Museum and spills out into the park in good weather. From inside you can see part of the exhibition, and the cuisine surpasses that of any museum restaurant in town. There are even appropriate theme menus during film festivals.

Hollandse Manege Café, Vondelstraat 140, overlooks the arena of the elegant 19th-century riding school. It's a quiet place to sip coffee and watch the horses, though there are occasional invasions of eleven-year-olds in jodhpurs. Coffee/beer ƒ1.75.

Café Américain, American Hotel, Leidseplein. Art-Nouveau grand café. Once the hangout of Amsterdam's literati, it's now visited mainly by tourists, but is just the right environment for a pot of fresh coffee and an extravagantly gooey cake. It also serves snacks and fuller meals. Beer ƒ3.75, coffee ƒ5.50 a pot.

Café Cox, beneath the Stadsschouwburg. Named after the theatre's director Cox Habbema. It serves scrumptious salads and light meals.

The Bulldog, Leidseplein. A 1970s institution. One of the first places allowed to sell marijuana on the premises. It's now a slick commercial enterprise with alcohol upstairs, dope downstairs and even a souvenir shop. Coffee ƒ2.75, beer ƒ3.00.

Le Soleil, Nieuwe Spiegelstraat 50. Traditional Dutch pancakes (sweet and savoury) served at communal tables. The chairs are painted in the pastel pink and green enamels you usually find in seaside tearooms and the walls are cluttered with Art-Deco knick-knacks. Coffee ƒ2.25.

Coffeeshop Françoise, Kerkstraat 176, in the Spiegelkwartier. Run and frequented mainly by women. It's calm and friendly, with classical

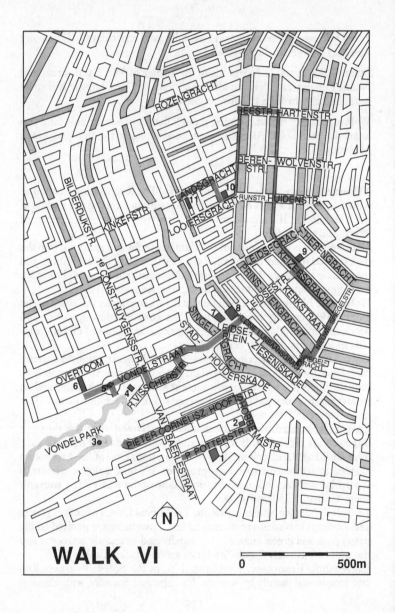

ROZENGRACHT

REESTR. HARTENSTR.

BEREN- WOLVENSTR.
STR.

RUNSTR. HUIDENSTR.

ELANDSGRACHT

BILDERDIJKSTR.

KINKERSTR.

LOOIERSGRACHT

1e CONST. HUYGENSSTR.

LEIDSEGRACHT

HERENGRACHT

KEIZERSGRACHT

PRINSENGRACHT

KERKSTRAAT

LEIDSESTR.

NIEUWE SPIEGELSTR.

SINGELGRACHT

LEIDSE-
PLEIN

MARN. LIJNBAANSGRACHT

SPIEGEL
GRACHT

ZIESENISKADE

OVERTOOM

VONDELSTRAAT

STADHOUDERSKADE

VAN BAERLESTRAAT

F. VISSCHERSTR.

6

5

4

3

PIETER CORNELISZ. HOOFTSTR.

P. POTTERSTR.

JOBBEMASTR.

2

1

VONDELPARK

N

WALK VI

0   500m

music, a speciality tea menu (from mango to Earl Grey) and home-cooked traditional dishes. Coffee *f*2.

The Metz Café, corner of Leidsestraat and Keizersgracht. Amsterdam from high up is a rare sight. The glass cupola on top of one of its poshest department stores is a good place to sip a coffee and change your perspective of the city—but not for a meal. It dishes up dull railway-station fare. Service is indifferent until you try to take a photograph. Coffee *f*2.75, beer *f*3.

Pompadours, Huidenstraat 12. A chocolaterie and patisserie. The interior—hardly bigger than an average kitchen—somehow incorporates carved oak panels, a staircase and a balustrade from an 18th-century town hall near Liège. You can sit in this matchbox splendour and choose from a selection of nearly 50 different hand-made choccies, or (and?) have a pastry with your coffee. Coffee *f*2.25.

Café Aas van Bokalen, Keizersgracht 335. Good brown café with an arty crowd and a restaurant-sized menu. Coffee *f*2, beer *f*2.25.

The alleys criss-crossing the canals, from Huidenstraat to Reestraat are a rich hunting-ground for good restaurants, should you wish to return for an evening meal (see Food and Drink).

☆   ☆   ☆   ☆   ☆

If you've arrived on Tram 2, 3, 5 or 12, walk down Paulus Potterstraat—the Van Gogh Museum is halfway down, on the right. If you've taken Tram 6, 7 or 10, then you'll need to cross the Singelgracht and Stadhouderskade and walk through the walkway under the Rijksmuseum. This brings you to Museumplein. A walk up the right-hand side of Museumplein will bring you to the museum.

The **Rijksmuseum Vincent Van Gogh** (National Vincent Van Gogh Museum, open Mon–Sat 10–5, Sun 1–5; adm *f*10) has really cornered the Van Gogh market with 200 paintings, 500 drawings, a collection of

---

KEY TO MAP OF WALK VI

1. Van Gogh Museum
2. Coster Diamonds
3. Round Blue Teahouse
4. Film Museum
5. Vondelkerk
6. Hollandse Manege

7. American Hotel
8. Stadsschouwburg
9. Metz Department Store
10. Indoor Fleamarket
11. De Looier Indoor Antiques Market

works by Van Gogh's contemporaries, the letters from Vincent to his brother Theo, Vincent's collections of Japanese woodcuts and 19th-century engravings, a press archive dating from 1899—and publishing copyright for the lot. The museum was completed in 1973 and is based on an initial drawing by the influential Dutch architect, Gerrit Rietveld (see p. 66), who died before working the plan through. Brave efforts by later architects to realize his rather sketchy ideas have produced a hard-edged and unsympathetic building. The paintings seem flung to the far sides of a vast, underventilated concrete box with an exhausting central stairway.

The building is not big enough to display the entire collection at any one time. Works from the permanent collection are displayed in rotation—usually in rough chronological order, though sometimes grouped according to subject matter. The most important works are, however, on display most of the time, and you're also quite likely to find a temporary exhibition highlighting some aspect of the painter's life or work. For ƒ6.50 you can get a cassette guide to the collection (you'll need a deposit—credit card, passport or ƒ50) and there's an insubstantial catalogue for ƒ12.50. The museum has an exceptionally good library, where you can view photographs of Vincent's letters to Theo. Training courses, and all sorts of activities to help working artists, are held regularly. (Details are available from the museum).

The darkened **Printroom** *on the second floor is a good place to begin.*

Here you can find Van Gogh's drawings and studies, and trace some of his influences—sketches by friends, pictures he copied and his collection of Japanese prints and magazine engravings. The selection on display changes frequently, but you can usually follow his development through some rather conventional Dutch landscapes, with all the expected perspectives, and studies of gnarled hands and heavily jowled peasant faces to the wild movement of *Women Dancing* (1885). Millet's *Labours of the Field* and woodcuts by Hiroshige and Kesai Yeisen clearly had an influence on some of Van Gogh's better known oils.

From the Printroom follow the signs to the start of the **Permanent Collection.**

Vincent van Gogh was born in 1853 in the tiny village of Zundert, near the Belgian border. We have an image of him as a wild, schizophrenic bohemian; a simpleton, out of touch with the world and reliant on his younger brother's handouts. This isn't the full truth. He came from an old Dutch family of clerics, naval officers and gallery owners. Though he was constantly at odds with his relations, and indeed offended almost everyone he met, he was in many ways part of the Establishment. He spoke three languages fluently, had a wide knowledge of European art and had the business acumen and connections needed to organize two exhibitions of friends' work in Paris. He signed himself 'Vincent' because he thought his surname, difficult for foreigners to pronounce, would be bad salesmanship. (You say it with two guttural 'gs'—'fun HGoHG'). Even the money he got from his art-dealer brother he excused as a business arrangement—an advance on the money Theo would one day make selling his work. Yet all his life he was desperately lonely, dogged by a sense of failure and frustrated by how few people appreciated his art. Towards the end he was beset by bouts of madness which left him exhausted and depressed. He was acutely sensitive to his surroundings. The colours, people, light or weather in one environment would become loathsome to him and the need to move would become consuming. Suddenly he'd up sticks and go—to the sun, to the city, to the country. These moves would often be reflected in a change in his work, so it's interesting to approach the paintings with some knowledge of what was going on in Van Gogh's life at the time.

Vincent's first job, at the age of sixteen, was as an assistant with the art dealer Goupil & Cie in The Hague. In 1873 he went to work at the London branch and was impressed by Constable, Turner and especially the Pre-Raphaelite John Everett Millais. An unhappy love affair made him grumpy at work. He began to be rude to customers about their taste, was shuttled between London and Paris and finally, despite family connections (his uncle was a partner in the firm), dismissed. Still obsessed by his English rose, he returned to Britain as a teacher, but was soundly rebuffed. She married someone else and he went back to Holland to work in a bookshop. He still didn't know what he wanted to do with his life. But in May 1877 it all suddenly seemed clear: following in his father's footsteps, he set off for Amsterdam to study theology. Greek and Latin proved an uphill struggle and he was entirely defeated by algebra; after less than a year he went to a crammer for evangelists in Brussels, where mathematical aptitude was not a prerequisite. But he couldn't preach either. Yet again the family pulled strings. The Brussels Evangelist Committee reluctantly sent him to prove his worth among the coalminers of the Borinage—a wasteland in south Belgium. After seven months he was dismissed for over-zealous involvement with the poor.

He stayed on in a hovel for another year, almost starving to death, and began to draw. He was 26 and had found his direction. His younger brother, Theo, rescued him and started to pay him the monthly allowance that was to be Vincent's only income for the rest of his life.

Van Gogh was largely self-taught, though he spent a brief period studying perspective and anatomy in Brussels in 1880. The following year he fell in love with his widowed cousin, Kee Vos. He walked to Amsterdam from his parents' home in south Holland, stormed into her father's house on the Keizersgracht and held his hand over a candle yelling: 'Let me see her for as long as I can hold my hand in the flame.' But Kee had fled. He left without seeing her and with a hole burned into his flesh. The incident caused a family row; he was thrown out of home and went to The Hague. Here he met members of the Hague School of painting, a movement characterized by muddy colours and gloomy skies. He was given lessons by one of its leading members, Anton Mauve (a cousin by marriage) and was also much influenced by Jozef Israëls' earthy studies of peasants. He was especially friendly with a young painter called George Breitner, who later became known as one of the best Amsterdam Impressionists. They discovered a mutual interest in Zola and together drew the street life in the seedier parts of town. An uncle who had commissioned twelve views of the city was horrified by Vincent's unconventional approach and refused to pay up. The relationship with Mauve grew tense when Van Gogh began to reject the older painter's advice, and family relations soured on a wider scale when it became known that he was living with the prostitute Sien Hoornik 'in order to reform her'.

In September 1883 Van Gogh suddenly left The Hague for the countryside of Drenthe in the north of Holland. He had begun to paint in oils, but still with a muddy Dutch palette. The good people of Drenthe thought him a dangerous lunatic and a tramp, and refused to pose for him—so this became a period of landscapes with small figures in the distance. After a few months, loneliness drove him to a reconciliation with his parents and he went back south to live with them in Nuenen. Weavers and peasants in the surrounding Brabant farmland were his dominant motif. The period culminated in the dim glow and gravy browns of *The Potato Eaters* (1885). Van Gogh loved this 'real peasant picture'—he felt you could smell the bacon, smoke and potato steam, and that the rough hands that dipped into the dish were the same hands that had dug the earth.

In *The Old Church Tower at Nuenen*, the tower stands crooked and solitary in a flat, empty churchyard. A few crows flutter against the overcast sky. Van Gogh painted it in May 1885, a few months after his father had been buried there, and just before it was demolished and all the wood—including the graveyard crosses—sold to peasants. His father had been an unpopular preacher in a declining sect. *Open Bible, Extinguished Candle and Book* (1885) has been seen as Vincent's homage to their difficult relationship. Next to the huge Bible and snuffed candle (a convention for death) is a French novel—something his father would not have allowed in the house.

Margot Begemann, a neighbour, took poison after her family had refused permission for her to marry Vincent. She survived, but Vincent got the blame and the village turned against him. He went to Antwerp, studied Rubens, covered his walls with Japanese prints and enrolled in the academy—which he left a few months later without ever learning of the academy's decision to demote him to the beginners' class. He then went to Paris. The first Theo (who was working there for Goupil & Cie) heard of the move was a note brought by a messenger asking him to meet Vincent in the Louvre. Vincent moved into Theo's tiny apartment, but was such a chaotic and irritating flatmate that Theo had to find somewhere bigger, with a separate studio space for his brother. The first few canvases in Paris (such as *View over Paris*, 1886) still use the Dutch browns and greys. But when Theo introduced him to a few Impressionist friends, the shock of their fresh, bright canvases changed Vincent for life. At first the colour creeps in gradually (*Woman Sitting in the Café du Tambourin*, 1887) but soon he is copying the flat colours of the Japanese prints and painting some of the familiar bright self-portraits. He began to long for a harder light and a less hectic milieu than Paris could offer. Writing to his sister Wil about *Self-portrait at the Easel* (1888), he draws her attention to his sad expression. He's had enough of Paris and wants the sun. He gives himself pinkish-grey skin against a greyish-white wall, his tightly drawn features contrast with a bristly, unkempt, bright red beard. On the palette he holds are all the colours of the painting except this fiery orange of the beard.

On 20 February 1888 Vincent escaped to the Mediterranean warmth of Arles in the south of France. Here in the famous 'Yellow House', which he shared for a while with Gauguin, his best known works were painted. It is hard to believe that the raucous yellows and bright reds and blues of *Harvest at La Crau* were painted only three years after *The Potato Eaters*. Look closely at one of the versions of *Sunflowers*. Between the greens and yellows are bright streaks of ice blues, mauves and reds—

colours you never notice in the reproductions. Portraits of the postman, Roulin, and his wife are drenched in sun and colour. Even the *Night Café* has a bright, steamy heat. The solitary *Sower at Arles* works under an enormous yellow orb in a green and pink sky. The most ordinary things around him evoke intense response. *Vincent's Bedroom at Arles* is filled with a brilliant light but the smooth paintwork, the mauves and blues of the walls have a calming effect. (The green splodge under the chair is the result of a botched repair job after the painting was damaged in transit to Theo).

Van Gogh was very excited by Gauguin's arrival on 20 October 1888 and went to great pains to furnish his room comfortably. The money to do this, of course, came from Theo. *Gauguin's Chair* shows a piece Vincent bought for his friend (elaborate in comparison with his own). On the seat are novels intended to indicate Gauguin's spirituality and modernism. A candle burns as well as the gas light, to suggest Gauguin's fiery nature. Together they visited nearby towns such as Les Saintes-Maries-de-la-Mer, where Vincent painted *Boats on the Beach*. The small red, green and blue boats had reminded him of flowers. He paints them with the flat colours and definite lines of a Japanese print, while the sea eddies and swirls with a shimmering complexity of colouring.

Gauguin's stay was not a happy one. The two artists had tempestuous arguments. After a particularly violent dispute on Christmas Eve, Vincent threatened Gauguin with a razor, then slashed off his own right ear and presented it to a prostitute who had complimented it. Gauguin left for Paris. Another nervous crisis followed Van Gogh's recuperation, and he was voluntarily admitted to the asylum of St-Paul-de-Mausole at Saint-Rémy. Paintings from this period—usually of fields around the asylum, the hospital garden or of individual trees and flowers—are in softer hues. In February 1890 Vincent painted *Branches of an Almond Tree in Blossom* for Theo's newly born son—blossom-laden branches stand out against an eggshell blue background. By May he felt well enough to leave the asylum, though he could only bear Paris for three days. He travelled to Auvers-sur-Oise where an eccentric art-lover, Dr Gachet, promised to keep an eye on him. But Vincent became more and more overwrought: his colours became harder, brush strokes more violent. In *Crows in the Wheatfields* (July 1890) it seems difficult for the birds to fly into the thick, dark sky. A path curves and goes nowhere. One of his last paintings, *Roots and Tree Trunks*, has even more disorientating perspectives and thick layers of paint in unexpected colours. The painter seems completely self-engrossed, and the viewer is quite alienated.

On 27 July Vincent went into the fields and shot himself, but he bungled even this. He staggered back to the inn where he was staying and died on 29 July, in Theo's arms. After a short illness, Theo himself died six months later, at the age of 32. The brothers are buried side by side in the churchyard at Auvers-sur-Oise.

Dedication, or desperation, drove Theo's widow—Johanna van Gogh-Bonger—to promote the works stacked all over her apartment. The art world began to take notice. In 1891 there was an exhibition in Brussels, followed by numerous others all over the Netherlands and in Paris. Paintings started to fetch high prices and national museums added Van Goghs to their collections. After Johanna's death in 1925 her son, Vincent's namesake, took over the collection and in 1931 put it on permanent exhibition in the Stedelijk Museum in Amsterdam. To prevent the break-up of the collection after his death, the Van Gogh Foundation was formed in 1960 and set about building the present museum. With three members of the Van Gogh family on the board of the foundation, there's a feeling that it's still very much a family concern—and Vincent, once the black sheep, is again part of the Establishment.

Turn right out of the museum past the quirky little statue of Van Gogh (by André Schaller, 1962) towards **Coster Diamonds**, *on the corner of Hobbemastraat (open daily 9–5; adm. free).*

Jews fleeing persecution in Antwerp set up the diamond-polishing industry in Amsterdam in the 16th century. Roaring trade with South Africa established it in the 19th century. (Diamond cutters would light their cigars with a ƒ10 note, more than the average weekly wage). The city is still a focus for diamond dealing and processing. What this means in practical terms is that you can buy the gems for half the price you'd pay in London or New York. All over the city factories invite you in to see the craftsmen at work in order to lure you into their salerooms.

Coster Diamonds is one of the biggest. The 'Koh-I-Noor' (Mountain of Light), one of the prize gems in the British crown jewels was cut here, and there's a glassy replica in the exhibition hall. Smart, uniformed hostesses conduct you on a short tour through the cutting and polishing works (done with whizzing discs coated with diamond dust and olive oil) and then propel you past a room temptingly labelled 'Self Service' (it turns out to be a café) into the jewellery shop. It's an interesting ten minutes, though if you want to buy it might be worth shopping around (see pp. 240–1).

Turn left down the side of the Coster building into Hobbemastraat, and left again into **Pieter Cornelisz. Hooftstraat.**

Amsterdam's *chic*est shopping street is named after a 17th-century poet. It's one of the few streets in the city where you can confidently window shop without fear of stepping in dog turds. There are a few exotic delis, mouth-watering pastries and chocolates at Oldenbergs (no. 97), certificated Delft porcelain at Focke & Meltzer (no. 65) and some elegant, but dull, cafés. Mostly it's clothes: shops for the hip toddler or the fashion-anxious adolescent. If you're past voting age then things range from well-cut classics to the outré (well, almost). All the favourite names (Armani, Gucci, Hamnet) can be found. Some (like MaxMara and Stephane Kèlian) have their own shops. P.C. Hooftstraat and Van Baerlestraat, which crosses it further up, are also home to some of the better Dutch designers—Edgar Vos, Rob Kroner and Sissy Boy.

P.C. Hooftstraat leads right into the **Vondelpark**.

Joost van Vondel (1582–1674; pronounced in the way an old English army officer might say 'fondle') is proclaimed the Dutch answer to Shakespeare. He excelled in ornate poems in celebration of public events, clocking up over a thousand lines for the opening of the Town Hall alone. The lack of action in his dramas is notorious: he went in for static pictorial representations accompanied by long flowery descriptions of anything exciting. His play *Gijsbrecht van Amstel* is a Dutch literary classic. It's said that one of the scenes inspired Rembrandt's *Night Watch*. By all accounts the Master would have had quite enough time to paint it during the performance. From humble beginnings in his father's busy hosiery shop on the edge of the red-light district, Vondel built up a considerable reputation and small fortune. The former counted for little in mercantile Amsterdam when his son squandered the latter. At the age of 70 he had to go back to work in the city pawnbrokers. He was sacked after 10 years service for writing poetry in office hours and finally, in his eighties, was granted a state pension. He died at 92 of hypothermia, and suggested his own epitaph:

> *Hier ligt Vondel zonder Rouw,*
> *Hij is gestorven van de kou.*
> Here lies Vondel, without regret [*or* unmourned],
> He was killed by the cold.

188

During the so-called 'Second Golden Age' at the end of the 19th century, when the butter market was turned into Rembrandtsplein and the neighbourhood around the museums was being developed as an upmarket residential area, some local burghers got together to commemorate the poet by creating the Vondelpark. It's a large park by Amsterdam standards and J.D. Kocher's informal English landscaping gives it calm, graceful lines and wide perspectives. Curved tree-lined avenues, irregularly shaped lakes and ponds, little furrow-like paths through shrubberies, hidden gardens and wide stretches of lawn attract Amsterdammers from all over the city—especially at weekends. A lone accordionist sits on a bench and plays for the ducks. Refugee guitarists from South America play heartrending tunes, homesick for a stronger sunlight. Jugglers meet to learn, practise and show off. There's a party atmosphere whenever the sun shines, and in the summer the festivities go on well into the night with concerts, theatre performances and an open-air cinema. On holidays (especially Queen's Day) enjoyment reaches carnival pitch.

There are dainty bridges, a few sculptural surprises and some odd architecture to catch your eye. As you enter the park, you can see, across the pond, one of the more attractive examples of Nieuwe Zakelijkheid (Functionalist) architecture: H.J. Baanders' **'t Ronde Blauwe Theehuis** (Round Blue Teahouse), a cross between a pagoda and a flying saucer that seems to hover over the water. Across the way Vondel himself, in badly fitting laurels, looks gouty, prosperous and entirely oblivious of the Muses playing about his ankles. His ornate pedestal was made in 1867 by P.J.H. Cuypers (architect of the Centraal Station and Rijksmuseum).

*The pavilion (to your right as you enter the park) was designed in 1881 by P.J. and W. Hamer, and is now the **Netherlands Film Museum** (Museum open Tues–Sun 1–8.30, adm. f2.50; Cinema Box Office open Mon–Fri 8.30am–¼hr before last film ends, Sat from 1pm, Sun from 11am; see press for details of film times; entrance from f6).*

The first director, Jan de Vaal, was a voracious but secretive collector. He hoarded his treasures and seemed wary of the outside world. The result was that not many people bothered about the film museum until the dynamic duo—director Hoos Blotkamp and film buff Eric de Kuyper—took over in the late 1980s and discovered an archive of world significance. Funding was secured, the building was revamped, the long

189

process of cataloguing begun (unearthing such gems as colour silent movies) and the occasional screenings were boosted to three shows a day. There are all sorts of special events and films are shown in the original language. On summer Saturdays there are free screenings on the terrace (around 10 pm), when you can buy a beer and have a giggle at Charlie Chaplin or Abbott and Costello. There are small displays of technical equipment and posters, and the main hall is worth a peek. The interior is from Amsterdam's first cinema, the Cinema Parisien built in 1910. The Parisien had declined ungracefully into a porn pit when the daughter of the original owner heard, in 1987, that it was about to be gutted by the hotel next door. Armed with coffee flask and screwdriver she went to rescue the interior (still intact after a 1930s redecoration) and, aided by the Monuments Trust, the old atmosphere was bottled and transferred to the Film Museum. The library, with a good selection of magazines and reference works and a stash of posters and publicity material, is in the building alongside the pavilion (open Tues–Fri 10–5).

Leave the park by the gate next to the Film Museum. The grand 19th-century Gothic of the **Vondelkerk** *(Heilige Hartkerk) fills a tiny oval in Vondelstraat. The architect, P.J.H Cuypers, was highly respected for his churches, and this is acknowledged as one of his best. Unfortunately it's been converted to offices, so the interior is lost. Turn left down Vondelstraat. The houses at nos. 73–9 were also designed by Cuypers. The tiled tableaux on the wall show the architect, the mason and the jealous critic. The motto translates as: 'Jan conceives it, Piet realizes it, Claes tears it apart. Oh, who cares?'*

Further up Vondelstraat, at no. 140, through the arch and up a long passage lies one of Amsterdam's best kept secrets. As you walk up towards the black door at the end of the passage, you'll notice a clue—the earth and cumin-musty smell of horses. Open the door and immediately you are in the vast, light and eerily silent **Hollandse Manege** *(open daily, usually from 10 am–midnight).*

The architect, A.L. van Gendt (who also designed the Concertgebouw), was influenced by the Spanish Riding School in Vienna. The beautifully plastered interior, with horses' heads worked into the classical design and elegant open iron roofing, comes as a complete surprise.

Walk up the wide staircase (to the left) past marble vases and gilded mirrors, and you come to two more doors.

190

The one marked 'Tribune' leads to a balcony overlooking the arena. Sawdust muffles all sound and the occasional sharp command from the instructor is all that breaks the thick silence. The door marked 'Foyer' takes you to a café that runs the width of the building. It has the relaxed grandeur of a palace stables. The wooden floor is dusty; there's even an odd wisp of straw. The tall smoke-yellowed walls are encrusted with plaster flowers and graces. An eighteen-stick brass candelabra hangs from the ceiling. A brass stallion shies at the clock on the mantelpiece. More gilded mirrors. You can see the horses in the arena through glass doors all up one side of the café—and the drinks are the cheapest in town.

> *Double back along Vondelstraat and onto the busy Stadhouders-kade. On the way you might like to duck down Roemer Visscher-straat (turn right at Eerste Constantijn Huygensstraat, then first left) to see a row of quaint 19th-century houses (nos. 20–30a) designed to illustrate seven national architectural styles: German, French, Spanish, Italian, Russian, Dutch and English.*
>
> *Across Stadhouderskade, in the lower branches of a tree opposite the Barbizon Centre Hotel, is another of Amsterdam's secrets. Once you've spotted it, cross the bridge over the Singelgracht to Leid-seplein. As you do so you come to the* **American Hotel**.

The jutting balconies and odd protruding windows are a Dutch interpretation of an original Art Nouveau design. The architect, W. Krom-hout, is considered a forerunner of the fanciful Amsterdam School (see pp. 169–70). The writers and artists who used the **Café Américain** (open daily 10 am–midnight) for most of this century have fled the tourist armies of the Leidseplein, but it's still worth a visit for the glass Japanese parasol lampshades and patterned windows that filter the hard Amsterdam light into a soft and playful kaleidoscope.

> *Next door is the* **Stadsschouwburg** *(Municipal Theatre, open nightly; backstage tours in summer daily at noon; entrance f5, duration 1 hour).*

State theatres in Amsterdam were usually out in the sticks, and kept burning down. The first one on this site was built in 1774 (when Leidseplein was on the edge of town) and, after suffering the usual fate, was replaced by the present building in the late 19th century. The new building was designed by Jan Springer, the bohemian kingpin of Architectura et Amicitia, a wickedly unrestrained artists' society. Budget cuts put a stop to his more florid decorations, yet still the public disapproved of the result. Springer went into a sulk and virtually abandoned his career. The building has a small stage and the new Muziektheater on Waterlooplein has rather stolen its thunder, but it continues to host local and international productions.

Leidseplein is Amsterdam's tourist vortex with more than the usual complement of British boys in Union Jack shorts learning the strength of Dutch lager. Fire-eaters and itinerant musicians busk while your pockets are picked, though at night the atmosphere improves a little as the square becomes the festive hub of late-night transport. As a 17th-century traveller cautioned, 'Here be sure to furnish yourself with money.' The neon-alleys leading off the square are lined with expensive and nasty restaurants and night clubs with names like 'Cash'. Leidsestraat, the northern exit, is clogged with pedestrians and bicycles travelling on no particular side until, bells clanging, a yellow tram hurtles down the central rails scattering all. Mainly airline offices, 24-hour bureaux de change and shops selling clogs and Taiwan Delft, Leidsestraat is happily avoided—though there is a good private photograph gallery and bookshop, the Canon Image Centre (no. 79). The famous delicatessen Dikker & Thijs (on the corner of Prinsengracht) has shrunk to corner-shop size and been largely replaced by an expensive brasserie.

> *Escape Leidseplein down Kleine Lijnbaansgracht. This you do by taking the main road opposite the Stadsschouwburg, but keeping to the smaller left-hand fork following the canal. This takes you to the* **antiques shops and galleries** *of the* **Spiegelkwartier**, *one of the two quarters in Amsterdam dedicated to one particular business (the only other one being the red-light district). Even the local dentist (Zieseniskade 20) has turned his waiting room into a gallery: spine-chilling sounds come from behind a screen in the corner. Turn left into Spiegelgracht and walk on to the Prinsengracht.*

The Spiegelkwartier has gone up-market in recent years—these days even museums buy here for their collections—but it hasn't lost its charm, and the prices are still lower than in most other major cities. (There are even cheaper antiques markets at the end of the walk, and it's not too far to double back to the Spiegelkwartier should you want to look those over before buying anything.) Here you'll find shops crammed with elaborate clocks, solemn rows of carved wooden dressers and ornate gilded furniture. Enormous chandeliers hang at eye-level, and gold, silver and colourful gems shine at you from all sides. Tucked amongst all this grandeur, you can still find idiosyncratic little shops, obviously the domain of a single collector. Spiegelgracht 20 doesn't even aspire to junkshop status—it's more 'bag lady unpacks'. Odd pieces of no possible value to anyone, with curled, yellowing price tags, are scattered about. It's just the sort of place you could imagine finding a lost Rembrandt. The proprietress is seldom in, but ring the bell and try your luck. In the cellar at Spiegelgracht 2a, Art Rages sells contemporary glass and ceramics. The bright, lumpy, gilded work of Rob Brandt (beginning to be snapped up by museums) is very much worth a look. Aalderink (no. 15) has a sparse but expertly selected range of oriental pieces and Africana.

> *Continue over the bridge to* **Nieuwe Spiegelstraat**, *where the price tags begin to get serious.*

If your souvenir budget runs to multiple noughts you could pop into Elisabeth den Bieman de Haas for a little Chagall litho or bright modern oil from COBRA, a post-war expressionist movement. Roel Houwink (no. 57) has one of those shops you could potter about in for ages—everything from musical boxes to escutcheons nicked from under the nose of a Prince of Orange. Kramers (no. 64) has tangles of old jewellery and trinkets, barrels of clay pipe bowls and a roomful of Delft tiles ranging from the 15th to 20th centuries and costing anything from the price of a sandwich to double your airfare. On the corner with Kerkstraat is Norman's Automatics: bubble gum vendors from the 1950s, old pinball machines and one-arm bandits—in fact anything that whirrs, clicks or flashes and looks as if it comes from a B-movie.

> *Turn left up the left-hand side of* **Keizersgracht**, *one of the three grand 17th-century canals, where there are a number of galleries showing 20th-century Dutch art.*

Even if you show no signs of buying, gallery-owners are usually friendly and informative and it's a pleasant way to learn. At no. 546 nothing of the façade, except the windows, has changed since it was built in 1760. The bell-gable is a good example of the playful cake-icing Louis XV decoration. Walk on as far as Leidsestraat. The ornately decorated building that cuts the corner with Leidsestraat is German inspired—the Dutch were more into solid right angles at corners. A frieze of fat naked babies, lurking in shrubberies and grumpily pushing carts and canoes, runs around the wall. The bust commemorates the 17th-century poet Pieter Cornelisz. Hooft.

Cross to the other side of the canal. The pompous building on this corner was built on the site of Van Gogh's uncle's art shop for an insurance company in the late 19th century, but is now the refined **Metz** *department store.*

Inside, you can mount stairs, passing racks of tasteful kitchenware and mounds of Liberty prints. As you climb, the atmosphere becomes increasingly rarefied and the floors emptier and emptier. By the time you're nearing the top, there's hardly anything for sale at all. The few pieces of designer furniture scattered about look more like museum pieces than anything you could put in the dining-room. At the top is a café designed by Gerrit Rietveld. Gazing through its glass cupola, you have a rare opportunity to view Amsterdam's spider's web from on high.

Carry on up the right-hand side of the Keizersgracht and across the Leidsegracht.

The startlingly large windows of the public library at no. 440 (built 1897) originally lit a clothing design studio and factory. It must have been the world's most gracious sweatshop. The bank at no. 452 was once a private residence. Designed by Outshoorn in 1860 it is one of the last of a series of grand canal houses, influenced by French and Italian architecture, that were built by the three great domestic architects—Vingboons, van Campen and Outshoorn—over a period of 200 years. One of Vingboons's early houses can be seen further up the canal at no. 319 (built 1639), the façade virtually untouched. It's the first one in which he combined classic elements (the Doric pilasters) with the traditional Dutch style.

Short streets lead off from both sides of the three bridges beyond the Leidsegracht. These alleys offer the most **intriguing shopping** *in Amsterdam. Keep a steady progress up the Keizersgracht, ducking down each in turn, only as far as the next canal.*

The first on the right, Huidenstraat, has trendy **second-hand clothes** stores and shops crammed with lamps and light fittings—from original Art Nouveau to bright and bulbous 1960s products. In the Third World Charity shop you can buy all sorts of cheerfully coloured clothes and Zulu weaponry, and Pompadours at no.12 sells impossibly tempting **hand-made chocolates**. Across the bridge in Runstraat is the Witte Tandewinkel (White Teeth Shop) for nothing but the tooth—psychedelic and electric toothbrushes, pastes galore, curious aids and sound clinical advice. Just the place to expiate your sins after Pompadours.

194

Furniture from **antiques shops** tumbles out into the streets, though they're not always as cheap as the image suggests. The Vignet Gallery 'of symbolic, erotic and magic art' seethes with suspicious shapes, spell-casting devices and esoteric sculptures.

> *On the way up to the second bridge, you pass the imposing* **Felix** **Meritus** *building (no. 324 on the left-hand side; open daily 5pm–midnight).*

It was built in 1778 to house an arts and scientific Society founded in the spirit of Voltaire and Rousseau. With an observatory, library, laboratories and a small concert hall, the Felix Meritus Foundation became the cultural centre of the Dutch Enlightenment. When Napoleon made his triumphal entry to Amsterdam, he was punted up the canal and ushered with pride into the building. He got no further than the foyer, spat on the floor, said the place stank of tobacco smoke, and strutted back to the boat. Towards the end of the 19th century the society went into terminal decline. The building was later used as the Communist Party headquarters, but won back its cultural prominence in the 1970s when it housed the Shaffy Theatre, in the forefront of the European avant-garde. The theatre lost some of its significance and impact during the 1980s, but the Felix Meritus Society has been revived. As an arts complex and the home of Amsterdam's Summer University, the building is once again playing host to artists and intellectuals from around the world.

> *Continue up the Keizersgracht.*

Wolvenstraat, to the right of the second bridge, has more second-hand clothes shops (one with Queen Mother hats) and a **button shop** (some in such shapes and sizes that their function is barely recognizable). Berenstraat, across the bridge is home to some of the younger, trendier **art galleries**. The newest, Animation Art: 'Name that Toon', sells storyboards and cels (the acetate originals from which cartoons are made) of everyone from Betty Boop to Winnie the Pooh. Hartenstraat (at the third Bridge) has more **fashion shops** and another eccentric collector's outlet—this time **vintage electronic equipment**. The jolly naked illustrations of Eddie Varekamp that have found their way onto T-shirts and coffee mugs are on sale from his studio shop (no. 30). Reestraat has a *poppendokter* (**dolls' doctor**). Puppets hang from the ceiling, dolls of all sorts crowd the window and a disconcerting catalogue of dolls' faces hangs on the wall. Next door is a **candle shop**. Coloured, scented, sculpted, altar candles and erotic candles hang from the ceiling, are

stacked on shelves or poked into odd candlesticks and elaborate candelabra—and they're not at silly prices.

> *At the end of Reestraat cross the Prinsengracht and turn left down*
> *the far side. Walk along to Looiersgracht. On the way down have a*
> *look at the house at no. 300, nicknamed 't Vosje (the fox) after a*
> *17th-century furriers on the site. Above the doors a red fox holds a*
> *bird in its mouth. There's another below the hoist beam. Turn right*
> *into Looiersgracht. At no. 38 is the* **Rommelmarkt** *(literally*
> *'rubbish market') an indoor fleamarket that seems almost sub-*
> *terranean.*

Entering through a small street door you seem to walk forever down a
long, dim corridor lined with piles of old toys, tea caddies, zippo lighters,
1960s records and magazines. The further you penetrate, the more
precious things become. You might even pick up some antique Japanese
lacquerware or an Art-Deco vase. Up the stairs you're assaulted by the
bright light that streams in through skylights. Here the real 'rommel' lies
spread out on tables. It all seems a bit unwanted: there's an air of dead
people's things. Perhaps it's the light. Perhaps it's time to leave.

> *If you double back down one of the alleys and turn left down*
> *Elandsgracht you come to the* **De Looier Indoor Antiques**
> **Market**, *a collectors' and dealers' market pitched halfway between*
> *Rommelmarkt junk and Spiegelkwartier splendour. Stall-holders*
> *have a lively communal spirit—they even have their own newspaper*
> *and weekly bridge drives. There are regular specialist fairs. In this*
> *honeycomb of little stands selling furniture, glass, old lace and even*
> *older Delftware, Walk VI fades to FINIS.*

Museums and Galleries

Rijksmuseum

Amsterdam has over 40 museums. You can admire world art treasures, take a peek at some unique collections or poke about in back rooms crammed with one hoarder's booty. All but seven of the museums are privately owned and nearly all charge an entrance fee. Most offer discounts to children, but not all offer reductions to students. If you intend visiting more than one or two, the **Annual Museum Card** or **CJP card** (youth pass) is a must (see Practical A–Z: Discounts).

Most museums are closed on Mondays, and swarm with school children on Wednesday afternoons. Many keep Sunday hours over public holidays, but some close entirely—so a quick phone call might save you trouble.

A **museum boat** will chug you pleasantly along the canals between 16 of Amsterdam's museums. Tickets valid for a day (*f*12, *f*10 to under 13s and CJP holders; available on the boat) also entitle you to discounts on some admissions. Boats leave every 45 minutes, 10–3.15 daily, from one of six stops: Centraal Station (main boarding point and office, tel 622 2181); Prinsengracht/Egelantiersgracht (Anne Frank Huis); Singelgracht (Van Gogh, Stedelijk, Rijksmuseum); Herengracht/Liedsegracht (Bijbels, Fodor, Amsterdam Historisch, Allard Pierson); Amstel/Zwanenburgwal (Rembrandthuis, Joods Historisch); Oosterdok/Kattenburgergracht (Tropenmuseum, Werf t'Kromhout).

Agnietenkapel, Oudezijds Voorburgwal 231, tel 525 3341; open Mon–Fri 9–1 and 2–5 (though phone first to check); adm. free, or nominal charge around *f*2. Prints and trivia relating to Amsterdam university life. The 15th-century chapel is infinitely more interesting than the collection it houses.

Allard Pierson Museum, Oude Turfmarkt 127, tel 525 2556; open Tues–Fri 10–5, Sat, Sun 1–5; adm. *f*3.50, children 11–15 *f*1, under 11s free. Superb archaeological collection, though poorly presented. Few English texts, but children like the repro Roman chariot.

Anne Frank Huis, Prinsengracht 263, tel 626 4533; open Sept–May Mon–Sat 9–5, Sun 10–5; June–Aug Mon–Sat 9–7, Sun 10–7; adm. *f*6, under 18s *f*3, under 10s free. Unfortunately the stream of visitors filing through the Frank family's hide-out destroys any remnant of the atmosphere evoked in the diaries (see Walk III).

Museum Amstelkring (Our Lord in the Attic), Oudezijds Voorburgwal 40, tel 624 6604; open Mon–Sat 10–5, Sun 1–5; adm. *f*3.50, under 15s *f*2. Magical 17th-century clandestine church and restored canal house (see Walk I).

Amsterdams Historisch Museum (Amsterdam Historical Museum), Kalverstraat 92, tel 523 1822; open daily 11–5; adm. *f*5, under 16s *f*2.50. DIY carillons, paintings that play music, and bits and pieces dug up around town make an accessible and well-presented introduction to the city's history (see Walk I).

Artis (Zoo Museum), Plantage Kerklaan 38–40, tel 523 3400; open daily 9–5; adm. included in zoo ticket: *f*16, under 10s *f*9. Slides and stuffed animals in a corner of the zoo.

Aviodome, Schiphol Centre, Schiphol Airport, tel 604 1521; open Oct–May Tues–Fri 10–5, Sat and Sun noon–5; May–Sept daily 10–5; adm. *f*6, under 13s *f*4.50. Aeronautics and space travel. Models of everything from a flimsy 1903 Wright Flyer to American Mercury capsules—some open to clamber about in.

Bijbels Museum (Bible Museum), Herengracht 366, tel 624 2436; open Tues–Sat 10–5, Sun 1–5; adm. *f*3, under 16s *f*2. Another museum worth visiting more for the building than the collection. The 17th-century Vingboons house and stunning 18th-century ceiling paintings by Jacob de Wit far outshine old Dutch Bibles and models of Solomon's temple.

Electrische Museumtramlijn (Electric Tramline Museum), Amstelveensewag 264, tel 673 7538; open Apr–Oct Sun 10–6, July–Aug Tues–Thurs, Sat 1–4; adm. *f*4 (return), *f*2.50 (single), under 11s half price. A museum on the move. Antique trams rattle along a 30 minute ride to the Amsterdamse Bos (Amsterdam Forest).

Nederlandse Filmmuseum, Vondelpark 3, tel 589 1400; open Tues–Sun 1–8.30; adm. ƒ2.50. Posters and vintage movie equipment.

Museum Fodor, Keizersgracht 609, tel 624 9919; open daily 11–5; adm. ƒ1, under 16s 50c. Contemporary art—usually by Amsterdam artists—of a high standard and tending towards the avant-garde.

Van Gogh Museum, Paulus Potterstraat 7, tel 570 5200; open Tues–Sat 10–5, Sun 1–5; adm. ƒ10, under 18s ƒ5. Over 200 of Vincent's paintings and 500 drawings as well as work by his contemporaries (see Walk VI).

Hash Info Museum, Oudezijds Achterburgwal 150, tel 624 0836; opening hours: laid back—phone first; adm. ƒ4. History of dope—exhibits are occasionally confiscated by the authorities.

Heineken Brewery Museum, Stadhouderskade 78, tel 670 9111; adm. ƒ2; guided tours only: Mon–Fri 9, 9.45 and 10 am; May–Sept also at 1, 1.45 and 2.30 pm. (Fewer tours in low season—phone to check). Copper vats, dray horses and a glass or two of free beer.

Joods Historisch Museum (Jewish Historical Museum), Jonas Daniel Meyerplein 2–4, tel 625 4229; open daily 11–5, closed Yom Kippur; adm. ƒ7, under 15s ƒ3.50, under 10s free. Converted synagogue complex, with displays focussing on Jews in Amsterdam (see Walk III).

Kattenkabinett (Cat Museum), Herengracht 497, tel 626 5378; usually open Tues–Sun noon–5, but phone to check; adm. varies. Art with a feline theme in a restored canal house.

Werf 't Kromhout (shipyard museum), Hoogte Kadijk 147, tel 627 6777; open Mon–Fri 10–4 (also Sat, Sun noon–5 in summer); adm. ƒ3, under 12s ƒ1.50. The working shipyard restores antique vessels—but most of the exhibits are rather esoteric bits of patent diesel engines.

Museum van Loon, Keizersgracht 672, tel 624 5255; open Mon only 10–5; adm. ƒ5, under 16s ƒ4. The most charming of the canal house museums, with a cosy, lived-in atmosphere.

Max Euwe Centrum, Paleisstraat 1, tel 625 7071; open Tues–Fri and first Sat of the month 10.30–4; adm. free. Chess memorabilia and the chance to play the game with live people or clever computers.

NINT (Technology Museum); Tolstraat 129, tel 664 6021; open Mon–Fri 10–5, Sat and Sun noon–5; adm. ƒ7, under 13s ƒ5, under 5s free. Soap bubbles big enough to stand in, games, video displays and lots of flashing lights and buttons to push—brings technology alive for anyone over the age of six.

Rembrandthuis, Jodenbreestraat 4–6, tel 624 9486; open Tues–Sat 10–5, Sun 1–5; adm. *f*4, under 17s *f*2.50, under 10s free. An unrelieved collection of 250 of Rembrandt's etchings in the house he lived in for 20 years (see Walk III).

Rijksmuseum, Stadhouderskade 42, tel 673 2121; open Tues–Sat 10–5, Sun 1–5; adm. *f*6.50, under 18s *f*3.50. Dutch art from its earliest moments to the 19th century, as well as a warren of rooms stacked with Delft, furniture and ecclesiastical knick-knacks (see Walk II).

Nederlands Scheepvaart Museum, Kattenburgerplein 1, tel 523 2311; open Tues–Sat 10–5, Sun 1–5; adm. *f*5, under 18s *f*3. The Royal Barge, a reproduction 17th-century sailing ship, and rooms and rooms of maritime models (see Walk IV).

Sex Museum, Damrak 18, tel 622 8376; open daily 10–11.30; adm. *f*3.75. Lurid evidence that the pornographer's imagination has changed little over the centuries.

Stedelijk Museum, Paulus Potterstraat 13, tel 573 2911; open daily 11–5 (4 pm on public holidays); adm. *f*7, under 17s *f*3.50, under 7s free. Lively municipal museum with an up-to-the-minute collection of modern art (see Walk V).

Spaarpottenmuseum (Money Box Museum), Raadhuisstraat 12, tel 556 7400; open Mon–Fri 1–4; adm. *f*1, under 12s 50c. Part of a 12,000-strong collection of piggy banks started by an eccentric bank manager (see Walk III.)

Nederlands Theater Instituut, Herengracht 168, tel 623 5104; open Tues–Sun 11–5; open *f*5, under 10s *f*3, under 4s free. A beautiful canal house (18th-century ceiling paintings by Jacob de Wit) with enticingly presented costumes, scenery and backstage equipment (see Walk III).

Tropenmuseum (Tropical Museum) Linnaeusstraat 2, tel 568 8200; open Mon–Fri 10–5, Sat and Sun noon–5; adm. *f*6, under 18s *f*3. Tapes, models and life-sized installations evoke the atmosphere of life in the Third World. The splendid 1920s building also houses exhibits of ethnic musical instruments and reminders of Holland's colonial past.

Madame Tussauds, Peek & Cloppenburg Building, De Dam; open daily 10–5.30; adm. *f*16, under 15s *f*13, under 5s free, family ticket *f*39. Waxworks; some good re-creations of 17th-century life (see Walk I).

Vakbonds Museum (Trade Union Museum), Henri Polaklaan 9, tel 624 1166; open Tues–Fri 11–5, Sun 1–5; adm. *f*5. One of the best examples of Berlage's architecture after the Beurs (see Walk I) houses a collection of interest only for those in quest of knowledge about the Dutch Labour movement (see Walk III).

Verzetsmuseum (Museum of the Resistance), Lekstraat 63, tel 644 9797; open Tues–Fri 10–5, Sat and Sun 1–5; adm. ƒ3.50, under 16s ƒ1.75. Newspaper clippings, photographs, tape-recordings and make-shift secret equipment give intimate insight into the 1940s Resistance movement.

Museum Willet-Holthuysen, Herengracht 605, tel 523 1822; open daily 11–5; adm. ƒ2.50, under 17s ƒ1.25. Grand, if over-embellished, canal-house museum (see Walk II).

Commercial Galleries

There are over 140 commercial art galleries in Amsterdam. They're scattered all over town, though you'll find a number of the more established ones along the Keizersgracht and in the Spiegelkwartier.

The listings magazine *What's on in Amsterdam* (ƒ2.50 from the VVV, newsagents and hotels) will guide you to mainstream exhibitions. For a fuller picture, pick up a copy of *Alert* (ƒ2.50 from most galleries), the monthly Amsterdam gallery diary. Although this is in Dutch, the pages of photographs, clear symbolic coding and detailed maps give you a good idea of what's showing around town and where to find it. The Amsterdam Gallery Guide (Laurierstraat 70, tel 625 2275) offers 3-hour **walking tours** around a handful of galleries in the centre for ƒ35 per person. Look out also for 'Open Atelier' posters—artists working in one neighbourhood will open their studios for a day, and you can wander in for a chat, a look and possibly (they hope) a happy purchase.

Ten Contemporary Art Galleries

Barbara Farber, Keizersgracht 265; open Tues–Sat 1–6. Has a reputation for picking out unknowns on the brink of glittering fame.

Galerie Rob Jurka, Singel 28; open Wed–Sat 12.30–5.30. One-time establishment rattler, now has a calmer more conventional approach.

Van Krimpen, Prinsengracht 629; open Tues–Sat 2–6. Works seem chosen at the owner's whim—but he has an eye for the exciting and a knack for picking up on current trends.

The Living Room, Laurierstraat 70; open Tues–Sat 2–6. Mainly new Dutch artists. Specializes in installations.

Mokum, Oudezijds Voorburgwal 334; open Tues–Sat 11–5. Dutch realistic art—a good place to find work by Magic Realists (see p. 62).

De Selby, Nieuwe Teertuinen 16; open Tues–Sat 11–5. Out-of-the-way gallery with a conspiratorial feel of 'this is where it's happening'.

SBK Kunstuitleen, Nieuwezijds Voorburgwal 325; open Tues 11–9, Wed–Fri 11–5, Sat 9–5. Art library that hires out original work by Amsterdam artists from *f*25 per month—and you get the option to buy.

Swart, Van Breestraat 23; open Wed–Sat 2–6, Sun 3–5. Run by the queen of the Amsterdam art scene. She rules with a rod of iron and her exhibitions seldom fail to excite.

Torch, Prinsengracht 218; open Thurs–Sat 1–6. Specializes in video and photography, but currently a leading light in other media too.

W 139, Warmoesstraat 139; open Tues–Sun noon–6. Cavernous space used by fledgling artists. Sometimes the work is dire, sometimes plain curious—but occasionally you'll find a gem, and will seldom be bored.

Some Specialists
ABK (Amsterdam Sculptors' Collective), Zeilmakerstraat 15; open Wed–Fri 10–5, Sat and Sun 1–5. Sculpture of all sizes (see Walk IV).

Animation Art, Berenstraat 19; open Tues–Fri 11–6, Sat 10–5. Original drawings of everyone from Popeye to Betty Boop.

Art Rages, Spiegelgracht 2a; open Mon 1–6, Tues–Fri noon–6, Sat 11–5.30. Zany ceramics.

Canon Image Centre, Leidsestraat 79; open Tues–Fri noon–5.45, Sat 11–4.45. Photographic exhibitions of consistently high standard.

Food and Drink

Erasmus, the great 16th-century Dutch humanist and man of letters, was pleased to note that his fellow countrymen were not given to much wild or ferocious behaviour, treachery or deceit, indeed were 'not prone to any serious vices except, that is, a little given to pleasure, especially to feasting'. Two centuries later the national ability to tuck in and drink up was still impressive enough to shock the British—themselves no mean feasters. In 1703 the seven or so deacons of the Arnhem guild of surgeons dispatched, at one sitting, 14 lb of beef, 8lb of veal, six fowl, stuffed cabbages, apples, pears, bread, pretzels, assorted nuts, 20 bottles of red wine, 12 bottles of white wine and some jugs of coffee. Today, eating is still a supreme Dutch enthusiasm, and one in which any visitor to Amsterdam can happily join.

Paradoxically, native **Dutch cuisine** is not all that inspiring. The Dutch culinary clichés are *hutspot* ('hotchpotch'), a well-boiled stew that was much appreciated by starving citizens after the siege of Leiden and still requires a similar state of ravenousness before it can really be enjoyed; and *erwtensoep*, a porridgy pea soup which comes (vegetarians beware) with bits of sausage floating in it and a side-dish of bread and raw bacon. The quality of *erwtensoep* is judged by testing whether or not your spoon will stand up on its own in the middle of the bowl. These are the staples of many a 'tourist menu', but (like the English) the Dutch have recently begun to explore more exciting avenues in their local cuisine—with game and fish especially. The tourist board is encouraging this: look out for red, white and blue **Neerlands Dis** signs which indicate a restaurant which serves regional specialities. Other palatable traditional foods include *pannekoeken* (pancakes) which come with sweet or savoury fillings and *haring* (herring) eaten raw by tossing your head back and dropping a whole fillet down your throat, holding it by the tail. If you can stomach it, this is a marvellous cure for a hangover. *Belegde broodjes* are crusty rolls filled with a delicious variety of fillings—travellers' tales of sliced beef layered on buttered bread pre-date anecdotes about Lord Sandwich's invention by about a century. Waffles, dripping with syrup or smothered with fruit and cream, are sold on the streets and are treacherously gooey and unmanageable, but quite irresistible. Cones of *frites* (potato chips), usually with a large dollop of mayonnaise, are ubiquitous. They're normally cooked with good-quality potatoes in clean oil and make a warming winter snack.

In the absence of a stimulating local tradition, Dutch chefs have looked further afield. **French cuisine** first came into fashion during the Napoleonic occupation, and remains the cornerstone of many of the best kitchens. Nowadays most menus are tantalizingly eclectic, showing influences from Japan, Indonesia, Surinam and Turkey. This makes for some curious—but usually delicious—combinations. Don't be surprised to find peanut sauce, saffron pasta and oysters on the same menu.

Specialist **ethnic restaurants** abound. Reasonable Indian and Italian food is to be had all over town, though the increasingly popular Thai and Japanese restaurants make a more exciting alternative. It's the culinary heritage of Holland's imperial past, however, that makes for the best ethnic binge. Treat yourself to an Indonesian *rijstafel*—a personal banquet of rice or noodles with a myriad of spicy side dishes. (See the section on Language for a selection of Dutch and Indonesian food terms.)

Vegetarians will have a difficult time in Amsterdam. The Dutch are great carnivores. Fish doesn't seem to count as meat, so if you enquire about vegetarian dishes you're usually offered *kabeljauw* (cod). However, in the 1970s the tastes of the hippies spawned a few vegetarian restaurants and more have opened recently. Chefs in better restaurants are beginning to be more imaginative with their vegetarian options.

Take-away foodstalls punctuate markets and shopping streets all over town. As well as *frites*, *haring* and waffles you can sample all sorts of foreign delights: Turkish kebabs, Israeli *falafel*, Japanese *sushi* and spicy nibbles from Surinam and Indonesia. Under signs flashing *Automatiek* you can select a deep-fried croquette from a row of tiny windows displaying this and similar wares: drop in your *f*1.50, pull a lever and collect your reward.

Budget eating is easy, and needn't be boring. Many restaurants offer a three-course 'Tourist Menu' for under *f*20, but you're generally better off looking out for signs advertising a *dagschotel* (dish of the day). You usually end up with an oversized white plate with some well-prepared meat and a constellation of pickles and salads. Many cafés serve food— menus change daily and often offer the best value of all.

Ingredients are usually market-fresh and microwave cookers are pleasingly thin on the ground. Food is cooked to order in most res- taurants, so expect an unhurried meal. The Dutch eat early in the evening—between 7 and 9 pm—and many kitchens are closed by 10 or 11 pm.

Amsterdam is very much a cash city. Most smaller restaurants don't accept credit cards, and there's an air of reluctance about those that do. Even some of the larger establishments don't like plastic—so it's always a good idea to check in advance. Feasting Amsterdammers and hungry tourists fill up most good restaurants pretty quickly, so it's wise to reserve a table by telephone.

Restaurant Categories
The following list is a very personal selection from the hundreds of good restaurants Amsterdam has to offer. An exploratory wander around the Jordaan or along Utrechtsestraat will reveal even more. Restaurants are listed in three areas. Central refers to the semi-circle bounded by the three main canals, the Jordaan is the area in the west of the city, just beyond the canals. Restaurants in the south and east will be found under Further Afield. They are all graded according to the approximate price of a three-course meal, without wine. You'll find eating out cheaper than in most large cities. Expensive means over *f*60 (though seldom more than *f*150), moderate means *f*25–*f*60 and cheap under *f*25. The bill will include tax and a 15 per cent service charge—though if you feel you've been well looked after you can leave a little extra. It's usual to leave behind any small change (or round up larger bills to the nearest *f*5).

Restaurants

Central

EXPENSIVE

Restaurant Chopin, Utrechtsedwarsstraat 107, tel 625 4189; closed Tues. Subtle Loire cuisine, endless Chopin in the background and a stone's throw from the Carré Theatre. ƒ80.

Excelsior, Hotel l'Europe, Nieuwe Doelenstraat 2–8, tel 623 4836. Grand without being pompous, Michelin star-rated French cuisine (with a delicate Japanese touch) and a superb view over the Amstel. ƒ80. Dress: Jacket and tie.

Koriander, Amstel 212, tel 627 7879; open till midnight; closed Sun/Mon. The view is even more sublime than from the Excelsior, but the menu and decor more down to earth. The *gezellig* atmosphere and no-nonsense (yet imaginative) fare are a great attraction to artistes from the nearby Opera House. ƒ60.

Van Harte, Hartenstraat 24, tel 624 3154. A modest image, yet an excellent kitchen. Berries and wild mushrooms in the sauces, tender meats and charming service. ƒ80.

Les Quatre Canetons, Prinsengracht 1111, tel 624 6307; closed Sun. Snug and stylish restaurant in a converted spice warehouse. Tickle your tastebuds with such French-inspired gourmet dishes as goose liver in Madeira sauce. ƒ90.

De Silveren Spiegel, Kattengat 4–6, tel 624 6589. The building, all Delft tiles and cosy corners, dates from 1614. The owner was a wine merchant and owns part of a French vineyard (this shows in the wine list). The visionary chef produces dishes like quail and chicory salad and dune rabbit stuffed with lobster. (The dessert soufflé is a dream.) Service is personal and friendly. A sublime combination that makes it one of the best restaurants in town. ƒ90.

't Swarte Schaep, Korte Leidsedwarsstraat 24, tel 622 3021. Up a steep staircase in a 300-year-old building you'll find oak beams, antiques, superb wines, an eclectic cuisine and passing members of the Dutch royal family. ƒ80.

Les Trois Neufs, Prinsengracht 999, tel 622 9044; closed Mon. Intimate atmosphere in a converted 17th-century warehouse. French cuisine with a heavier Dutch hand—try the beef in honey and thyme sauce. ƒ90.

Vasso, Rozenboomsteeg 12–14, tel 626 0158. Fresh pasta and fine

Italian food in a restaurant that has the lively atmosphere of the kitchens of a faded palazzo. *f*70.

D'Vijff Vlieghen (The Five Flies), Spuistraat 294–302, tel 624 8369. An intriguing conglomeration of antique-filled rooms in a wonky 17th-century inn. It gets its unfortunate name from the original owner, Jan Vijff Vlieghen. In the 1950s and 1960s it was frequented by the likes of Orson Welles, Benjamin Britten, Jean Cocteau and Walt Disney. These days the restaurant rests on its laurels, and doesn't give good value for money. *f*90.

MODERATE

1e Klas, Platform 2B, Centraal Station, tel 625 0131 (see Walk I Lunch/Cafés). Well-prepared (though not wildly adventurous) Dutch fare in the beautifully restored First Class restaurant. *f*50.

Centra, Lange Niezel 29, tel 622 3050. Busy, garish, cafeteria-like atmosphere, and the best Spanish food in town. *f*30.

't Fornuis, Utrechtsestraat 33, tel 626 9139. Friendly staff and good-value French cuisine. *f*35.

Hemelse Modder, Oude Waal 9, tel 624 3203; closed Mon. Haunt of writers and journalists. Before you get to the divine chocolate mousse that gives the restaurant its name ('Heavenly Mud'), try some of the delicious fish dishes. *f*40.

Kort, Amstelveld 2, tel 626 1199. Freshly prepared food with simple sauces. Somewhere for the health-conscious gourmet. Quiet terrace on the water's edge. *f*60.

De Impressionist, Keizersgracht 312, tel 627 6666. Stark decor, but a creative team of chefs who come up with dishes from all over the world—including good vegetarian meals. *f*45.

Lucius, Spuistraat 247, tel 624 1831. This restaurant deserves its reputation as the city's best place for fish, but it can be an eerie experience for the queasy—tucking into fresh fish while their cousins swim about in the aquariums that line the walls. *f*55.

Het Melkmeisje, Zeedijk 19, tel 625 0640. An 18th-century dairy with a converted fairground organ for a bar. The menu varies daily, depending on what's good at the morning markets, but the *vispot* (a sort of fish stew) is a regular treat. *f*50.

Oshima, Prinsengracht 411, tel 625 0996; closed Mon. Tranquil Japanese restaurant with the freshest *sushi* in town. *f*60.

Pier 10, De Ruyterkade Steiger 10 (behind Centraal Station), tel 624

8276. A little wooden hut, once a shipping line office, right on the end of a pier in the IJ. Watch the boats chug past as you devour scrumptious Dutch/French food. ƒ50.

Rose's Cantina, Reguliersdwarsstraat 38, tel 625 9797. Crowds of Bright Young Things, tasty Tex-Mex food and lethal margaritas. ƒ25.

Sluizer Visrestaurant, Utrechtsestraat 45, tel 626 3557; and **Sluizer**, Utrechtsestraat 41–3, tel 622 6376. Two adjacent trendy restaurants, evocative of the thirties with marble-topped tables and fringed lamps. Both are usually packed, and the fish restaurant especially has a good reputation. Both open till midnight. ƒ50.

Tempo Doelo, Utrechtsestraat 75, tel 625 6718. Indonesian restaurant where the waiters specialize in dire warnings about the heat of the food. Sometimes they're justified. Rijstafel ƒ49.

Sukabumi, Geelvincksteeg 2, tel 625 1446; closed Sun. Cosy, plain but inexpensive Indonesian restaurant. Rijstafel ƒ29.50.

Zuid Zeeland, Herengracht 413, tel 624 3154; closed Sat/Sun. Specializes in fish dishes from Zeeland, but also meat dishes with a French and Japanese influence.

CHEAP

Anda Nugraha, Waterlooplein 339, tel 626 6046. Tasty home-cooked Indonesian food. Rijstafel ƒ38 for 2 people.

De Blauwe Hollander, Leidsekruisstraat 28, tel 623 3014. Cheap and cheerful, if rather heavy, Dutch cooking. ƒ25.

Keuken van 1870, Spuistraat 4, tel 624 8965; kitchen closes 8 pm weekdays, 9 pm Sat/Sun. Began as a soup kitchen in 1870. Still serves enormous, superbly cooked meals for under ƒ10.

Casa di David, Singel 426, tel 624 5093. Wooden beams and canalside charm give this pizzeria a special edge. The food is good too—pasta made on the premises and fragrant, crusty pizzas cooked in a wood-burning oven. Pizzas around ƒ15.

Fantasia, Marnixstraat 417, tel 638 5665. Wholemeal pizzas and vegetarian lasagne. Pizzas around ƒ15.

Haesje Claes, Spuistraat 273–5, tel 624 9998. Touristy, but unhurried. Solid tasty Dutch food, lots of salad and vegetables. Tourist menu ƒ19.50.

Pancake Bakery, Prinsengracht 191, tel 625 1333 (see Walk III Lunch/Cafés). The best pancakes in town. Pancakes around ƒ10.

Upstairs Pannekoekenhuis, Grimburgwal 2, tel 626 5603 (see Walk I Lunch/Cafés). Teeny pancake parlour suspended above a bustling lane. Pancakes from ƒ10.

The Jordaan

EXPENSIVE

Bordewijk, Noordermarkt 7, tel 624 3899; closed Mon. Germolene pink walls, black furniture and self-concious punters. Not everyone's cup of tea, but the French-inspired cuisine is tasty, if a little faint-hearted. ƒ70.

Christophé, Leliegracht 46, tel 625 0807. Currently *the* place to be seen. The atmosphere can be a little frigid, but the superb Dutch/French cuisine makes up for all. ƒ100.

De Kikker, Egelantiersstraat 128–30, tel 627 9198. Most of the Art Deco interior comes from the 1920s Parisian department store 'Au Bon Marché'. French haute cuisine with Dutch, Italian and Japanese eccentricities. There's cabaret at weekends. ƒ80.

MODERATE

Caramba, Lindengracht 342, tel 627 1188. Lively South American restaurant where an arty crowd consumes piles of tortilla and gets pole-axed by vicious margaritas. ƒ40.

Burger's Patio, 2e Tuindwarsstraat 12, tel 623 6854. An Italian restaurant (despite the name) serving good fare in a cheery atmosphere. ƒ40.

Lafitte, Westerstraat 200, tel 623 4270. Hearty cajun cooking. Lip-smacking gumbo soup and blackened fish—and some very fine American wines. ƒ50.

De Luwte, Leliegracht 26, tel 625 8548; closed Mon. Banquets of salads and meat dishes with classic sauces. Candlelight, wooden tables and chairs and a pleasant, unpretentious atmosphere. ƒ50.

El Naranjo, Boomstraat 41a, tel 622 2402; closed Mon. Wide selection of tapas. Rousing Spanish sing-a-longs on Friday nights and live classical music on Sunday afternoons. ƒ40.

Mango Bay, Westerstraat 91, tel 638 1039; closed Thurs. Filipino cuisine—rice and spicy dishes cooked with exotic fruit. ƒ50.

Speciaal, Nieuwe Leliestraat 142, tel 624 9706. Many say the best Indonesian restaurant in town. Rijstafel ƒ39.50.

Het Stuivertje, Hazenstraat 58, tel 623 1349. Quirky French-orientated restaurant. Just the place for wild boar with tamarillo sauce. ƒ40.

Ristorante Toscanini, Lindengracht 75, tel 623 2813; closed Tues. Cavernous, rowdy and very Italian. A gastric and sensual delight. ƒ40.

CHEAP

De Eettuin, 2e Tuindwarsstraat 10, tel 623 7706. Forests of greenery, generous Dutch portions and a groaning salad bar. ƒ20.

Moeders Pot (Mother's Cooking), Vinkenstraat 119, tel 623 7643. Meat and ten veg cuisine. A one-person affair run by a huge hairy man who *must* have 'mother' tattooed somewhere under his white T-shirt. Main dishes under ƒ15.

Further Afield

EXPENSIVE

Beddington's, Roelof Hartstraat 6–8, tel 676 5201; closed Mon. Austere decor, but sumptuous meals by a chef who combines culinary experiences from her Derbyshire background, life in the Far East and the summits of French haute cuisine. ƒ75.

Bols Taverne, Rozengracht 106, tel 624 5752. A large restaurant of nooks, small rooms and odd floor levels. Classically simple fresh fish, with the occasional Japanese grace note. ƒ75.

Ciel Bleu, Okura Hotel, Ferdinand Bolstraat 333, tel 678 7111. God's-eye view of Amsterdam from the 23rd floor of the city's most hideously ugly monolith. The cuisine is appropriately *haut*, and the highpoint of the menu is the Soufflé de Homard en Cocotte. ƒ100. Dress: Jacket and tie.

De Kersentuin (The Cherry Garden), Dijsselhofplantsoen 7, tel 664 2121; closed Sun. An oriental setting in which to sample the works of a chef rated by people in the know as one of the best in the country. ƒ100. Dress: Jacket and tie.

De Gouden Reael, Zandhoek 14, tel 623 3883. A 17th-century house on a quayside in the Western Islands (see Walk IV). Renowned for its French provincial cuisine—a different area every three months. ƒ70.

De Groene Lanterne, Haarlemmerstraat 43, tel 624 1952. The narrowest restaurant in the world—in places just a doorway wide. Rich fare such as smoked duck and stuffed guinea fowl. Quaint, but over-priced. ƒ80.

De Knijp, Van Baerlestraat 134, tel 671 4248; open till midnight. Near the Concertgebouw and popular with local concert-goers. Fresh oysters are a speciality. ƒ75.

MODERATE

La Brasa, Haarlemerdijk 16, tel 625 4438. One of the more intimate of the Argentinian grills. Very much a place for carnivores: hairy cowhide seats and juicy beef on a wood grill. ƒ35.

In Dubio, Entrepotdok 36, tel 625 4845. A new restaurant owned by one of the founders of the Sluizer (see above). Modern decor, a quiet waterside terrace and superb menu that changes daily. *f*60.

Bodega Keyser, Van Baerlestraat 96, tel 671 1441; closed Sun; open till midnight. Writers and musicians have been coming here for nearly a century to eat smoked eel and fresh sole. (The Concertgebouw is right next door.) *f*50.

Mijnlieff, Rapenburgerplein 6, tel 638 5912. Simple, fresh, home-cooked food in a trendy atmosphere. *f*40.

The Movies, Haarlemmerdijk 159, tel 626 7069. Crowded restaurant attached to an old Art Deco cinema offers 'Cuisine Sauvage'—challenging concoctions such as rabbit stewed in ale with a pesto sauce. *f*40.

CHEAP

Lucullus 2e van der Helststraat 7, tel 679 3138; closed Mon. For a special occasion on a low budget. Relaxed candle-lit ambience and delicious, lovingly presented dishes. Excellent value. *f*20.

Le Petit Restaurant, corner of Laagte Kadijk and Kadijksplein; no telephone bookings. The restaurant was set up and run by squatters. They built up such an enthusiastic following that when the authorities tried to hold a sale of their equipment, regular customers bought it all and gave it back. Come early to get a table, and be prepared to wait a long time for your food. You'll have two choices (meat or fish), but when it comes you'll be rewarded with one of the tastiest meals of your visit. (Be warned though: if the manager takes a dislike to you, you won't be served.)

Vegetarian

Bolhoed, Prinsengracht 60, tel 626 1803. Pleasant, rather trendy, decor and good vegetarian and vegan cuisine. *f*20.

The Egg Cream, St Jacobstraat 19, tel 623 0575; closes 8 pm. An Amsterdam institution. Cooks from all over the world present a menu that changes daily. *f*15.

Green Cuisine Slow Food, Beulingstraat 9, tel 627 5755. Lots of new ideas for the vegetarian gourmet. *f*35.

Late Night

Of the restaurants listed above, a few keep their kitchens open until midnight: Bodega Keyser, De Knijp, Koriander and the Sluizer.

Homolulu (Kerkstraat 23), a disco with a largely South American and gay clientele, has a restaurant that serves palatable food until 3 am. **Bojo** (Lange Leidsedwarsstraat 51) is an Indonesian restaurant open until 2 am during the week and until 5.30 am on Fri and Sat. **Maoz** (Reguliersbreestraat, near Tuschinski Cinema) serves scrumptious *falafel* and salads on the street all through the night.

Cafés and Coffeeshops

Cafés are at the centre of an Amsterdammer's social life. Wooden floors and furniture, and walls stained by years of cigarette smoke, have inspired the name **brown café**. Here you can have a drink or just a coffee, nibble snacks or plough through hefty Dutch meals. But most of all you sit and talk, or while away the time paging through the day's papers or glossy magazines. There's seldom any grating background music—though in friendly neighbourhood bars the clientele may burst into song. Whether it's in a tiny café supported by a handful of locals, or a stylish new bar with an arty crowd, you'll find that Amsterdammers create an atmosphere where they can relax and feel both *uit* and *thuis* ('out' and 'at home').

The term 'café' covers a wide range of establishments. At one end of the spectrum are the poky bars, where you go to knock back a few beers (with the odd *jenever* chaser); you might also be able to buy bread rolls, *tostis* (rather pale toasted sandwiches) or *bitterballen* (balls of meat purée, coated in breadcrumbs and deep-fried). At the other end you'll find enormous, airy **grand cafés** and places that offer such sumptuous fare that they're really indistinguishable from small restaurants. These often call themselves **eetcafés** (literally 'eating cafés') or even **petit restaurant cafés**. Some rather startling newcomers made an appearance during the 1980s: the **designer bars** are the complete antithesis of the brown café—hard metal furniture, bright light and colours and loud music—but seem very much here to stay.

Most Amsterdammers drink beer. Ordering *een Pils* at the bar will get you a small glass of lager topped with a finger or two of froth. Or you might prefer a *jenever* (Dutch gin—oilier and weaker than its British counterpart, with a whiff of juniper berries). In this case ask for a *borrel*. You can have either *oud* (old—more mellow) or *jong* (young—sharper). *Jenever* may also be flavoured: *citroenjenever* (lemon) or *bessenjenever* (blackberry) are popular. Ask for a *kamelenrug* (camel's back) and your glass will be filled to the rim. Traditionally, you knock back all of your *jenever* with a single gulp. Should you require both beer and gin simultaneously, request a *kopstoot* (literally: 'knock on the head').

On freezing winter's days a quick visit to a **proeflokaal** will warm your blood. These were once free tasting houses attached to spirit-merchants and taphouses. These days you have to pay, but the procedure is much the same: walk in, drink up, walk out.

Coffeeshops serve only tea, coffee and wonderful cakes and pastries. Sometimes they serve snacks and fuller meals, but never alcohol. Tea is seldom served with milk, unless you specifically ask for it. Coffee will come black or with strange processed *koffiemelk*, unless you order *koffieverkeerd* (literally 'coffee wrong'), in which case you'll get a delicious 50:50 mixture with fresh milk.

Since the 1970s some coffeeshops (the so-called **smoking coffeeshops**) have openly sold marijuana. These are easily distinguishable at first glance/sniff. They are painted psychedelic colours, often have leaf designs on the windows and emit loud music and fazed customers.

Café-crawling is the best way to discover Amsterdam: between museum visits, on rainy afternoons, on long hot summer evenings. There are nearly 1500 cafés to visit, and you're sure to rootle out a few favourites for yourself—but here is a list of a few special ones to help you on your way. Most cafés close at 1 or 2 am over weekends. They begin opening their doors around 11 am, though some don't get it together until 3 or 4 pm. An asterisk (*) indicates cafés particularly recommended for their food. The letters after the address give you some indication of where the café is: C—the central area bound by the main canals; J—the Jordaan and north-western Amsterdam; S—south and south-east of the centre.

Cafés

*Aas van Bokalen, Keizersgracht 335 (C). Arty brown café. (See Lunch/Cafés, Walk VI.)

Int Aepjen, Zeedijk 1 (C). A 'rariteitencafé', crammed with antiques. (See Lunch/Cafés, Walk IV.)

*Américain, American Hotel, Leidseplein (C). Splendid Art-Deco grand café. (See Lunch/Cafés, Walk VI.)

Het Beervat, Raadhuisstraat 17 (C). Over 150 varieties of beer. (See Lunch/Cafés, Walk III.)

*Belhamel, Brouwersgracht 60 (J). Art-Nouveau decor on a pretty canal. (See Lunch/Cafés, Walk II.)

213

*Beurs van Berlage, Beursplein 3 (C). For a view of the Father-of-Modern-Dutch-Architecture's brickwork. (See Lunch/Cafés, Walk I).

De Blaffende Vis, Westerstraat 118 (J). Cheery Jordaan café. (See Lunch/Cafés, Walk III.)

Chris, Bloemstraat 42 (J). So small you have to flush the loo from behind the pool table. (See Lunch/Cafés, Walk III.)

Cul de Sac, Oudezijds Voorburgwal 99 (C). Tucked away down a side alley—one of the few really good bars in the red-light district.

*De Doffer, Runstraat 12 (C). Crammed with students, and open late (2.30 am Sun–Thurs, 3.30 am Fri/Sat.)

Doll's Place, Vinkenstraat 57 (J). Open until 3 am (4 am over weekends). Carouse with locals under the beady eyes of 1000 dolls. Wild sing-songs often develop as dawn draws near.

De Druif, Rapenburg 83 (near Maritime Museum). Dates from 1631. (See Lunch/Cafés, Walk IV.)

*Dulac, Haarlemmerstraat 118 (J). Fantasy grand café, inspired by the French fairy tale illustrator Edmund Dulac. (See Lunch/Cafés, Walk IV.)

De Eik en Linde, Plantage Middenlaan 22 (near Zoo). Local brown café with mixed, arty crowd. (See Lunch/Cafés, Walk III.)

Eland, Prinsengracht 296 (C). Traditional brown café.

*Engelbewaarder, Kloveniersburgwal 59 (C). Writers gulp down pasta and scribble away on wooden tables. Heated discussions about art and life echo from the corners.

First Class, Platform 2B, Centraal Station. Lose yourself in the great age of rail travel. (See Lunch/Cafés, Walk I.)

Gollem, Raamsteeg 4 (C). Another home of a hundred (or more) beers.

De Gijs, Lindengracht 249 (J). Tiny two-tier bar with an edge of Jordaan eccentricity.

Het Hok, Lange Leidsedwarsstraat 134 (C). A refuge from the hordes on Leidseplein. Filled with quiet people playing chess.

Hollandse Manege Café, Vondelstraat 140 (S). Overlooks an exquisite 19th-century riding school arena. (See Lunch/Cafés, Walk VI.)

Hoppe, Spui 18–20 (C). Dates from 1670. These days it's an after-work watering hole. (See Lunch/Cafés, Walk I.)

*Huyschkamer, Utrechtsestraat 137 (C). Trendy café in a former male brothel. (See Lunch/Cafés, Walk II.)

De IJsbreker, Weesperzijde 23 (S). Attached to Amsterdam's leading venue for serious contemporary music, with appropriate background sounds. Tranquil riverside terrace.

De Jaren, Nieuwe Doelenstraat 20 (C). Light and airy grand café. Home of the arts and media set. (See Lunch/Cafés, Walk I.)

Karpershoek, Martelaarsgracht 2 (C). Claims to be Amsterdam's oldest café (this is challenged by Café Chris). (See Lunch/Cafés, Walk IV.)

De Kat, Lindengracht 160 (J). Quiet and friendly Jordaan café.

Koophandel, Bloemgracht 49 (J). Converted warehouse that only begins to fill up around midnight, then throbs till dawn.

*Kort Amstelveld 2 (C). Modern café with a quiet canalside terrace. (See Lunch/Cafés, Walk V.)

*De Kroon Royal Café, Rembrandtsplein 17 (C). Historic meeting place of variety artistes and their agents, with a view over Rembrandtsplein. (See Lunch/Cafés, Walk V.)

Luxembourg, Spui 22–24 (C). Grand café that attracts well-heeled office workers. (See Lunch/Cafés, Walk I.)

*Het Molenpad, Prinsengracht 653 (C). A brown café that frequently crams a live jazz band into one corner. A smoky, dreamy place to while away a Sunday afternoon.

Nieuwe Lelie, Nieuwe Leliestraat 83, (J). One of the quieter Jordaan bars—it's even possible to get a table late at night. Chess players take advantage of the tranquillity.

Nol, Westerstraat 109 (J). Outrageously kitsch Jordaan bar. Locals, gangsters and astonished visitors get swept into uproarious sing-songs.

*L'Opera, Rembrandtsplein 19 (C). Sedate Art-Deco café on a bustling square. (See Lunch/Cafés, Walk V.)

Papeneiland, Prinsengracht 2 (C). Built in 1642, with a secret passage to the house across the canal. (See Lunch/Cafés, Walk III.)

De Prins, Prinsengracht 124, (C). Pretty canalside pub popular with students.

*Van Puffelen, Prinsengracht 377 (C). Sawdust on the floor, and cherubs on the ceiling. A good restaurant at the back, a terrace on a barge on the canal in front, and a very smart clientele.

*De Reiger, Nieuwe Leliestraat 34 (J). Bursting with Jordaaners and visitors all having a good time.

*Rosereijn, Haarlemmerdijk 52 (J). Cosy brown café with a good selection of magazines and cheap, tasty food.

*Schiller, Rembrandtsplein 26 (C). Cosy Art-Deco bar tucked away from the rumpus of Rembrandtsplein. (See Lunch/Cafés, Walk V.)

't Smackzeyl, Brouwersgracht 101 (J). Draught Guinness attracts

English and Irish ex-pats who sit around the bare tables and subside into drunkenness.

't Smalle, Egelantiersgracht 12 (J). An 18th-century *proeflokaal* converted into brown café. Gets packed most evenings. (See Lunch/Cafés, Walk III.)

De Tuin, 2e Tuindwarsstraat 13 (J). Dim light, board games and a twinge of eccentricity. All the ingredients of a classic brown café.

Twee Prinsen, Prinsenstraat 27 (C). Heated terrace and a friendly, alternative Jordaan crowd who profess great rivalry with the 'yuppies' at the **Vergulde Gaper** on the opposite corner.

Twee Zwaantjes, Prinsengracht 114 (C). Electric organ music, accordions and fat ladies with big voices from the Jordaan will make any visit unforgettable.

*Vertigo, Vondelpark 3 (S). Wonderful terrace on Vondelpark for good weather, cosy cellar under the Film Museum for bad. (See Lunch/Cafés, Walk VI.)

Welling, J.W. Brouwerstraat 32. Traditional brown café convenient for the Concertgebouw. (See Lunch/Cafés, Walk V.)

De Wetering, Weteringstraat 37 (C). A real log fire in winter and an ancient television that is used only for crucial football matches.

*Wildschut, Roelof Hartplein 1–3 (S). Art-Deco interior and noisy, smoky but none the less popular terrace.

Designer Bars

*Dantzig, Zwanenburgwal 15 (C). Attractive corner of the ugly new Stadhuis. Frequently filled with wedding parties. (See Lunch/Cafés, Walk III.)

Esprit, Spui 10 (C). Plateglass and aluminium showcase for the trendy. (See Lunch/Cafés, Walk I.)

Krull, Corner of 1e van der Helststraat and 1e Jan Steenstraat (S). Friendly café near the Albert Cuyp market.

*Morlang, Keizersgracht 451 (C). Brittle trendier-than-thou atmosphere.

*Paris Brest, Prinsengracht 375 (C). Hangout of the icy cool.

*Het Land van Walem, Keizersgracht 449 (C). Friendlier than the Morlang next door, with a bigger terrace and view through to a garden at the back.

Weltschmerz, Lindengracht 62–74 (J). Austere late-night bar for serious drinkers and snooker players.

Proeflokaalen

De Admiraal, Herengracht 319 (C). Enormous, with comfy chairs—stretches the definition somewhat. (See Lunch/Cafés, Walk II.)
De Drie Fleschjes, Gravenstraat 18 (C). More traditional *proeflokaal*. Some nearby offices have their own marked barrels. (See Lunch/Cafés, Walk I.)
Hooghoudt Proeflokaal, Reguliersgracht 11 (C).
House of Liquors, Damstraat 36 (C). Tiny and piled high with barrels.

Coffeeshops

Artemis, Keizersgracht 676 (C). You may have to ring the doorbell to get in to this arts and dancers' centre. Then you can sit in the bright coffeeshop, watch dancers in class through a glass wall at one end, or listen to their tales of aches and pains as they stretch their legs over your table.
Backstage Boutique, Utrechtsedwarsstraat 65–7 (C). The zaniest coffeeshop in town. (See Lunch/Cafés, Walk II.)
Berkhoff, Leidsestraat 46 (C). Little mauve-haired old ladies silently devour mounds of delicious creamcakes.
Françoise, Kerkstraat 176 (C). Classical music and good home cooking. (See Lunch/Cafés, Walk VI.)
Greenwoods, Singel 103 (C). *Real* English afternoon tea for the homesick. The English owner is most frequently seen up to her elbows in flour making the next batch of scones or sponge cake.
Granny, 1e van der Helststraat 45 (S). Near Albert Cuyp market. Some of the best *appelgebak* in town.
Pompadours, Huidenstraat 12 (C). Refined hand-made chocolates in a splendid setting. (See Lunch/Cafés, Walk VI.)

Smoking Coffeeshops

The Bulldog, Leidseplein 13–17/Oudezijds Voorburgwal 90 (C). Oldest and most commercial.
Prix d'Ami, Haringpakkersteeg 5 (C). Deeply respectable-looking branch of a chain of coffeeshops.
Rusland, Rusland 16 (C). Privately owned, intimate and relaxedly scruffy.
Pink Poffertje, moored at southern end of Oude Schans (C). Cosy boat that even sells marijuana beer.

217

Where to Stay

Canal House Hotel

It's a summer Friday afternoon, the VVV Information Office opposite Centraal station is brimming with hopeful weekenders looking for accommodation. But by 4 o'clock Amsterdam is full. Frustrated visitors are being despatched to surrounding towns like Leiden or Haarlem—pretty towns, and commuting is swift and cheap, yet this is always going to be second best....

The truth is, to really relish Amsterdam you need to stay right in the centre, preferably on a canal, and to do that you should **book a hotel room well in advance**—two to three weeks at least, more in the summer or over holiday weekends. There is, of course, always the chance of catching a cancellation, and some hotels do keep back a room or two until the last minute. If you cannot book in advance, try calling the hotel direct just before noon—the witching hour between check-out and check-in—and try your luck.

Standards of cleanliness and service are high, and unless you're scraping along at the very bottom of the price range, you're unlikely to find yourself sharing your room with local fauna, thumping faulty electrical equipment or speculating about the origins of the hairs on the sheets. Facilities can be quite spartan, however, and a lot of the smaller hotels offer rooms of the bed/bedside table/wardrobe only variety. Yet even these are usually tastefully done up and almost invariably impeccably

218

clean. Hotels are graded by the Benelux star system (one to five stars), though this isn't a particularly useful guide as it is based on an inventory of facilities and tells you nothing about location, service or ambience. Facilities vary in direct relation to price—you get what you pay for. Around the top end of the moderate range (ƒ150–ƒ200) you should be assured of a TV and telephone in your room. Beyond that lies the world of mini-bars, *en suite* jacuzzis and telephones in the loo.

All sorts of canal houses—poky, grand and resonantly historical— have been given new life as hotels. Many of these are privately owned and have been lovingly turned into little havens of *gezelligheid* or storehouses of antiques. These are the best places of all to stay—but most have built up a dedicated clientele and require booking some time in advance. Rooms in the same house will vary enormously in size and *en suite* bathrooms tend to have showers only. If you hear of a particularly desirable room, try to book it specifically by number.

Reservations can be made, once you're in the country, through the VVV (see Practical A–Z: Tourist Information). They charge a ƒ3.50 booking fee and a ƒ4 room deposit which is later deducted from your bill. The Netherlands Board of Tourism in your home country can give you a list of hotels, but can't make bookings. If you want to make a reservation before you leave, contact the hotel direct or make use of the free reservation service: Netherlands Reservations Centre (PO Box 404, 2260AK Leidschendam; tel (070) 320 2500, fax (070) 320 2611, telex 33755; open Mon–Fri 8–8, Sat 8–2). You pay the bill at the hotel as usual.

Accommodation Categories

Because accommodation is at such a premium, you'll find that most hotels will ask for a deposit or the security of a credit card number. Some simply won't accept weekend reservations unless you book, or at least pay for, Friday, Saturday *and* Sunday night.

As Amsterdam is such a compact city, hotels in this list are graded by price rather than area. Nearly all of them are within easy walking distance of the main tourist sites, and have been chosen because of their pleasant atmosphere, location or historical significance. An asterisk indicates hotels that are especially recommended. The hotels in the 'Expensive' range tend to be business hotels. Here you're paying for facilities like fax, telex and meeting rooms. Such places are briskly efficient, but are often soulless and used to expense-account customers. You can be just as

219

comfortable, and probably far happier, in a more idiosyncratic hotel from the top of the 'Moderate' range. Price ranges given in this guide are as follows:

Luxury	ƒ300 and over
Expensive	ƒ200–ƒ300
Moderate	ƒ100–ƒ200
Cheap	under ƒ100

These prices are for a double room with bath or shower *en suite* in season, and include services and taxes and (unless otherwise stated) Dutch breakfast. For prices of single rooms deduct 15–20 per cent. The addresses given below include the Amsterdam post code.

Luxury

American Hotel, Leidsekade 97, 1017 PN; tel 624 5322, fax 625 3236, telex 12545. An Art-Deco extravaganza overlooking the thronging Leidseplein. The café downstairs was once the meeting place for Amsterdam's literati (see Walk VI). From ƒ385, breakfast ƒ29 extra.

*Amstel Hotel Intercontinental, Professor Tulpplein 1, 1018 GX; tel 622 6060, fax 622 5808, telex 11004. A gracious and sedate hotel on the banks of the Amstel. If you're stuck for transport you can use the hotel's motor yacht or Rolls Royce. ƒ525 excl. breakfast (closed for renovations until spring 1992).

Doelen Karena Hotel, Nieuwe Doelenstraat 24, 1012 CP; tel 622 0722, fax 622 1084, telex 14399. One of Amsterdam's oldest hotels, though fading in grandeur. Rembrandt painted *The Nightwatch* here in 1642. ƒ320 excl. breakfast.

*Hotel de l'Europe, Nieuwe Doelenstraat 2–8, 1012 CP; tel 623 4836, fax 624 2962, telex 12081. An elegant 19th-century hotel in the grand old style. Knocks spots off the Doelen down the road. ƒ525. Breakfast from ƒ22.50.

Grand Hotel Krasnapolsky, Dam 9, 1012 JS; tel 554 9111, fax 622 8607, telex 12262. Right in the centre of town and very grand from the outside, but disappointingly renovated. From ƒ400.

*Hotel Pulitzer, Prinsengracht 315–331, 1016 GZ; tel 523 5235, fax 627 6753, telex 16508. Twenty-four canal houses linked up to form a warren of oak-beamed rooms. There's a peaceful garden and a magnificent 18th-century dining-room. ƒ375, breakfast ƒ30.

Amsterdam Hilton, Apollolaan 138–140, 1077 BG; tel 6780 780, fax 662 6688, telex 11025. In the south-west of the city, not in the centre. From ƒ460 excl. breakfast.

Hilton International Schiphol, Herbergierstraat, 1118 ZK; tel 603 4567, fax 648 0917, telex 15186. Part of Schiphol complex around the airport. Shuttle bus from airport. ƒ450 excl. breakfast.

Holiday Inn Amsterdam, De Boelelaan 2, 1083 HJ; tel 646 2300, fax 646 4790, telex 13647. In the far south of the city, conveniently close to the ring road. From ƒ390.

Holiday Inn Crowne Plaza, Nieuwzijds Voorburgwal 5; tel 620 0500, fax 620 1173, telex 15183. Centrally located for the Euro-business-person. From ƒ455 excl. breakfast.

Expensive

Acca International, Van de Veldestraat 3a, 1071 CW; tel 625 5262, telex 10840. Modern, functional hotel near the main museums. From ƒ280.

Hotel Ambassade, Herengracht 335–353, 1016 AZ, tel 626 2333, fax 624 5321, telex 10158. Eight converted houses, dotted about with antiques and with a magnificent breakfast-room overlooking the canal. ƒ240.

*Hotel Dikker & Thijs, Prinsengracht 444, 1017 KE; tel 626 7721, fax 625 8986, telex 13161. Intimate but opulent with a reputation for good food, and with a famous delicatessen attached. In a central, hectically busy area of town. From ƒ290, breakfast ƒ20 extra.

Jan Luyken Hotel, Jan Luykenstraat 58, 1071 CS; tel 676 4111, fax 676 3841, telex 16254. Smart, efficient business hotel in quiet area near the Concertgebouw. From ƒ260.

Hotel de Molen, Prinsengracht 1015, 1017 KN; tel 623 1666, fax 622 6736. Friendly staff, all mod cons and canal views, though the decor is a little bland. From ƒ200.

*Schiller Karena Hotel, Rembrandtsplein 26–36, 1017 CV; tel 623 1660, fax 624 0098, telex 14058. Decorated with the paintings of its 19th-century owner, it was once the meeting place of actors and artists. It overlooks a lively square, and has one of the Amsterdam's best bars downstairs. From ƒ295.

phone: 31 - 20 (Amsterdam)

Moderate

Hotel Aalders, Jan Luykenstraat 13–15, 1071 CJ; tel 662 0116, fax 673 4698, telex 14041. Old-fashioned hotel with a gloomy charm. Near the main museums. ƒ165.

Hotel Acro, Jan Luykenstraat 44, 1071 CR; tel 662 0526. Sparkling, simple, if a little soulless. Set in the quiet museum district. ƒ130.

Hotel Adolesce, Nieuwe Keizersgracht 26, 1018 DS; tel 626 3959. Cheerful, simple hotel with a sunny breakfast-room. A good one if you have children. From ƒ100, some rooms without bathroom.

*Hotel Agora, Singel 462, 1017 AW; tel 627 2200, fax 627 2202, telex 12657. The owner is interested in fine furniture—and it shows. Rooms overlooking the canal or back garden are the best. Good value from ƒ165.

Hotel De Admiraal, Herengracht 563, 1017 CD; tel 626 2150. Friendly owner, views over *two* canals, and a slap-up breakfast. Around ƒ135 (ƒ90 without private bathroom).

Hotel Belga, Hartenstraat 8, 1016 CB; tel 624 9080. Unpretentious, family-run hotel in a quaint shopping alley. ƒ125 (ƒ110 without shower).

*Het Canal House, Keizersgracht 148, 1015 CX; tel 622 5182, fax 624 1317, telex 10611. Stunning converted canal houses, filled to the brim with the owner's carefully chosen antiques. A breakfast-room with a piano and drippingly beautiful crystal chandelier. The hotel has the feel of a tastefully (if somewhat grandly) decorated private home. From ƒ190—superb value.

Hotel Engeland, Roemer Vischerstraat 30, 1054 EZ; tel 612 9691, fax 618 4579. The English representative in a quaint row of 19th-century houses built to show seven different national architectural styles. From ƒ130 (ƒ100 without bath).

*Hotel De Filosoof, Anna Vondelstraat 6, 1054 GZ; tel 683 3013. Each room is named after a well-known thinker, and decorated accordingly. The hotel can arrange consultations with one of 16 philosophers practising in Holland, many of whom frequent the bar. From ƒ100.

Hotel De Gouden Kettingh, Keizersgracht 268, 1016 EV; tel 624 8287. Larger rooms than most canal house hotels, and some good views. From ƒ150 (ƒ110 without bathroom).

Hotel Maas, Leidsekade 91, 1017 PN; tel 623 3868, fax 622 2613, telex 12899. Well appointed hotel on quiet canal. As you ascend the price scale you could end up with (in addition to the usual business facilities) a waterbed or whirlpool bath. From ƒ175.

Owl Hotel, Roemer Visscherstraat 1–3, 1054 EV; tel 618 9484, telex

13360. Smart family hotel with large garden. In the museum neigh-bourhood. ƒ175.

Hotel Prinsenhof, Prinsengracht 810, 1017 JL; tel 623 1772, fax 638 3368. Quiet, thoughtfully decorated hotel with friendly management. ƒ140 (ƒ95 without bathroom).

*Hotel Seven Bridges, Reguliersgracht 31, 1017 LK; tel 623 1329. The most charming of the small hotels. Beautifully decorated rooms—and breakfast served in bed. ƒ100 (without bath) to ƒ145.

Hotel Toren, Keizersgracht 164, 1015 CZ; tel 622 6352, fax 626 9705, telex 18118. Seventeenth-century canal house with high moulded ceil-ings, and antiques scattered among the modern furniture. From ƒ160.

*Hotel Wiechmann, Prinsengracht 328–330, 1016 HX. tel 626 3321, fax 626 8962. Carefully converted canal houses with an air of old world charm, and a noble breakfast-room. From ƒ150.

Inexpensive

Hotel de Harmonie, Prinsengracht 816, 1017 JL; tel 625 0174. Bright, jolly, family run hotel. ƒ95 without bathroom.

Hotel Impala, Leidsekade 77, 1017 PM; tel 623 4706. Clean, laid-back hotel with young crowd. From ƒ85.

Hotel Liberty, Singel 5; tel 620 7307. Tiny, but clean with amiable management. ƒ80 without bathroom.

*Quentin Hotel, Leidsekade 89, 1017 PN; tel 626 2187. Popular with musicians playing at *De Melkweg* around the corner. Posters of past (now famous) residents adorn the walls. There's also a faithful gay clientele (mainly women). Spotless, tastefully decorated and good views over the canal. From ƒ65 excl. breakfast, shared bathrooms.

Hotel de Westertoren, Raadhuisstraat 35b, 1016 DC; tel 624 4639. Well-kept, if a little noisy. From ƒ85.

Hotel Ronnie, Raadhuisstraat 41, 1016 DD; tel 624 2821. One of the better of a strip of hotels along frantic Raadhuisstraat. ƒ90 without bathroom.

Hostels

The two official International Youth Hostel Federation hostels are:

Vondelpark, Zandpad 5, 1054 GA; tel 683 1744, telex 11031.
Stadsdoelen, Kloveniersburgwal 97, 1011 KB; tel 624 6832.
Members ƒ19.50 per person (incl. breakfast); sheet hire ƒ5.50; May–Sept supplement ƒ2.50; day membership ƒ5.

There are also:

Amstel, Steiger 5 (Pier 5), De Ruijterkade; tel 626 4247. The last remaining of Amsterdam's barge hotels, moored behind Centraal Station. Clean, though a little cramped. From *f*25 per person.
*Eben Haezer Christian Youth Hostel, Bloemstraat 179, 1016 LA; tel 624 4717. Spotless, not oppressively religious and the best value of the lot. *f*13.50, including breakfast and bed linen. No membership required.

Campsites

Het Amsterdamse Bos, Kleine Noorddijk 1, 1432 CC, Aalsmeer; tel 641 6868; open April–Oct. Bus 171, 172. Good facilities but far out. *f*7 per person, *f*2.50 per car, *f*3.35 per night electricity charge for campervans.
Vliegenbos, Meeuwenlaan 138, 1022 AM; tel 636 8855; open April–Sept. Bus 32 (10 minutes from Centraal Station). 'Youth Campsite'—all ages welcome but be prepared for late-night high spirits. From *f*5 per person, cars *f*3, electricity *f*3.

Apartments

Amsterdam Apartments, Nieuwezijds Voorburgwal 63, 1012 RE; tel 626 5930. Privately owned flats around town from *f*600 per week.
Intercity Room Service, Van Ostadestraat 348, 1073 TZ; tel 675 0064. Flatshares from *f*50 per day.
GIS Apartments, Keizersgracht 33, 1015 CD; tel 625 0071. From the simple to the luxurious—usually flats let by Amsterdammers away on holiday. From *f*500 per week.

Entertainment and Nightlife

Statue of 'The Unknown Violinist'

Amsterdam's nightlife centres on **cafés**. They offer everything from a quiet evening over the backgammon board to jolly sing-songs in just about any language you choose. There are even some cafés where you can dance, though a handful of good **nightclubs** serve those who really like to bounce and sweat. The more genteel spectator entertainments are quite accessible to foreigners. **Films** are usually shown in their original language, with Dutch sub-titles; there's a strong tradition of highly visual **theatre**, and many performances in English; the new Muziektheater provides a venue for touring **opera** and **dance** companies and Amsterdam has high international status in the various **music** worlds. Up and coming British **rock** bands test the water here before facing jaded audiences at home; there are some good **jazz** festivals, and recent immigration has upped the quality of **salsa** and **Latin American** music. The acoustically superb Concertgebouw attracts leading **classical** artists and conductors, and there's a very healthy **contemporary music** scene.

Information

The various **listings magazines** will guide you through the maze. The tourist office publish a fortnightly *What's On In Amsterdam* (f2.50, available at VVV and around town). The free monthly *Uitkrant* (from VVV, AUB, libraries, museums and theatres) is more comprehensive

225

and, although it's in Dutch, fairly easy to follow. *Agenda* (free Dutch monthly to be found in cafés) aims at a younger crowd and is good on live music. *WILD!* (f3.50 from WILD! Boutique, Kerkstraat 104) is a monthly English guide to trendy dancing Amsterdam. *Oor* (available from newsagents) is the Dutch equivalent of *NME*, the British rock music newspaper. Both the VVV and the AUB booking office (see Practical A–Z: Tourist Information) can reserve tickets. The AUB also has an up-to-the-minute What's On noticeboard (good for pop music) and a few rainforests' worth of leaflets. (For a guide to some of the city's arts festivals see Practical A–Z: Festivals and Events.)

Film

The Dutch are avid movie-goers. Most cafés and some restaurants and take-aways have a list of the week's films pinned up on the wall. Home-grown products haven't, however, made much of an impact on the international scene—though director Paul Verhoeven is known for *Robocop* and *Total Recall*, and the British director Peter Greenaway operates largely with Dutch funding.

You'll find most of the multi-screened **commercial cinemas** in the area around Leidseplein, where they offer pretty standard fare. The six-screen Tuschinski (see Walk V, p. 175) must be a hot contender for the most beautiful cinema in the world and is worth a visit no matter what's showing.

Cinema prices range from f10–f13 and there are often discounts on weeknights. In the rare cases where an English film has been dubbed over you'll see *Nederlands Gesproken* on the publicity.

Amsterdam offers nothing to rival the internationally important **Rotterdam Film Festival** (held Jan/Feb; information from any VVV), but **art movies** get a good showing in some rather romantic old cinemas.

Art Houses

Alfa Kleine Gartmanplantsoen 4, tel 627 8806. Cannon-owned art cinema showing mainly English films.

Desmet, Plantage Middenlaan 4, tel 627 3434. Ornate Art-Deco cinema used by a Jewish cabaret company in the early years of the Second World War. These days known for its imaginative mini-festivals and weekend gay screenings.

Film Museum, Vondelpark 3, tel 589 1400. Frequent changes of programme, usually with something from the museums unique and extensive archive—such as tinted silent movies (see Walk VI p. 189).

Kriterion, Roeterstraat 170, tel 623 1708. Cult American movies and erotic French late-nights.

The Movies, Haarlemmerdijk 161, tel 624 5790. Some of the programming verges on the mainstream, but the 1920s interior is a delight and there's a vibrant café/restaurant (see Food and Drink, p.211).

Rialto, Ceintuurbaan 338, tel 662 3488. Good on retrospectives, science-fiction, animation and children's films.

De Uitkijk, Prinsengracht 452, tel 623 7460. Amsterdam's oldest cinema (dating from 1913) squashed into an even older canal house. It features a white grand piano that has long since tinkled its last notes, but is too big to be removed.

(See also **De Melkweg** p. 234.)

Theatre

Like England, the Netherlands experienced a 17th-century Golden Age of the theatre. Playwrights of that era, such as Vondel, Hooft and Bredero, are still performed in Holland. The 18th and 19th centuries saw the growth of extravagant stage spectacles. (On the nights they went to the theatre, wealthy families would send their maids and cooks on ahead to swell the ranks of the extras.) By the end of the 19th century, theatre had ossified from a popular into an élitist form. The 'Tomato Action' of 1968 put an end to that. A disgruntled new generation of actors began throwing tomatoes at their older colleagues during performances and sparked off a theatrical revolution. In the decade that followed, Amsterdam theatres like the Mickery and the Shaffy earned a world-wide reputation for high quality avant-garde work. Government cuts and changing tastes have curtailed the mud-wading and body-painting, but there is still a strong tradition of excellent, highly visual theatre (look out for work by Orkater theatre company and spectacular outdoor romps by the Dogtroep).

There is no national theatre company; the chief mainstream company is the rather stolid Toneelgroep Amsterdam, resident at the Stadsschouwburg. Two local English-speaking companies compete with foreign touring productions for the Amsterdam audience. Panache presents small-scale productions, usually upstairs in a converted prop room at the Stadsschouwburg, and the Stadhouderij Theatre Company produces contemporary work of a consistently high standard. The Nes (off Damstraat) and the banks of the Amstel are traditionally Amsterdam's theatreland, but these days no old warehouse, factory or stable is safe from troupes of eager actors.

If you want to go to the theatre, the best thing to do is check the listings magazines for touring companies—but here's a short list of venues where you're most likely to find good work in English.

't Fijnhout Theater, Jacob van Lennepkade 334, tel 618 4768. A popular theatre with English-language touring companies.

Koninklijk Theater Carré, Amstel 115–125, tel 622 5225. Built for a circus—a function it still performs over the Christmas period when Dutch children regard a visit as *de rigueur*. It's the home of most big Amsterdam musicals, but more off-the-wall performances slip into gaps in the programme. (See Walk II, p. 119.)

Shaffy Theater, Felix Meritus Building, Keizersgracht 324, tel 623 1311. Unlike the Mickery, the Shaffy has (just) survived the 1980s and looks set for a new lease of life. Housed in a building with a rich cultural past. (See Walk VI, p. 195.)

De Stadsschouwburg, Leidseplein 26, tel 624 2311. Amsterdam's municipal theatre. Director Cox Habbema is expanding the programme to include a wide range of national productions, and is attracting more international companies. There's a good **theatre bookshop** near the main entrance. (See Walk VI, p. 191.)

De Stadhouderij, 1e Bloemdwarsstraat 4, tel 626 2282. A converted stable that seats around 40 people. Home to one of Amsterdam's English-speaking theatre companies.
(See also **De Melkweg** p. 234.)

Dance

Until recently, Dutch dance was sagging rather sadly, propped up by a rather unvivacious Nationale Ballet and the practically moribund Scapio Ballet. Only the Nederlands Dans Theater had the verve and energy to prevent complete artistic prolapse. But at the moment the Netherlands is rising towards the crest of a new wave of dance, inspired perhaps by the big stage at the new Muziektheater, an influx of foreign dancers and traditional rhythms from the former colonies. The Nationale Ballet has expanded its repertoire, and is benefiting from the visits of touring companies who, on the larger stage of the Muziektheater, now have a suitable Amsterdam venue. The Scapio is dusting off the cobwebs and under new artistic direction has appointed Ed Wubbe as their daring new choreographer; the Nederlands Dans Theater keeps up a salvo of fine ballet and modern dance. Look out also for work by Djazzex (jazz dance), Dansproduktie (Cunningham-inspired modern dance) and Dansgroep Krisztina de Châtel (vivid, fairly theatrical style).

Once again the listings magazines will tell you what's on, but the following venues are worth checking out:

Bellevue, Leidsekade 90, tel 624 7248. Often plays host to modern dance touring companies.

Captain Fiddle, Kloveniersburgwal 86, tel 626 0363. The spot to catch the newest companies (theatre and dance).

Frascati, Nes 63, tel (day) 626 6866/(night) 623 5723. A venue for more established modern dance companies.

Muziektheater (Stopera), Waterlooplein 22, tel 625 5455. If you want to see something in this new opera house, ballet may be the best choice as the acoustics are a little iffy. (See below.)

Studio Danslab, Overamstelstraat 39, tel 694 9466. Another place to catch interesting new work, as well as more established performers.

If you're a dancer yourself and want to keep up with classes or attend courses, visit **Artemis Kunstcentrum** (Keizersgracht 676, tel 623 2655; open Mon–Sat 10–3.30; *f*12 per class, professionals only). It's a friendly dance centre, run by English and American ex-pats, and housed in a beautifully converted church. Famous dancers passing through town are often persuaded to give short courses in the summer. Non-dancers can enjoy the coffeeshop (see Food and Drink) and should keep an eye open for the evening music recitals.

Music

Classical and Opera

After a lull during the 1980s, when government cuts guillotined five of the Netherlands' thirteen major orchestras, and public interest began to wane, Dutch music seems to be undergoing a renaissance. Baroque and period instrument orchestras are reaching particularly high standards (try to catch the Amsterdam Baroque Orchestra, or the Orchestra of the 18th Century when they are not on tour). The Nederlandse Opera repeatedly comes up with sharp, adventurous productions, often of 20th-century works, and the contemporary music scene is very lively (look out for pieces by Louis Andriessen and performances by the refreshingly unorthodox Ricciotti Ensemble).

The famed **Royal Concertgebouw Orchestra** first established its reputation before the Second World War under the baton of Willem Mengelberg. He built up a close working relationship with Mahler and Richard Strauss and devoted 50 years to establishing his orchestra as one of the greatest in the world, only to be sacked after the war for pro-German sympathies. In the 1960s the orchestra was propelled to even greater heights by Bernard Haitink. It too has been through a dry patch recently, but conductor Riccardo Chailly is giving it new life.

Tickets will seem cheap if you're used to London or New York prices, but they sell out quickly. You can try for returns half an hour before a performance, but there are no last-minute discounts and systems of selling return tickets (especially at the Muziektheater) can be disorganized. Churches are favourite venues for concerts and recitals. Scan the listings magazines to find out what's on at the Oude Kerk, the Nieuwe Kerk, the Engelse Kerk and the Oude Lutherse Kerk. Other venues include:

AGA Zaal and Wang Zaal, Damrak 213, tel 627 0466. Home to the Netherlands Chamber Orchestra and the Netherlands Philharmonic respectively. Beautifully converted concert halls in the old Beurs van Berlage (see Walk I, p. 95).

Concertgebouw, Concertgebouwplein 2–6, tel 671 8345. The Grote Zaal (Large Hall) has perfect acoustics and is used for orchestral concerts and also visiting pop stars and jazz bands. Nervous students from the Sweelinck Conservatorium across the road make their professional debuts in the Kleine Zaal (Small Hall). There are free lunchtime concerts on Wednesdays. (See Walk V p. 167.)

De IJsbreker, Weesperzijde 23, tel 668 1805. A deservedly famous centre for contemporary music. It brings out its own news-sheet and offers a stimulating programme of local and international composers and improvisers.

Muziektheater (Stopera), Waterlooplein 22, tel 625 5455. Home to the national ballet and opera companies, but subject of one of the biggest architectural and property development controversies of the century, and of angry complaints by musicians and audience alike about the bad acoustics (see Topics, pp. 72–6). It does, however, have an attractive, cosy auditorium—rare for a modern theatre. There are organized backstage tours (Wed and Sat 4 pm; ƒ8.50; book in advance on 551 8103 for English guide). (See also Walk V p. 176.)

De Rode Hoed, Keizersgracht 102, tel 625 7368. Varied programmes in a converted church.

Rock and Pop

Chart-busters and stadium-packers like Madonna and Prince usually give Amsterdam a bye and head for the larger venues of Rotterdam, though Dutch stars who have made it internationally—such as Mathilde Santing, Eton Crop and the not so gently aging Golden Earring—have a loyalty to the old town and come back for a gig or two. Young British bands (who see an Amsterdam tour as the penultimate rung on the ladder to fame and glory) are often the best bet if you're looking for good rock. Many of these head for Paradiso or De Melkweg, though they often also strain the sound systems of smaller venues around town. Amsterdam's large Indonesian and Surinamese populations swell many a bar with pulsating ethnic rhythms—the Latin and South American music scene is especially lively. In the summer everyone heads for the **Vondelpark**, where good musicians give free concerts and the park swings with a party atmosphere.

The listings magazines *Oor* and *WILD!* are your best guide to what's on. Prices range from free entrance to around *f*20 and starting times are usually between 9 and 11 pm.

Akhnaton, Nieuwezijds Kolk 25, tel 624 3396. Recording studios, rehearsal facilities and a forum for much of the liveliest new music, hip-hop and and ethnic bands.

Cruise Inn, Zeeburgerdijk 272, tel 692 7188. Flotsam and jetsam from the 1950s shake, rattle and roll in an old wooden clubhouse.

Korsakoff, Lijnbaansgracht 161, tel 625 7854. A venue for head-banging post-punks, which nods towards heavy metal and gothic teeny-boppers.

Paradiso, Weteringschans 6–8, tel 626 4521. An Amsterdam institution. A gloomy looking church that has been converted into a bright and buzzing venue for good music—anything from big rock names to jazz, African, Latin and even contemporary classical.

PH 31, Prins Hendriklaan 31, tel 673 6850. A bare box of violent sound in the middle of a rather sleepy residential district.

(See also **De Melkweg** and Nightclubs below.)

Jazz, Latin and Folk

The mellow tones of jazz seem to suit the atmosphere of the brown cafés, and many will have a live band on a Saturday night or Sunday afternoon. There are often special gigs around the same time as the Holland Festival (see Practical A–Z: Festivals and Events) and the excellent North Sea Jazz Festival in The Hague (see Day Trips p. 271). Surinamese and other South American immigrants crowd out a number of vibrant drinking and dancing venues around town. Bars and cafés with live music usually don't charge entrance, but have more expensive drinks.

Jazzcafé Altó, Korte Leidsedwarsstraat 115, tel 626 3249. Live jazz every night in a cosy brown café tucked away in a brash touristy street.
Bamboo Bar, Lange Leidsedwarsstraat 64, tel 624 3993. Live Latin music or jazz every night. Some say the trumpeter Chet Baker used to live upstairs and come down to play for his rent.
Bimhuis, Oudeschans 73, tel 623 3373. The city's major jazz venue plays host to visiting artistes and the cream of the locals, and has free sessions on Mondays and Wednesdays.
Canecão Brazilian Bar, Lange Leidsedwarsstraat 68–70, tel 626 1500. Live Samba and a gyrating throng of Latin ex-patriots.
Iboya, Korte Leidsedwarssstraat 29, tel 623 7859. Small theatre café that often has live South American bands.
Joseph Lamm Jazz Club, Van Diemenstraat 8, tel 622 8086. Traditional and Dixieland jazz and free jam sessions on Sundays.
Odeon Jazz Kelder, Singel 460, tel 624 9711. Trad jazz in an intimate atmosphere.
Rum Runners, Prinsengracht 277, tel 627 4079. Glitzy, crowded Caribbean bar/restaurant with live Latin bands on Sunday afternoons and early evening.
Rembrandt Bar, Rembrandtsplein 3, tel 623 0688. Plays Dutch folk music. But for a real knees-up and noisy accordion rather visit **Café Nol** or **De Twee Zwaantjes** (see Food and Drink: Cafés).

Nightclubs and Dancing

Amsterdam night-clubbers don't suffer the fashion neuroses of their London or New York counterparts. You can dress up, down, wild or straight: there's no need to shock or impress some desperately cool doorman before you're let in. Entrance prices are low enough—and the city small enough—for you to wander from one club to the next. The mood is carefree and unpretentious—late-night clubbing seems just an extension of early-evening café life. There *is* a new club-culture scene that holds all-night warehouse parties in deserted areas of town, yet even here you'll find playful Dutch touches. The *WILD!* magazine and boutique (see above) are good sources of information about one-nighters and parties.

The commercial discos (chart music, plastic palm trees, expensive drinks and posses of drunken men) cluster around Leidseplein. What follows is a list of places for those with rather different tastes. Most venues close at 4 am (5 am over weekends). You should tip the doorman as you leave (about ƒ5), and avoid using cabs cruising outside. Legal cabs will be found at a nearby rank—or the club may phone for one for you.

Dansen bij Jansen, Handboogstraat 11, tel 620 1779. A bit like a Students' Union bop. You usually need to prove membership of a college or university to get in. Frequent theme and fancy-dress nights.
Escape, Rembrandtsplein 11, tel 622 3542. Mirrors, theatrical decor, video screens, lasers, a young crowd and fairly bland music.
't Heerenhuys, Herengracht 114, tel 622 7685. Café and cocktail bar where you can hold a conversation at a normal level. A dance-floor where thirty-somethings can hop about to soul, jazz, blues and rock and roll.
Julianas, Hilton Hotel, Apollolaan 138, tel 673 7313. As you would expect from the location, muted, elegant and sedate.
Mazzo, Rozengracht 114, tel 626 7500. Once hyper-trendy, now eclipsed by the Roxy (see below), it's a comfortable club with a good atmosphere. There's live house at weekends and local bands on Tuesday.
36 Op de Schaal van Richter, Reguliersdwarsstraat 36, tel 626 1573. Earthquake-shattered mirrors on the walls and good soul/disco music—but most of the interesting clientele have moved across to the Roxy.
Roxy, Singel 465–7, tel 620 0354. Currently the city's trendiest club, this is the one place where you need a little pzazz (or a friend who's a member) to get past the doorman. Once you're inside you'll find the old cinema grandly decked out and the clientele strutting their stuff. There's an upstairs bar where you can sit and watch it all.
Star-Sky, Warmoesstraat 151, tel 627 1545. Dress snappily, practise your steps and join Amsterdam's South American population for an evening of soul and salsa.
Zorba the Buddha, Oudezijds Voorburgwal 216, tel 625 9642. Marble dance floor, chic ambience and mainly young crowd.
(See also **De Melkweg** below.)

Multi-Media Centres

De Brakke Grond, Nes 45, tel 626 6866. Attractive venue for Flemish art and performance. Dance programmes are especially worth catching.
De Meervaart Centrum, Osdorpplein 205, tel 610 7393. A modern arts centre that stages a good variety of film, theatre, dance and music (classical and jazz).
De Melkweg, Lijnbaansgracht 234a, tel 624 1777. Converted from an old dairy in the 1960s, De Melkweg (Milky Way) has managed to slough off its old hippie image, and emerge as a vibrant centre for the arts. The theatre has an extraordinarily imaginative programme and plays host to companies from around the world (performances are often in English). There is a small cinema that shows a range of films from mainstream to cult; and a concert hall that stages excellent African and South American bands, and acts as a try-out venue for a lot of up-and-coming rock groups. At weekends, when the bands have finished, an alternative disco takes over. The coffeeshop was one of the first where the sale of marijuana was tolerated by the authorities. If you're going to use the centre a lot, it's a good idea to take out membership (f5, valid three months) which gives you considerable discount on admission prices.
RAI Congrescentrum, Europaplein 12, tel 644 8651. A business congress centre which frequently houses large concerts and touring musicals. It is also the venue for KunstRAI, an annual fair of contemporary art (see Practical A–Z: Festivals and Events).

Shopping

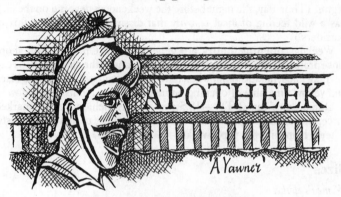

A Yawner

What is there that's not found here
Of corn; French or Spanish wine
Any Indies goods that are sought
In Amsterdam may all be bought
Here's no famine ... the land is fat.
—*Constantijn Huygens, 17th-century*
Dutch poet

Amsterdam's prosperity in the Golden Age turned it into an exotic *emporium mundi*. The little shops below the decorative *uithangborden* (painted signs) were crammed with Nuremberg ceramics, Lyons silk, Spanish wines, mysterious Egyptian potions and an abundance of local pastries, cheeses, linen and boots. When Marie de Médicis made her grandiose entry into Amsterdam in 1638, the first thing she did when she had a moment's spare time (amidst the lavish ceremonies celebrating her arrival) was to swoop down on the Amsterdam shops where, apparently, she haggled with the adept confidence of someone reared in a market-place.

Amsterdam's markets, boutiques and eccentric speciality shops are still one of the city's greatest allures. The range of goods and oddity of the shops can keep you browsing for hours. The only barriers against your absolute financial ruin are the inconvenient opening hours.

Calvinism wins over tourism—you'll find very few places at all open on a Sunday. Amsterdammers enjoy their weekends, and the fun tends to overflow into Monday: many shops also stay closed on Monday mornings, if not for the whole day. However, most stay open late on Thursday nights. (Thursday, the night before the weekenders descend on the city, has a wild feeling of local festivity that dissipates under the influx of outsiders.)

Weekday **opening hours** are generally 9–6. On Saturdays shops close around 5 pm, some as early as 3 pm. Many of the smaller shops can be quite idiosyncratic about when they open, but all will have a little black and yellow timetable of opening hours posted on an outside window.

Dutch **sales tax** (BTW—18.5 per cent) is included in the marked price, though many stores offer **tax-free** shopping to non-EC tourists. They'll help with the paperwork.

Sizes

Women's clothes

UK	8	10	12	14	16	18
US	6	8	10	12	14	16
Eu	38	40	42	44	46	48

Men's Shirts

UK/US	14	$14\frac{1}{2}$	15	$15\frac{1}{2}$	16	$16\frac{1}{2}$	17	$17\frac{1}{2}$
Eu		36	37	38	39	40	41	42	43

Men's Suits

UK/US	36	38	40	42	44	46
Eu		46	48	50	52	54	56

Men's shoes

UK	6	7	8	9	10	11	12
US	8	9	10	11	12	13	14
Eu	39	40	41	42	43	44	45

Women's shoes

UK	4	5	6	7	8
US	5	6	7	8	9
Eu	37	38	39	40	41

After-hours Shopping

Most neighbourhoods have one or two shops that open around 5 pm and stay open until between 11 pm and 1 am. Here you can buy, at a suitably inflated price, emergency bottles of wine, groceries and gooey cakes for late-night munchies. Some of the more up-market establishments sell gourmet meals and chocolates to bring tears to your eyes. Look out for signs reading *Avondverkoop* or *Nightshop*. Here's a selection of the more up-market ones:

Baltus, Vijzelstraat 127.
Big Bananas, Leidsestraat 76. Big price tags.
Heuft's First Class Nightshop, Rijnstraat, 62. Late-night oysters and champagne.

To locate a **late-night pharmacy** contact the Central Medical Service (tel 664 2111).

Antiques

The **Rokin** (the street running from the Dam to Muntplein) was once the traditional stretch for antique dealers. Now there are only a few crusty die-hards here—the sort of shop where you have to comb your hair and ring a bell before they let you in. These days the most stylish, outlandish and enticingly chaotic treasure-troves are to be found in the **Spiegelkwartier** (see Walk VI pp. 192–4) and around the **Looiersgracht** (see Markets).

Artists' Supplies

J.Vlieger, Amstel 52. Pencils, pigments and piles of inspiring paper.

Beauty Shops

The Body Shop, Kalverstraat 157–9. Ubiquitous, environmentally-friendly British chain store with an aroma that reaches right down the street.
Jacob Hooy & Co., Kloveniersburgwal 12. Pre-empted the Body Shop by over two centuries. Barrels and boxes of herbs and cosmetics and modern Green products.
Palais des Parfums, Van Baerlestraat 74. Top of the range perfumes, cosmetics and facial pampering.

Books

Good **antiquarian bookshops** pop up all over the city, but especially around the university at the southern end of the red-light district. New books in English are usually quite expensive in Amsterdam.

American Discount Book Center, Kalverstraat 185. Best stock in town of English fiction and non-fiction, magazines and children's books. Musicians use the basement tea-room as an informal labour exchange.

Architectura & Natura, Leliegracht 44. Just what it says, with an impressive collection of books on Amsterdam.

Atheneum Nieuwscentrum, Spui 14–16. Stamping ground of the city's intelligentsia. Good selection of magazines and English non-fiction.

N.C. van den Berg, Oudeschans 8–10. Untidy, eccentric and a feast of second-hand bargains.

The Book Exchange, Kloveniersburgwal 58. Essential in this town of outrageous prices.

Canon Bookstore, Leidsestraat 79. Abundantly-stocked photographic bookshop above a gallery.

à la Carte, Utrechtsestraat 110–112. Maps, streetplans and guide books.

Castafiore, 1e Looiersdwarsstraat 12. Period LPs and underground comics.

The English Bookshop, Lauriergracht 71. Carefully selected range.

Intertaal, Van Baerlestraat 76. Everything you need to learn Dutch or to teach English.

Lankamp & Brinkman, Spiegelgracht 19. Children's books in English.

Lambiek, Kerkstraat 78. Cheery comic shop. Collectors' pieces and a cartoonists' gallery.

Robert Premsela, Van Baerlestraat 78. Art books a cut above the museum shops.

De Slegte, Kalverstraat 48–52. Discount and antiquarian megastore.

W.H. Smith, Kalverstraat 152. A large up-market branch of the British chain.

Bicycles

John's Inn, Nieuwe Keizersgracht 64. Second-hand bikes. Parts, repairs and sympathy when your machine falls to bits or the front wheel gets caught in the tram lines.

Tweewieler Centrum, Linnaeusparkweg 142. New and used sales and repairs.

Cameras

Foto Professional Nieuwendijk 113. Official dealer for all the big names.

Clothes

Dutch designers don't cause many tremors in world fashion, but you will find tasteful, well-cut clothes in fine natural fabrics at much lower prices than in other capitals. The second-hand clothes shops attract stall-grubbers from around the globe.

DESIGNER

P.C. Hooftstraat and **Van Baerlestraat** are the corridors of high fashion—here you'll find international labels as well as Dutch designers.

Antonia, Gasthuismolensteeg 12. Young designers strut their stuff.
Edgar Vos, P.C. Hooftstraat 134. Nifty suits for the high-powered businesswoman.
Modegalerie Summat, Zeedijk 39. Clothes and accessories so striking that the shop promenades as a 'gallery'. November is men's month.
Sissy Boy, Van Baerlestraat 15. Middle-of-the-road elegance at fast-lane prices.

EYE-BROW RAISERS

Expectations, Warmoesstraat 32. Leather, rubber and denim fetishwear.
Tothem, Nieuwezijds Voorburgwal 149. Swimsuits and sexy underwear for men.
Victoria's Secrets, Leidsestraat 32. Pricey, sensuous silk lingerie.
WILD!, Kerkstraat 104. Clubwear for the brave and the beautiful.

SECOND-HAND CLOTHES

Clusters of second-hand shops rub elbow patches with each other in the zig-zag of lanes from **Huidenstraat** to **Hartenstraat**. You could also try:

Hans en Grietje, Overtoom 255. Ethnic and colonial bits and bobs.

Rose Rood, Kinkerstraat 159. For that little 18th-century bodice or 1960s leatherette mini-skirt.

If you're into something tasteful or demure, head for P.C. Hooftstraat again. Alternatively try:

Shoebaloo, Koningsplein 7–9. Glitz, ruffs and teetering heels for the oddly shod (unisex).
Big Shoe, Leliegracht 12. For big feet (either gender).
Candy Corson, St Luciensteeg 19. Stylish leather bags and belts.

Wampie, 2e Anjeliersdwarsstraat. Imaginative, original, affordable clothes for the under sevens.

Department Stores

De Bijenkorf, Dam 1. 'The Beehive'—aptly named. Bustling shop with a wide range of good-quality merchandise, and no pretensions to being Harrods.
Hema, Reguliersbreestraat 10 (and all around town). The Dutch Woolworths or five-and-dime. A good one-stop shop to stock up on essentials.
Metz & Co, Keizersgracht 455. Liberty prints, stylish kitchenware and design-museum furniture. Superb view of Amsterdam from the glass-walled café on the top floor.

Delftware, Clogs and Gifts

Rinascimento Gallerie d'Arte, Prinsengracht 170. Old and new Delftware, (the real thing, not souvenir shop tat). Watch the designs being painted on by hand.
De Klompenboer, Nieuwezijds Voorburgwal 20. Clogs and other wooden goodies carved on the premises. Also pewter and lace.

Diamonds

Where you buy depends very much on your personal taste, but do shop around and stick to established dealers. You can watch diamonds being cut in a number of shops.

Coster Diamonds, Paulus Potterstraat 2–6. (See Walk VI.)

Gassan Diamond House, Nieuwe Uilenburgerstraat 173–5.
Rokin Diamonds, Rokin 12.
Van Moppes, Albert Cuypstraat 2–6.

Food

BAKERIES

Look out for two kinds. A *warme bakker* sells breads and biscuits and a *banketbakker* sells pastries and all the wonderful creamy things that the doctor forbids. Many also sell hand-made chocolates.

Pool, Ceintuurbaan 278. Delicious ryebread, crispy white rolls and healthy wholemeals—which cause Moscow-like queues along the pavement.
Hendrikse, Overtoom 472. Tarts and cream cakes fit for Queen Beatrix.
C.O. Hottkamp, Vijzelgracht 15. Mouthwatering goodies closer to the centre of town.

CHEESE

In the better cheese shops you'll be given a sliver to taste before buying. Choose from mild *jong* (young), or the more tangy *belegen* (matured) or *extra belegen*.

Wegewijs Kaas, Rozengracht 32. 100-year old family cheese shop.

DELICATESSENS

Dikker & Thijs, Prinsengracht 444. Unrivalled. A gourmet's paradise.
A Taste of Ireland, Herengracht 228. British provisions for the homesick.

HEALTH SHOPS

Manna, Spui 1. The biggest and best, with a café and take-aways too.

SPIRITS, BEER AND WINE

De Bierkoning, Paleisstraat 125. Cosy shop behind the palace. Glasses of all shapes and around 750 brands of bottled beer.
Hart's Wijnhandel, Vijzelgracht 3. Wide range of wines and spirits.

SUPERMARKETS

Albert Hein is the most popular chain. You'll find branches on

Waterlooplein and Vijzelstraat. **Mignon** is more expensive, but has a centrally-situated branch in Leidsestraat.

TEA AND COFFEE
Keizer Prinsengracht 180. Wondrous aromas and odd utensils in an early 19th-century setting.
Geels & Co, Warmoesstraat 67. The city's oldest tea and coffee specialist, in the middle of the red-light district.

Markets

Albert Cuyp Markt, Albert Cuyp Straat; Mon–Sat 9–4.30. Foodstuffs, clothes and hardware (see Walk V).
Bloemenmarkt (Flower Market), Singel, between Muntplein and Koningsplein; Mon–Sat 9–6. Amsterdam's floating flower market (see Walk III).
Boerenmarkt, Noordermarkt; Sat 10–3. Organic produce, ethnic crafts.
Lapjesmarkt, Westerstraat; Mon 7.30–1. Bargain clothes and spectacular fabrics.
Lindengracht; Sat 9–4. Small general market, but the best.
De Looier Indoor Antiques Market, Elandsgracht; Mon–Thurs 11–5, Sat 9–5. Mid-price antique market. There's also a *rommelmarkt* (junk market) just around the corner. (See Walk VI.)
Nieuwmarkt; May–Sept, Sun 10–5. The seedy square gleams briefly with good quality antiques.
Noordermarkt; Mon 7.30–1.30. Pile upon pile of junk. Get there early for a treasure hunt.
Oudemanhuis Book Market, Oudemanhuispoort; Mon–Sat 10–4. A dim alley smelling of musty binding and yellowing paper.
Stamp Market, near Nova Hotel, Nieuwezijds Voorburgwal 276; Wed, Sat 11–4. Grizzled collectors swap stamps, currency, medals and esoteric jokes.
Waterlooplein; Mon–Sat 10–4. Amsterdam's famous fleamarket. (See Walk III.)

Services

CAMERA HIRE
Ruad Foto, Overtoom 371. Cameras, computers and camcorders to hire.

DRY CLEANING, LAUNDRY AND REPAIR
Clean Brothers Laundrettes, Kerkstraat 56/Rozengracht 59/Westerstraat 26.
Self-service laundrettes open daily 7–9.
Cleaning Shop Express, Huidenstraat 22. Dry cleaning, laundering, repairs.

FLORISTS
Gerda's Bloemenwinkel, Runstraat 16. Flowers with flair—a sensual delight.

FORMAL DRESS HIRE
Joh. Huijer, Weteringschans 153. The works, from cuff-links to bow tie.
Maison Van Den Hoogen, Sarphatipark 88–90. Ball gowns, cocktail frocks and little black numbers.

HAIR SALONS
H.B. Hairstylers, Amsterdam Hilton, Apollolaan 138, tel 679 0599. Expensive, but expert, classic service for men and women.
Kunsthaar, Berenstraat 21, tel 625 9912. Trendier styles in a salon-cum-art gallery.
Wim Patberg, Schippersgracht 13, tel 638 0929. One-man business in a light, attractive salon. Superb cuts at a reasonable price. (Men and women.)

LUGGAGE AND SHOE REPAIR
Wentholt Exclusive Luggage Repair Shop, Nieuwezijds Kolk 4.
Mr Minit, Leidsestraat 71. While-you-wait repairs to shoes and handbags.

PHOTO PROCESSING
Capi, Leidsestraat 77. Colour film ready in an hour. Two days for slides.

Specialist Shops

Amsterdam abounds in idiosyncratic speciality shops: old family businesses, outlets for some personal obsession or the fantasies of quixotic visionaries. Here are but a few:

Condomerie Het Gulden Vlies, Warmoesstraat 141. Condom as consumer item.

Egosoft Psychoactive Tools, Nieuwe Kerkstraat 69. Aids to moulding your psyche.

Flying Objects, 2e Tuindwarsstraat 8. Kites weird and wonderful.

Hangmat, Herengracht 265. Bright and breezy hammocks from around the world.

P.G.C. Hajenius, Rokin 92–6. Tobacconist with famed house-brand cigars.

The Head Shop, Kloveniersburgwal 39. Accessories for dope devotees.

Knopenwinkel, Wolvenstraat 14. Buttons of all shapes and periods.

Kramer, Reestraat 20. Candles and candlesticks—ethnic to high altar.

Mosquito Nets Siam, Prinsengracht 232. The best way to ward off the pests.

Miniature Furniture, Prinsengracht 293. Open Sat noon–4.30. Everything on a one-twelfth scale.

Poppendokter, Reestraat 20. Dolls and parts of dolls.

Waterwinkel, Roelof Hartstraat 10. Over 100 types of mineral water from around the world, and mud from the Dead Sea.

De Witte Tanden Winkel, Runstraat 5. Champagne-flavoured toothpaste and toothbrushes, toothbrushes, toothbrushes.

Sports

The rivers in the Netherlands are covered with a candy
sugar-like layer at certain times of the year, strong enough
to carry a horse and carriage, and a milling throng of people
amuse themselves by rushing across this layer at the speed
of an ostrich, doing so by means of sharply ground irons
bound under their feet.

—17th-century Moroccan envoy to The Hague

Amsterdam is not a very hearty, sporting city. Most people seem to get
the exercise they need from all the walking and cycling they do every day.
However, if you're wandering down Prins Hendrikkade on a weekend
afternoon, you might be astonished to see brightly dressed figures,
swathed in ropes, scaling the walls of the old firemen's barracks. This is
the **Netherlands Mountaineering Club** acting out of desperation.
They are not alone. Every year, from May to October, squads of eager
'horizontal mountain climbers' don shorts and sneakers and slop
knee deep through sucking quagmires of black mud off the Frisian coast.
This they do for two to four hours at a time, before returning home.
Another odd national pastime is **pole sitting**. Every year, around the
beginning of August, men sit on poles in the North Sea (at Noorderwij-
kerhout just north of The Hague) until they fall off. The last one to do so
is the winner. **Korfball** is an indigenous hybrid of netball and volleyball

played between teams comprising equal numbers of men and women. It's a rule-bound battle of the sexes where players have to toss a ball around at great speed and try to shoot it into a hoop 11½ feet (3.5 m) off the ground. The nation does, however, also participate in less esoteric sports.

Spectator Sports

The most popular national sport is **football**. The Dutch team have not had many resounding international successes, but the local Amsterdam team, **Ajax**, has a vociferous and enthusiastic following. Important matches have even been known to cause the city council to adjourn sessions, and will almost certainly turn your neighbourhood brown café into a silent room of tense men fixated on a flickering screen. Ajax won European Cups three times in the 1970s, but was recently banned after someone threw an iron bar at the opponent's goalie. If you want to see the team for yourself, the stadium is at Middenweg 401, tel 694 6515. **Hockey** (field hockey), on the other hand, is a sport in which both the men's and the women's national teams have been world champions. Many national home matches and some good club games are played at Wagener Stadium, Nieuwe Kalfjeslaan, tel 640 1141. If your taste inclines towards the faster and more furious, a good **ice hockey** team (S IJ S Amsterdam 89) plays at the Jaap Edenhal rink (Radioweg 64, tel 694 9652) from Oct–Feb. The local **basketball** team, Canadians Amsterdam, is one of the best in the country. They play at the Apollohal, Stadionweg (tel 671 3910).

Do-it-Yourself

The 1980s health mania hit Amsterdam as soundly as it did other major cities in the Western world, and you can find a number of well-equipped gyms and **fitness centres** around town. Two of the best are: Splash (Looiersgracht 26–30, tel 624 8404; open Mon–Fri 9–10, Sat and Sun 11–6; weights, machines, sauna, steam, massage and aerobics; f25 per day/f110 per month all inclusive) and Garden Gym (Jodenbreestraat 158, tel 626 8772; mainly, though not exclusively, for women; weights, dance, sauna, solarium, massage, self-defence; day pass f13.50, with sauna/shower f20). Sauna Deco (Herengracht 115, tel 623 8215; adm.

ƒ13.50 before 2 pm, ƒ21.50 after 2 pm) is an exhilarating experience. You sweat away those extra inches in a stylish Art-Deco interior rescued from a famous 1920s Parisian department store.

Swimming pools in Amsterdam are clean, well-maintained and supervised. They often have small bars or coffeeshops at the water's edge so you can top up the calories after an energetic swim. Opening times are complicated, with periods set aside for club and naked swimming, so it's a good idea to phone first. The Marnixbad (Marnixplein 9, tel 625 4843; adm. ƒ3.80) has waterslides and a whirlpool. The Mirandabad (De Mirandalaan 9, tel 642 8080; adm. ƒ5.25) has tropical temperatures, a pebble beach and a wave machine. There's an outdoor pool for good weather and a slide and whirlpool. The Zuiderbad (Hobbemastraat 26, tel 679 2217; adm. ƒ3.80) is just a plain, rectangular pool of water for swimming quietly up and down in. It was built at the beginning of the century and still has most of its original features, including some beautiful tile work and a neat perimeter of wooden changing cubicles opening onto the edge of the pool.

Walking and **cycling** are the two great national pastimes, and the attractive canals and well-laid out cycle paths make both a joy. If you want to be more serious about things, or would like an uninhibited jog, head for the Vondelpark (see Walk VI) or the Amsterdamse Bos (see Day Trips). The VVV can offer suggestions for cycling or walking tours (see p. 8–9 for bicycle hire). They will also be able to give you information on the *Grachtenloop* ('canal walk'), Amsterdam's equivalent of the London Marathon. One Sunday early in June thousands of people come together to spend the best part of the day jogging set distances up and down the main canals.

In the winter walking gives way to **skating**. If you're lucky you may be in Amsterdam in a year when the canals freeze over, and everyone whizzes around the city on skates. (Be careful, though, the ice can be thin and sometimes doesn't freeze under bridges.) Every winter, from November to February, a free outdoor rink is erected on Leidseplein. If you don't have your own skates, head for Jaap Edenhal (Radioweg 64, tel 694 9652), a large indoor rink where you can hire skates for under ƒ10 (you'll need your passport or a ƒ100 deposit). If the weather is really cold you'll hear talk of nothing else but the *elfstedentocht* ('eleven city marathon') which takes place on the canals and waterways between 11 towns in Friesland. It is only rarely that the freeze is good enough—if you hear it's happening, then it's certainly worth a trip north.

If bats, rackets and balls are your forte, you'll find **squash** and indoor **tennis** courts at the Frank Otten Stadion (Stadionstraat 10, tel 662 8767; tennis open 9–9, squash open 9–11; tennis ƒ22.50 per hour/ƒ30 after 5 pm, squash ƒ15/ƒ17.50 per half hour; racket hire ƒ5). There are 36 tennis courts, most of them outdoor, at the Amstelpark (Karel Lotsylaan 8, tel 644 5436; open 8 am–midnight; indoor courts ƒ 30 per hour, outdoor courts ƒ25; rackets loaned free). Squash City (Ketelmakerstraat 6, tel 626 7883; open Mon–Fri 8.45–11.15, Sat and Sun 8.45–9; ƒ25/ƒ30 after 5 pm and on Sun; racket hire ƒ3) also has a weights room and sauna for players to use. For **table tennis** enthusiasts, there's the Table Tennis Centre Amsterdam (Keizersgracht 209, tel 624 5780; open daily 1 pm–1 am; ƒ9 per table per hour).

As gentler form of relaxation, you might try a little **billiards, snooker** or the pocketless Dutch variation called **biljart** (countless volunteers willing to explain the rules and offer advice around every table). You'll find all three played at the Biljartcentrum Bavaria (Van Ostadestraat 97, tel 676 4059; open daily 11 am–1 am; snooker ƒ9 per hour until 2 pm, then ƒ13.50, carambole ƒ7.50 per hour). The Snookercentrum de Keizer (Keizersgracht 256, tel 623 1586; open Mon–Thurs and Sun noon–1 am, Sat noon–2 am; ƒ11 per hour before 3 pm, then ƒ16) is in a 17th-century canal house. The tables are in private rooms and you can phone down to the bar for drinks.

Gay Amsterdam

In the heady social upheaval of the 1960s and 70s, when pixie-hatted members of the Gnome Party held protest meetings on the Dam and troupes of hippies camped out in the Vondelpark, Amsterdam's lesbians and gays joined in the frolic. Homosexuality had been decriminalized in 1811, but the gay community wanted a city free of the petty prejudices and subtle discrimination they ran up against in day-to-day life. In many ways they succeeded. Today Amsterdam is known as the Gay Capital of Europe. Gay bars and cafés, though often in clusters, aren't in ghettos. Nobody bats an eyelid if two men kiss or hold hands in public. The city was quick off the mark in coping constructively with AIDS, the council housing department gives gay couples the same status as married hetero-sexuals, and in 1987 the world's first memorial to persecuted lesbians and gays, the **Homomonument**, was unveiled (the three triangles of pink granite between the Westerkerk and the Keizersgracht are the focal point of many a party, protest or commemoration service.)

There are gay bars, clubs, hotels, bookshops and restaurants all over town. You'll find most of the heavier leather bars lurking up the north end of **Warmoesstraat**, ribbons of coffeeshops, restaurants and bars along **Kerkstraat** and **Reguliersdwarsstraat**, a jolly throb of clubs and pubs along the **Amstel** off Rembrandtsplein, and scores of local neigh-bourhood cafés. Gay tourists flock to the city. Over weekends, the hunk at the end of the bar is more likely to be a computer programmer from

South London than a local lad. Many Amsterdammers respond to this invasion by staying at home; venturing out on Thursdays and Sundays when the occupying forces are thinner on the ground.

The atmosphere, though, is friendly and welcoming. Most gay venues distribute free **maps of gay Amsterdam** and leaflets giving you an idea of what's on about town; but as people are so open and chatty, word-of-mouth is often the best way to find out what the evening might have in store. If you're spending some time in Amsterdam, you might invest in one of the specialist guides, like *Top Guide* (see Further Reading).

Here is an idiosyncratic selection of places to go; some are well-known but others are quirky, local establishments, out of the tourist maelstrom.

Cafés, Coffeeshops and Restaurants

Adrian, Reguliersdwarsstraat 21, tel 623 9582; open daily 6 pm–midnight. Classic, up-market French restaurant—soft candlelight and subtle sauces. Around ƒ55 a head with wine; major credit cards accepted.
COC, Rozenstraat 14; coffeeshop open Wed–Sat 1 pm–5 pm. Spartan but amiable haven in Amsterdam's lesbian and gay 'culture centre'.
Downtown, Reguliersdwarsstraat 31; open daily 10–8. A friendly daytime coffeeshop, popular with tourists and locals, in one of Amsterdam's gay streets. It serves food and has a sprawl of pavement tables on sunny days.
The Eighties, Brouwersgracht 139; open daily 10–8, but closes 6 pm Oct–Mar. Trendy hi-tech café, well stocked with magazines, with a terrace on one of Amsterdam's most tranquil canals.
Le Monde, Rembrandtsplein 6; open daily 8 am–midnight. Tiny, cheery snack café with a terrace on Rembrandtsplein. The sister restaurant along the square does good Dutch food.
Backstage Boutique (a.k.a. 'The Twins'), Utrechtsedwarsstraat 75; open Mon-Sat 10 am–6 pm. Not exclusively gay, but brothers Greg and Gary Christmas create an atmosphere of stratospheric camp that shouldn't be missed. (See Lunch/Cafés, Walk VI.)

Bars

Argos, Warmoesstraat 95; open Mon–Thurs 9 pm–3 am, to 4 am at weekends. Amsterdam's oldest leather bar sweats with bikers' jackets, cowboy chaps and denim. As you wander into the dimmer recesses, what the gay guides coyly term 'action' becomes quite lively.

April, Reguliersdwarsstraat 37; open daily 2 pm–1 am. Popular with young Amsterdammers during the week. Over the weekend tourists swell numbers until the bar bursts into a street party.

Amstel Taveerne, Amstel 54; open daily 3 pm–1 am, to 2 pm at weekends. Beer mugs and bric-a-brac hang everywhere. Dutch reproductions on the walls. Dutch originals around the bar. A provincial pub in the middle of the city with sing-a-longs and good cheer (all Dutch).

Le Shako, 's Gravenlandseveer 2; open daily 9 pm–2 am, to 3 am at weekends. A minuscule bar that attracts students, writers, academics and a good load of local scruffs. Cheap beer on Tuesdays and free snacks on Thursdays.

Doll's Place, Vinkenstraat 57; open daily 10 pm–3 am. Mixed lesbian, gay men and assorted others. Decorated with Marilyn Monroe photographs and over 1000 dolls (mostly hanging from the ceiling). Spontaneous sing-songs around the piano. Donate a doll and you might get a free drink.

Havana, Reguliersdwarsstraat 17; open daily 4 pm–1 am, to 2 am at weekends. Comfortable café/bar with an exhausting constellation of beautiful people. There's a small dance floor upstairs, so you can pop up for an early evening bop.

Montmartre, Halvemaansteeg 17; open daily 4 pm–1 am, to 2 am on Fri and Sat. Dancing barmen, original 1920s decor, loud music and a tight squeeze.

Clubs

COC, Rozenstraat 14. Amsterdam's Gay Centre runs a disco on Friday nights (10 pm–2 am) which attracts a local crowd and ingénues from the provinces.

C'ring (or Cockring), Warmoesstraat 96; open daily 11 pm–4 am, to 5 am on Fri and Sat. Steamy, sweaty, swarming venue for emergency sex.

De Club, Amstel 178; daily 10 pm–5 am, to 6 am on Fri and Sat. More a bar with a dance floor than a club, but a friendly (mainly local) crowd of lesbians and gay men.

IT, Amstelstraat 24; open daily 10 pm–4 am, at weekends to 5 am. Euro-Disco with a large dance floor, light show, numerous bars and boys who dance in cages.

De Trut, Bilderdijkstraat 165; open Sun 11 pm–4 am. A trendy, but relaxed and pose-free club with a wide range of music, a (mainly) young crowd and a mix of lesbians and gay men. The Trut is in the cellar of what was once one of Amsterdam's biggest squats. The entrance is unmarked, but if you turn up between 11 and midnight, you'll see where to go.

Accommodation

Hotels are forbidden by law to discriminate against gay couples, but here's a selection of specifically gay places to stay. Prices are for a double room with shower in season, breakfast included. (Addresses given with Amsterdam postcode.)

International Travel Club/ITC, Prinsengracht 1051, 1017 JE; tel 623 0230. Quiet hotel overlooking one of Amsterdam's finest canals, popular with lesbians. Pity about the management. From ƒ130.
Hotel New York, Herengracht 13, 1015 BA; tel 624 3066. Swish hotel with all mod cons, hiding behind three 17th-century canal houses at a tranquil end of Amsterdam's grandest canal. From ƒ145.
Orfeo, Leidsekruisstraat 14, 1017 RH; tel 623 1347. Large hotel popular with English visitors. ƒ100.
Waterfront Hotel, Singel 458, 1017 AW; tel 623 9775. Attractive converted canal house, popular among lesbians and gay men. ƒ195.

Interhome Sevices (Keizersgracht 33, 1015 CD Amsterdam; tel 625 0071) or **Drake's** (Keizersgracht 669, NL 1017 DV; tel 627 9544) offer furnished apartments from ƒ500 per week.

Many of Amsterdam's best 'straight' hotels are gay owned, and are sympathetic places to stay. See especially the **Quentin Hotel** (which has a large lesbian clientele), **Seven Bridges Hotel** and **Hotel Engeland** under Where to Stay.

Lesbian Amsterdam

Lesbians are not as well catered for as gay men in Amsterdam, but there's a lively, friendly scene in places such as:

Coffeeshop Françoise, Kerkstraat 176; Mon–Sat 9 am–6 pm. Offers good Dutch meals in a relaxed atmosphere. Not exclusively gay, but popular with local women.

Café Saarein, Elandsstraat 119; open Mon 8 pm–1 am. Tues–Thurs and Sun 3 pm–1 am, Fri and Sat 3 pm–2 am. A cosy local café, currently the citadel of Amsterdam's lesbian life.

Café Vandenberg, Lindengracht 95; open daily 4 pm–1 am, Fri and Sat to 2 am. Situated in the middle of the Jordaan, with a sunny terrace.

Café Vie-la-Vie, Amstelstraat 5; open daily noon–1 am, to 2 am at weekends. Sociable crowd in a vaguely Art-Deco bar with music that increases in volume as the night wears on.

COC (see under clubs above) holds a women-only disco on Saturdays from 8 pm–2 am.

De Brug, Kuiperstraat 151; open 8.30 pm–2 am, first Sat of the month. Disco for lesbians over 35.

PH 31, Prins Hendriklaan 31; open Sun only 9 pm–2 am. The evening starts with music and theatre, and around 11 pm develops into a disco.

Other Attractions

If the sun's shining, the place to be is **Zandvoort**, on Amsterdam's **gay beach**. Zandvoort is not the forgotten patch in the dunes that such places usually are, although it's a bit of a trek to reach it. There's a gay restaurant nearby (Zeezicht, tel (02507) 123 14) and two gay bars (Eldorado and Sans Tout) on the beach. All three are open from 8 am until midnight. You can get there by train from Centraal Station (about 30 mins, frequent trains right through the day). Once you get to the beach, walk south along the promenade and then on past the 'Naakt Strand' (nudist beach) for about 5 km.

There's a **gay cinema** every Saturday and Sunday at Desmet (Plantage Middenlaan 4a, tel 627 3434). It shows a selection of popular and independent films and attracts a local crowd.

You can spend hours browsing around **gay bookshops** like Intermale (Spuistraat 251)—mostly for men—or Boekhandel Vrolijk (Paleisstraat 135), which has a wide selection of literature, biographies and non-fiction of interest to lesbians and gay men. The American Discount Bookshop (Kalverstraat 185) has a good gay section.

Mandate (Prinsengracht 715; open Mon–Fri 11 am–10 pm; Sat noon–6 pm, Sun 2 pm–6 pm; daily membership *f*20) is a well-equipped **gay gym** with a busy coffee bar; and the notorious Amsterdam **saunas** are Thermos Day (Raamstraat 35; open Mon–Fri noon–11 pm, Sat and Sun noon–6 pm; entrance *f*21) and Thermos Night (Kerkstraat 60; open daily 11 pm–8 am; entrance *f*22.50).

Information

Gay and Lesbian Switchboard (tel 623 6565; open 10 am–10 pm) gives information and advice in English.

COC is Amsterdam's lesbian and gay social centre (Rozenstraat 14; tel office 626 3087/information 623 4079; open Mon–Thurs 9 am–5 pm; for disco and coffeeshop hours, see Clubs and Lesbian Amsterdam above).

Living and Working in Amsterdam

If you mention that you're considering living and working in Amsterdam, people will tell you that you won't be able to find an apartment or a job. Believe them. You'll need all the energy, imagination and cunning you can muster if you want to prove them wrong. Until recently it was very difficult for foreigners to find work. Things are a little easier now, but Amsterdam is still struggling to absorb masses of immigrants from Indonesia, Surinam and Turkey. Traditional options for English speakers—such as language teaching and work in the service industries—barely exist in Amsterdam because the locals speak English so well.

It's a small city, and new urban development projects are only slowly chipping away at an enormous housing backlog. Reasonably priced accommodation is very hard to come by—though, of course, once you cross the magic boundary into the world of company lets and luxury rents, problems vanish. However, if you have stamina and tenacity, or lead a charmed life, you might just find yourself in that little apartment overlooking a canal, in one of the most congenial cities in the world.

Amsterdam has most of the advantages of a metropolis and hardly any of the disadvantages. It's safe, clean, unpolluted and so compact that you'll probably be able to walk to work. Yet it's never boring. There's a rich mix of nationalities and a vibrant cultural life. You'll find yourself readily accepted by the residents, and before long you'll be behaving with an Amsterdammer's relaxed urbanity.

Long-term Residence and Finding a Job

Neither EC nor American citizens need a visa for stays of under three months. If you want to stay longer than that you will need some proof of financial independence—usually that means a job in the Netherlands.

The situation for **EC citizens** is going to change with the open European market in 1992, but at the time of going to press no-one yet knows how—except perhaps the relevant government ministers, and they're not letting on. Unless your local Dutch consulate can tell you otherwise, the first thing to do is to get your passport stamped when you enter the country. This won't be done automatically, and sometimes you have to be quite insistent. A stamped passport is the only proof of duration of that residence most authorities will accept. Then within five days you should report to the Aliens Department of the main police station (Elandsgracht 117) with a letter from your employer and your passport. The police will grant you a residence permit. It's your employer's responsibility to get you a work permit. This effectively means that you have to have a firm offer of a job before you enter the country—or at least have to leave and come in again once you have sorted out some employment.

American citizens are the only non-EC citizens permitted to apply for a residence permit once they're already in the country, rather than before they leave home. The procedure once you arrive is the same one outlined above.

The place to start **looking for a job** is an *uitzendburo* (employment agency) or in newspapers such as *De Volkskrant* (which has a very good jobs section on Saturday). But be warned, unless your Dutch is excellent you're up against very stiff competition from poly-lingual locals. Two useful employment agencies are Manpower (Van Baerlestraat 16, tel 664 4180; general office/secretarial/computer) and Tempo Team (Rokin 118, tel 622 9393; academic/catering/medical/secretarial/technical).

Finding Somewhere to Stay

Shared accommodation is not as common in Amsterdam as in other large cities. Houses and apartments are small, and people tend to be jealous of their space. Your energy would be better spent trying to find an apartment. A dawn raid on the nearest newsagent for a copy of *De Volkskrant* or *De Telegraaf* might bear fruit, if you act quickly. Both newspapers have 'Rented Accommodation Offered' columns (*Woonruimte te huur aangeboden*), though you usually find only a miserable handful of letting agency ads. The *gevraagd* ('wanted') column, however, stretches on depressingly. The weekly freebie *De Echo* is also a good bet. The noticeboards in libraries, supermarkets and tobacconists' windows are a good source of medium-term accommodation: many Amsterdammers off on a long holiday will advertise here for someone to look after an apartment. You could leave an ad yourself—but return to check it daily. Competition is fierce and ads tend to disappear overnight. Word of mouth is really the best way to house hunt. Just be prepared to be a bore at parties until you finally find someone who has a friend whose neighbour is moving out.

As a last resort try one of the accommodation agencies (see under Where to Stay). Be prepared to fork out a whacking fee—one or two months rental at least, and consider yourself lucky if you're offered something for under *f*1500 a month.

If, after living in Amsterdam for two years, you still haven't found suitable accommodation, you can get an *urgentie bewijs* ('urgent need certificate'). You will need to be a legal resident and have registered at the Bevolkings Register (Stadhuis, Waterlooplein; open 8.30 am–3 pm). This will entitle you to a council flat.

Accounting and Tax Services: Amstelraede (Bouwerij 7, Amstelveen, tel 647 5383) will guide you through the labyrinth.

Business Services: Kamer van Koophandel (Chamber of Commerce, De Ruijterkade 5, tel 523 6600) will tell you most of what you want to know about import/export and the ins and outs of doing business in Amsterdam. The World Trade Centre (Strawinskylaan 1, tel 575 9111) offers a broad range of office facilities and services, and at Buro Jenny Spits (Prinsengracht 909, tel 624 7635, fax 620 3499) you can get anything from a photocopy to a new bookkeeper.

Computers: Apple Center (Hogehilweg 10, tel 697 6166) Offers computers for hire and desk-top publishing services. De Vakman (Nieuwe Hemweg 6N, tel 684 2425) will try to repair temperamental computers; 24-hour service.

Customs: Douane Amsterdam (Leeuwendalersweg 21, tel 586 7511).

Dating Service: Dinnerdate (tel 600 3730) will set you up for anything from dinner to a walk around the galleries.

257

Detective Agency Randata (tel 617 3622) will send round a man with spy-holes snipped out of his newspaper.

Domestic Emergencies (of a mechanical nature): A Reparette Team (Freefone 06 0455) will fix anything from a blocked loo to a recalcitrant CD player at any time of day or night.

Heating: Jaspers (2e H de Grootstraat 64–70, tel 684 2729) sell all the stoves, boilers and pipes you need to keep you comfortable through the winter. Bode (Van Hallstraat 637, tel 684 7281) will repair them when they wheeze to a halt.

Language Courses: Volksuniversiteit Amsterdam (Herenmarkt 93, tel 626 1626) has high standards and is not expensive. Day and evening courses from ƒ175.

Legal Services: Bureau voor Rechtshulp (Legal Advice Centre: Spuistraat 10, tel 626 4477) give free legal advice on immigration and civil matters.

Library: The Centrale Bibliotheek (Prinsengracht 587, tel 623 5065; open Mon 1 pm–9 pm, Tues–Fri 10 am–9 pm, Sat 10 am–5 pm) has some wonderful reading desks overlooking the canal, an excellent collection of books on Amsterdam and a coffeeshop stocked with newspapers from around the world. Anyone can use the library, but you need to show proof of Amsterdam residence before you can take books out.

Limousine Hire: Limousine & Airport Service (tel (030) 444 411) can whisk you off in a Cadillac, Bentley or Rolls-Royce chauffeured by a 'discreet and uniformed' driver.

Locksmiths: Amsterdam Security Centre (Prinsengracht 1097, tel 671 6316) will open doors at all times of day or night if you've locked yourself out.

Messengers: DHL (tel Freefone 06 0552) will whisk your package anywhere in the world. All-Ride (tel 613 4804) offer a 24-hour local service.

Mortgages: Financial Advice Centre (Valeriusstraat 133, tel 671 1643) will tie up mortgages, life insurance and pension plans.

Moving: Cors de Jongh Int BV (Sloterweg 312 Badhoevedorp, tel (02968) 97155) do worldwide removals; Geytenbeek BV (RAI Congresgebouw, Europaplein 8, tel 644 8551) specialize in business removals and tackle the customs officers for you.

Pets: You can bring your cat or dog into the country if it has a rabies vaccination certificate. If it looks peaky when it arrives take it along to the Dierenopvancentrum (Polderweg 12, tel 665 1888).

Post and Telephone Services: Mail & More (Nieuwezijds Voorburg-wal 353, tel 638 2836) will rent you a private mailbox, a portable phone, or print business cards in 5 minutes.

Schools: The British School of Amsterdam (Jan van Eyckstraat 21, tel 679 7840) offers a traditional British education for boys and girls.

Tax Free Cars: A. Van de Braak BV (Burg v Leeuwenlaan 31, tel 613 0727).

Translation: Language Solution (Corellistraat 11, tel 675 4698) use trained native-speakers of major European languages with business experience.

Day Trips from Amsterdam

The model town in The Hague

Gouda

Gouda (pronounced with an aspirated guttural G, 'HGowda') is not all cheese and ersatz medieval markets. There's a thriving crafts industry, an imaginative historical museum and, in the longest church in the Netherlands, stained glass so beautiful that even the iconoclasts left it alone.

Getting There
Gouda is 29 km (18 miles) south-west of Amsterdam. The easiest way to get there is by train from Centraal Station. The journey takes about 50 minutes and it's a 15-minute walk from Gouda Station to the market square. Trains average two an hour and a day-return costs ƒ23.50. By car take the A2, then the A12.

The VVV tourist office is on the market square (Markt 24, tel (01820) 13666) and can provide you with maps and further suggestions for walking tours. The main tourist sights are clustered around the market square and are just a few minutes' walk apart.

LUNCHES/CAFÉS
Just behind the Grotekerk, **Het Goudse Winkeltje** (Achter de Kerk 9a) sells delicious pancakes and sandwiches; **Van den Berg** (Lange

260

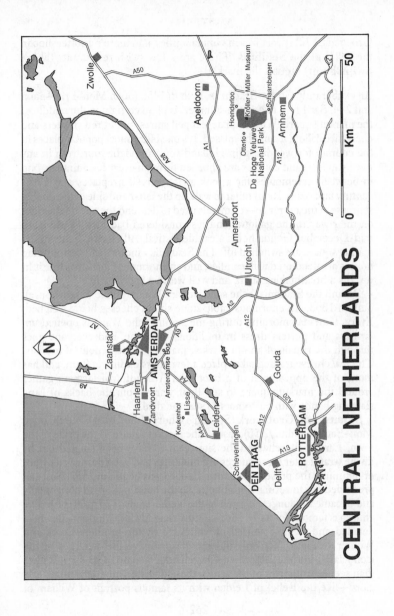

CENTRAL NETHERLANDS

Groenedaal 32) specializes in Gouda waffles, and there's a coffeeshop in the cellar of the **Stadhuis**. There are a few swish restaurants (like **'t Swijnshooft**) around the market.

An exuberantly Gothic **Stadhuis**, built in 1450 (open Mon–Fri 9–noon and 2–4, Sat 11–3, to 4 in the summer) is plonked right in the middle of the market square. With its pixie-capped spires, bright red shutters and cheerful carillon, it can't be missed. It's one of the most popular places in the country for weddings (in Holland you can plight your troth in any town you like) and couples are churned through every few minutes. Nip in between ceremonies for a look at the carved fireplaces and 17th-century tapestries. Remember to walk up the left-hand side of the double staircase at the entrance—criminals used to descend the one on the right on their way to the gallows, and it's considered bad luck to use it. In mid-December Gouda holds a candle festival. All electric lights in the market square are switched off. The Stadhuis windows and surrounding houses are decorated with candles, and an enormous Christmas tree is lit up. It's a breathtaking sight, and well worth a special trip.

Behind the Stadhuis is the solid, square **Waag** (public weigh-house), built in 1668. An enormous gable stone shows cheeses being weighed. Every Thursday morning during the summer the Waag is opened up, farmers and porters dress in traditional costume, and everyone goes through the rituals of an old market, mainly for the benefit of tourists. The *real* cheese trading takes place a few hours earlier, at 9 am, and has more of the appearance of a boot sale. A handful of farmers gather around the market square to sell their wares from the backs of cars, slapping hands with customers to seal the deal.

St Janskerk/Grotekerk (St John's Church/the Great Church, open Mon–Sat 9–5; adm. ƒ2.50), just off the market square, is the pride of the town. Earlier churches on the site seem to have been singled out by divine wrath: after three successive buildings had been destroyed by fire or lightning, the present cruciform basilica was begun in 1552. Soft soil precluded any towering Gothic spire, so the building spread horizontally and became the longest church in the Netherlands (123 m/403 ft). The church is famous for its 70 16th-century stained glass windows, the most detailed and richly coloured of which are by the brothers Dirck and Wouter Crabeth. Not only did the glass survive the scourges of the iconoclasts, but the Reformed Church added some of its own. Rather than scenes from lives of the saints, these depicted moments of historic glory—like the Relief of Leiden with its famous portrait of William of

Orange. During the Second World War the windows were taken out and stored safely, and so survive beautifully intact.

In the quiet lane behind St Janskerk you may see an old worker from the nearby stonemason's yard chipping away at an enormous block of sandstone, right up against the church wall. With his dusty leather apron and white hair he could be a medieval master craftsman rebuilding the nave. On this lane (helpfully called Achter de Kerk—'Behind the Church') is the tall red-brick **Lazaruspoortje** (Lazarus Gate) with a relief showing poor, pustule-ridden Lazarus and the rich man who will never make it to the bosom of Abraham (Luke 16:19–31). This 17th-century entrance to a Lepers' Hospice was transferred here in the 1960s to serve as the back entrance to **Het Catharina Gasthuis** (St Catherine's Hospital, now a municipal museum, open Tues–Sat 10–5, Sun noon–5; adm. ƒ3.50—ticket also valid for De Moriaan Museum), an intriguing collection of 14th–17th-century buildings. You can see a reconstructed 19th-century apothecary's shop (very much in demand as a period film set) and a medieval surgeon's room, a torture chamber and a lunatics' cell. There's a frightening similarity in the instruments used in each. The torture chamber sports an ingenious designer execution block. The victim was strapped down spread-eagled, there are holes for the blood to run through and a spike to display the head on afterwards. The museum also has a good collection of paintings from the French Barbizon school and from the Hague School (see pp. 60–1) and a fine collection of medieval silver (especially the ornate 15th-century *Chalice of Jacoba of Bavaria*). The new director stages vigorous and adventurous exhibitions of contemporary art.

Five minutes' walk down the canal from the Catharina Gasthuis, you'll find **De Moriaan** ('The Blackamoor') at Westhaven 29, a 17th-century merchant's house and tobacco shop named after the carving over the door (open Mon–Fri 10–5, Sat 10–12.30 and 1–5, Sun 12–5). It has a vast collection of pipes, tiles and pottery. The **Goudse Librije** (Gouda Library, Spieringstraat 1, off the square behind the Catharina Gasthuis; open Mon–Fri 2–4; adm. free) was used as an orphanage from the 17th century up to the 1940s. Now it houses a collection of 16th–19th century books which you can take down off the shelves and page through.

Gouda bustles with craft industry. It's famous for its candles, and claims to produce 85 per cent of Holland's 'Delft' china. At **Het Tin en Keramiek Huis** (Lange Groenendaal 73, open Tues–Sat 10–5; adm. free) you can see award-winning designers paint the blue and white Delft patterns onto jugs and plates. Gouda also has its own ceramic style, which uses richer colours, is far more beautiful and considerably more expensive. At Peperstraat 76, you can watch the luxuriously moustachioed Adrie Moerings make **clay pipes** in the traditional way (Mon–Fri 9–5, Sat 11–5; adm. free). Try to persuade him to make a *doorroker*. This pipe has a plain bowl, but as you use it, a pattern begins to emerge in the clay. At **De Roode Leeuw** (the windmill at Vest 65; open Tues–Sat 9–5; adm. *f*1.50) you'll meet Marcel Koop, a real rosy-cheeked, flour-covered miller. In the early 1980s he gave up his job as an engineer to renovate the 17th-century windmill. Now it's the only working mill in the Netherlands also lived in by the miller. You can climb almost to the top, accompanied by the deep organic grumbling of the grindstones. And, of course, there's **cheese**. As well as the Thursday market, there are excursions and short bicycle rides to nearby dairy farms where you can follow the whole cheese-making process from cow to bulging yellow cartwheel (contact the VVV for details of what farms are open).

Haarlem

Just fifteen minutes by train from Centraal Station, Haarlem has a cosy, provincial atmosphere quite different from Amsterdam—but it's by no means dull. You'll find hordes of friendly cafés, the much-painted St Bavo's church, tiny *hofjes* tucked behind over-the-top public architecture, and the Frans Hals Museum.

Getting There
Trains leave Centraal Station about every ten minutes. A day-return costs *f*8. By car, it's a few minutes up the A9.

The VVV tourist office is outside the railway station (open Mon–Sat 9–6; tel (023) 319059) and can supply you with maps and public transport information.

LUNCH/CAFÉS
Brinkman Brasserie (Grote Markt 9–13) is an elegant Art-Deco establishment overlooking St Bavo's. The street behind the church, at the far end of the market, is a good place to look for restaurants and cafés. The *proeflokaal* **In den Uiver** (Rivier Fischmarkt 13) and Italian restaurant **Piccolo** (Grootmarkt 31) are particularly worth a try. For light snacks and sandwiches try the cheery **De Karmeliet** (Spekstraat 6),

264

though you really need go no further than the wood panelling and hanging lampshades of the beautifully restored **Station Restaurant** (on Platform 2).

Most people arriving in Haarlem head straight for the **Grote Markt** (Market Square) and the imposing Gothic **Grote of St Bavokerk** (Great or St Bavo's Church; Mon–Sat 20 am–4 pm; adm. *f*2). The view across the square hasn't changed much over the centuries, and on a quiet morning you feel you could be looking at one of Gerrit Berckheyde's 17th-century paintings of the church. The interior is bright and painted white. A gleefully ostentatious Baroque organ upstages even the soaring Gothic arches. It was built by the Amsterdammer Christiaan Muller in 1738, and is said to be one of the biggest in the world. Clusters of musical putti and graceful maidens cling to the pipes. Handel, Mozart and Albert Schweitzer have all had a go on the ivory and tortoise-shell keyboard. Before you go, have a look at the fading tapestry designs painted on the columns at the side of the church and the fluid lines of a marble relief by The Hague sculptor Xavery: Poetry and Music paying homage to the town patroness. In the centre column of the Brewers' Chapel (near the south transept) two little lines mark the heights of past Haarlem residents: Giant Cajanus (2.6m/8ft 8ins) and Paap (94cm/37ins).

Outside the church is a statue of Laurens Coster. Local legend has it that while he was carving his lover's name in a tree trunk, a letter fell into the sand. He was inspired by the imprint to invent printing. Though Haarlem is proud of him today, his contemporaries took him for a sorcerer and drove him out of town. He went to live in Germany—which might explain why the rest of the world believes that printing began with Gutenberg.

The oldest part of the **Stadhuis** across the square is a 14th-century hunting lodge built for the Count of Holland. It's been altered and expanded over the years, and the present complex incorporates a medieval monastery. During office hours you can have a look at the old heavy-beamed **Gravenzaal** (Count's Hall). On the south side of the square is the relentlessly ornamented **Vleeshal** (the former Meat Market, built in 1602). Sacheverell Sitwell remarked that we should 'regard it less as a building, than as Dutch cabinet work on a most capricious scale'.

Haarlem is renowned for its **hofjes**—secluded almshouse courtyards dating from the 15th century. Most are still lived in, but if you're discreet you can have a quick look around. The best ones are in the western part of the city around Barrevoetestraat and Tuchthuisstraat. One of the grander *hofjes*, a 17th-century Old Men's Home, is now Haarlem's star attraction—the **Frans Hals Museum** (about 15 minutes' walk from the market square; open Mon–Sat 11 am–5 pm, Sun 1 pm–5 pm; adm. *f*4). The museum isn't devoted entirely to Hals—there's a batch of other Golden Age painters, a wide range of furniture and applied art and an extensive modern collection. The corridors are pervaded by a steady ticking of clocks, and the displays give you some sharp surprises. In a dim 17th-century period room, you'll see an enormous drawing by the 1930s Magic Realist, Pyke Koch. Bright contemporary pieces hang alongside Old Masters or in rooms displaying antique silver. All this gives the museum a quirky liveliness. Don't miss the exquisitely crafted 18th-century dolls' house or the Restoration Workshop. (You stand behind a glass wall and watch painters work painstakingly on the tiny patch of an Old Master that will occupy them for months.) The most intriguing of Frans Hals's works in the museum are the portraits of the *Regents* and *Regentesses of the Old Men's Home*, painted in 1664 when Hals was in his eighties. The story that he was a bitter occupant of the almshouse is not true, but he certainly seems to be taking some sort of revenge with his brush. The Regentesses, in particular, are a sour and terrifying lot. Their expressions range from rosy stupidity to pure evil, and the white faces are thrown into stark relief by the sombre surround. (You can see why Van Gogh said that Hals had at least 27 shades of black).

The **Provinciehuis Noord-Holland** (North Holland Provincial Government Building; guided tours by arrangement, contact the VVV) is slightly out of the centre of town, but certainly worth the 20–30 minute walk. It was built as a home and private art gallery by an eccentric Amsterdam banker in 1796, and during its chequered history has been a palace to Louis Bonaparte and a museum. It's a sumptuous neo-classical building with exquisite stucco work, gorgeously moulded ceilings and patterned parquet flooring. The rooms abound with marble statues and period furniture.

Before you leave Haarlem you might also like to pay a quick visit to the Netherlands' oldest museum, the **Teylers Museum** (Spaarne 16, open Tues–Sat 10 am–5 pm, Sun 1–5 pm, winter until 4 pm; adm. *f*4). It's the best sort of small museum—one based on the taste of an erudite, eccentric private collector, in this case the 18th-century merchant Pieter Teyler van der Hulst. A succession of astute directors have, in making new acquisitions, skilfully developed the diverse themes of Teyler's original collection. You'll find a fascinating hoard of old scientific instruments and machines, fossils, paintings and drawings (including some by Michelangelo and Rembrandt).

Leiden

Leiden is famous for its ancient university, for its siege in the 16th century, for housing the Pilgrim Fathers in the 17th century and for being Rembrandt's birthplace. Today it's a lively little town with friendly student cafés, good specialist museums and some pretty canals. All of the main tourist sites are within easy walking distance of the centre and the railway station.

Getting There

Leiden is only half an hour by train from Centraal Station. There's a train every 15–20 minutes and a day-return is ƒ17.50. By car, it's 40km (25 miles) along the A4.

The VVV Tourist office is right near the railway station at Stationsplein 210, tel (071) 146846. Here you can pick up a map and advice on routes of walks around the town.

LUNCH/CAFÉS

The best place for cafés and restaurants is around **Pieterskerkhof** and **Hooglandskerk**. **Annie's Verjaardag Brasserie** has a dripping cellar full of students and a waterside terrace. The **Koetshuis**, a converted 17th-century carriage house at the foot of the Burcht, serves good light lunches.

Locals ('Leijenaars') like to claim that the Leiden grew from the Roman settlement of Lugdunum, but it's safer to pinpoint the town's origin at the appearance of **De Burcht** (The Stronghold) around AD 1000. This dumpy fortress was built on a mound between two branches of the Rhine to protect a small settlement of fishermen and farmers from marauding Vikings, fractious local lords and the fickle water levels. You can still march around its sturdy battlements and look out over the whole city. Around 1050 the powerful Counts of Holland moved into town, so ensuring Leiden's prosperity for centuries. At the beginning of the Eighty Years' War, the Spanish besieged Leiden (1573–4). The starving town was eventually relieved by William the Silent, who broke down the dikes and, to the Spaniards utter surprise, came sailing across the fields with the Dutch navy. The Spanish made off with such haste that they left their dinner—an enormous pot of stew—still simmering on the fire. It

267

was found by a city marksman (romantics say a wandering orphan). He carried it back to the hungry Leijenaars who were already laying into the white bread and herring that the navy had brought. Every year, on 3 October, the town celebrates the anniversary of its relief with festive public consumption of bread, herring and 'hotchpotch'. As a reward for their endurance William offered the people of Leiden either eternal relief from taxation, or Holland's first university. With characteristic farsightedness they chose the latter.

The **University**, founded in 1581, is now the most prestigious in the Netherlands. The part most worth visiting is the **Hortus Botanicus** (open April–Sept Mon–Sat 9–5, Sun 10–5; Oct–March Mon–Fri 9–5, Sun 10–5). Planted in 1594, it is one of the oldest botanical gardens in Europe. A 17th-century traveller described the gardens as 'ravishing in rare curiosities'. When you tire of the elegantly laid-out shrubberies, you can push your way through hothouses of sticky exotica, past signs warning you to 'Beware of the Butterflies' to the massive *Victoria Regia* lily that can support the weight of three men on its pads and flowers but one night a year. To the left of the main gate is one of the oldest parts of the university. Once a nunnery, it has for centuries been used as an exam hall. Inside, up a spiral wooden staircase, you'll find the 'Sweat Box'— the room where anxious candidates sat before exams and later awaited their results. The room is now hermetically sealed to protect the generations of signatures they left behind them on the walls.

From 1609 to 1620 a group of Puritans, finding the religious atmosphere in Holland more congenial than in England, settled in Leiden with their preacher, John Robinson. **Jean Pesijnshofje** (Pieterskerkhof 21), a late 17th-century almshouse, now marks the site where Robinson lived and preached. The congregation felt the need for an even freer climate, so in 1620 they headed back to Plymouth, boarded the *Mayflower* and set sail for the New World. Robinson didn't go with them. He died in 1625 and is buried in the Pieterskerk. You can watch a slide-show and find out more about the Pilgrim Fathers in the **Leiden Pilgrim Collection** (Vliet 45, near the Hortus Botanicus; open Mon–Fri 9.30–4.30; adm. free).

The 15th-century **Pieterskerk** (open daily 1.30–4) is in the heart of the student quarter. The surrounding cafés are favourite places to meet and relax, and on a fine summer's day there appear to be more live bodies stretched out in the former cemetery than dead ones. The church was originally called St Pieters, but was stripped of its saintly title, and any other papist ornamentation, during the Reformation. By far the most interesting thing to see in the plain, cavernous church is a mummified body. It was found, dried out by the draught, in a secret room under the pulpit and now lies in the church with its ankles neatly crossed and its head on a pillow. No-one knows how it got there, or even how old it is. Some suspect murder, or a priest's secret lover; members of the older generation mutter darkly about Nazis and the Occupation. Pieterskerk's other attractions include George Bush's family tree—showing his descent from the Pilgrim Fathers, and the tomb of Jan Steen, the 17th-century Dutch painter.

Rembrandt's parents are also buried at Pieterskerk, though their graves are unmarked. Very little remains in Leiden to remind you of the painter's early years in the town. A plaque on the side of a 1960s block of flats in Weddesteeg, halfway between the railway station and the university, marks the spot where he was born, and nearby at the **Rembrandt Studio** (Kort Galgewater; open Tues–Sat 10–5, Sun 12–5; adm. f2) there's a panorama and light show inspired by his painting *The Painter in his Studio*.

Leiden's other museums offer more exciting fare. The **Rijksmuseum Van Oudenheden** (Antiquities Museum) at Rapenburg 28 is the country's leading archaeological museum (open Tues–Sat 10–5, Sun 1–5; adm. f3.50). In 1960 the Egyptian government donated the entire 1st century AD *Temple of Taffeh* to the Dutch in gratitude for their contribution to UNESCO excavations in Abyssinia. The squat stone building is in the museum foyer (it was a condition of the gift that no-one should pay to see it) and overhead lighting simulates the passage of the sun (a second stipulation). The museum has a thrillingly gruesome collection of mummies, good stores of Greek and Roman antiquities and finds from local excavations.

On the other side of town, yet no more than 20 minutes' walk away, is **De Lakenhal** ('The Cloth Hall', Oude Singel 32; open Tues–Sat 10–5, Sun 1–5; adm f2.50) which was built in 1640 as the administrative centre of Leiden's prosperous cloth industry. In 1874 it was converted into a municipal museum. There are good collections of silver and furniture, but the star attractions are the paintings. Look out especially for Lucas van Leyden's fine and delicately coloured triptych, the *Last Judgement* (1572); works by the young Rembrandt and his studio-mate Jan Levens; Gerard Dou's tiny, intense oils (which established a Leiden style) and the lecherous abandon of Jan Steen's *Amorous Couple* (1660). There's a painting depicting the brave Burgemeester van der Werff who, at the height of the siege, offered his own body as food to the faltering citizens.

They refused but were fired by his courage to hold out even longer. (In the painting they look well-fed and a little embarrassed by the offer).

The **Rijksmuseum Voor Volkenkunde** (National Museum of Ethnology) at Steenstraat 1, a few minutes from the station, has a such a good collection of Japanese art and artefacts that people travel from Japan to see it (open Tues–Sat 10–5, Sun 1–5; adm. *f*3.50). The nearby **Molenmuseum de Valk** (2e Binnenvestgracht 1a), a restored 18th-century grain mill, is something the children might appreciate (open Tues–Sat 10–5, Sun 1–5; adm. *f*3); and the **Museum Boerhaave** (Lange St Agnietenstraat 10), a museum of scientific and surgical instruments, contains a reconstruction of a wooden operating theatre—a mini-colosseum with steep rakes of spectators' seats surrounding the central table (open Tues–Sat 10–5, Sun 1–5; adm. *f*3.50).

Den Haag (The Hague)

A 17th-century travel guide describes The Hague as 'the fairest village in the world, both for the pompous buildings, and for the largeness thereof'. Two centuries later Matthew Arnold wrote: 'I never saw a city where the well-to-do classes seem to have given the whole place so much of their own air of wealth, finished cleanliness and comfort; but I never saw one, either, in which my heart would so have sunk at the thought of living.' Little has changed. People still call The Hague 'the largest village in the world' and the many ex-colonials who have retired here have generated another nickname: 'The widow of Indonesia'.

The wide boulevards and graceful architecture *do* speak of quiet, established wealth, and Amsterdammers, in particular, complain that The Hague is a stuffy domain of diplomats, civil servants and businessmen. (Though Amsterdam is the capital of the Netherlands, The Hague is the centre of government and the chosen seat of the present Queen.) It may not be the place you would go to bop until dawn or throng singing through the streets, but the spotless architecture, acres of greenery and inimitable museums give it an atmosphere of tranquil refinement which is rather alluring. Most of the main sites are centrally situated, though if you really want to appreciate all The Hague has to offer, you'll need more than a day.

The Hague lets its hair down with some lively summer festivals. In June there's a 10-day long Indonesian market, the *Pasar Malam Besar*; the International Kite Festival at Scheveningen; and a two-day international horseshow on the Lange Voorhout, a large green square in the middle of town. The North Sea Jazz Festival, held annually in The Hague in mid-July is becoming one of the world's most important jazz festivals.

Getting There

The Hague is 48 km (30 miles) south-west of Amsterdam. By car take the A4, then the A44. Trains from Centraal Station take 50 minutes. There are about four an hour and a day-return costs *f*13.50.

The Hague has two railway stations: Den Haag H.S. (Hollandse Spoor) and Den Haag C.S. (Centraal Spoor). There are frequent tram and rail links between the two, but the C.S. is the more convenient, and it's there you'll find the VVV tourist office (Koning Julianaplein, open Mon–Sat 9–8/9 pm in summer, Sun 10–5; tel (070) 354 6200). They can supply you with maps and information about public transport.

You can use your Amsterdam *Strippenkaart* on the public transport, or buy a *Dagkaart* from the VVV.

LUNCH/CAFÉS

De Posthoorn (Lange Voorhout 39a) serves light snacks and sandwiches and has a pleasant terrace overlooking the tree-lined market place. The **Oesterbar Saur** nearby (no. 47–53) has good sea-food. The side streets and canals to the east of Lange Voorhout are well stocked café hunting-grounds. Noordeinde (which runs past the Noordeinde Palace) is a stretch of rather good restaurants. Try the **Brasserie Renoir** for something light; or **Restaurant Turner** in Molenstraat 9a–11, a medium priced, small French establishment. For something a little more quirky try **Achterommetje** (Achterom 71, an alley behind the 'Passage' shopping arcade in the city centre). They play jazz, sell good, healthy, home-cooked food and delicious cakes.

The Hague is famous for its Indonesian restaurants. Try **Bogor**, (Van Swietenstraat 2, tel (070) 346 1628)—fine cooking in an elegant *Jugendstil* house—and **Tampat Senang**, Laan van Meerdervoort 6, tel (070) 363 6787), slightly more pricey, but with a live *gamelan* orchestra.

William II, Count of Holland, built his official residence on the North Sea dunes in 1247. The settlement that grew up around it was known as '*s-Gravenhage* (the Count's Hedge), and this is still The Hague's official name. The count's courtyard, the **Binnenhof**, remains the centre of town, though now it's an amalgam of architectural styles. On the third Tuesday in September, Queen Beatrix sweeps into the courtyard in a gold carriage to open parliament. The ceremony takes place under the high oak ceilings and delicate turrets of the **Ridderzaal** (the 'Hall of Knights') in the centre of the Binnenhof. The Ridderzaal, the oldest building in the complex was built to host the early Counts of Holland's hunting parties. The two chambers of the States General actually meet in more sober halls around the edge of the courtyard. (Guided tours, Mon–Sat 10–4; in July–Aug also Sun noon–4; adm. *f*4, from the Information Office, Binnenhof 8a). By far the best view of the Binnenhof is from the outside—across the **Hofvijver** (Court Pond), a glassy expanse of water with a softly spraying fountain.

Next to the parliament buildings, on a corner of the Hofvijver, you'll find the **Mauritshuis** (open Tues–Sat 10–5, Sun 11–5; entrance *f*6.50), a grand 17th-century mansion, built for a favoured general and now home to the Royal Collection of paintings once owned by *stadhouders* William IV and William V. Highpoints of three centuries of Dutch and Flemish art cover the walls stacked one above the other (a fashionable way of displaying pictures in the 18th century). There's hardly an inch of wood-panelling or flock wallpaper to be seen between the gilt frames, there are no labels and the pictures hang in no particular order—but it's a heady experience. You can see Rembrandt's first Amsterdam commission, *The Anatomy Lesson of Dr van Tulp* (1632). (The corpse, like the painter, had just arrived in Amsterdam from Leiden; and the erudite surgeon was renowned for his advice that patients drink 50 cups of tea a day.) You can see three of Vermeer's rather minimal oeuvre, Frans Hals's manic *Laughing Boy*, Paul Potter's nightmarish, meticulously finished *Young Bull* (complete with frogs and flies) and works by Rubens and Holbein. There are nine paintings by the 17th-century inn-keeper Jan Steen. His post-card sized cheekily lascivious **Girl Eating Oysters** would alone make a visit to the museum worthwhile. The remainder of the royal collection is housed across the pond in the **Schildergallerij Prins Willem V** (Prince William V Gallery, Buitenhof 35, open Tues–Sun 11–4; entrance *f*2.50). More work by Jan Steen and Paulus Potter and also paintings by other 17th and 18th century masters are on display, but the Mauritshuis has creamed off the best of the collection. Next door you'll find the **Rijksmuseum Gevangenpoort** (Prisoners' Gate Museum), which houses a gory collection of torture instruments (open Mon–Fri 10–4, Apr–Oct also Sun 1–4; entrance *f*4). The building was a prison for over 400 years, though warders seldom managed to outwit The Hague's maidservants, who were notorious for their ability to spring incarcerated lovers and brothers.

The Counts of Holland were incorrigible palace-builders. In the centre of town you can see the neo-classical pile of the **Paleis Noordeinde** (built 1553) and the smaller 18th-century **Paleis Lange Voorhout**. A few minutes' ride from the centre, in the thickets of the Haagse Bos, you can peer through the trees at the present Royal residence—the dinky, domed **Huis ten Bosch** ('House in the Woods', built 1654). None of these is open to the public. You can, however, join other commoners in the **Vredespaleis** (Peace Palace, Carnegieplein 2; tours Mon–Fri 10, 11 am, noon, 2 and 3 pm; entrance *f*3; about 10 minutes from the centre on Tram 4). The 1899 Hague Peace Conference established the Permanent Court of Arbitration—a court with global jurisdiction, still widely respected and considered neutral—but gave it a rather dingy home. In 1903 the American millionaire, Andrew Carnegie donated $1.5 million to build a more appropriate palace for the court. Countries from all over the world contributed ironwork, stained glass, statuary and furniture to create a quirky hotchpotch of a building.

Nearby the Vredespaleis, you can drop in on the **Panorama Mesdag** (Zeestraat 65; open Mon–Sat 10–5, Sun 12–5). You walk about under a canvas canopy and look out on all sides, across sand dunes littered with clogs and empty gin bottles, at a huge, circular view of Scheveningen painted in 1881. Another 10 minutes on Tram 4 will take you to a 1990s version of a panorama, the **Omniversum** (President Kennedylaan 5, programmes on the hour: Tues, Wed, Thurs 11–4; Fri, Sat, Sun 11–9, except 6 pm; adm. *f*14; tel (070) 354 7479 or contact VVV for programme details). Lasers and films (such as *Speed* and *The Future of Time*) are projected onto a dome-shaped screen, sounds explode all about you and special 'sub-woofers' produce bass notes so deep you can only feel them. Next door is the superb **Gemeente Museum** (Municipal Museum, open Tues–Sun 11–5; adm. *f*6). Designed in 1935 by the influential architect H.P. Berlage, the spacious tiled interior looks, at first glance, like a bank—or a very up-market public lavatory. It houses a beautiful collection of glass and silverware, some important 19th-century paintings, superbly reconstructed period rooms and one of the best modern art collections in the country. You'll find lots of familiar names from the first half of the century—Monet, Picasso, Egon Schiele—as well as the pick of modern Dutch artists like Jan Toorop, Pyke Koch and the painters of the COBRA movement, Karel Appel and Constant (see p. 63). There are a number of early works by Mondriaan—realistic landscapes and bright impressionistic studies—that hint only slightly at the abstract style for which he later became famous (see p. 61–2).

The collection of contemporary work gives you the rare impression of a healthy budget being intelligently spent. Don't leave without visiting the **music department**, which displays instruments ranging from exquisitely crafted harpsichords and viols to Mauricio Kagel's whirring, wobbling, resounding 250-instrument two-man orchestra.

The Gemeente Museum is on the edge of the **Scheveningse Bosjes**, an urban forest so rambling that you can quite easily get lost in it. If you make your way across the wilds you'll come to the miniature town of **Madurodam** (open daily March–May 9–10.30; June–Aug 9–11; Sept 9–9.30; Oct–Jan 9–6; adm. *f*11). You can see models of landmarks from all over the Netherlands, little residential canals, football grounds, an airport, railways and a harbour—all on a scale of 1:25. By far the most enjoyable sight, however, is from up on the coffee terrace where you can watch the visitors tramp, Gulliver-like, up and down the paths.

At its northern end, The Hague merges with the fishing port and seaside resort of **Scheveningen**. (Don't worry if you can't pronounce it—only the locals can. During the Second World War Dutch Resistance fighters made suspected German infiltrators say it as a test of their true nationality). It's a tacky resort, thronged mainly by German visitors, but you will find the **Kurhaus**, a gracious *grande dame* of a hotel, built in 1885 and now a national monument. The Kings and Queens of Europe have stayed here; Dietrich, Piaf, Chevalier and even the Rolling Stones have played in the concert hall. If you feel like escaping the crowds, **Kijkduin**, a few kilometres up the promenade, is a quieter spot where you can sit undisturbed on the windy dunes and look out over the grey North Sea.

Kröller-Müller Museum and De Hoge Veluwe National Park

Hélène Müller loved art. Her husband, Anton Kröller, loved nature. She was heiress to a blast-furnace industry; he married the boss's daughter. Together they developed the family firm into a prosperous multinational and used their fortune to realize a dream. Between 1909 and 1914 Anton bought up tracts of wild land near Arnhem. Hélène built up a superb and inspired collection of late 19th and early 20th-century art. They restocked the land with game, planted copses, built a lodge to live in and a museum for the paintings. Today the Kröller-Müller Museum, set in the vast and varied landscape of De Hoge Veluwe national park, is one of the most delightful places to visit in the Netherlands. The estate now covers 5500 hectares (13,000 acres) of land, the art collection is still growing and there really is something for everyone. You can picnic in forests or lie about on dunes, gallop through the fens on horseback or cycle sedately along leafy lanes. You can bird-watch, look for wild boar or nestle in animal hides waiting for red deer. The airy, intimate museum is a pleasure to walk around, and the collection is one of the best in the country. The sculpture park could detain you for hours and the Lodge is unstuffy and well-preserved. There are all the cafés, restaurants and children's playgrounds you could wish for, without the horrid ambience of a theme park or tourist trap.

Getting There

The easiest way to get there is by car. You can drive about in the park, and abandon the car where you wish. Take the A1 to Apeldoorn or the A2 and A12 to Arnhem. There are gates to the park at the villages of Otterlo, Schaarsbergen and Hoenderloo. The journey takes about 1¹/₂ hours.

The nearest railway stations are at Arnhem and Appeldoorn. Both are served fairly frequently from Centraal Station (though less so over weekends) and the journey takes around 1¹/₂ hours. The Netherlands Railways often offer special excursion tickets (check at Centraal Station information desk). From late June to early August there's an hourly excursion bus from Arnhem railway station. Once in the park you can get about on the (free) white bicycles. Out of season you'll need to take the VAD bus 107 from Arnhem, or the 110 from Apeldoorn.

Information is available from the Visitors' Centre (Hoenderloo Gate), tel (08382) 1627, or the local VVV tourist office, tel (085) 420330. Maps are for sale at all the entrance gates.

LUNCH/CAFÉS

The **Museum Café** sells light snacks and cakes and has a sunny terrace, the **Koperen Kop** (open daily) is the main restaurant and serves fuller meals, the smaller **Rijzenburg** closes during the week over winter. The best thing to do is to take a picnic—you can have it anywhere you like.

De Hoge Veluwe national park (open daily 8 am–sundown; adm. ƒ6.50 per person, ƒ6 per car—includes admission to museum and sculpture park) is a curious amalgam of drifting sand dunes, watery fens, thick cultivated forests and open heathland. Mrs Kröller-Müller loved autumn colours—so you'll find forests of oak, birch, beech and rowan trees as well as the older plantations of pine and junipers. In the summer there are gloriously coloured thickets of rhododendrons and purple heather covers the heath in August and September. Anton Kröller filled the park with magnificently antlered red deer, moufflons (a curly horned wild sheep from Sardinia), wild boar, roe deer and even kangaroos. All, except the poor roos, survive in multitudes and have such violent fun in the rutting season (Sept–Oct) that you're confined to your car in some parts of the park. There are marked walks throughout the area, though you don't have to keep to the paths. The Visitors' Centre can put you in touch with a local stables if you'd like to hire a horse, or you can pick up a bicycle (free, no deposit necessary) from the shelter in the central square.

The **Kröller-Müller Museum and Sculpture Park** are now state-owned (museum open Tues–Sat 10–5, Sun 11–5 (Nov–Mar 1–5); sculpture park open 1 Apr–1 Nov 10–4.30, Sun 11–4.30). A collection of exceptional quality is growing around the core of Hélène Kröller-Müller's bequest. It's a far more pleasant place to see Van Goghs than the crowded museum in Amsterdam—and Mrs Kröller-Müller had nearly 300 of the painter's works: a version of *The Potato Eaters*, fine self-portraits and landscapes and some of his best drawings. You'll find good examples of Braque, Picasso and the rather neglected Cubist, Fernand Léger, colourful stippled Pointillist paintings by Seurat, and a touching study of an aging clown by Renoir—in fact most major movements and artists of the last 100 years are represented. Before you leave have a look for Dutch artist Jan Toorop's eerie fairy-tale drawings and a dreamy pink and green screen by the French Symbolist painter, Odilon Redon.

Out in the Sculpture Park you'll find pieces not only by old familiars like Rodin, Henry Moore and Barbara Hepworth, but also exciting work by contemporary artists. The Park reflects Hélène Kröller-Müller's vision of the way art, nature and architecture can interrelate. The long, low, stone and glass museum blends perfectly into the surrounding landscape. In the pond outside, Marta Pan's enormous, curvaceous, abstract white *Swan* is gently blown about by the wind. In a little hollow, over a hill, rusty iron sheets seem to grow up from the soil. Boulders hang suspended in rope hammocks between the trees; giant, seed-shaped balls of clay, slate igloos and odd tent-like stuctures are scattered about open grass patches. A frail needle of aluminium pipes and steel wire towers 28 m (92 ft) into the sky, higher than most of the trees. Anyone under the age of 12 makes a bee-line for Jean Dubuffet's *Jardin d'Email* (1972/3). From the outside it's a tall white wall, but once you climb the narrow stairs you're in a big, bumpy white landscape cut up by irregular black lines. Bemused adults sit around the edges, while children tear about, trip over the mounds and bang their heads.

Before leaving De Hoge Veluwe, pay a quick visit to the **Jachthuis St Hubertus** (St Hubert Hunting Lodge, open May–Oct, guided tours every half hour 10–11.30 and 2–4.30). The Kröller-Müller's family home and its artificial lake were built in 1914 by H.P. Berlage, the father of modern Dutch architecture (see p. 66) It's a compact brick building with an ugly, incongruous tower. Inside, however, the house has a cosy 'lived-in' atmosphere—and some superb Art-Deco furniture. Monstrous carp swim about in the lake and devour anything you drop in with a nightmarish 'plop'.

Bulbs, Woods and Beaches

If you'd like to escape museums and city life, there is plenty to enjoy in the countryside around Amsterdam.

Flowers

In spring, the fields of North Holland blaze with the colours of millions of tulips and other bulbs, and attract nearly that number of tourists. Coachloads pour out of Amsterdam, to return traumatized by the sight of great cutting-machines churning through the bulbfields scrunching up the flowers. (Most plants are grown for the bulb rather than the bloom, and a swift blade to the stalk makes the bulb subdivide). The VVV tourist office and various agencies around the station can help with organized tours (see p. 26), but it's a far better idea to go on your own by train or car. The town to head for is **Lisse**, and the garden to see is the **Keukenhof** (open late March–late May, daily 8–6.30).

> *Centraal Station will usually have details of special discount offers on a combined rail/bus ticket to the Keukenhof. Alternatively, you could combine a visit to the gardens with a trip to Leiden or Haarlem—there's a bus connection from both to the Keukenhof in the season (details from VVV). The cafés around the Keukenhof are crowded and unexciting. Pack youself a picnic.*

The Keukenhof (literally 'Kitchen Garden') was, in the 15th century, the herb and vegetable patch of the Countess Jacoba van Beieren. Whatever she grew there enabled her to get through four husbands (including a Duke of Gloucester and a Dauphin of France) before her own death at the age of 35. In 1949 a group of Dutch bulb-growers took over the land as a shop-window for the bulb industry. It turned out to have a much wider appeal. Today there are some 30 ha (74 acres) of nearly 7 million plants and a further 5000 sq m (54,000 sq ft) of flowers under glass. The best time to go is from mid to late April, when tulips, daffodils, narcissi and hyacinths are all flowering at once.

Amsterdamse Bos

You don't have to go so far afield for a bit of greenery. The wilds of the Amsterdamse Bos (Amsterdam Woods, open 24 hours; adm. free) are only a tram ride away from the centre of town.

You can get there by bus—nos. 170, 171, 172—but a quainter way to go is by antique tram. On Sundays, and some other afternoons from March–September, a variety of old trams run from Haarlem-mermeer Station in west Amsterdam. There's one every 20 minutes (but contact the VVV for full details).

The Amsterdamse Bos was created in the 1930s, providing jobs for the hundreds of unemployed needed to produce it, and a new recreation space for the expanding city. The **Bos Museum** (Koenenkade 56, in the north-east corner of the Bos; open daily 10–5; adm. free) tells the story of how it all happened. You can go for secluded walks, cycle (there are bikes for hire at the main gate), go boating on one of the vast stretches of water, or visit the buffalo reserve. There are lots of places to picnic, or you can have a pancake amongst live peacocks on the terrace of the **Boerderij Meerzicht** (open summer months 10–7), an old farmhouse near the museum. The Bos is the ideal place to go if the children are getting small-space fatigue.

The Beach

Canal water can be pretty poisonous, so if the weather is hot and you feel like an outdoor swim, you can join the flocks of Amsterdammers heading for the beaches at **Zandvoort**. Although Zandvoort is just beyond Haarlem (another 15 minutes on the train) it has achieved the honorary status of being 'Amsterdam's beach'. It's a crowded and commercial resort, though if you wander further up the coast you'll find a nudists' beach, a gay beach and lots of quieter spots among the dunes.

Language

The language spoken in the Netherlands is *Nederlands*. In the Middle Ages it was known as *Dietse* or *Duutsc* (hence the English 'Dutch'), an equivalent of the German *Deutsch* meaning 'the language of the people' (as opposed to Latin—the language of scholars and the Church). You can hear variations spoken in Belgium (Flemish or *Vlaams*) and South Africa (*Afrikaans*). *Vlaams* has retained some older forms, and was at one time influenced by Old English, but it is essentially a dialect of the root language. *Afrikaans*, on the other hand, will send a Dutchman into fits of giggles. It's a highly simplified Dutch forged by isolated pockets of farmers in the South African outback, and sounds to the modern Hollander's ears like a sort of archaic baby-talk. *Nederlands* is also the administrative language of Surinam and the Netherlands Antilles.

The standard form of the language goes by the rather grand title of *Algemeen Beschaafd Nederlands* (General Cultured Netherlandic—or ABN), though there are a multitude of regional dialects. Most of the Dutch you'll hear in Amsterdam will be ABN. But relax in a neighbourhood bar, or wander through one of the markets, and you'll hear the noisy rasping vowels of what detective story writer Nicolas Freeling called the rooks' caw of the Amsterdam dialect.

Historically, Dutch is the same language as German, a descendant of the language spoken by West Germanic tribes and the Salic Franks. Even today there are many similarities of sentence structure and vocabulary between the two languages. But Dutch doesn't have the gloss and edge of German. It's a softer, cosier, muddy language that seems to have grown out of the bogs and polders. Dutch is not an easy language to grapple with, and the difficulties are compounded by a topsy-turvy (to English speakers at least) word order, similar to that of German. However, to a short-term visitor to Amsterdam this need present no problem, as nearly everyone you meet will speak such good English that you could almost consider it to be the city's second language. The list of words and phrases below will help the polite and adventurous who wish to master everyday courtesies, interpret the menu, or disentangle themselves from sticky situations.

Pronunciation is a question of tackling some rather difficult vowel sounds. Happily, spelling is phonetic, so once you've learned the sounds, you'll be able to make a pretty accurate stab at pronouncing anything you read. The stress in Dutch, as in English, generally falls on the first syllable of a word.

Consonants: Most consonants are pronounced the same as they would be in English. However, *p*s, *t*s and *k*s aren't aspirated (i.e. they're pronounced without the accompanying puff of air usual in English speech). Say *ch* and *g* as in the Scottish 'loch' (*g* is more strongly voiced in northern parts of the country). Good luck in getting your tongue around the combined *s* and *ch* sounds in words like *schip* (ship), *school* (school) or *schrijver* (writer). You have a choice for *r*—you can roll it at the back of your mouth or trill it behind your teeth, but you must *always* pronounce it. Say *w* halfway between the English 'w' and 'v', except before *r*, when you pronounce it 'v'. The Dutch *v* is closer to English 'f'. Say *j* as English 'y'; *sj* as English 'sh' and *tj* as English 'ch'.

279

Vowels: Pronounce the basic *a, e, i, o, u* sounds the same as you would in English, but *much shorter* (*a* as in 'hard', but shorter). Say *ie* as in 'neat', *oo* as in 'boat' and *oe* as in 'pool', but make all the sounds shorter. *aa* is like the 'a' in 'cat', but longer and *ee* is similar to the vowel sound in 'hail'. Say *eu* to rhyme with 'err', but round your lips tightly, and say *uu* as English *oo* in 'hoot'. *ui* is pronounced like the vowel sound in 'house', but with round lips and a mouth full of tongue.

Here are some practice sentences:

Dag! Ik wil graag een fles wijn
darHg! ik vil HgrahHg ayn fles veyn
(Hello, I'd like a bottle of wine, please)

Waar is de wc?
Vahr iss de vay say?
(Where is the loo?)

Echt? Wat leuk!
EHgt? Vut lerk!
(Really? How nice!)

Useful Words and Phrases

do you speak English?	*spreekt u Engels?*
I don't understand	*Ik begrijp het niet*
could you speak more slowly please?	*kunt u wat langzamer spreken, alstublieft?*
hello/good-day/goodbye	*dag*
hi	*hoi* (grating to some ears)
'bye	*doei* (grating to some ears)
goodbye	*tot ziens*
see you later	*tot straks*
good morning	*goede morgen*
good afternoon	*goede middag*
good evening	*goedenavond*
good night	*goede nacht*
yes	*ja*
no	*nee*
maybe	*misschien*
please	*alstublieft*
thank you	*dank u wel*
thanks	*bedankt*
thank you very much	*hartelijk dank*
don't mention it	*niets te danken*
there is/there are	*er is/er zijn*
there isn't/there aren't	*er is geen/er zijn geen*
I have	*Ik heb*
I don't have any	*Ik heb geen*
I'd like	*Ik wil graag*
we'd like	*wij willen graag*

280

I like it	*Ik vind het leuk*
I don't like it	*Ik vind het niet leuk*
where	*waar*
what	*wat*
when	*waneer*
which	*welk*
who	*wie*
why	*waarom*
where is the lavatory?	*waar is het toilet?*
may I	*mag ik*
can you	*kunt u*
how much is this/that?	*hoeveel kost dit/dat?*
expensive	*duur*
cheap	*goedkoop*
can you help me please?	*kunt u mij helpen, alstublieft?*
I'm hungry	*Ik heb honger*
I'm thirsty	*Ik heb dorst*
I'm in a hurry	*Ik heb haast*
I'm lost	*Ik ben verdwaald*
call a doctor quickly	*roep vlug een dokter*
call an ambulance	*roep een ambulance*
please call the police	*roep de politie, alstublieft*
entrance/exit	*ingang/uitgang*
push/pull	*duwen/trekken*
open/closed	*open/gesloten (dicht)*

MEETING PEOPLE

how do you do?	[say your name and surname clearly]
how are you?	*hoe maakt u het?*
how are things?	*hoe gaat het?*
very well, thank you	*uitstekend, dank u*
fine thanks	*heel goed, dank je*
and you?	*en u/jij?*
my name is...	*mijn naam is...*
may I get you a drink?	*mag ik u iets te drinken aanbieden?*
what are you having?	*wat neem je?*
do you have a light?	*hebt u/je een vuurtje?*
are you enjoying yourself?	*amuseer je je?*
where can we go dancing?	*waar kunnen we gaan dansen?*
where shall we meet?	*waar spreken we af?*
how nice	*wat leuk*
really?	*echt?*
I won't be long	*ik ben zo terug*
shall we go?	*gaan we?*
Africa	*Afrika*
America	*Amerika*
USA	*VS (Verenigde Staten)*
UK	*VK (Verenigde Koninkrijk)*
Great Britain	*Groot-Brittannië*

England	*Engeland*
Australia	*Australië*
Canada	*Canada*
France	*Frankrijk*
Germany	*Duitsland*
Ireland	*Ierland*
Italy	*Italië*
Netherlands	*Nederland*
New Zealand	*Nieuw-Zeeland*
Scotland	*Schotland*

HOTEL

single room	*eenpersoonskamer*
double room	*tweepersoonskamer*
with private bath/shower/toilet	*met privé bad/douche/toilet*
may I see the room?	*mag ik de kamer zien?*
did anyone telephone for me?	*heeft er iemand voor mij gebeld?*
may I see the manager, please?	*mag ik de directeur spreken, alstublieft?*

TRANSPORT

airport	*luchthaven/vliegveld*
customs	*douane*
railway station	*trein station*
train	*trein*
platform	*perron*
platform five	*spoor vijf*
car	*auto*
bicycle	*fiets/rijwiel*
ticket	*kaartje*
occupied/reserved	*bezet/gereserveerd*
where can I get a taxi?	*waar kan ik een taxi krijgen?*
what's the fare to …?	*wat kost het naar …?*
take me to this address	*breng me naar dit adres*
I want to go to …	*Ik wil naar …*
how can I get to …?	*hoe kom ik bij …?*
where is …?	*waar is …?*
where's the ticket office?	*waar is het loket?*
I'd like a ticket to …	*Ik wil graag een kaartje naar …*
single/return	*enkeltje/retourtje*
change (trains)	*overstappen*
when does the next/first/last train leave?	*wanneer vertrekt de volgende/eerste/laatste trein?*
how long does it take?	*hoe lang duurt het?*
near/far	*dichtbij/ver weg*
left/right/straight ahead	*links/rechts/vooruit*

DRIVING

car hire	*auto verhuur*
petrol/diesel	*benzine/diesel*
leaded/unleaded	*lood/loodvrij*

filling station	*benzinestation*
garage (for repairs)	*garage*
parking place	*parkeerplaats*
parking garage	*parkeer garage*
no parking	*verboden te parkeren/niet parkeren*
speed limit	*snelheidslimiet*

FOOD/DRINK/RESTAURANTS

a beer, please	*een pilsje, alstublieft*
I'd like a bottle of wine	*Ik wil graag een fles wijn*
red/white/sweet/dry	*rode/witte/zoete/droge*
may I see the menu/wine list?	*mag ik de spijskaart/wijnkaart zien?*
bon appétit	*eet smakelijk*
it tastes good/bad	*het smaakt lekker/niet lekker*
may I have the bill, please?	*mag ik de rekening, alstublieft?*
waiter/waitress	*ober/serveerster*
service	*bediening*
starter	*voorgerecht*
soup	*soep*
main course	*hoofdgerecht*
dish of the day	*dagschotel*
dessert	*nagerecht*

MENU GUIDE

Drinks

coffee	*koffie*
coffee with milk	*koffie verkeerd*
tea (with milk/lemon)	*thee (met melk/citroen)*
fresh orange juice	*jus d'orange*
tomato juice	*tomatensap*
fizzy mineral water	*spa rood* (brand name)
still mineral water	*spa blauw*

Fish

cod	*kabeljauw*
bass	*zeebaars*
eel	*paling*
halibut	*heilbot*
herring	*haring*
trout	*forel*
salmon	*zalm*
sole	*tong*

Meat

veal	*kalfsvlees*
lamb	*lamsvlees*
beef	*rundvlees*
pork	*varkensvlees*

283

Poultry and Game

chicken	*kip*
duck	*eend*
turkey	*kalkoen*
rabbit	*konijn*
venison	*wildbraat*

Vegetables

garlic	*knoflook*
mushrooms	*champignons*
carrots	*worteltjes*
asparagus	*asperge*
spinach	*spinazie*
potatoes	*aardappelen*
potato chips	*patat frites*
salad	*sla*

Dessert

whipped cream	*slagroom*
icecream	*ijs*
icecream and chocolate sauce	*dame blanche*
fruit	*vrucht*

Preparation

poached	*gepocheerd*
fried	*gebakken*
roast	*gebraden*
boiled	*gekookt*
braised	*gestoofd*
grilled	*geroosterd*
stuffed	*gevuld*
rare	*rood*
medium	*half doorbakken*
well-done	*gaar*

Dutch Specialities

amandelbroodje	sweet roll with almond-paste filling
appelgebak	world-famous apple pie
appelmoes	apple sauce (with everything)
belegd broodje	bread roll with variety of fillings
bitterbal	ball of meat purée covered in breadcrumbs and deep fried
blinde vink	slice of veal rolled around stuffing
boerenomelet	omelette with vegetables and bacon
drie-in-de-pan	fluffy pancake with currants
erwtensoep	thick pea soup with sausages in it
frikandel	meatballs
hete bliksem	potatoes, bacon and apples cooked in butter, salt and sugar
Hollandse nieuwe	freshly caught filleted herring
hutspot	hotchpotch (beef and vegetable stew)
kroket	croquette (with any filling imaginable)

pannekoek	pancake
poffertjes	mini doughnut-like pancakes
rolpens	fried slices of beef and tripe with apple
speculaas	spiced almond biscuit
uitsmijter	bread, ham and fried eggs (and variations)
vla	custard—served with everything that doesn't have *appelmoes* (q.v.)
Vlaamse karbonade	braised beef and onions—usually with beer
wentelteefje	bread dipped in egg batter, fried, then sprinkled with cinnamon and sugar

Indonesian Dishes and Terms

Ajam	chicken
babi pangang	roast suckling pig with sweet and sour sauce
bami goreng	casserole of noodles, vegetables, pork and shrimps
daging	beef
gado gado	vegetables with peanut sauce
goreng	fried
ikan	fish
kroepoek	fluffy deep-fried prawn crackers
loempia	enormous spring roll
nasi	rice
nasi goreng	fried rice (with meat and vegetables)
nasi rames	mini *rijsttafel* on a single plate
pedis	spicy (tongue-searing)
pisang	banana
rendang	beef stewed in a dry, fiery sauce
rijsttafel	plain rice, and up to 30 side dishes of spicy meats, vegetables, sauces and fruit
sambal	hot chilli paste
saté	skewered meat with peanut sauce
seroendeng	spicy, fried coconut
tauge	bean sprouts

NUMBERS

nought	*nul*
one	*een*
two	*twee*
three	*drie*
four	*vier*
five	*vijf*
six	*zes*
seven	*zeven*
eight	*acht*
nine	*negen*
ten	*tien*
eleven	*elf*
twelve	*twaalf*
thirteen	*dertien*
fourteen	*veertien* (etc.)

twenty	*twintig*
twenty-one	*eenentwintig*
twenty-two	*tweeëntwintig* (etc.)
thirty	*dertig*
forty	*veertig*
fifty	*vijftig*
sixty	*zestig*
seventy	*zeventig*
eighty	*tachtig*
ninety	*negentig*
hundred	*honderd*
two hundred and twenty	*tweehonderdtwintig*
thousand	*duizend*
two thousand	*tweeduizend*
million	*een miljoen*
first/1st	*eerste/1e*
second/2nd	*tweede/2e*
third/3rd	*derde/3e*
fourth/4th	*vierde/4e*
eighth/8th	*achtste/8e*

TIME

what time is it?	*hoe laat is het?*
one o'clock	*een uur*
a quarter past one	*kwart over één*
half past one	*half twee* [sic]
a quarter to two	*kwart voor twee*
ten to/past three	*tien voor/over drie*
twenty past five	*tien voor half zes*
twenty-five to eight	*vijf over half acht*
I'll come at 2 o'clock	*Ik kom om twee uur*
today/yesterday/tomorrow	*vandaag/gisteren/morgen*
morning/afternoon	*morgen/middag*
evening/night	*avond/nacht*
Monday	*maandag*
Tuesday	*dinsdag*
Wednesday	*woensdag*
Thursday	*donderdag*
Friday	*vrijdag*
Saturday	*zaterdag*
Sunday	*zondag*
day	*dag*
week	*week*
month	*maand*
year	*jaar*

286

Further Reading

HISTORY/GENERAL

Bakker, B. (ed.), *Amsterdam: the history of a city and its people* (Waanders, 1988). A short, anecdotal, well illustrated glossy pamphlet. Good café reading.

Cotterell, Geoffrey, *Amsterdam* (Saxon House, 1972). Readable romp through the history of the city right up to the 1960s.

Geyl, Pieter, *The Revolt of the Netherlands 1555–1609* and *The Netherlands in the 17th Century 1609–1648* (Cassell, 1988). Definitive histories of the uprising against Spain, the unification of the Netherlands and the Golden Age.

Hibbert, Christopher, *Cities and Civilizations* (Weidenfeld & Nicolson, 1987). Interesting chapter on everyday life in the 17th century.

Kistemaker, Renée and Van Gelder, Roeloef, *Amsterdam: The Golden Age* (Abbeville Press, 1975). Lavishly illustrated and wittily written account of 17th-century Amsterdam.

Schama, Simon, *The Embarrassment of Riches: An interpretation of Dutch culture in the Golden Age* (Abbeville Press, 1975). An erudite book that wears its immense research very lighty. A wonderful read.

ART

Clark, Kenneth, *Civilisation* (BBC Publications, 1969). Accessible and perceptive chapter on the Golden Age.

Fromentin, Eugène, *The Masters of Past Time: Dutch and Flemish painting from Van Eyck to Rembrandt* (Phaidon, 1981). An articulate art critic wanders about the towns and galleries of 19th-century Netherlands, and notes down his impressions. A gem.

Fuchs, R. H., *Dutch Painting* (Thames & Hudson, 1978). A good general introduction, if at times a little disjointed.

Jaffe, H. L. C., *De Stijl 1917–1931* (Alec Tiranti, 1956). Comprehensive history of the Netherlands' most influential modern art movement.

Kloos, Maarten (ed.), *Amsterdam: An architectural lesson* (THOTH, 1988). Lectures by renowned architects on modern Amsterdam architecture, and the city's planning problems.

McQuillan, Melissa, *Van Gogh* (Thames & Hudson, 1989). The life, the letters and the works.

Rosenburg, Jacob et al., *Dutch Art and Architecture 1600–1800* (Penguin, 1978). Comprehensive, clearly written account of the Golden Age and beyond.

Stone, Irving, *Lust for Life* (Methuen, 1980). Interesting semi-fictional (though at times cringingly awful) biography of Van Gogh.

White, Christopher, *Rembrandt* (Thames & Hudson, 1988). Easy and wide-ranging account of Rembrandt's chaotic life and his work.

287

GUIDES

Kemme, Guus, *Amsterdam Architecture: A guide* (THOTH, 1989). Photographs and brief accounts of important buildings in the city—from the oldest standing, up to the late 1980s.

Stoutenbeek, Jan, and Vigeveno, Paul, *A Guide to Jewish Amsterdam* (De Haan, 1985). Every nook and cranny of the city with a significance to Jewish people listed and discussed.

Top Guide to Amsterdam (Excellent Publications, 1991). Exhaustive guide to gay clubs, cafés, restaurants and bordellos.

Amsterdam in Cameracolour (Ian Allen, 1980). Good photographs and witty snippets of text.

FICTION

Dutch fiction is unjustifiably neglected by the English-speaking world. Authors mentioned below are very much worth exploring further. Penguin Books has a good Dutch list.

Carmiggelt, Simon, *I'm Just Kidding* (publ. in English 1972). Wry observations on life in Amsterdam—an anthology of pieces he wrote weekly for the newspaper *Het Parool* under the penname 'Kronkel'.

The Diary of Anne Frank (Pan). No matter how many times you read it, you'll be moved by its honesty and awed by its perception.

Freeling, Nicolas, *Because of the Cats, Love in Amsterdam* etc. (Penguin, 1963). The creator of Van der Valk of the BBC TV series writes good classic detective stories—many set in Amsterdam.

Hillesum, Etty, *Etty* (Triad Grafton, 1985). War diary of a young Jewish woman who died in Auschwitz. More knowing than Anne Frank's diary, and not as compelling.

Mulisch, Harry, *Last Call* (Penguin, 1985). From one of Holland's foremost authors. The story of an old actor unearthed to play Prospero in *The Tempest*—it examines the national guilt about the lack of intervention to save the Jews in the Second World War. (Mulisch also wrote *The Assault*, which was made into an Oscar-winning film.)

Multatuli, *Max Havelaar: or the coffee auctions of the Dutch Trading Company* (Penguin, 1987). Neglected Dutch classic, a satirical indictment of Dutch colonialism which shocked 19th-century Holland.

Nooteboom, Cees, *A Song of Truth and Semblance* (Penguin, 1990). Two different fictions, separated by centuries, interweave. A witty novel that seems to reveal the essence of Dutch writing. (Try also *Rituals* and *In the Dutch Mountains*.)

Wolkers, Jan, *Turkish Delight* (Marion Boyars). Deliberately offensive misogynistic work by one of Holland's most provocative writers and artists.

Chronology

AD 50	Roman occupation
AD 70	Local 'Batavians' revolt against Romans
AD 600ff	Gradual Christianization. Eventual unification under Charlemagne
AD 814	Charlemagne dies. Kingdom divided into areas roughly corresponding to France, Germany and the Low Countries
AD 922	King of France creates first Count of Holland
1100ff	Appearance of fisherman's huts and Gijsbrecht van Amstel's castle at the mouth of the Amstel
1275	First recorded reference to city. Floris V grants toll tax exemption to Aemstelledamme
1296	Gijsbrecht IV rebels against Floris
1300	Amsterdam granted first charter
1384	Willem Beukels guarantees future trading prosperity by discovering how to salt herrings efficiently
1419	Philip the Good of Burgundy begins to unite the provinces
1421	First Great Fire of Amsterdam
1425	Singel, the first girdle canal begun
1452	Second Great Fire of Amsterdam
1467	Philip the Good dies, his son Charles the Bold assumes power
1477	Charles's daughter Mary in power, marries Maximilian of Austria
1482	Mary dies and Maximilian rules alone
1494	Maximilian becomes Holy Roman Emperor, transfers power to his son Philip the Handsome, and later to grandson Charles V
1516	Charles becomes King of Spain
1535	Anabaptists briefly occupy the Town Hall but are executed
1555	Charles abdicates, handing over Spain, Italy and the Low Countries to his fanatical son Philip II
1559	Reaction to Philip II's campaigns of persecution of Protestants force Philip into tactical withdrawal, leaving sister Margaret to rule
1565	Winter famine. Wave of iconoclasm
1566	City Regents protest to Margaret. They persuade her to sign the 'Moderation' offering greater religious tolerance
1567	Philip sends the Duke of Alva to take over. He establishes the Council of Blood and begins a reign of terror
1568	William of Orange attempts invasion, but receives little support from terrified Protestants. This marks the beginning of the Eighty Years' War with Spain
1573	Alva and his son Frederic massacre Calvinists at Haarlem. Dikes cut and Netherlanders use superior naval power to force a withdrawal. Philip replaces Alva with De Resquesens
1574	William relieves Leiden

289

1576	De Resquesens dies. Unpaid troops mutiny, slaughtering the inhabitants of Antwerp—the 'Spanish Fury'. Outrage at this gives William wide support. Various provinces unite behind him in the Pacification of Ghent
1578	The 'Alteration'—Calvinist coup in Amsterdam. Town Hall taken over and Catholics expelled
1579	North–south divide reasserts itself. The Union of Utrecht unites the seven northern provinces as the United Provinces with William as *stadhouder*. The southern provinces declare allegiance to Spain in the Union of Arras. Duke of Parma takes control of cities in the south
1584	William assassinated. Aggression continues from south
1585	Fall of Antwerp. Refugees flood Amsterdam
1588	Maurits (William's son) becomes *stadhouder* of the United Provinces
1597	Compagnie van Verre (The Far Away Company) formed. The Dutch are beginning to look East
1602	East India Company formed
1609	Beginning of the 12-year truce with Spain
1613	First phase of canal extension (Heren/Keizers/Prinsengracht)
1622	Northern provinces renew war with Spain (part of the Thirty Years' War)
1624	West India Company formed
1648	Final defeat of Spain. Peace of Westphalia formally recognizes Dutch independence. Closure of the Scheldt waterway means end of Antwerp as trade centre.
1650	William of Orange unsuccessfully attacks Amsterdam (which is showing too much independence in foreign affairs).
1652	First Anglo-Dutch War (for sea-supremacy)
1658	Second phase of canal expansion
1664	Second Anglo-Dutch War
1665	Completion of Town Hall (later Royal Palace)
1667	Dutch Fleet reaches the Medway. Peace of Breda ends war. Louis XIV of France invades Spanish Netherlands. Holland, England and Sweden form Triple Alliance
1688	William of Orange crowned King of England after secret negotiations to replace James II
1701	War of Spanish Succession. Restoration of Grand Alliance of England, Dutch Republic, Austria and German States
1702	William dies heirless
1713	Treaty of Utrecht ends war—both sides exhausted. France renounces all claim to Spanish Netherlands, passes control to Charles VI of Austria
1713ff	Growing conflict between Orangists ('Loyalists') and pro-French ruling families—the 'Patriots'
1734	Dutch Republic unwillingly enters the war of Austrian Succession
1778	Trade treaty in support of rebellious American colonies
1780	England discovers this. War
1780ff	Near civil war between Patriots and Loyalists. Growing Francophilia
1786	Patriots riot, momentarily victorious, but defeated by Prussian invasion

1791	West India Company ends and East India Co goes into liquidation
1792	France defeats Austria in southern Netherlands. Schelde re-opened, Antwerp can become trading city again
1793	France declares war on England and the Dutch Republic.
1795	French enter Amsterdam and set up the Batavian Republic—end of the Dutch Republic
1806	Napoleon's brother, Louis, installed as King. Town Hall becomes Royal Palace
1810	Louis forced to abdicate. Holland is incorporated into France.
1813	Prince of Orange returns after riots and Napoleon's retreat from Moscow
1814	Unification of Netherlands under Prince of Orange by Congress of Vienna
1815	Belgium is joined to Netherlands
1824	North Holland Canal built to bypass the Zuider Zee, to allow bigger ships to reach Amsterdam
1831	Conference of London recognizes Belgium's independence after riots
1839	First railway line—Amsterdam to Haarlem
1848	William panics at European revolts and rushes through liberal constitution
1876	North Sea Canal opens to supplement ineffectual North Holland Canal
1880	Amsterdam University founded. Bicycles and trams begin to appear
1889	Central Station built
1890	Queen Wilhelmina ascends the throne
1903	Berlage's Beurs opened
1914	The Netherlands neutral in First World War
1921	The world's first air travel booking office opens at Schiphol
1928	Olympic Games held in Amsterdam
1930s	Amsterdam School of architecture develops New South
1939	Attempt to remain neutral in Second World War
1940	German invasion
1941	Round-up of Jews begins. General strike in protest
1943	Resistance burns Amsterdam Registry Building
1945	Canadians liberate Amsterdam
1948	Queen Wilhelmina abdicates and is succeeded by Queen Juliana
1953	Disastrous flooding of Zeeland leads to beginning of Delta project
1965	Provo 'happenings' begin
1966	Confrontation with police leads to riots. Provos win enough votes for a council seat
1967	Provos disbanded
1970	Kabouters adopt Provos policies and win seats in five Amsterdam municipalities
1975	Riots over plans to build the Metro
1980	Metro opens
1980/4	Rise of squatter movement and squatter Battles
1981	Kabouter movement winds up
1986	Stopera (city hall and opera house) opens, despite protest

INDEX

Note: **Bold** figures indicate main references. *Italic* figures refer to maps. Names beginning with 'van' or 'de' will normally be found under the main part of the name.